Projections 6

In the same series:

PROJECTIONS 6

Film-makers on Film-making

edited by John Boorman
and Walter Donohue

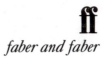

faber and faber

First published in 1996
by Faber and Faber Limited
3 Queen Square London WC1N 3AU

Typeset by Faber and Faber Ltd
Printed in England by Clays Ltd, St Ives plc

A CIP record for this book
is available from the British Library

ISBN 0-571-17853-7

10 9 8 7 6 5 4 3 2

Contents

Introduction

John Boorman

I am preparing a movie at present that includes a number of fantasy creatures, which has drawn me into the realm of digital effects and animatronics. Jim Acheson is designing it, and together we journeyed to Los Angeles to visit the magical workshops of the great Stan Winston. He entertained us in a gallery dedicated to the goblins, ghouls, monsters and dinosaurs he has built and brought to life – from *Aliens* to *Jurassic Park*. He was very impressed by the coloured drawings of our characters: 'These are great. Who's the artist?'

Jim became very English and self-deprecating. 'I did them, but we don't call ourselves artists in England – craftsmen.'

Stan folded Jim in a fraternal embrace. 'Wrong. We are the true artists of the twentieth century. We are the new Renaissance men.'

Well, over here we know it is dangerous to talk about art, to take what we do too seriously. And the Renaissance men didn't know they were Renaissance men, presumably. I recall an interview Michel Ciment conducted with Billy Wilder. Michel became exasperated as Billy turned away all his serious questions with quips and sallies. 'Don't you want to be taken seriously at all?' Michel asked. 'Michel,' the master replied, 'the only thing worse than being taken too seriously is not being taken seriously at all.'

Projections is concerned with the practice of our craft, but it is often hard to describe visual processes without sounding pretentious, arty and risking ridicule. Walter and I always encourage contributors to take risks, to be open, to write from the heart in the knowledge that they are not laying bare their bosoms to the knives of the critics but addressing fellow film-makers.

It would be easy to ridicule Lawrence Bender's *crie de coeur*, that having produced *Reservoir Dogs* and *Pulp Fiction* he did not achieve the satisfaction and happiness he expected, finding that in the drive for success, he had lost touch with his feelings. He wonders how he can function in the cut-throat world of Hollywood and not cut throats himself. His honesty in confronting this dilemma is very touching and raises disturbing issues about the mental condition of the people who decide which films get made. One issue he does not raise is that the films he has produced are extremely violent. Can you send violence out into the world without doing violence to yourself?

Mike Figgis, wittily describing his tour of the awards circuit, also deals with the nature of success and reward. Is it ever enough? Is it always a let-down? Is there a given moment with a hit picture when the makers can say: 'This is it'? I don't think so. I have had my share of hits and failures, extravagant praise and harsh criticism, and I offer this advice: take your pleasure from the process, enjoy the making and, best of all, be shooting the next one when the last one comes out.

In this edition, we include edited transcripts of a fascinating experiment at the Edinburgh Festival in which film-makers described the construction of particular scenes from their films. In another section a number of cinematographers discuss their methods. It is a rich array of styles and techniques. I'm delighted that Vittorio Storaro feels free to be uninhibitedly intellectual, Terence Davies extravagantly modest, Freddie Young defiantly down to earth, the Coen brothers unrepentantly quirky. And, in all our contributors' attempts to communicate (dare I say it) art, we crave on their behalf your indulgence should they veer, however fleetingly, into the dreaded domain of pretension.

Reflections On . . .

Mike Figgis with Nicolas Cage and Elisabeth Shue (photo by Suzanne Hannover).

1 The Award Season

Mike Figgis

I am now a member of the award circuit. *Leaving Las Vegas* has been noticed and endorsed by groups of critics. It started at Toronto in September of last year and it will culminate in just over a week with the Oscars. I have been invited to attend most of these award events and in most cases, wherever possible, I do. Here are some of my observations.

15 September 1995, Toronto

Having been turned down by every other major festival, MGM is pinning a lot on this screening. I am told that we have a great spot, closing the festival. In fact, it turns out that *Devil in a Blue Dress* has this moment. Nevertheless, the screening goes well and the venue is packed. Afterwards a party is given in our name at a disco. Inside, the place is heaving and hot and the music so loud that you cannot have a conversation – which is exactly what everyone wants to do. We (Nic Cage, Elisabeth Shue, etc.) leave as soon as is polite and head back to the hotel to have a drink. The bar is closed but under pressure they open it again and we drink and talk. I think we were all excited about the reaction to the film.

The next night the Q Tarantino gang arrive with *Four Rooms* and are greeted like rock stars, but apparently the film plays badly. I feel sorry for them. When *Pulp Fiction* came out, there was so much hype that I knew that his next film would be very difficult for him. Look what happened to both Steven Soderberg and David Lynch. Americans are so desperate to find a home-grown genius that they smother all candidates in childhood.

The next day we do press junkets all day. The publicity people have the smart idea of having just one film crew. Interviewers come and go and are handed a tape as they leave. Average interview time is ten minutes and questions range from:

'Oh boy, that's some dark movie you made.'
'What made you think of Nic Cage?'
'What made you think of Elisabeth Shue?'

'What was it about the book that interested you?'

'So, Mike, you wrote the script, you directed the film, you did the music and you're gangster number three. Is it difficult to wear four hats?'

After four interviews I become acutely aware that the crew is listening to the same answers over and over again. I become embarrassed at the banality of my answers and so I begin to vary them. I try never to give the same answer twice. At the end of the day the sound man tells me it has been an interesting day for him and I feel genuinely pleased at the compliment.

The British Airways terminal was anarchy. The flight had been diverted because of engine failure. We had to get to the next festival, San Sebastian. Air India was the only choice. Images of explosions over the sea flashed into my mind as we checked in free-form anarchy style. The flight was . . . interesting. Good curry, old jet, worn carpets (metal fatigue?). This has to be one of the oldest jumbos in service. Anti-rust paint around the door. We were given a free CD of film themes from the sixties. I knew one of the titles. I lost my signed poster and have never had the nerve to ask everyone to sign another.

19 September, San Sebastian

I arrived at the festival and attended the screening of the film. It seemed to go well. There were parties with a lot of alcohol and the town itself is very pretty. I was last here with *Stormy Monday* in '88 or '89. I still have a press clipping on my wall of me and Melanie Griffith doing a press conference. She had lost her bags and was wearing a borrowed tuxedo and looked very beautiful. *Leaving Las Vegas* was in the competition and so there was an element of anticipation. Two of the jury members were known to me and were inevitably present at some of these drinking sessions. They were tight-lipped at all times and studiously refused to mention the film. The results were to be announced on the final Friday of the festival, the day we were due to fly back to London. Nothing was said. On arriving in London, there was a message saying that the film had been awarded Best Actor and Best Director and asking whether we could all come back as soon as possible; the presentation was taking place the next day. So we all set off for the airport at first light and in due course arrived back at the hotel just in time for a quick nap and the award ceremony. Oh, there was also a rehearsal for Spanish TV, where I met Emma Thompson, who was to give me the award.

Back at the hotel dressing for the event, I was drawn to the balcony by the noise of a large crowd. I was impressed. Over a thousand people had gathered outside the hotel and were making strange noises. A chant began and I think the word whore (*puta*) was fairly dominant. Suddenly, without any warning, the crowd exploded into action and from out of nowhere riot police appeared. People running everywhere and screaming and shouting. Police chasing them into side streets. Just as quickly as it started it was all over. Downstairs in the lobby, as we gathered for our red carpet walk we were assured that it was nothing.

The award is a silver conch shell in a velvet-lined display case. As we go on stage at the end fake snow, made from soap suds, begins to fall and the stage is very slippery. I notice that my award is actually for Victoria Abril and she has mine. Spanish friends later tell us that they saw it live on TV and were excited. It was here in San Sebastian that I first came across the 'gift bag'. At dinner, each chair has on it a very smart carrier bag saying Hermes or Chanel, or something like that. The bag contains some cosmetic freebie, or maybe a T-shirt, hip flask or cigarette box. It is possible to amass hundreds of these items, as all seasoned festival folk leave them untouched. The food is of the club-class airline variety. Talking of which, on the way back to London the next day we travelled with Christopher Hampton and Emma Thompson. On the BA flight we all tucked into the *Sunday Times* and I read with horror a particularly vicious attack on *Carrington* and in particular on Emma Thompson, now sitting two rows back and about to announce to the world the break up of her marriage. I don't think English critics are a very nice bunch and I'd love to start a new film magazine that would put them all out of business.

7 January 1996, New York Critics' Circle

As I go through immigration at JFK, the passport man scrutinizes my photo and then stares at me, then back at the photo. I'm innocent of anything that he might suspect, but still I'm nervous. He looks at me, then back at the photo, he tap taps on the computer keys and then looks at the screen. Eventually, I get my passport back and he says, 'Good luck with Oscar nominations!'

The morning of the awards I woke early, jet-lagged and looked out of the window to see my first American blizzard. Quite beautiful. The snow was dry and serious. By the time the limo arrived it was laying thick and fast. Stretch limos are not ideal for blizzards and it was touch and go whether we would make it. Of course, we did. At the Rockefeller Center some die-hard camera crews had turned up and we were all asked to do interviews as we came in. In the coming months the questions would become more than familiar.

We have the airline-style dinner and the ceremony begins. They had asked me who I would like to present the Best Film award and I'd suggested Woody Allen. Woody Allen doesn't do that sort of thing so I suggested Richard Gere. Richard accepts but is delayed by the snow and for a while it seems that Quentin T is going to do it, but then Richard makes it after all. Other winners include Terry Zwigoff (director of *Crumb*) and Mira Sorvino, who's here accepting an award for Woody Allen. Over the season they become very familiar faces. Speeches are made, some long, some short, some funny, some extremely boring. Nic is very nervous and anxious. I realize that Catherine Deneuve is sitting at the next table. Eventually our turn arrives and Nic, accepting his second award for Best Actor, makes a nice short speech thanking all the right people and gets off the stage. I look out of the window and see that the snow is blowing sideways and upwards. The wind howls and I wonder if we are going to get out of the venue and back to the hotel. Everyone by now is pretty ripped and it's a nice feeling. I'm glad to be in New York with all these critics, but I realize that I have not prepared a speech and try to think of something clever to say.

Richard is announced and makes his way on to the small stage. He speaks. First he announces that he is not sure why he accepted to come at all, given that the New York critics have not been very kind to him in the past. There is some laughter, slightly nervous. Next he points out that the Brazilian man who has just been given a special award for running an alternative cinema still owes him money for some air fares from some fifteen years ago when he went to the Rio Film Festival. Then he talks about me and says what a great guy I am and that the four films I have made – I point out that it is actually seven – OK, seven . . .

Then I have to go and speak. I decide to be different. I propose a toast to Buñuel's *Exterminating Angel* (Catherine D visibly perks up). The glasses go up and I point to the window and the blizzard and suggest that as we are all going to be spending the night together, we had better choose a partner (laughter). I say that my first choice would be Catherine D. I'm still not sure whether she was offended or not.

We make it back to the hotel and get very drunk with many actors, directors and producers. Fifteen inches of snow falls and a siege mentality sets in. Rivalries are momentarily forgotten. It was very romantic and memorable for three days, but frustrating when we tried to leave New York. Eventually MGM-UA put us on Concorde, figuring that it was still cheaper than the room service bill at the Four Seasons. At the terminal I am spotted by Terry Gilliam, who looks at me, then looks out of the window at Concorde, then back at me. 'Not bad for 16mm, Figgis!'

17 January, LA Critics' Circle

I'd been surprised that the LA critics had been so generous, there being such rivalry between New York and LA. The *LA Times* review was not good. We'd been named Best Picture and also been given Best Director, Best Actor and Best Actress.

Turning up in the stretch I was surprised by how many press and TV crews were waiting outside the hotel. Autograph hunters with photographs to be signed. Where do they get the photographs? The flashes go off and it's blinding. It occurs to me that a lot of the photographs must be useless because of the double flashing bleaching the neg. More interviews of the 'Did you ever imagine this little picture would get this far?' variety. But now a new question starts to emerge: 'What hope for the Oscars?'

Inside, the format is consistent. Honorary awards are given for this and that. Some of the speeches are funny, some are not. All are long and the food is still of the airline variety. This is a weekday lunch and people have to go back to work so the awards are given out while we eat. Several hundred people trying to use a knife and fork quietly is a very interesting sound. At one point a journalist was making a plea for Third World disease awareness and spoke passionately about diarrhoea. At this point the tonality of the massed utensils became momentarily muted. The Best Director award was presented at the end and again I'd decided not to write a speech but to wait for inspiration. Late in the meal it came. Just before my moment, I borrowed a hardback book from one of the critics, took off its dust jacket and walked on to the stage with it. I said that I felt that everything that had to be said had already been said and at times like this there was no better thing to do than fall back on the classics (this being the year of Jane Austen). I opened the book and announced that I was going to read the third chapter of *War and Peace*. The look of horror on the audience's faces was pretty good and their laughter due to sheer relief.

21 January, Golden Globes

On a cold wet day in London the news came through that the film had been nominated for the Globes. This is an event that up until fairly recently had been thought of as a bit of a joke – the Hollywood Foreign Press Association's annual get-together. Now, like all the other awards, it has taken on weight and is another excuse for everyone to practise for the Oscars. It also has a significant effect on the marketing of the film. MGM pump in more P and A money and the film goes a little bit wider. Annie Stewart, the producer of *Leaving Las Vegas*, calls me from LA to tell me that Armani would like to be my tailor for the event. This is interesting. Armani has not been so aggressive in the past, but in recent years Hugo Boss has been and Quentin T and the boys are wearing his stuff (as well as Nic). Thank God, say I, it's time the guys like me got some attention and I accept his offer with indecent haste in case he was kidding or changes his mind. A couple of days later I get a little card from Versace with the same offer. Too late, my friend, I'm playing on Giorgio's team now. I have a fitting and choose a fab tux. Wanda, my new best friend, tells me that Giorgio would like to make me something special for the Oscars. I point out to her that the nominations have yet to be announced and she gives me an old-fashioned look and says that Giorgio has seen the film and is in no doubt that I am going to be nominated. This is one of the nicest things that has ever happened to me . . . in my life . . . so far. Have you ever tried to wear an award?

The day arrives and the limo turns up at the hotel to pick up my wife Bienchen and me. Unfortunately, LA is having a biannual rain storm. Tropical stuff. The limo is old. On days like this they must get every stretch ever built out of mothballs, a bit like a Battle of Britain fly-past. As we set off in the storm it strikes me as funny that in NY it snowed and here it is still raining. But I'm feeling damned good in the tux from Giorgio (and the shoes and the shirt and the beret). Suddenly a huge deluge of water comes through the roof on to us. The sun roof has a leaky seal and a backlog of rain water must have been building up for some time. Leaks appear at other points in the roof and we do our best to dodge them as we make our way to Annie's house to pick up her and her date, Danny Huston. The limo driver is an extremely nice man from the East Coast who doesn't know his way around town so I, the Brit, direct him . . .

We eventually arrive at the Hotel, the Beverly Hilton, the venue for a lot of these awards. They have laid out a massively long red carpet on which we walk into the hotel. It is now at saturation point and as we step on to its thick luxuriance, we sink up to our ankles in wet carpet, stopping every three or four yards to chat to the press, the way we've all seen Charles and Di do on walkabouts. The press are safely cordoned off behind rope barriers. Flash, flash, flash, flash. Mike . . . Mike, this way, CNN, Mike, BBC, Mike. Did you ever think this little old film would? . . . Are you nervous? (No.) What do you think your chances are at the Oscars? (Haven't a clue.)

Once inside we make our way to the table, which has a number and place names. Apparently some early arrivals, not happy with their table's proximity to the stage have switched table numbers and a modicum of anarchy and confusion is rife. Seasoned waiters seem to have spotted the ruse, but are unable to find the culprits. Heads are swivelling as celebs are spotted, Tom, Nicole, Mel, Michelle, Nic, Patricia, Tom (the other one), Sean (the elder), Pitt (the younger), Meryl and, of course, Sharon. Without wanting to name-drop, I can tell you that I'd spent the afternoon just the day before with Ms Stone and she'd shown me her outfit (Valentino, of course) and her closet. She also gave me a brooch to wear for good luck, but I couldn't find anything to pin it on to so I brought it in my pocket in case we bumped into each other, at which point I would have whipped it out, so to speak, and held it to my chest or somewhere.

The airline food was served and the wine wasn't too bad, until they took it all away. This was because the event was being sponsored by a champagne company and they'd insisted that the only alcohol in evidence had to be theirs. Huge bottles of champagne were opened and placed on every table. I never saw anyone drink any. What a waste. Water, on the other hand had to be paid for. The live telecast began and I watched the cameramen and crew with real admiration as they wiggled their way through the sardine seating and lined up the correct shot for the next nomination. 'Excuse me, are you so and so?' 'No, that's him there.' 'Thanks a lot, pal.' For some reason the director awards were very early on and I clapped heartily as Mel Gibson went up to thank the world. 'I see,' I thought to myself, grinning cheerfully to the cameras in case they wanted a reaction shot, which they didn't.

Next we went into TV award hell, something that blissfully will be absent from the Oscars, and which alone makes the Oscars special. 'And the award for child acting in a day-time soap goes to . . .' Elisabeth doesn't get her award, Sharon does and she says exactly what she'd told me she'd say, 'No one is more surprised than I am.' She says a lot more and the tele-prompter behind us (but in front of her) starts to flash something like 'Get off! Get off!' Sharon has had to deal with far worse than that and takes her time. Nic does win and makes a nice speech, but forgets to mention Annie until the last moment where his mind clearly goes quite blank. Travolta forgets to thank his wife but does thank Ron Hubbard (which later is put forward as a theory as to why he doesn't get nominated for an Oscar). Brad thanks his woman and the manufacturer of an anti-diarrhoea product and then it is all over, and about a thousand people head for the exit and their stretch limos. If you lined up all the stretch limos in LA . . .? We never find ours and have to cadge a lift with someone else. This limo driver also doesn't know LA so we have to direct him via the intercom phone in the back. We party hop for a while. Celebs everywhere and they treat me as if . . . I was a celeb. Amazing. I notice that I'm leaving much bigger tips. You need balls to get out of a stretch limo in an Armani suit in front of a bunch of photographers without giving a large tip to an incompetent driver. It does lead to a more profound understanding of the workings of the culture of the town known as LA. I return to England to rest. I work on the rewriting of a Joe Eszterhas script and show a dance documentary to Billy Forsythe for his approval (which he gives). My family show concern for my health and tell me to rest.

24, 25 January, Brussels and Amsterdam Festivals

My first chunnel crossing. I didn't like it much. They serve airline food, and lunch is at 11 a.m. At the hotel in Brussels the interviews begin immediately. Elisabeth is here. One French-speaking TV crew wants to do the interview running around the corridors of the hotel with a steadi-cam. The interviewer is a hip chick in leather trousers who reads the questions in broken English from a piece of crumpled paper. Her strange accenting and phrasing leads me to suspect that English is not her strong suit. I ask the cameraman at what speed he wishes the walking interview to be conducted and he says that he doesn't care. So I set off at a brisk pace and they begin running backwards. The hip chick never looks back (a mistake, in my opinion) and bounces off the many right-angle turns in the corridor, this being a Euro hotel built around an atrium. I take them into an open lift and the interview concludes. I'd love to see it one day. That evening we miss the end of the screening because dinner (airline style) has taken too long and then we go to do a Q and A session in the middle of a beer tent, where the noise level is intense. The translator is a very shy, quietly spoken man. Everything has to be translated and it takes for ever. Next morning I sleep in and miss breakfast and have to start without even coffee. That evening we drive to Rotterdam and on the way I try to conduct an interview with an Irish journalist by mobile phone. On arrival we go to eat in a restaurant. It is bitterly cold and snow is trying to fall. We catch the end of the screening and I notice that the film is running at the wrong speed and so all the voices are like Donald Duck. No one else seems to mind but I am very angry at the sloppiness and wonder how many times this happens around the world without anyone monitoring it. However, they seem to like the film and the interviews the next day are stimulating and different, and I remember why I always liked working here in the past.

13 February, Academy Nominations

For the past week I have been on another junket, this time a tour of some American universities. Annie Stewart accompanies me. Philadelphia, Washington, Michigan, Atlanta, Austin and finally UCLA in LA. The screenings have been huge, almost two thousand students in some places and the enthusiasm has been very invigorating. Endless talks with students and good interviews for college newspapers and campus radio and TV stations. In LA the nominations are announced very early in the morning in LA so that they can be watched in New York. For some reason I do not set my alarm clock and wake up twenty minutes late. I turn on the TV in time to hear the announcer say: 'And that must be a huge disappointment for the *Leaving Las Vegas* team.' I flick from channel to channel and only hear snippets. *Sense and Sensibility* seems to have done well. *Babe* seems to have done very well. *Dead Man Walking* seems to have done well. *Il Postino* seems to have done very well. *Leaving Las Vegas . . .* 'What happened there, Pete?' I turn on the radio and begin dialling through the waveband while channel hopping on the TV. The phone rings and my assistant, Amancia, congratulates me from London. I ask her to put me out of my misery: four nominations but no Best Picture. The next day the trades all have big stories asking why we did not get the Best Picture nomination. As I avidly scan them I realize, sadly, that I have become an award junkie and Polanski's advice has been temporarily cast aside. Actually his advice was about reviews: 'If you believe the good ones then you have to believe the bad ones too.' TV crews arrive at my house. The phone rings immediately. Everyone wants a quote or a funny 'What were you doing when you heard the news?' story. I tell them I was asleep, but no one prints it. They all want to know if I am upset about the absence of a Best Picture nomination. The truth is I am not. It all seems slightly insane and I have a terrible headache. It makes hardly a ripple in the English press, who have now decided that Emma is a bit of all right again. I can't work out if I am insulted or not. Have I really become an award junkie?

I return to England to rest.

2 March, DGA Awards, New York

This time we arrive on Concorde. The film is now doing very well at the box office, over a thousand screens and $20,000,000 in the bank. Again we are at the Four Seasons Hotel. The awards are to be held simultaneously in LA and New York. Everything proceeds as usual. Limo turns up, we arrive at the venue, cocktail party, some interviews for CNN, Entertainment TV, gossip columns and then into the ballroom for the airline dinner. This is going to be a long evening, I think to myself, as the third cabaret act takes the stage. All of the winners of all the categories are in LA, but still we go through the motions of announcing the nominees and opening the envelope. Endless TV awards and commercial awards and news awards. At our table we maintain a jolly ambience, but I notice a lot of watch gazing. During the fifth or sixth cabaret act I become aware of someone crouching by my side in the gloom. It is a man from the DGA, who tells me that the three film director nominees present – me, Ron Howard and Ang Lee – will all be getting some kind of nomination 'thing', and that when our names are called, we should go on to the stage to pick it up and that if we want we can speak but it is not a requirement. I nod at him in acknowledgement and he scurries off in the gloom. A long while later I hear my name being called over the PA and I spring to my feet and get on the stage to receive this huge open box with a silver plate-type thing in it. There is warm applause which I thank the audience for. In my short speech I tell the audience that I'm aware of the novelty factor, i.e., I tell them I am proud to be a member. And I get off. Next, they call Ron (it's alphabetical, you see) and he bounds on to the stage and immediately says that he agrees with me, that it is indeed an honour to be recognized by one's peers. He goes on to say that he'd like to thank . . .

. . . ten minutes later, having worked his way through the crew, the producers, the distributors, his daughter, his best pal (his wife), he gets off. During this time I become increasingly uncomfortable and nervously glance around the table at the men from MGM-UA and their wives. None of whom I have thanked or even mentioned. It is they who specifically asked that I be in New York for this event so that they could share it with me. But to make a speech for being nominated, not even knowing who the winner is? My feelings become increasingly ambiguous. Next they call Ang Lee's name. He has had time to think about this and in hesitant English he thanks everyone in the world as well. Call me paranoid, but I'm telling you, the temperature around my table has become very chilly. It seems to me that suddenly everyone is gazing intently at the stage and not returning my calls. I begin to pray for victory so that I can get back up there and make things all right again. I was told beforehand that it was between me and one other director; I know that Mel Gibson was the favourite and that he is in LA. A woman comes on stage and opens an envelope. She looks at the card inside and begins smiling. 'The great news is that the winner tonight is here with us in New York . . .' I let out my breath and am halfway out of the chair as she finishes the sentence. 'And the winner is . . . Ron Howard.' Ron Howard? Yes, Ron, and he bounds youthfully on to the stage and continues to demonstrate his ability to memorize entire phone books.

I don't recall anyone saying goodnight to me and the ride back to the hotel was strange. I was angry with myself and felt that I had let the side down badly. The next day I rang Frank Lomento at MGM and asked him to apologize to everyone for my gaff. He assured me that it wasn't a big deal, but the words 'big deal' further convinced me that it was. I was also angry at not being told what the form was beforehand.

The next night I flew to LA. As we were coming in to land I was watching *The Scarlet Letter* and dozing. I opened my eyes and the entire staff of stewards was standing in front of me holding a bottle of champagne, two glasses, some chocolates and some aspirin. They wished me luck at the Oscars and said how much they'd loved the film. I had a little tear in my eye.

13 March, Academy Nominees' Lunch, LA

Back to the Beverly Hilton, same room, different decor, same food, quick waiters. No stretch limo today; I drive myself. Lots of cameras and press. People have told me that today will be fun. Annie Stewart is my guest. We find ourselves at a table with Sid Ganis, who I know from *Internal Affairs* days, when he was an executive at Paramount. There seems to be a policy not to put people with their friends. Nic is at one table, Elisabeth at another. Quincy Jones, who is running the show this year, gives us a lecture on how to receive the award, how to walk (quickly), how to talk (quickly) and what not to do, which turns out to be what everyone will do, namely thank everyone in the world. We all pose for a huge group photograph and then one by one, in alphabetical order, we all walk on to the stage and get a certificate proving that we are nominated, a sweatshirt and a poster. I, being a double nominee, get two certificates (but only one sweatshirt).

17 March, Writers' Guild Awards, LA

The limo picks me up at 3.15 p.m. and we then pick up Evgenia Sands (Julian Sands's wife), who has kindly agreed to sit at the *Leaving Las Vegas* table. Lastly we pick up Annie Stewart. We arrive at the Beverly Hilton. This is now the third time I have been to this venue. We have deliberately turned up a little bit late to avoid the cocktail party and I'm hoping that this will be a short event. From the limo I see the line of photographers and camera crew. I decide to sneak past them and I almost succeed before I'm stopped by an official, who politely tells me to go and talk to the girl from the BBC radio. She has some difficulty getting her Sony recorder to work, but eventually we get going. Other news types see me talking and they request soundbites also. I discover why it was so easy to sneak past. None of them has any idea who I am. They all ask me to spell my name and the name of the film. Clearly the Writers' Guild is not being given too high a profile. Inside we are give a table number, 126, and we sit down and wait for the event to start. Dinner is served; some salad, some steak and then some very sweet desert. A bottle of wine is thrown in, but everything after that has to be paid for. The waiters are a very tough bunch and plates are hurled around and whipped away if you show any hesitation. My guess is that they are all airline staff moonlighting. I say hello to Kalli Khouri and tell her I like her movie (*Something to Talk About*), which I do.

The evening begins with a long speech about the importance of writers and I think to myself that the speaker should have used a writer. Next we meet the MC who is a female sketch writer and comedienne. She has a thankless task ahead of her. She has to be funny and keep things moving. She also has to introduce the personalities, who in turn will introduce the nominees and then open the envelope and announce the winning names. Most of the jokes are about Joe Eszterhas.

There are honorary awards which entail watching montages of work interspersed with specially shot interview material. The honorary awards take the longest and there seem to be a lot of them. The film writing awards are the final two events. I find myself drinking. In fact, I find myself getting quite drunk and it crosses my mind that if I win I might make a spectacle of myself. This option does not arrive and Emma's producer again thanks everyone in her absence.

23 March, Spirit Awards, LA

The limo arrives. My whole family is here for the Oscars. They get into the limo and I cross around and get into the other side. It's actually quite difficult to get into one of these monsters. As I open the door, Steve, our driver, says something which sounds like a warning. In fact, it is a warning. The entire door panel falls away. Another example of mothball limo syndrome. We put the door back together and set off for Santa Monica. It crosses my mind that if there are a lot of photographers the door falling off might be a good entrance.

The event takes place in a tent on the beach and it is a clear, windy day. Several hundred press and TV people are waiting and it is very difficult to get into the tent without talking to all of them. As this is only a couple of days before the Oscars, nearly all the questions are about how this event compares with the big one. The Spirit Awards are for independent films only. Once inside I see that the free gift factor is again at work, this time it's a rucksack full of magazines, cosmetics and two CDs, one of which is *Leaving Las Vegas*, the other *Dead Man Walking*. The food is comfortably familiar and I don't eat any of it. Today the film is nominated for Best Actor, Best Actress, Best Screenplay, Best Director and Best Picture. Yesterday someone rang me with a rumour that we'd swept the awards, but I don't trust rumours. The MC is Samuel Jackson and he is pretty good and scathing in some of his comments, many of which are aimed at Miramax. Jodie Foster is a leading figure in the indie world and she says a few words to get things going. The ceremony is blissfully quick and the big upset is that Nic loses to Sean Penn. This is the only time, so far, that Nic has lost to anyone. This time Elisabeth does win. Throughout she was unfailingly loyal and generous towards Nicolas and me and the film, and continues to be so even though she did not win many of the awards. When she accepted her Spirit award she also thanked Jennifer Jason Leigh for inspiration via her performance in *Last Exit to Brooklyn*. Declan Quinn wins the cinematography award – which is great. Also, Annie and Lila share the producing award. I win for directing and make quite a long speech about how difficult it is for the low-budget film because of the restrictive practices of the unions. This is slightly sensitive ground, but it gets a good response and I do my best to avoid treading on too many toes. This time I remember to thank MGM-UA, but forget to thank my family who are all present. The event finishes and it is very difficult to get to the car because so many people want to say something personal. We get to the car eventually and as we pull up at a light four young men in the car next to us say something like, 'Fucking stretch, I don't give a fuck who it is, fuck 'em.' I poke my head out and loudly agree with them as the light turns to green and they turn left and we go straight. This throws them because they never get to see who said it. Nic must be getting very nervous in this home stretch; he and Sean are big rivals. Didn't get a chance to say hello to him afterwards.

25 March, Oscars, LA

Some time ago I went to the Armani store in Beverly Hills and had a fitting for my special tuxedo. I think the design I chose was something they were hoping to get Quentin T to wear but he went over to Hugo Boss. It's a long coat with a velvet collar and silver lining. The lining was my idea; I have an ego as well. The week before the Oscars the coat turns up but it's all wrong, not a long coat but standard length. They are very contrite in the store and fax Milan and promise me that it will be made in time for the big night. Eventually it does turn up and is very special, but the day I go to pick it up they tactfully ask me to leave before Mel Gibson arrives. The fitting room has racks of clothes in it waiting to be picked up by the chosen.

On the morning of the Oscars I try to sleep late and have a normal breakfast. In fact, I am not in the slightest bit nervous and am in complete agreement with David Thomson's predictions (which, for the most part, prove to be entirely accurate). My entire family has joined me at the Château Marmont and it is interesting to see what my two sons look like in tuxedos. My daughter chooses to wear an antique dress that I bought a long time ago in a shop in Devon. My wife has borrowed a diamond necklace from the appropriate store in Beverly Hills and my two sons set off in a taxi armed with IDs to pick it up. The necklace is valued at about $650,000 and it's handed over without a murmur. The boys decide to go to another store and leave the necklace in the taxi for a while.

The inevitable stretch limo turns up and we depart at about 3.00 p.m. It's very hot in the back and the driver, a young girl called Laura, sets off over Laurel Canyon, which is a very winding road. The windows do not open from the back and we have to ask her to do it. It feels like we're schoolchildren on an outing. We drive into The 'Valley' and get on a freeway and about forty minutes into the journey we drive past the Sunset Boulevard exit, about a half mile from the hotel. We see lots of other limos heading in the same direction. As we get closer to the theatre we see some helicopters circling. We join a huge line of limos and creep forward. Out of the window we see a huge crowd. Some people are holding banners with religious right-wing statements: 'Homo Sex Is a Sin', 'Sex Is a Sin', etc., etc. Jesse Jackson is boycotting the event because there are no black nominees. There are also no Hispanic nominees or Asian, for that matter. Our windows are dark but people press their faces against the glass, trying to work out if we mean anything. It's very hot in the back. Suddenly we are there and doors are opened violently by a team of red-coated flunkies. The noise of the helicopters is incredible and we are urged onto a red carpet and announced over a PA system. The rest of my family go ahead while my wife and I walk the line from camera to camera. Live interviews start. It's impossible to hear properly or to think straight and I have no recollection of any conversation. As I wait behind Claudia Schiffer and her magician, I become aware that my foot is stuck to the red carpet, courtesy of a huge wedge of bubble gum which some celebrity has dropped. The gum dogs my footsteps all evening. Eventually we get into the theatre. It is impossible not to peer into the faces for a famous name. We make our way to our allocated seats. It seems that all nominees have aisle seats. Rod Steiger makes himself known as a fan of the film. Anthony Hopkins says hello. Tom Cruise and Nicole Kidman say hello. Sharon Stone says hello. I wish everyone luck and realize afterwards that half of them are guests and not nominees.

At this point it is still exciting. An atmosphere of something about to happen. The show starts. Three and a half hours later it finishes and by that time I am very depressed and bored. Nic wins his award and Elisabeth and I do not. It's a huge relief that it is over and that this is the final ceremony. Here are a few images from the three and a half hours:

Christopher Reeve is revealed in the middle of the stage in a wheelchair. He makes a very moving speech and I find myself in tears. He gets a standing ovation, but as he finishes we go into a commercial break and a barrier slowly comes down between him and us. As the barrier is coming down we see on a huge TV screen a Revlon commercial by Cindy Crawford. I found the two images together quite disturbing. At the break there is a stampede for the bar, the only place where smoking is permitted. Substitute guests come in to fill all the empty seats.

Richard Dreyfuss is sitting in front of me. He has his teenage daughter with him. During every break she gets a mobile phone out of her bag and makes calls. Later, Steven Spielberg does a nice speech leading up to Kirk Douglas's honorary award. Kirk walks with difficulty and has problems with his speech after his recent stroke. A mobile phone rings and young Ms Dreyfuss makes a cute 'whoops' gesture and turns it off. A camerman fights his way down our row to get a shot of someone behind us. He shoulders my wife aside and supports his weight on her shoulder. She tries to get out of his way and he tells her, annoyed, 'Relax.' The only moment of genuine audience response was to the English group, Stomp, who managed to get something cooking for a short moment. There seemed to be a bit of an obsession with death; the idea that film gives some kind of immortality and that the ageing or the dying of actors is some kind of special event, different from ordinary folk.

It was also clear that the technical awards seemed to reflect some kind of internal carve up. Personally, I thought that the editing and sound and music on *Leaving Las Vegas* were special and certainly as good as anything being fêted that evening.

When the Best Actor award came up, I had a feeling that Nic was not going to get it. When he did I experienced a huge drop in energy and a wave of depression, which I suppose was due to relief that it was now all over at last. It has been a somewhat uncomfortable period to be in, and yet not in, this special club.

After the awards there was a 'Governors Ball', to which my kids were not invited. We made plans to meet up later. The ball was chaos. Winners walked around with heavy trophies not quite knowing what had hit them and not knowing what to do with the things. Much hugging, congratulating and consoling. A man approached me and wanted to know why there was no 'back story' in *Leaving Las Vegas*. I sat at a table with Nic's mother and his grandmother. The food was good, but they were not hungry so quite sensibly took it home with them in a plastic bag. I said a quick thing or two to Nic and then gave him back to the mob. We ate quickly and left.

Outside there was anarchy as everyone tried to find their limo. I gave my number and waited for an hour and a half. During that time, waiting in harsh tungsten light, I said hello to Robin Williams, another fan, it seems. We fell into conversation with lots of people, the way you would waiting for a bus. A mugger's paradise. Eventually we found our driver, who informed us that she had been parked twenty yards away waiting for her call. We set off for the next rendezvous. More traffic jams, more circuitous driving. Spago and the Miramax party. We got in, but my kids were held back. I kicked up a fuss and they got in. As I did so, it crossed my mind that as a loser I might not have the same clout I had as a nominee, but my change in status had not quite filtered through yet. I attempted to get drunk and, with Stephen Rea, eventually succeeded.

The next morning I had a complete hangover. Part alcohol abuse, part award season abuse. But I survived.

2 Credits and Debits

John Boorman

There was a time, not so long ago, when movies concluded with a simple caption saying 'the end', with the possible addition of 'released by MGM' or whichever. Those brief words would be accompanied by sounds of the audience stampeding for the exit. Of course, the resolving chords of the swelling music would warn that the end was nigh, so the exodus would often begin earlier still. In Britain, we wanted to get out before the National Anthem would freeze-frame the auditorium.

John Boorman (photo by Steve Pyke).

Today, those end credits go on for three, four, even seven minutes. And surprisingly, many people stay and sit through them. Are they really interested in the names of the drivers, the neg. cutters, the caterers and accounts assistants? No. They are listening to the music. Interminable end-credits at least give the composer a chance for a substantial cue which does not have to follow action. Often it is a reprise of the music in the film, a sort of 'afterture'. If people liked the picture, it becomes a way of savouring the experience.

How has it come about, this ever-sprawling crawl? Partly from trade unions' ever-upward demands, and partly it is a kind of boast by the producers about the huge scale and complexity of their movie.

This mysterious litany is probably becoming familiar to regular movie-goers, although they can surely have little idea of what many of these functions are: ADR Editors, Foleys, Best Boys, Gaffers, Key Grips. In the big special-effects pictures, a whole new slew of functions appears: the computer nerds.

Since the humblest runner or gofer is mentioned, I often wonder why the session musicians are seldom named – a soloist or two, but not the orchestra. Perhaps another eighty names is too daunting even for the vainglorious producer who wants you to count heads. They are certainly more deserving than most. I always marvel how they can walk into a recording studio and play the first time from a score they have never seen before.

John Seale, with whom I worked on *Beyond Rangoon*, told his agent that he did not want the credit of Director of Photography because there is only one director on a picture. His agent told him that the union had fought for years for this dignified title and that he would be a traitor to his brethren to forgo it. Except on the credits, few of us use that title. We say cameraman or lighting cameraman. However, some Directors of Photography are pressing for more. Finding that they are often working with inexperienced directors who expect them to choose the lenses and break down the scenes into component set-ups, they want to be called Technical Directors.

The escalation of titles causes problems. There used to be an Art Director who had an Assistant Art Director. Art Directors are now called Production Designers and the Assistant Art Director becomes the Art Director. When it comes to awards, the Art Directors clamour to share the honours. In the Oscars, the Set Decorator is linked with the Production Designer, the Art Director omitted.

The Production Co-ordinator used to be the Production Secretary. Co-ordinators now require assistants as behoves their status.

The Production Manager has now become the Line Producer, whose assistant is now naturally called the Production Manager.

The Accountant has become the Financial Controller and, with the help of several high-powered computers, now needs three or four accountants to do what he or she formerly did alone with a calculator.

Writers have sloughed off the indignities of such credits as 'adapted for the screen by' or 'screenplay by' for the magisterial 'written by'. Many writers are now insisting that they receive additional credit as Associate Producers or Co-Producers. This started out as a way for the writer to ensure he can be around when the film was shot to protect the integrity of his material. Now it has simply become a status symbol. If the writer has enough clout, his agent will negotiate the title for him.

Which brings us to Producers. What technicians and sundry toilers have done to swell the end-roller, producers have done to the opening credits. There used to be one producer on a film, sometimes two if they were partners. Now, Producers, Executive Producers, Associate Producers, Co-Producers and Line Producers often bring the toll up to seven, eight, ten. This is the only credit that can be handed out willy-nilly, there being no union to curb excesses. So these titles often reward a lawyer or a faithful wife for support along the way.

The fact is that in American Studio pictures, the Studio itself is the actual producer: supplying the money, exercising financial control, making the ultimate decisions about casting and script. The Producer in these cases should really be called the Developer. Once the picture is going, the Developer engages a Line Producer (Production Manager) to hire the crew and organize the logistics with the Director. But as budgets get bigger, deals become more complex and Producers proliferate.

There was a time when you hired an actor, you picked them up in a car, they acted and you took them home. Now when a star actor is hired for a role, an extra $250,000 has to be allowed for their 'comfort' costs. There are assistants, a trainer, a nanny for the kids, a masseur, a make-up artist, a hairstylist and (a new wrinkle) an assistant director designated to stand by the director, relaying by walkie-talkie to the star in their trailer the state of affairs on the floor. You will see all these helpers further extending the end-credits.

For the Director to have nothing more than the simple title 'Directed by' indicates to the initiated that he was hired for the job, had no real power and his was not the dominant vision on the movie. To enjoy respect he must have a possessive credit: 'A so-and-so Film' or 'A Film by'. This was once a title hard-earned by an experienced Director and indicated that he or she had shaped the script, cast it, composed the images, edited the film. Now first-time directors want it as by right.

I wonder how long it will be before a writer, director or producer will claim the credit often used in TV series, 'Created by', suggesting a God-like responsibility for the film which casts all other credits into the cosmic shadows.

Lawrence Bender

3 Struggling with Success

Lawrence Bender

When I was younger, some of my friends told me, 'Lawrence, quit acting and become a producer.' It's funny, but as an actor in New York, I never knew what a producer was, and was obviously not happy to hear them say that. However, after years of being an out-of-work actor, I decided to try something different – I had a new mission in life: to become a producer – only to find myself out of work again. I figured at least I would have more control over my life. I soon found how much control producing actually meant. As an actor in New York – even if you weren't working – people gave you respect because they assumed you were an artist working at your craft. I soon found out that in Hollywood it was the exact opposite; as an out-of-work actor, I was at the bottom of the evolutionary scale. So when I started to try to produce – with this background – I didn't find a lot of support and found myself out of work again. I struggled a long time to make it in Hollywood and then suddenly after making *Reservoir Dogs, Fresh* and *Pulp Fiction*, I found myself in the middle of it. I had finally become a producer and had become part of the Hollywood circle – I had reached my goal, had gotten what I wanted. I was driven for so long, and thought I would find happiness once I had achieved my goal. In reality, once I got there, the conflicts within my basic nature were not resolved; in fact, they seemed accentuated.

Throughout my life I have found there is a distinction between two types of people: the driven types who set goals in their lives at the expense of their feelings, and those who are naturally emotional, but who are ineffective achievers. As I was growing up, I felt a conflict within myself between a constant force driving me to achieve and, simultaneously, a yearning to feel and experience life deeply.

Now as a producer in Hollywood, I'm living in a world which magnifies this polarity, because the movie industry is about getting results. It is a culture that recognizes the person who gets things done; it values the achiever. It seems as if everyone in Hollywood is trying to get on a long train which has one direction and one goal – power, money and fame. There are those who are fighting to get on, while those who are already on are fighting their way to the front.

Most of the people I know wake up at 7 a.m., have a breakfast meeting, go to the office, have a lunch meeting, go back to the office, spend the entire day on the phone either signing a client, making a deal, finding the next hot writer/director/actor or trying to resolve the problems they created in the process. Then they go to a screening of a movie in which they have some involvement, go out to dinner afterwards, go home, read a script, maybe look at the budget or list of directors or actors attached to that script. Finally, you go to bed, kissing your kids and your partner goodnight. You wake up in the morning and realize that you only read the first ten pages of the script before you fell asleep, so you read the coverage from the reader on the way to your breakfast meeting with the writer.

Where is the experience of life or intimacy with your loved ones? No wonder for most people in this situation when they reach their goals, they feel so empty inside. When I finished *Reservoir Dogs* and *Pulp Fiction*, people said I must be so happy and feel so fulfilled about what I'd done. The sad thing is, that though I felt the excitement of the achievement of what I had done, there was something missing.

Most people in Hollywood spend their lives trying to become a bigger and bigger part of the machine and, in the end, the machine simply consumes them. I feel, in part, that this is what is happening to me even though I am very happy with what I've produced. I am making movie after movie; I've just created a commercial production company and have many plans for the future. The problem is that the demands of my work do not allow much room for anything except reaching my goals. The world of Hollywood is all about taking action after action – just doing. There is nothing about experiencing love or just being. If you spend your life constantly on the run, how can you ever experience vulnerability and creativity?

For myself, the solution is to find a balance, and not to let my driven self determine my experience of life. Therefore, what I want to create is a new relationship between the 'doer' in me and the part of myself that just 'is', so that I am not only a man of action. It's really difficult because my work not only pulls me away from this ideal, but accentuates this duality within. So, I've had to find things outside my work to help me get to that place.

Throughout my twenties I completely committed and disciplined myself to study dance, singing and acting. When I was growing up, I was the type of person who never showed my emotions, who held everything in. But by immersing myself in the performing arts, I began to connect with the emotional part of myself.

I had so little money that I used to clean my teacher Sandra Seacat's house in exchange for acting classes. I spent my life either going to voice classes, speech classes, singing classes, dance classes, acting classes, acting workshops – or working as a waiter to pay for them. I spent hours every day in my room practising not only these disciplines, but also meditation and relaxation. I was driven to be not just a driven person. In addition to all this, I spent hours in traditional therapy where I learned to recognize the difference between what I had become, due to the conditioning of my childhood, and who I really was.

Through all of this, I became a warmer person, more available to people, more at ease with being in the world; I simply became less afraid to express myself. Years later, when I became a producer, I realized that this had been a part of the training that has led me to what I do. In my twenties, I used my willpower to become attuned to myself. In a sense, I was spending my batteries in order to recharge them, but at least I was recharging them. Up until recently, as a producer, I felt I was spending lots of energy and depleting myself; I felt burned out – as if my batteries needed to be recharged. Producing had only satisfied one half of me, and because of the insane amount of time it requires, it consumed me. In order for me to be finally happy in my producing, I needed to incorporate that other half of myself. All the work I did in my twenties was to get closer to my heart, and it's that work which had helped my drive to succeed as a producer. I need to rekindle my heart again, but I need to do it differently from how I did it before.

I chose to begin this new process by working with Alvaro Lopez Watermann and Dominique Sire. Over the years both have developed their own personal forms of teaching. The core of Alvaro's work is to take the inner life of a person revealed through dreams and help the person channel them into a creative form. Dominique, in her workshops, uses the language of the body to identify and transform the unconscious, self-defeating patterns that run our lives.

Dominique was doing her workshops in San Francisco during the making of *Pulp Fiction*. It might sound crazy to fly to San Francisco to do workshops after working all week on a movie, but, in fact, they were very supportive. A film set is like a family – one in which the emotional and dysfunctional aspects can become intensified. There are about one hundred people working together to make something happen under the pressure of time and money. The problem is that there is never enough of either. Every person in each department has a specific job, and at the same time, each person depends on others to fulfil his or her own part. Ultimately, this creates an emotional pressure cooker. Add the physicality of the job and lack of sleep to the equation and it's understandable why insane things can happen. People get defensive and go in fear. There are breakdowns in communication. People become manipulative or abusive because they don't know how to handle their frustration and anger. This results in more resentment, which leads to disempowerment and makes it more difficult to get to the goal. There are also many times when people feel unappreciated and unsupported by those in charge. I feel personally that as a producer it is my job to create an environment where this happens as little as possible. I have found it's possible to do this not by damage control, but by creating another type of environment. As I worked with Dominique, I began to learn not to be at the effect of my own emotions, and consequently it improved my ability to work with people on the set.

Dominique's philosophy is that we live in a world that tends to emphasize the development of the mind at the cost of our heart and instinctual self. The nature of the mind is to oppose; it is rigid, linear and controlling. The mind resists experiencing feelings such as fear, pain and anger by trying to control or deny them. To achieve this, the mind separates us from our emotional self. Consequently, this creates an internal war. The mind wins, leaving us with a semblance of safety and power, but ultimately with a sense of disconnection from life.

It is inevitable that throughout life we will have to confront fear, pain and anger. Dominique believes that when you learn not to resist those experiences but to include them, you can have both your feelings and your goals – and a fuller experience of life. Through this new way of being you can access a different type of intelligence: your intuition, instincts and creativity. By learning not to be at the effect of your emotions, you learn not to be at the effect of your circumstances. In other words, you don't need to separate yourself from life in order to achieve in life. You become powerful in a different kind of way. You discover the power of the heart, a power that is not based on overpowering.

Dominique has developed specific exercises that use conscious movements to bypass the censoring, editing and controlling mind. Through these exercises we begin to integrate mind and heart and to live accordingly. It is no longer is a mental concept, but becomes a place from which to operate.

Inherent in the role of the producer is power and authority. Because producers are responsible for money and time, they are obliged to pressure people and make demands. It is difficult for a producer to hold that kind of power without becoming overpowering; to be demanding without being abusive. The irony is that this kind of power makes you removed and separate from the people on the set, and this, in turn, disempowers you.

Through my work with Dominique I'm learning to use my direct will to achieve my goals without having to put on hold my experiences, moment to moment; I've become more receptive to those around me, which results in me having a clearer understanding of their desires and goals. By existing in the moment, on the set, I am becoming more competent at solving conflicts by responding to people instead of reacting to them. The result is that my power empowers people. Through this technique I am learning to become available to my own creative impulses.

This led me to realize how important it was for me to come up with a more personal story for me either to direct or produce. That's when I decided to work with Alvaro Lopez Watermann. By analysing my dreams, he has helped me with my scriptwriting. I needed help to find that voice in me which gets lost in the sheer noise of the world in which I'm so immersed. Dreams are a way to do this.

Alvaro has devised a method of extracting, through a set of programmed dreams, the theme, plot, structure and characters of a script. Because I'm actually using my own dreams to create a story, I'm getting two things: I'm coming up with an interesting story, but also one that's very pertinent to my own life.

Before I started this dream work with Alvaro, I – like a lot of people – didn't understand how dreams related to my life. I knew, of course, that people like Freud and Jung had explored them, but had no idea how I could get insight from them or use them practically in my personal or professional life. I found that the dream work could become confrontational at times, because dreams don't necessarily tell you what you want to hear; they tell you what you *need* to hear. Dreams identify the issues within ourselves that are manifested as negative patterns in our outer lives. In our subconscious lives that part of us that is the healer. Dreams are a vehicle for transporting that knowledge from the unconscious to the conscious. They are a way to listen to the healer. In the waking state throughout the day, it is hard to hear because of all the external voices that surround us and are inside us. At night, they all go to sleep and the unconscious then talks to us through our dreams.

About twelve years ago, I was going out with a woman and we were having a lot of problems. Alvaro suggested that I write a note to myself before I went to bed asking what I needed to know about this relationship. I had this very vivid dream about a rap star on stage at Radio City Music Hall singing 'Games People Play'. Alvaro said, 'That's you, Lawrence, you were the one playing the games.' Of course, I had thought *she* was the one doing all the game playing.

Many people interpret their dreams literally, but on a deeper level they show us larger patterns that affect all areas of our life. In the dream about the rapper, I had to take a look at not only how I played games with my girlfriend, but also how it showed up in other areas of my life. One of the things I learned from this dream is that I didn't know how to be direct about asking for the things because of personal fears. Consequently, I would unintentionally manipulate my communication to get what I wanted. By recognizing this pattern, I learned to be more direct – something which became indispensable in my life as a producer. I always had this quality within myself, but I didn't know it because it was hidden and, therefore, not available for use in my life. The process of the dream work helped me to access it.

Over a period of several months, Alvaro and I met on a daily basis to use my dreams to come up with a plot and theme on which to hang a story. This was a great tool for two reasons: first, it helped me deal in a clear way with my daily situation and, second, it channelled my own thought process into the creation of the script.

It all came together after a very intense weekend workshop with Dominique. The next day I was working with Alvaro on my story and had finally reached the end of it. I said to Alvaro, 'You know, I loved the process, but when I read what I came up with, I don't like the story enough to make the movie.' Alvaro said, 'Well, you came up with a good structure, just make up another story.' It was an obvious and simple thing to say, but it was just what I needed to hear at that point. All of a sudden my defences dropped, and I felt a deeper connection to a part of me I hadn't felt before. It felt like a spigot had opened up and for the first time I was doing what I feared I couldn't do – create something out of nothing. I felt I had finally tapped into my creative source. So many times I've heard people say that stories just come to them or I've heard Quentin say that the characters write themselves, but this was the first time that I had actually experienced it myself. It felt like a turning point in my life, like I was reaping the rewards of a lot of hard work.

Since then I've faced up to the fear that it will never happen again. However, I've come to realize that this fear may surface at any time. That's life. Therefore, instead of fighting it, why not just accept it? It makes life a hell of a lot easier!

Notes

Tom DiCillo in Knoxville, Tennessee (photo by Bill Bettencourt).

4 Notes from Overboard:
The *Moonlight* Diary

Tom DiCillo

During the summer of 1995, I spent three months in Knoxville, Tennessee, directing my third feature, *Box of Moonlight*. It was supposed to have been my second film; the one I'd hoped to make immediately after *Johnny Suede* (1991). The tale of its torturous journey to celluloid would be of vague interest only to drunken shoe salesmen stranded in an airport lounge.

The film was a 'Go Picture' five times. And five times the film fell apart (once two weeks into pre-production). In the months and years between each 'Go Picture', I managed to keep my hopes alive by strenuously imagining myself sitting in some greasy spoon in Knoxville, eating a breakfast of scrambled eggs, grits and a tiny glass of watered-down orange juice. Although I am not particularly fond of these traditional southern breakfasts, I savoured this fantasy meal for five years, telling myself, 'Don't give up. One day you will actually be sitting down eating this breakfast and when you are, then you will know without a doubt that this film is really getting made.'

However, it wasn't until I had given up making the film completely and made another film, about the horrors of making a film, that I finally got the Real Green Light to make *Box of Moonlight*. I finally arrived in Knoxville in August 1995 to begin pre-production. I chose this small city, nestled in the foothills of the Smoky Mountains, for its tattered, disturbing beauty. Sections of the city seemed stopped in time, combining a Gothic Americana with a numbing, contemporary blandness, epitomized by endless strips of fast-food suburban wasteland. In contrast, the surrounding countryside is stunningly beautiful; lush rolling hills, spacious forests, meadows, streams and clear blue lakes. I was looking for a landscape that suggested America in a primeval state, before Europeans arrived.

The film is about a young father, Al Fountain, who is away from home, supervising a construction job in this small, unnamed American town. Each night Al calls his wife to tell her the job is on schedule and he will be home in a week. Suddenly the job is cancelled. All the workers go home except Al. He calls his wife and tells her the job is still proceeding on schedule and he will be home in six days. He rents a car and for the first time in his life takes a hesitant step out into the void of Free Time. By accident (a car crash) he meets The Kid, a comical, slightly disturbed young man dressed in a grimy Davy Crockett outfit. A series of unexpected events forces Al to spend six days with The Kid, who lives in a dilapidated mobile home out in the woods. At the end of those six days, Al returns home. John Turturro plays Al and the rest of the cast includes Sam Rockwell as The Kid, Catherine Keener as a phone sex operator fired for not being sexy enough and Dermot Mulroney as a menacing small-town bully.

The shoot was exhilarating but brutal. I thought after making *Living in Oblivion* that I'd learned a few things and this one would be a little easier. In actuality, it was like falling overboard in the middle of the Atlantic. In the middle of a hurricane. With fifty-foot waves, 100-mile-an-hour winds and lead shoes. We worked six-day weeks and shot the entire film in thirty-four days. I could only keep notes on my days off.

It wasn't until well after I'd returned to New York that I realized the whole time I was down in Knoxville I never once sat in a greasy spoon and ate a breakfast of scrambled eggs, grits or a tiny glass of watered-down orange juice.

Knoxville, 4 August 1995

Location scouting all day. Found The Kid's trailer, which is an old mobile home someone was actually living in until a year ago. It is perfectly situated in a clearing, with a grove of trees at the back. It was bizarre standing in front of it, finally seeing for the first time what had been real only in my mind, and seemed forever to be an impossibility.

Got back to the hotel more exhausted than from a day of shooting. At 8 p.m. I went to a 'class C' wrestling match at the Knoxville Coliseum, right across the street from the hotel. I was hoping to cast some of the wrestlers as Uncle Samson, Saddam Insane and The Castroater, the three wrestlers Kid watches on his TV. Walked into an unexpectedly intense dose of contemporary Americana. Primarily white people, all ages, from the very young to the very old. Most of the males, boys and men alike, had the same kind of modern haircut – long on top, shaved to the skull around the sides – which made their heads look like half-peeled potatoes. Made a note to have Dermot's character, Wick, wear a similar haircut.

T-shirt: 'I'm politically incorrect and fuckin' proud of it'. Another: 'My kid beat up your honour student'. On their way to the ring the wrestlers walked through a gauntlet created out of portable metal railings. Escorted by beefy State Troopers in skin-tight blue uniforms. Teenage girls and small children leaning over the railing, screaming, taking flash pictures, reaching to touch the wrestlers as they pass.

Young women in tight tube tops, tiny shorts and pantyhose, delivering plastic jugs of beer. They were called Hooter Girls because they all worked at a sportsbar chain called Hooters featuring waitresses with large breasts. One wrestler got in the ring and bleated into the microphone, 'Any of you Hooter girls wants to go home with a real man tonight, just call my name!'

All the teenage girls alongside the aisle beside me erupted in a spasm of high-pitched squeals.

One tag-team match was between two beefy, all-American hunks with long, blond hair, and two scrawny white guys name PG-13 and NC-17. (These are rating codes for films in the US; Parental Guidance for children under 13, and No Children under 17.) PG-13 and NC-17 turned the crowd against them by fighting dirty and incensed them further by winning the match. Two fat guys in front of me, dressed in biker gear – leather pants, boots, arm bands, sunglasses, and bandannas wrapped over their heads – lurched to their feet and screamed, 'No way, man!' at exactly the same time.

The matches were uniformly dull; however, at every pre-choreographed body slam the crowd leapt to its feet with a roar. At one point it seemed to me this utterly fake spectacle of churning emotion and drama was the American working-class equivalent of opera. I found it charming for a few minutes until three guys threatened to punch a woman behind them who'd asked them to sit down.

Outside the arena, sullen, overweight women sat behind tables selling colour photos of the wrestlers in various poses. One photo showed a long-haired wrestler flexing on a small pedestal against a sky-blue background. He was heavily oiled and wore white boots and red satin bikini briefs. Oddly, a German shepherd dog was posing on another pedestal beside him. A moment later this wrestler came out in the flesh, wearing the same boots and red briefs, and wrote his name with a black laundry marker on the thin white inner forearms of two teenage girls.

Saturday 5 August 1995: The Donut

Driving back from a long day of location scouting with Chip and Nelson, my two location managers. Around 7 p.m. we passed a bright pink strip joint with the word 'Bambi's' painted in six-foot-high black letters on the wall facing the highway. Nelson informed me the place was locally famous for an attraction called the 'Donut Dance'. He did not reveal the details of this dance or how he came to know about it. Thinking it would be a perfect location for the bar where Al and Kid get beaten up, I told Chip to pull over.

Gene, the club's owner, was behind the bar selling Budweiser by the can. He immediately agreed to let us shoot in his parking lot and plonked down three beers, 'on the house'. While he and Chip discussed the details, I took a glance around.

About fifteen men sat at tables scattered around a small, elevated runway with a mirrored ball rotating feebly above it. Strangely, the men all looked identical. If most of them weren't sitting alone, I would have thought they were members of a family comedy troupe featuring overweight white guys with long hair, floppy wide-brimmed hats and mirrored sunglasses. They were all staring intently at the young blonde who was dancing at that moment. She was extremely limber; her body moved like a firehose the firemen have let go of.

Off to the side I noticed four or five other dancers, sitting in a quiet cluster, wearing only their bras and G-strings.

As the blonde finished, a hidden male DJ urged the audience into tepid applause by saying, 'OK, that's right. OK, now. Isn't that something? Put your hands together for Tiffany all you gentlemen out there watching these lovely ladies dancing for your pleasure and enjoying pleasing you with their sensuous dancing.'

Tiffany strode up to the bar, refastening her bra behind her as Gene introduced her to us. 'Ain't she sweet? Tiffany just turned twenty-one yesterday. Now she's legal.'

Another blonde in her underwear slid onto the barstool beside me, introducing herself as Mimi. In contrast to Tiffany, Mimi seemed tired and somewhat nervous. My own uneasiness contributed quite a bit to the dullness of our conversation. I actually heard myself ask her if she had seen any good movies lately. She said she had just taken her two-year-old son to see *Pocahontas* that afternoon.

Just then Tiffany took Nelson's hand and led him to a dark corner of the lounge. They approached a large, white, circular couch with a hole in the centre about four feet in diameter. To my amazement, Nelson stepped up onto the seat, put a leg over the back and settled into the hole with only his head protruding.

Then I realized; he was in the Donut. Tiffany removed her bra and commenced what I deduced was the Donut Dance. Essentially this dance consisted of her climbing up onto the circular seatback surrounding the hole, spreading her legs on either side of Nelson's head, and moving her G-stringed pelvis around in front of his face. Nelson appeared quite entranced, though it was somewhat hard to gauge his expression as most of the time his head was completely engulfed by Tiffany's thighs.

At that moment Mimi leaned closer and spoke into my ear. Her breath was warm and scented like baby powder.

'When are you getting in the Donut?' she whispered.

'Oh, not for a while,' I said.

'That's the biggest hole you'll ever be in,' she said.

I turned to her quickly, surprised by her sudden shift to sarcasm. In fact, she had been absolutely serious. She wasn't even looking at me. She was staring intently across the room as Nelson took out his wallet and handed several bills to Tiffany.

As we were driving back to the production office, Nelson quietly asked Chip and me to 'be cool and don't go spreading this around'. We assured him that went without saying.

The next morning as I passed Nelson's office, I saw that someone had already posted a small sign on his door, reading 'Donut Disturb'.

Friday 25 August 1995

John Turturro and Sam Rockwell arrived this week. Had my first rehearsal with them yesterday, followed by another four-hour session today. Turturro immediately had me on the floor laughing. He jokingly accused me of laughing at my own script; I assured him my laughter was merely my delight at watching him work.

Actually, I am delighted my instincts were correct in casting him. I knew I needed an actor of his strength and commitment to pull off some of the more risky moments of humour. In fact, the stronger and more committed he is the funnier the scene. I told John I wanted him in great shape, suntanned, with impeccable posture. I suggested a combination of a young Burt Lancaster and Ward Cleaver (the father on the 1950s TV show *Leave it to Beaver*).

He is gentle and patient with Sam, who at the moment is a little nervous. He's had the script for so long (four years) that he's worked on it too much. He's devised little actions he plans to do. Some of them are very funny, but some take him out of the scene. I told him if his behavioural ad-libs have nothing to do with intensifying The Kid's interaction with Al, then we're not going to use them.

Sam knocked on my door tonight just as I was getting into bed. He wanted to show me what he had worked out for the scene after Wick beats him up. He jammed a paper towel into his mouth, explaining that this was to help him suggest 'the whole swollen mouth and broken teeth thing'. Then he did the scene as if in such agony from the beating he could barely move. The wad of soggy paper towel made his words completely unintelligible.

When he was done I asked him to take the paper towel out of his mouth. I told him it was not a scene about his considerable dexterity in depicting physical pain but about the thrill of revenge: 'Kid is in such an agitated state here that I seriously doubt if he feels any pain at all. Ever seen an animal with a hurt leg? In trying to get away from danger they'll get up and run on it, their fear completely overwhelming their pain. Try it again and this time show me no pain. Just show me how intensely Kid wants to get back at Wick. Show me the thrill he would feel in finally being victorious over him.'

The next time he did it the speech had a wild, jagged thrust that had me riveted. He left at 1 a.m. We are one week away from shooting.

28 August 1995

First day of shooting. Last night I had two calls from executive producers 'just calling to wish me good luck' at 12.30 a.m. It was a little difficult fully to appreciate their graciousness, especially since I'd gone to bed at 10 p.m. in preparation for my 5 a.m. call time.

On set, I was so groggy I barely knew what I was saying. But the shooting went well; we finished all of the bus shots, interior and exterior. Had an unexpected spat from Turturro after our last shot. I listened carefully to his complaint, judged it to be unfounded, and called it a wrap. He walked away, still angry. An hour later I met him coming into the hotel and we worked it out.

He is a tough one to read. At times he is amazingly warm, supportive and giving. Then at the most unpredictable moments there is suddenly a wall that is impenetrable. During his swimming lesson yesterday, he took off his ring and set it by the edge of the pool. It was slightly too large and he was afraid it might come off in the water. His father had given it to him shortly before he died and he valued it greatly. While he was swimming someone stole the ring.

As distraught as he was, he continued the lesson. The film calls for him to jump into a pool of water and swim leisurely, speaking several lines of dialogue. John never learned to swim and is a little uneasy being in water over his head. The swimming instructor spent most of the lesson yesterday showing him how to hold his breath. Physically he looks great: slim, tanned, muscular; amazingly similar to photos of my father as a young man.

Originally, the location for the swimming hole was to be a small mountain stream. But I had problems finding one deep enough and ultimately scrapped the whole idea because in every one of the streams the rushing water was freezing and very loud. Last week we decided on an abandoned quarry. This solves a lot of problems. It's quiet. The water is warm and we can shoot on our own time, unimpeded by the public.

On the down side, the water is 350 feet deep. I'd originally told Turturro, on the basis of the mountain stream concept, that the maximum depth would never exceed six feet. He asked me today how deep the quarry was and I said, 'Twenty-five feet in some places.' Which is not strictly a lie. I've instructed everyone on the film to repeat exactly the same thing if asked.

Matters were not helped by a headline yesterday in the local newspaper: 'EXPERT SWIMMER DROWNS IN QUARRY'. The details were pretty gruesome. The rescue diver, who brought him up from the bottom of the quarry, discovered the victim had been bitten by a poisonous snake.

Sunday 10 September 1995

Just finished second week of shooting. The intensity of the work is unending. Every day accelerates into a wild, chaotic scramble to get the shots before the light goes. Turturro is having more and more consistent moments of brilliance. His concentration is staggering. He agreed with a note I gave him that the vocal inflection he was using tended to deflate Al's energy and make him too tortured. A hard thin line for us both to walk. While I never want Al's turmoil to be depressing to the audience, it still has to be real for John.

In the film, Al returns to Splatchee Lake, a water park he had visited as a child. He discovers it is now in ruins and shares his memories with Luvven and Wynelle Coddle, two elderly strangers strolling along the polluted shoreline. We shot all the Coddles' coverage first, then turned around for John's coverage in the afternoon. I told him only one thing: 'Convince these two that nothing is bothering you.'

It is immediately obvious when one of my suggestions stimulates John. He jumped and said, 'OK, OK, let's go!' We started the shot. From the opening moment Turturro was like a living man right in front of us. The pretext of small-talk my note suggested, actually prompted him to dig deeper into the emotion of the scene. The story he was telling was so convincing that everyone on the set stopped and stared as if they were hearing if it for the first time. Luvven and Wynelle, though off-camera, were staring and reacting like no-one was at the lake but the three of them.

Al Fountain cuts loose (Sam Rockwell, Catherine Keener, John Turturro and Lisa Blount).

As he neared the end of the scene John trembled and his eyes filled with tears. I was staring, transfixed. Out of the corner of my eye I suddenly saw the Assistant Cameraman look at the footage counter and shake his head. John was about to finish the last few lines of the scene when I heard the camera run out of film. The AC glanced at me in question. I shook my head and continued, as if we were still filming. When John had finished the scene I yelled, 'Cut!' We did several more takes. Fortunately, John filled the last moments of the scene again in these later takes. I did not tell him about the camera running out of film until the end of the day.

Box of Moonlight: The dinner scene (John Turturro and Tom DiCillo standing; Lisa Blount and Catherine Keener sitting).

Sunday 17 September 1995

The pace is taking its toll. Turturro is yelling at people. I am yelling at people. Yesterday Turturro yelled at me. During the Swimming Hole Scene where Al and Kid meet Floatie and Purlene, played by Catherine Keener and Lisa Blount, I asked Turturro to quicken the pace by walking over some rocks. He stumbled during the shot, then went on to finish the scene. As soon as I yelled 'Cut!', he exploded. He'd broken two toes. My sole directorial accomplishment for the rest of the day was to keep him from flying back to New York. When we resumed shooting the next morning, his toes were the size and colour of two small eggplants. Nonetheless, he did all of his swimming scenes with no outward signs of nervousness.

Sam, on the other hand, was completely at ease in his flirting scenes with Catherine and Lisa. He was hilarious, strutting around in his wet underwear like a scrawny, hairless squirrel. My sense is that he enjoyed the momentary change of pace of acting with someone besides Turturro. There is an escalating tension between the two. He and John could not be more opposite in technique. Turturro attacks every moment with a concentration and discipline that leaves no detail unexplored. Sam careens through each scene like a new-born colt, stopping suddenly, then racing off in a completely different direction. At times, Turturro scolds him for being unfocused. Sam stiffens and ignores him like a rebellious teenager. Although this real-life battle perfectly mirrors their relationship in the film, I have to be careful it doesn't stifle their sense of play with each other.

Walkie-talkies keep going off right in the middle of the most delicate dialogue scenes. I told the AD I was very upset about this and nearly went insane when I heard him reply, 'Well, now, you know, Tom, sometimes these things are inevitable.'

My response, a high-pitched shriek about where on his anatomy the next walkie-talkie would end up, appeared to have some effect. There were no walkie squawks during shooting for the next six days.

For four years the opening line of the script has read, 'Camera emerges from foliage into a clearing to reveal a wide-eyed ceramic Bambi.' All during preproduction I stressed to the Art Department that I wanted a 'ceramic Bambi, a fawn right out of a Walt Disney cartoon'.

Yesterday we set up for the two shots involving this ceramic Bambi. Just before we were to shoot I walked past the Art Department van and jumped suddenly, seeing a real deer, an adult doe, nosing in the grass behind the van. It took several moments for me to realize it was fake and several more to realize this was the 'ceramic Bambi' the Art Department had produced. There was nothing cartoonish about it at all. It was not Bambi, it was a real deer, a plastic hunter's decoy.

My infuriated confusion was met by profuse apologies from the Art Department. After weeks of searching, this deer was the closest they could come to 'a wide-eyed ceramic Bambi'. As we had one hour of daylight left to shoot two lengthy scenes, I made the decision to shoot with the new deer.

Halfway through filming the scene where Al walks up to the deer and thumps it in surprise, saying, 'It's a fake! It's a statue!' I suddenly realized that this realistic-looking deer was actually perfect for the scene. If it had been a cartoon Bambi, Al would never have thought it was real, even from afar. Which placed me in a particularly paralysing dilemma. Part of me wanted to rage at the Art Department for not getting me the ceramic Bambi specified in the script. The other part of me wanted to hug them all in desperate gratitude for saving the scene.

20 September 1995

My wife, Jane, flew down for the weekend. I feel like it's been twenty years since I last saw her. Her visit was very sweet, though we spent most of the few hours we were together discussing my frustration. As usual, her advice and encouragement was astute: 'You are the captain of the ship,' she said. 'Whether you like it or not, you are responsible for everything.'

'Broken toes?!'

'Broken toes, walkie-talkies; everything. The sooner you accept this, the better off you'll be.'

She flew back to NY this morning. When we got back from dailies tonight at twelve, I found a note she left me. Inside was a drawing of me on a boat in the middle of the ocean. The word 'action' was coming out of my mouth. Although the drawing was meant to be encouraging, portraying me as 'captain of the ship', I couldn't help noticing that I was alone on the boat, which looked alarmingly like a rudderless toy and none too seaworthy. I also noticed the waves were approaching tsunami height and seemed about to crush the boat and wash me overboard.

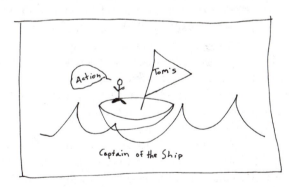

23 September 1995

Catherine Keener appeared and disappeared like a brief flash of sun on a dreary day. Her performance as Floatie was as magical and effervescent as anything she's ever done. Everyone misses her.

Had an odd experience filming her phone-sex scene. We constructed a tiny set for her 'office' and spent a rare day shooting indoors. At one point I looked up and saw her sitting there on that tiny, fake set, surrounded by lights, the camera and the boom operator hovering with the mike just out of the frame. Just then Catherine glanced up and smiled at me. In that instant I had a sudden rush of memory of filming *Living in Oblivion*: the joyful carelessness, the intimacy, the comforting, insular world created by that clan of crazy, trusting friends. I valued it then. I treasure it now.

Dermot will stay another two weeks to finish his last two scenes. His prosthetic burn looks startlingly realistic. He liked my idea of the haircut shaved to the scalp around the sides. He's come up with some physical actions that work well for Wick: an odd, bow-legged strut and a compulsion always to be eating ice of some kind.

The last night Catherine was here, she, Dermot and I went out to dinner. The young waitress recognized Dermot and asked for his autograph.

'You were, like, good friends with River Phoenix, weren't you?'

'Yes, I was,' Dermot replied. He and River had grown extremely close following the film they did together, *A Thing Called Love*.

'Oh, that's like excellent.' A tight, nervous giggle. 'Were you, like, really bummed when he died?'

'I was pretty upset,' Dermot answered quietly, with a restraint that astonished me and sky-rocketed my respect for him. My impulse would have been to take a butter knife and tattoo the words 'bummed' and 'excellent' across her forehead.

1 October 1995

Filmed the Tomato Field Sequence yesterday. This included the tomato fight between Al and Kid, and the scene where Kid pushes the police car down a hill. Started shooting at first light and ended in a frantic rush to get the last shot as the sun went down. Should have had at least two days to film this sequence. The Tomato Fight itself took over two hours to choreograph. We shot the whole thing with a Steadicam in a series of long, uninterrupted takes. The heat was intense. Sam was exhausted after the first take, running full tilt in his heavy buckskin costume. Turturro seems to love this physical activity; he just kept going. He had a wickedly accurate arm, nailing Sam repeatedly with hard, straight shots from all the way across the field.

In a medium shot of Turturro, we needed to have a big tomato hit him right in the chest, as if Kid had thrown it from off-camera. A prop girl stood a few feet away and hurled several wet, mushy tomatoes at John, missing each time. John had requested she do it, 'because it would be more humiliating to have a woman hit me'. After the fourth miss I grabbed two tomatoes and said, 'Alright, I'm doing this.' As I aimed at John, standing three feet away, I heard someone mutter, 'A pretty accurate representation of the relationship between director and actor.'

My first shot missed John completely. My second hit him hard in the shoulder, raising a welt the size of a pancake.

The runaway police car was a complicated set-up involving a stunt driver steering the car straight at the backs of the sheriff and patrolman, who were actors and had to jump out of the way at the right time. My excitement at shooting my first real movie stunt was obliterated by my conviction that we would never finish on time and that someone would die because we were all running around like frenzied lunatics on speed.

We used three cameras (one operated by a truck driver), which only complicated matters and created three times as much yelling because each camera seemed unable to set up a shot without both the other cameras in frame.

The tomato field belonged to Wagner Forelock, a gracious and dignified older man with wavy white hair and a small white moustache. I'd invited him to watch us filming. He stayed out there all day, along with his wife and son.

At the end of the day I dragged myself into the front seat of the crew van, about to depart, and was almost asleep when I saw Wagner Forelock standing in front of his house with his wife, son and some neighbours. I got out and went up to Wagner, thanking him for his hospitality and generosity. Oddly, he barely shook my hand and did not look me in the eye. Alarmed, I asked him what the matter was. After a heavy sigh he turned to me and said, 'I like you, Tom, but I have to tell you I won't be able to recommend this movie to my friends.'

'Why not?' I asked

'The language.'

I racked my brain trying to recall some vulgarity Sam or John may have screamed during the tomato fight.

'What language?' I asked finally. 'Did someone on the crew say something?'

Wagner sighed again. 'No, Tom, it was the sheriff. He used the Lord's name in vain. He said, "Jesus, we killed 'em." Do you remember?'

I nodded in astonishment as he went on.

'You see, Tom, Jesus is my dearest, closest friend. Jesus is my light and my life. And you used his name in a bad way. And now I won't be able to tell my friends to see this movie or go see it myself. I like you and I don't hold it against you, but these are my beliefs and I take them very seriously.'

It really bothered me that I had caused him such distress. I told him I respected his beliefs and I would never in any way want to insult him or cast aspersions on his spiritual convictions. In conclusion I told him how sorry I was that we had to end our brief relationship on a note of disappointment.

'It's OK, Tom,' he said, putting his arm around me. 'I'll tell you what; to prove there's no hard feelings, let me show you something inside.'

As he led me into the house, I glanced back at the waiting crew van. Everyone inside was glaring at me in vexed exhaustion, wanting to get the hell out of there. At that moment there was nothing I wanted more than to be inside that van.

Inside the small house, Wagner opened a door and ushered me into a dark room, whispering confidentially, 'This is where we make our own Smoky Mountain BBQ sauce.'

A huge stainless-steel vat stood gleaming in the centre of the room. Wagner pointed to it proudly and said, 'That's where it happens, right there, in my brand-new vat. It holds eighty-five gallons.'

'Jesus! You're kidding me!' I blurted in amazement. The silence that filled the tiny room was endless and excruciating. Finally Wagner turned away and led me back outside. I crawled into the van and waved goodbye to him as we pulled out. In the side-view mirror I saw Wagner say something to his wife with a slow, sad shake of his head.

Sunday evening 10 October 1995

Living in Oblivion opened last night at the Knoxville arthouse theatre. I was tempted to go, but opted instead to rewrite a scene and do some food shopping. It was a good thing I didn't go. I found out today that the reels had been projected out of order. It was not much consolation to hear that no one in the audience appeared to notice.

Went to a local supermarket to buy some groceries. On the way out I was met by a homely, obese white woman in her thirties, dressed in a knitted sweat suit grey with age and grime. She shook a can at me that contained several coins and said, 'Can you help my daughter win the Homecoming Princess?'

Glancing behind her, I saw a little girl, about nine, short, fat and, despite her delighted grin, painfully unattractive. She held a ragged black and white pompom in her hand and as her mother said 'Homecoming Princess' she raised the pompom and shook it once.

I realized suddenly that what her mother wanted from me was not advice about posture or grooming but money. After dropping some coins in her can, I moved away but turned back to look, still somewhat amazed. Just then an old man came out of the store. The mother shook her can, the little fat girl shook the pompom and the old man dropped a coin in the can with a clink. As he walked off he exclaimed loudly, 'Good luck, and I hope she wins!'

'Oh she will,' the mother called back. 'She's talented. It's only money is all she needs.'

Thursday 12 October 1995

Finished shooting the film at 9 a.m., about two hours ago. What day is it? When did this day begin? Hard to recall. I've been up for twenty-eight hours. Started yesterday with pick-ups for some daytime exteriors, then the whole company moved to the parking lot at Bambi's Bar to shoot the Fight Scene. We started as soon as it was dark and worked steadily through the night.

The scene was short but complicated. Wick (Dermot Muroney) and his partner Doob get out of their truck and move to enter the bar. Passing Al and Kid, someone throws a match at Wick who immediately assumes it was Kid and punches him hard in the face. As Al moves to help Kid, Doob punches him in the stomach then smashes his head against a car headlight. While Al is stretched out on the pavement, Wick props up the nearly unconscious Kid and knees him hard in the face. The fake blood was so realistic that at one point I glanced at Sam sprawled on his back with his eyes closed and jumped because he looked like he was dead.

Around 4 a.m. the AD whispered in my ear that we'd just shot Turturro's last shot. I told him to make the announcement to the company and waited for the applause to end with a rising apprehension. The last few days have been tense for both of us. Suddenly, however, as Turturro walked towards me I was startled by an intense rush of emotion. He had given the role everything, there was no question of that. And there was also no question he would be brilliant in the film. But the toll was enormous. As he got closer I recalled my first letter to him, two years ago, in which I'd urged him, in naked desperation, to read my script. Then we embraced and he was gone. It struck me again, the only constant in this business is the continuous cycle of drawing together and breaking apart.

Half an hour later Dermot was gone. Then Sam. I got fake blood all over me as we said goodbye. It was still pitch black outside when we moved inside Bambi's to do the last shot of the film: a slow motion shot of a grey hair falling to the floor. Although it was only a brief, locked-off camera shot, it was still quite complicated and tedious. I had several sizes and shapes of hair to decide upon, in addition to getting the hair to fall at the right speed and land at the right spot.

As Orvis, the prop man, stood dropping single grey hairs in the dead silence of the closed bar, I looked up and saw that Orvis, the DP and myself were the only ones awake. All around us in the darkness, on the floor, on tables, on the white circular Donut couch, the entire crew was asleep. At that instant my own exhaustion washed over me like a gigantic wave and almost pounded me to sleep on my feet.

Some time later, we finished the shot and the film was over. I walked around like a zombie shaking people's hands and thanking them. Someone handed me a plastic cup of champagne and after two sips I was completely wasted. I staggered out of the bar and was dumbfounded to see the sun was already over the trees at the far end of the parking lot, shining pale and diffused through the thin mist that was hanging in the air. I sat down on a magazine case lying on the cracked sidewalk in front of the bar. The film was over.

Out in the parking lot the equipment trucks were being loaded. Two grimy electricians paused after coiling a mound of cable to exchange phone numbers. A wardrobe assistant walked by carrying Kid's blood-stained buckskin costume in one hand and a cup of champagne in the other. Someone in the camera truck turned on a radio, low, and the faint music seemed to rise and mingle with the pale yellow mist. The film was over.

A laugh echoed across the parking lot. Around the side of the bar two crew members were throwing a football in the dew-wet grass. Beyond them, a steady stream of traffic was moving on the highway, commuters on their way to work.

Eleanor Coppola (photo by Sofia Coppola).

5 Further Notes

Eleanor Coppola

Even though I have seen Francis making films for over thirty years, I always find it a curious profession, an exotic process. I never tire of observing life on the set. I am usually away from home then, and far from friends. I find myself wanting to tell someone about my experiences, so I write notes like those that follow.

Kurosawa

11 November 1979 Hokkaido, Japan

It was raining in Tokyo as we drove to the airport. The traffic was bumper-to-bumper all the way. Crowded into orange-and-cream-coloured buses, we were taken out to the plane. The flight to Hokkaido was full, every seat occupied. The plane waited a long time on the runway before it was cleared to take off in the rain. The visibility was very low; the hangars and buildings were grey shadows. Mexican music played over the PA system. During the hour-and-twenty-minute flight, two stewardesses hurried to serve everyone a paper cup filled with orange juice or green tea.

My mind travelled to Napa and thoughts of fall and the children. Sofia is eight; I felt badly about leaving her again. She was upset the night before I left. I had made a calendar for her with each day marked with her activities and coloured on the days that she would stay overnight with a friend. I got into bed with her, read and talked and rubbed her back until she fell asleep. The next morning I took her to the bus stop. We were a little early; as we sat in the car I asked her how she felt about my going away. She started to laugh and couldn't stop. It scared me. Then her friend came over to the car; she hugged me and jumped out. I watched her until the bus came. She seemed to be OK.

On the plane, I closed my eyes and felt the conflict run through me: wanting to go with Francis, wanting to be home with Sofia. I noticed that it was when the trip was tiring or boring that I most wished I was home.

The plane landed at six in the evening. It was already dark. We were hungry; we hadn't had any lunch. Francis wanted to stop at a little noodle shop in the airport, but the people who met us said we had to hurry; Kurosawa had invited us to the set and wanted us to arrive in time to see the last shot. The production assistant bought a box lunch with egg salad sandwiches and orange soda, and put us in a waiting car. We were both grumpy on the ride. We were driven for over an hour in the darkness, through what I thought was flat farmland. At one point we came to a lit intersection where we could see shops. There were strips of small fish drying, hanging outside like curtains.

The car turned off the highway on to a rutted, sandy road. As we bounced up and down, the headlights shone on sand dunes. Finally, in the distance, we could see lights on a hill. As we got closer I could see scaffolding towers with huge arc lights on top. The car stopped in an opening where more than twenty buses and horse trailers were parked. When we got out of the car, I could smell the sea. We walked about a quarter of a mile to the bottom of a hill, into an area lit by the immense lights. As we left the shadows, I could see cables, supply boxes and assistants with walkie-talkies. We walked up the hill. The road was steep, and I watched where I stepped, trying not to stumble and shaking the sand out of my open-toed shoes. As we got to the crest of the hill, I looked up. I felt the same rush of excitement I felt going on the set during a big night-shot for *Apocalypse Now*. Every cell of my body seemed suddenly awake. In front of me was a samurai army in full vintage armour. Hundreds of foot soldiers stood in formation guarding a shogun seated on a throne at the top of an enormous sand dune. There were lines of mounted samurai on either side. The riders in the rear carried tall banners that flapped in the wind; horses pawed the sand restlessly. The lights on the towers had green gels casting an unearthly tint over the scene.

A short woman in a fur hat, seal boots and a down jacket hurried towards us. It was Nogami, Kurosawa's assistant and producer. She greeted us and led us through the samurai to a place by the B camera. The last shot of the evening was about to begin. I was standing near a pole made from a fir tree, bracing the scaffolding of the lighting tower. I could hear someone talking about a shot the previous week that had required 200 dead horses on the field after a battle. Over forty veterinarians had to be hired to tranquillize all the horses at the same time. The man was saying that the horses on the picture had cost more than the extras, and that it had taken over a year to train them to get used to the spears and armour.

Each samurai had a banner on a thin bamboo pole up his back. Someone was saying that the black banners represented the mountains, the emblem of the mounted troops who protected the shogun. Green banners representing the forest were worn by the foot soldiers who mopped up. Red banners for fire and banners representing the wind were worn by the attack forces.

Everyone was still, waiting for the signal that the cameras were rolling. In a few minutes the walkie-talkies must have received the signal and directions went out over the PA system. A charge of mounted samurai, which I hadn't noticed, came out of the dark shadows at the foot of the hill and rode up the

Akira Kurosawa with Francis Coppola and George Lucas.

side of the huge dune in clouds of sand to attack the forces defending the hill-top where the shogun was. There was a flurry of swords, sand and samurai in military manoeuvres. The attacking charge was apparently rebuffed by the shogun's army. When the shot ended, everyone immediately began packing their equipment, preparing to leave for the evening.

In a few minutes Nogami appeared with Kurosawa. He had been by the A camera at the foot of the hill with the angle up on the attacking forces. He was all bundled up in a heavy parka and hood. Through the interpreter he said he was glad to see us, but wasn't feeling well and would meet us the following afternoon. He was hurried away and we began to walk back to the car. I suddenly noticed how really cold it was. I had been so absorbed I hadn't noticed that my body was shaking. When we got to the parking area, I could see the samurai, still in their armour, sitting inside the buses, and the horses being loaded into vans.

12 November 1979 Hokkaido

Francis and Kurosawa are seated by a small table. White tissue reflectors, lights, photographers and journalists surround them. The room is hot. Kurosawa is wiping his face with a cloth and writing in a book of his drawings with a brush. He is drying the ink by holding it in front of one of the lights. He gives the book to Francis, showing him certain drawings. Francis says that it reminds him of the way Eisenstein drew. 'I draw sometimes, but not as well as my daughter Sofia. I was a theatre director, Kurosawa-san, you were an artist. We each work in our individual ways to achieve the results we want.' Kurosawa said he remembered that Francis carried a copy of *Heart of Darkness* in his pocket while making *Apocalypse Now*. He said that he is carrying a copy of *War and Peace* in his pocket while making *Kagemusha*.

The Godfather, Part III

8 October 1989 On an airplane

I am flying with Francis to New York on the first leg of the journey to location for *Godfather III*. I feel emotions moving through my body along old paths.

Yesterday I said goodbye to Roman on the sidewalk in front of Francis's office building as we left for the airport. I won't see him until Christmas. I can still feel the imprint of his thick hair in my hand as my arms reached around his neck in a lingering hug. A wave of pain mixed with fear pierced my body. I remembered the moment Gio hugged me as I left for the airport. I never saw him again.

Last evening, when we arrived at our house in Los Angeles, Fred Roos, the casting director, was waiting on the front porch with a box of video tapes. We settled into the living room. I watched as they went through the casting process, picking some actors for parts, eliminating others. I thought about how each person would feel when they got the news. I fell asleep on the couch, exhausted from the last weeks of cast rehearsals in Napa and preparations to leave home for five months.

20 October 1989 Rome

At Fumicino Airport a VIP car and escort met us on the tarmac and took us to the terminal ahead of all the other passengers. Our escort said, with excitement and a heavy accent, 'Welcome to Roma. You are the director of the film *Stepfather*.' When the young woman took our passports and read Francis's name, she called to the girl in the next booth and they giggled excitedly.

21 October 1989 Rome

I am in a second-floor office at Cinecittà, the Italian film studio near the outskirts of Rome. New offices have been prepared for Francis's production here in the space that used to be Fellini's. A handsome new door says 'Zoetrope/Italia'. I can hear Francis's voice, loud and urgent, as he conducts a script conference. In a few hours, when it will be morning in LA, he must submit the script for *GFIII* to Paramount. He is making the last changes before it is faxed to meet the delivery deadline.

23 October 1989 Rome

Once again I find myself in a familiar situation; Francis is excited, creative and impatient in the throes of the production preparations, while I deal with domestic problems. The furnished apartment rented for our location stay was overflowing with dusty clutter. After the cleaning lady worked for half a day and left, my friend Paula came and helped me pack up seven cartons of the owner's personal junk. The faucet dripped and the toilet-seat hinge was broken. It was chilly in the apartment and the heater didn't work. Now that several days have passed, I have nearly gotten things in order. Today, only the kitchen sink is stopped up. To me, my domestic chores feel very frustrating, but they are completely insignificant to everyone around me. Today, Francis is facing the problem that although he has rewritten the part many times to please Robert Duvall, every offer has been turned down. Now Francis must write Duvall out of the script.

Uprooted from my friends and my life at home, attending to the mundane tasks, getting settled in a foreign place, I am feeling a familiar wave of sadness. I try to lift my spirits by noticing what is around me. After all, I am in Rome. We live on a narrow cobblestone street. The courtyard of our building is filled with push carts and crates of produce for the open-air market in the piazza near by. Hungry cats dart from doorways; laundry hangs from second-storey windows. We met the man the neighbours tell us is the local king of the thieves: a burly man in his undershirt who lives on the first floor of our building. He told me to watch out for my purse until I am known in the area.

25 December 1989 Rome

It is cold. We made a fire in the fireplace. The Christmas tree is shedding needles on the grey carpet. Francis is in bed listening to the news in English on his short-wave radio. Roman and Sofia are asleep on the scruffy leather sofa. I am completely happy to have them here.

Last night, Christmas Eve, we went to Tally's. Talia Shire, Francis's sister, is renting an apartment on the sixth floor of a building near by. She has a huge terrace with views of the city in every direction. Al Pacino, Diane Keaton, Andy Garcia and his family, and all of us were there. Francis's mother made her traditional seafood sauce with octopus for the spaghetti. It was Tally's son Robert's birthday. At 10 p.m. a group of us walked to the French Church for mass. I was anticipating hearing wonderful music resounding within the beautiful space. Instead, thin voices of the congregation choir evaporated in the arched nave. There were two memorable moments, one when lights came on dramatically illuminating the vast, elaborately painted ceiling and the remarkable carvings above the altar. The second was when all the children came to the back, near where I was sitting. They lit candles and formed a procession to carry a baby Jesus doll forward to the altar. As they stood with their cherub faces, holding their candles and fidgeting, waiting for the signal to begin, they looked so fresh and beautifully expectant. Diane's hat bobbed in the row in front of me. Gia, our two-year-old granddaughter, fell asleep in the stroller. When a droning sermon began, we left rather conspicuously.

This morning we opened presents for hours. At one point we took an intermission and made an American breakfast with fried eggs and bacon. Then Tally and her family arrived. We were twenty people spending the day together in a two-bedroomed apartment. At 1 p.m., I put the twelve-kilo turkey in the oven. There was no roasting pan in the apartment that would hold a twenty-five-pound turkey. Paula told me to roast it the Italian way, in the broiler pan on the bottom of the oven. After several hours of cooking, the grease overflowed and caught fire. Francis lifted the turkey out of the flaming oven; it slipped off the pan and slid in a pool of grease across the kitchen floor. I wiped up the grease with paper towels, and mopped the floor by hand with a cloth and hot soapy water. Then I went out to a local restaurant with a bottle of our wine from California and asked the owner to lend me a lasagne pan. Eventually I got the turkey back in the oven. By four in the afternoon, all the sodas had been drunk and the carpet was a sea of nut shells, Christmas candy and wrappings. Members of the family pitched in to clean up a bit now and then, but there was a continuing messiness to the day. Somehow everything got done, more friends arrived, and twenty-five of us sat down to a good dinner. All through the meal I tried to get the taste of chaos off my palate.

28 December 1989 Rome

After Christmas with so many relatives, Francis seemed relieved to go back to work. Gia is here with us this morning. I played with her a long time in the bathtub, making desserts of foamy bubbles in her plastic dishes. Sofia got up late. Around noon the phone rang. I was surprised to hear the voice of Casey, the assistant director, calling in the middle of a shooting day. A little wave of panic flashed across my heart. He is a jovial guy, full of fun, but today he sounded serious. He said very quickly that the production doctor had just returned from seeing Winona Ryder, who was playing Mary, the daughter of Michael Corleone. She was too sick to work and was being sent home. Francis had decided to cast Sofia in her part. He asked if Sofia could come to the studio immediately, because a scene with her character was scheduled to shoot in a few hours and they needed her for a costume fitting. I told Sofia as evenly as I could, but tears of emotion were welling up in my eyes. She was very excited at first. Then, as it sank in, she became anxious. I could see how worried she was about letting her father down. I said I was sure he would never have cast her if he didn't believe she could do it. We took the subway to the station in front of Cinecittà; then we walked fast to the costume shop.

1 January 1990 Rome

Last night we went to a cast and crew party on our piazza in the rambling apartment of a man who played a member of the board of directors in the stockholders' scene. Francis had a heated exchange with an executive from Paramount who was questioning his wisdom in casting Sofia so quickly in the part of Mary Corleone. I went out on to the terrace that overlooked the piazza and watched the fireworks. Several fireballs whizzed within inches of Roman and the kids at the front of our balcony. I heard someone shout through the smoke, 'Incoming! Hey, this is like *Apocalypse Now*.'

Today is Gia's birthday. She came in the afternoon with all the family. Francis held her up to blow out the three red candles on her cake. She opened presents on the fat sofa, tearing through the wrapping paper with gusto.

The phone rang intermittently. Milena Canonero, the costume designer, called to arrange to have Sofia picked up in the morning to go to a fitter for body pads to make her look older for her part. Winona Ryder called from her family's home in California and apologized to Francis for getting sick and having to leave. Roman and Sofia talked to friends in California. Roman sounded homesick. Sofia told her boyfriend that she was going to get tits tomorrow.

2 January 1990 Rome

We got up early. Roman went to the studio with Francis. At 9.30 Sofia went downstairs to a waiting taxi and drove off, first to be fitted with body pads and then to go to the studio for costume fittings and to have her hair dyed darker. I did the shopping in the piazza. I stood in the light in front of the vegetable stalls absorbing the colours of the carrots, crates of shiny egg plant, zucchini, broccoli, dark green spinach, fennel bulbs, and long-stemmed artichokes. Shafts of light reached into our narrow street. It looked like a theatrical set. I had the day to myself, the first in a long time, a treasure.

10 January 1990 Rome

I am waiting for Sofia to wake up. As usual, Francis left early. The last few days have been exhausting. Francis and Sofia have been under enormous pressure, which overflows and affects my emotions. A number of people on the production think Sofia at eighteen is too young and too inexperienced for the part, and have made their opinions known. Francis has been shooting an extremely demanding scene with Sofia. Every moment Sofia isn't on the stage she is taken to costume fittings, or the hairdresser, or the diction teacher. Several times she has burst into tears. Well-meaning people tell me I am permitting a form of child abuse. They say she is not ready, not trained for what is being asked of her, and that in the end she will be fodder for critics' bad reviews which could scar her for years. They tell me that Francis can't afford to take a chance on a choice that could weaken his work at this point in his career.

The night before last, Francis went to sleep in a cold sweat and got up at five in the morning to go to the studio. By the time his new production manager arrived at eight, Francis had decided to hire an editor immediately and cut together the scene with Sofia in order to make a final decision based on what was actually on the screen. During the day his lawyer called to tell him that his contract gives him final artistic control. He shifted the schedule and shot the rest of the scene, which included Sofia's close-up. Roman and I went to the studio with her and spent the day there. I didn't hover; I was just there. I took the accusation that I was being a negligent parent very seriously. I could see that at times Sofia felt courageous and excited and eager to do it, and at other times she was tired and utterly miserable. But I didn't feel she needed me to help her get out of it. I didn't feel I was ignoring her and pushing her on.

16 January 1990 Rome

I am in Francis's office at Cinecittà. It is lunch break. He is at the computer writing a letter to the Paramount executives. I am huddled next to the heater. The costume I am wearing is a thin silk-brocade party dress. The day is bright, but cold. Today I am playing an extra in the party scene set in Michael's New York apartment. After rehearsing for hours, we are now in a holding pattern while Gordon Willis, the director of photography, lights the big master shot. This involves two cameras covering action that moves through several rooms.

I arrived today at wardrobe just after 8 a.m., late because of the bumper-to-bumper traffic along the Via Appia Antica. We were stopped for a number of minutes at the Porto San Sebastiani, where the cobblestone road goes under the old Roman aqueduct. It still amazes me to travel over the same roads that were used by chariots. This morning I was taken into a private fitting room, where I found Francis's mother. She talked about what great legs she has, not a vein visible, and she's in her seventies.

My costume consists of a short black skirt with a Nehru-style brocade overblouse. It closes up the front with more than three dozen difficult-to-button buttons. I buttoned forever, but they never came out even. Gia's mother Jacqui, who is working in the costume department, came in, pulled the extra button off and sent me to hairdressing. Two hairdressers consulted in Italian and then a young man began to curl my hair with a hot iron. He was remarkable to watch, but I ended up very frizzy. When Milena saw me she said, 'No, no, the look is all wrong.' They misted it with water, combed it straight back, and added a hairpiece swirled at the back of my neck. It was the first time I thought I looked truly grandmotherly. When Milena returned, I could see she didn't like it, but there was no time to change it again. I went into make-up where I received a very complete make-over, concluding with a lot of powder and bright red lips painted larger than my natural lip line.

I went to the set. The rooms of Michael's apartment had been dressed for an elegant party. Tables were set throughout, with beautiful flowers, glassware and silver. The orchestra was in the main room, which included the dais and round tables for guests. There were perhaps a hundred extras and many children. When I found Francis I could see that he was surprised by my look. He said he thought I looked older than usual and that I reminded him of my mother. He introduced me to the others at my table as Aunt Delphine, Tom Hagen's sister. My character's two nephews and a niece were at the table with my sister-in-law, Hagen's wife. The actors, led by John Savage, who was playing Tom Hagen's son, stayed in character and spoke to me as their aunt. I could see Francis's mother at the next table seated next to Eli Wallach and laughing at his jokes. Sofia was on the dais next to Al Pacino, Tally was standing near her dad, who was conducting the orchestra. The shot was of Tally leading the guests in singing 'O Compare'. All of Tally's shots will be done first, because she has to leave in a few days to be in *Rocky V*.

17 January 1990 Rome

This morning at the studio there is frost, white like snow, on the driveways and lawns. I am wearing the top of my long underwear under my costume, but my legs are freezing. I am the last one in make-up. (The sign on the door says 'Trucco', which is Italian for 'make-up' and also 'trick'.)

The extras and principals are being set for the scene where Mary Corleone gives the Archbishop the cheque for $100 million. Gordy is building the composition person by person for the camera, moving a press person a bit more to the right, Al a half-step forward. The camera assistant is putting tape Xs on the floor to mark the actors' first positions and moves. The extras are chatting and the assistant directors are frequently telling them to be quieter. A little boy near me tucks his adult-size tie into his seven-year-old's trousers and carefully buttons his jacket. Everyone is dressed for a party. Several production assistants are wearing tuxedos so they can work in the crowd cueing extras. Sofia looks lovely, with her dyed dark hair slightly waved and a beautiful dress. I can see hints of her anxiety from time to time, but she seems strong enough to handle it. For days she has been practising her speech with her coach Fret Vreeland, Diana's son. I notice how much of my emotional life is caught up in vicarious turmoil, with Sofia's anxiety and Francis's tension.

19 January 1990 Rome

Today Sofia did the scene where she waltzes with Al. It was so sweet, so reminiscent of Marlon waltzing with Tally. She did the rehearsals in her stocking feet. During the shot, Gia ran on to the dance floor and grabbed hold of Sofia's skirt. Francis let the cameras roll. I would wager that spontaneous moment will end up in the final cut.

Tomorrow I am returning to California to attend a family wedding I don't want to miss and catch up on my life there.

3 March 1990 Rome

Last week I went straight from the airport to the studio. I found Francis on the opera set. We were so happy to see each other! He was working on a scene from *Cavalleria Rusticana* for the final sequence of the film. The opera set was lit beautifully with very theatrical lighting. The costumes were a rich palate of Renaissance colours: golds, burgundies and Madonna blues. After the second take I heard a high little squeal. Gia ran across the floor over cables, around equipment and into my arms.

The next day I got up with Francis at 5.45 a.m. We went to the coffee bar in the side street off the piazza. It was just opening. The walk through the narrow streets looked new to me, fresh with the scent of bread cooling at the bakery, and the vegetable and flower vendors setting up their stalls. We ate breakfast and read the *Herald Tribune*, before Francis left for the studio and I returned to the apartment to start packing for the move to Sicily.

6 March 1990 Rome

I rode to the studio with Francis yesterday morning to see Sofia in the first shot. I found her in her dressing room at 7.30. She had already been to hair-dressing. We visited while the wardrobe assistant hung up her costume and laid out her accessories, which included two boxes containing falsies – heavy cold silicon blobs. I warmed them on the radiator before Sofia stuffed them into the pockets of her special bra. We walked over to the stage and I found Francis sitting on the big sofa in Michael Corleone's living room. We talked while the crew set up the shot on the main stairway. Francis was very depressed. He spoke with such conviction about all the things wrong in his life, how he hated that he was doing the same material he had done nearly twenty years ago, how he hated the process of making movies, and all the time it took. He said the only thing he liked about film-making was the technology. He talked about his family and complained about me. I sat there while he ran it all out, not agreeing, and not yielding to the temptation to give my point of view. I just tried to be present and listen.

8 March 1990 Rome

It is 6.30 in the morning. I can hear Francis's fingers flying over the keys of his computer at the kitchen table. He types faster than a court stenographer. I am still tucked under our down quilt this chilly morning. Today the production moves to Sicily. Yesterday I finished packing and a truck picked everything up. In the late afternoon I walked to the metro, savouring the last walk through the old city.

I emerged from the subway at Cinecittà just as the sky was turning a deep peach colour. I felt the familiar sadness of a location ending, mixed with excite-ment of moving to the next. I passed by the offices to say goodbye to people. Packing-boxes were stacked in the hallways, all the pictures were off the walls and the bulletin boards were bare. I found Francis outside in his editing trailer, the Silverfish, talking to the assistant director on the set over the intercom while the last shot in Rome was prepared. It was a close-up of cutting the cake at the party in Michael's New York apartment. When they were ready to shoot, we went on to the stage. Andy Garcia's daughter was the cake cutter, with the help of Al's stand in. Francis was looking forward to having a piece of the cake and celebrating the final shot. The cake trolley was moved into position about six times before it hit the mark for the camera exactly and the cake was actually cut. Everyone was disappointed to find that under the real icing, the cake was cardboard.

14 March 1990 Palermo

We took the overnight train from Rome to Palermo. It started out disastrously when we discovered that Francis's new briefcase had been stolen by gypsies who came up to us as we were unloading our luggage in front of the station.

In Palermo, we were met by the production staff at 8 a.m. and driven to the hotel with a police escort. The hotel was old and grand, and slightly shabby. Francis told me Lucky Luciano lived there when he was deported to Palermo after the Second World War. We spent the day looking at locations. First we went to the Villa Malfitano, where Michael stays while he is visiting Sicily. It was a huge, somewhat rundown villa in its own park inside the city. The art department had refurbished the great gardens in the back of the house. There were new plantings in the flower beds and four men were working on the fountain. New lawn furniture and umbrellas were in place. Tables and chairs had been added to the veranda. Gordon, Dean, Francis, and the ADs walked the premises, deciding where the first set-ups would be. I went inside the house and a security guard showed me a number of upstairs rooms. I saw bedroom upon bedroom, each left intact, filled with personal things of the original owner. Old family pictures and photos hung on the walls, and silk damask spreads covered the beds. Downstairs the set dressers followed Francis, Gordy and Dean as they decided where scenes were going to be shot and what furniture would be needed. The side and back walls of the garden room were painted with windows and views out to tropical foliage that matched the real windows and views. Its tile floors were spectacular. I loved seeing these rooms as they were before the cables were laid, and sand bags, light stands and all the other equipment was brought in.

Next we went to the Teatro Massimo where they will shoot scenes in the entrance, the lobby and opera boxes. The art department had covered the mirrors in the ante room outside the grand box with panels of red damask. Rolls of red carpet and newly upholstered theatre seats waited to be installed. The thick grey dust that had settled over everything during the twenty years the theatre had been closed had been vacuumed, but it wasn't completely gone.

On the first day of shooting in Palermo, I rode to the set with Francis. Our police escort moved us through the thick traffic to Michael's villa. I watched

The Godfather, Part III: Andy Garcia, Francis Coppola and Eli Walach.

the preparations for the first shot. Gary Fetis, the set dresser, told me that he had spent a day with a flower man working out all the flower arrangements for the different rooms and the man had made samples that were outstanding. Today he had been told that he had to use someone sent by the people 'sponsoring' the production. A man had arrived with a load of flowers and stuck them in vases with not the slightest artistry. Outside I saw a very large man in a black suit and dark sunglasses accompanied by a smaller man dressed identically. They looked like two guys sent by central casting to play Mafiosi. I asked the production manager if they were Mafiosi. He said, 'Yes, they are here to help us.' Later I heard there had been two groups who had wanted to 'help' the production and there had been some difficulties arranging for only one.

19 March 1990 Villa Malfitano, Palermo

I can smell fumes from the generators and the trucks starting up. Shooting at this location has been completed and there is a rush to pack up equipment and move to the next location at the Teatro Massimo. This evening the family that owns the huge villa invited everyone for a farewell glass of champagne on the beautiful enclosed veranda. To our hosts' surprise, the cast and crew gulped their drinks in minutes and returned to packing.

27 March 1990 Palermo

Last night I walked from the hotel to the set at 1 a.m. There was no one on the sidewalk and no traffic. Palermo seemed like a different city. Inside the Teatro Massimo, the crew was preparing for a wide shot of the Corleone family in the royal box. The red velvet upholstery and gold-leafed woodwork glowed in the light of cranberry glass lamps. I watched for a while and then went down into the Silverfish, where Francis was giving directions to the set and editing between shots. After the production wrapped at 3 a.m., Francis and I watched footage on the monitors for more than an hour.

Today we got up late and left for the set just after noon. I went to the costume workroom to see how the designers were progressing on the pad for Sofia's dress that is supposed to allow the special-effects blood to form a stain like a rose when she is shot. On the first test, the bloodstain didn't move through the lining fabric, so a patch with different but matching lining material and padding had to be added to each of the three identical gold tulle dresses. Next I stopped by the hairdressing trailer to say hello to Sofia. George Hamilton came into the trailer to have his hair dyed grey. He was dressed perfectly, with an elegant suit and a beautiful overcoat with a fur collar. He wanted us to see the wig made for him to use if his hair was back to normal next July, when they do retakes. The wig, made of real hair, was neatly pinned to a form. The colour was a good match, but the hair was wavy and George's hair is quite straight.

I went across the street to the coffee bar with Milena and we ate sandwiches standing up at the counter. John Savage came in wearing his black priest's costume. He looked carefully at all the Sicilian pastries in the glass cases and said that what he really wanted was a bran muffin. He began talking about how well everyone treats him when he is in costume. A production assistant with a walkie-talkie arrived looking for actors who were supposed to be on the set. John looked sheepish and left.

4 April 1990 Palermo

Last night I watched the big shot outside the Teatro Massimo with 450 extras. They rehearsed until 10 p.m., then took a meal break. It took the crew several more hours to complete the lighting. The first shot was gotten around 1.30 in the morning. It was of the large crowd arriving at the opera house, the Corleone family getting out of their fine cars and ascending the stone steps for the evening performance. It took a long time between shots to get the cars and all the people back into their starting positions. By 3 a.m. they had completed three takes and everyone was released except the camera crew, who had to move to the starting position for the next day's work.

Today was a perfect spring day. I walked out to buy fresh milk, fruit and dry cereal. We are so tired of the continental breakfast, all that is available at the hotel. I always have a moment of feeling tacky as I cross the lobby with my lumpy shopping bags full of food. For days Francis has been feeling great anxiety about the ending, which he shoots tonight. Many people think the film should end with Al Pacino dying in a burst of gunfire on the steps of the Teatro Massimo, as Francis wrote it in the original script. Now Francis feels it should be more unusual; it should end like *King Lear*, where his daughter dies, though in this case he is left to live with the horror of his life.

As we were finishing breakfast, Sofia came into our room. She is sore from working with Buddy Joe, the stunt co-ordinator, on her death scene. She has to fall on the steps and although she will wear body pads under her dress, she has to fall correctly in order not to get hurt. She is scared, which scares me. I rubbed her shoulders and hugged her, feeling an echo of fear. Finally she said, 'Oh, Mom,' and pushed me away.

5 April 1990 Palermo

Last night I wrote letters and sent faxes. When I finally arrived at the set to see Sofia's big scene, it was over; she was getting out of her wet, fake-bloodied dress. Perhaps I was late because some part of me couldn't watch even her make-believe death.

16 April 1990 Taormina

The production has moved. Sofia's work in Sicily is finished; she has returned to California. Yesterday was Easter. Francis and I went to lunch with a group of twenty-five cast and crew. I couldn't remember an Easter without any of our children. I hid eggs in the hotel room in Trieste during *Godfather II*, in the tropical foliage at our house in Manila during *Apocalypse Now*, in the city park in Tulsa during *The Outsiders*, and in the apartment in New York City during *Cotton Club*.

17 May 1990 New York City

Today it is raining intermittently; Central Park is shrouded in mist. I feel anxiety in the pit of my stomach. Francis is supposed to be shooting outside, a scene with an Italian fiesta and procession culminating in a complicated killing. The production hired 200 extras and over thirty street vendors with stalls filled with food. Because of the weather they will have to go to the cover set, a scene with Sofia. She has been preparing with Greta, a drama coach, but I know she is scared. It is an important scene opposite Andy Garcia. Rationally, I know my anxiety serves no purpose, but even alone in the hotel I am linked to them.

On Saturday I went to the cast and crew hotel to get Gia. Jacqui had left for an early call to work. Her babysitter hadn't arrived and she left Gia in Sofia's room. I didn't get there until noon. Sofia was cranky, because she had stayed out late. The drapes were drawn and the only light came from the television tuned to cartoons. Gia was in bed with Sofia, wearing only a T-shirt. Something about the clutter, Gia's bare bottom, the darkened room at midday with the TV going made my heart ache. It reminded me of days in the past when the children were sick on location in a hotel room somewhere with windows that didn't open, and with the smell of leftover room-service food and wet diapers. I dressed Gia in the clothes Jacqui had left for her. There was no belt for her jeans and they kept slipping down. She fussed when I tried to brush her tangled hair. Sofia confided that she was depressed because she had read an article in a magazine about the circumstances under which she got the part. It said the other actors had not wanted her, which she knew was true.

27 May 1990 On an airplane

Francis finished shooting in New York City on 25 May. There was a wrap party that was soulful, rather than the usual wild and crazy bash. Members of the cast and crew who had been together for 125 shooting days were gathered for the last time, celebrating the conclusion of shooting, and mourning the end.

13 July 1990 Napa

Last week I went with Francis on the Paramount jet from Napa to LA for a screening of *GFIII*. In the hottest part of the afternoon, we stepped into the cool cabin of the jet, the only passengers.

In the early evening we drove to the studio and settled into our plush chairs in an upstairs screening room with perhaps a dozen people. I noticed the screen had been masked down to a small size. The film started and I was very disappointed to realize that it was a video projection of an editing dub, with very

The Godfather, Part III: Andy Garcia and Sofia Coppola.

poor visual quality. I found it frustrating to strain to see who the characters were, when I knew that the footage was so beautiful on film. At the end everyone got up and started talking about what needed to be done. A group took the tape to another room to look at it on a different monitor and make their notes. I could feel Francis's despair. They weren't leaping out of their seats enthusiastically, saying it was great.

18 July 1990 San Francisco

Two days ago we came to San Francisco to see the first rough-cut of *GFIII* on film. The screening for Paramount was in the morning at the North Point theatre. The print was beautiful and its impact overwhelmed me. Tears streamed down my face at the end. I had to exit before the lights came up and go to the lounge to regain my composure. For lunch, we went to a Chinese restaurant where I sat at the table with sixteen men. They were excited by what they had seen and talked about marketing strategies. They discussed dates when a locked print would have to be ready in order for the sound-effects cutters to be able to complete their work, and the prints struck. They wanted a new scene clearly showing that Michael Corleone turns over the family to Vincent (Andy Garcia), so there would be a set-up for another movie. Francis responded strongly, wanting the focus of the film to be on Michael and not be obligated to the character of Vincent.

Francis had been up all night working on the last reels of film for the screening. After he fell asleep at 7 p.m., I drove to Berkeley to have dinner with a friend. As I drove up University Avenue, I noticed the flowers blooming in the central street dividers. They looked absolutely beautiful. I realized that I was outrageously happy, so utterly relieved that the film was well received. I hadn't realized the level of tension I had been carrying around in my body, in my mind. Tension was draining away, revealing normal life around me.

4 September 1990 Napa

Yesterday was Sunday. I drove to George Lucas's ranch and met Francis and Roman at 9.30 in the morning. We went into George's beautiful big screening room with the editors and watched *Godfather I*. When it was over I went for a walk on the grounds, past the vineyard to the main house and through the gardens. I needed to be alone in the fresh air and sunshine to regain my balance. It was very emotional to see the movie again on a big screen, to watch film events so interwoven with my real life and especially to see Sofia as the baby baptized at the end. When I returned, I found Francis and Roman having lunch in the atrium. Tally, Milena and Francis's father had arrived. We went into the screening room to watch *Godfather II*. I could hardly separate my own memories from the drama of the film. My heart ached seeing a forgotten moment when I was an extra on the boat of immigrants headed for Ellis Island, two-year-old Sofia on my lap, and Gio and Roman beside me.

After the film there was a lively discussion. Roman video-taped most of it. More food was served. Al, George, Sofia and her boyfriend arrived. Finally we saw *Godfather III*. I was sitting next to Sofia. She sucked in her breath and squirmed in her seat when her scenes came on the screen.

At the end, I knew that everyone felt they had seen a genuine continuation of the Corleone family's saga, rich and resonant, even though it was still unfinished. I felt Francis's deep relief. Al came over to talk to him. On the way he stopped and told Sofia that she was good, really good.

Today I am still feeling little aftershocks of emotion. In my mind's eye I see images from the films intertwined with moments of my life, all going by like a movie.

May 1995 Napa

Sitting here in my little octagon writing room five years later, I realize that during the production of *Godfather III*, I watched Sofia grow from a sheltered child into a young woman on a very difficult project. She recognized that she couldn't quit and worked through all the challenges until the film was completed. That creative and strengthening experience gave her a firm foundation for work in the arts. Today she is a published stills photographer; writer/producer/host of a four-part series on TV's Comedy Channel, and designer for her own clothing company.

At the time *Godfather III* was released, many reviewers were critical of Sofia. Francis and I advised her not to read the reviews, to let time pass before she attempted to evaluate her work. She got wonderfully encouraging letters from Woody Allen, Angelica Houston and other industry professionals she admired, but as much as she tried to avoid reviews, some negative ones got through her defences and were very painful. Francis said he felt those criticisms were meant for him, and that Sofia received them the way Mary Corleone got the bullets intended for Michael.

Dracula

19 October 1991 Los Angeles

This evening we watched rushes of *Dracula* in video projected on to the big screen in the bedroom. I was mesmerized watching a scene with Lucy and Mina over and over for many takes. Last week, on the first day of shooting, I went on to the set. It was inside a huge stage at Columbia. They had built a grand Victorian mansion. I loved seeing the furnishings, all the beautiful silks and brocades in a perfect harmony of muted colour. Francis took me to the bedroom to see the incredible round headboard with its delicate bat design and thick tassels.

The room opened on to a terrace overlooking the garden. We walked down two flights of wide stone steps to a fountain and a pond with waterlilies blooming. Beyond, I could see the entrance to the crypt and a hill with family gravestones. There was a rose arbour and a maze of high hedges. Francis told me that the garden was constructed in the pit of the stage that had originally been Esther Williams's swimming pool. He was called to the camera first position in the great hall. I roamed around, fascinated with the way real and plastic plants were interwoven in the garden. The painted stone walls had drifts of real ivy and moss. A greens man was burying the last pots of flowering shrubs next to the pathway.

I went back up to the main house set and was happy to find Eiko Ishioka, the costume designer. She pointed out an arrangement of flowers that she wanted the set dresser to change because the colours of the blossoms were too bright for the subtle scheme of the room. We walked to the bedroom set, which she hadn't seen. She said she had asked the art department to get many collections of exotic things, since it was the room of a rich girl who would have travelled a great deal and brought back trinkets from around the world. There were small oriental masks, cut-glass bottles with ornate silver tops, boxes of unusual butterflies, little silk purses, ivory carvings, hat boxes and many things still wrapped in tissue paper. Eiko pointed out the fake blossoming wisteria vines over the door to the terrace and said the shade of lavender was too strong and needed to be softened. When we got back to the camera position, Winona Ryder had come on to the set for a rehearsal in her costume. She had a perfect Victorian figure: a tiny wasp waist and full bust. Eiko observed every detail of her dress. I looked at its craftsmanship and construction. The pale, absinthe-green silk taffeta had intricate embroidery on the bodice, the full skirt had hundreds of tiny knife pleats at the waist, and the draped bustle had yards more cascading fabric. It was a work of art.

9 November 1991 Los Angeles

I flew from New York to LA and took a taxi to the studio. As I passed by the big open doors of Stage Thirty, I could see bulldozers pulling down the last of the beautiful mansion set. There was a dark gaping hole where the English garden had been. I found Francis in Stage Twenty-three on the asylum set. I was so happy to see him and excited to see the new set. The crews were rushing between their supply areas and the set, working on last-minute details before the first shot. The cavernous dungeon-like rooms were wonderfully horrifying, with rock walls oozing slimy water. Francis pointed down a long musty corridor and said, 'See that? It's a mirror.' Suddenly I realized that the set was quite small and the vastness was created by a huge wall of mirror, partially covered in rock at the edges.

Tom Waits stepped out from one of the chambers in his costume. His hair had been shaved up the back in odd little ridges. The front, left long, had been sprayed grey and stuck out from his head. His teeth had been stained black and brown, and he wore filthy long underwear and a torn, dirty Victorian coat. He had pointed period shoes, unbuttoned, flapping open on his dirty bare feet. Each of his hands was covered with a bizarre cage-like thing – dark-stained leather around his wrist and thin bent metal rods over his fingers, with leather caps at the tips. He held a battered tin plate with his asylum food, a mouldy crust of bread covered with a squirming mass of maggots, strange orange worms, dead flies, a large potato bug and a selection of beetles. Tom was gently pushing them around the plate and talking to them, saying, 'Hey, you, move over.' The bug wrangler was standing near by. He had several additional tins of maggots and beetles. He occasionally prodded the contents of Tom's plate to make sure they were all moving. He had an assistant with several boxes of candy beetles that were added to the plate so that when Tom picked up something to eat in a scene he could select the candy. Tom was having difficulty picking up anything with his caged fingers. Eiko and the prop man were called in. They tried putting honey on Tom's leather fingertips so the insects would stick. It didn't work. They tried double-faced sticky tape and then spray adhesive. Tom was very patient and tried hard to pick up worms from the wiggling mass. Finally the shot set-up was complete and they had to shoot. They decided to frame over Tom's shoulder and let the second unit get the shots of him actually eating from the plate.

12 November 1991 Los Angeles

This morning I drove to the studio and went down into the underground screening room to see rushes shot by *Dracula*'s second-unit director, our son Roman. The director of photography and the camera operator were already there. We sat down in the plush seats. Roman arrived with his briefcase and his hair mussed from riding his black studio bicycle hurriedly across the lot. He leaned over the seat and gave me a quick kiss. The lights were dimmed. The first shot came on the screen. It was a series of spiders and beetles crawling over Tom Waits's eye glasses on the asylum floor. The last shots were of Tom putting the live bugs and worms in his mouth and chewing. One shot ran over and you could see him spitting out a beetle and laughing.

Dracula: **Tom Waits and Richard E. Grant.**

The Career

(in association with the
Drambuie Edinburgh Film Festival)

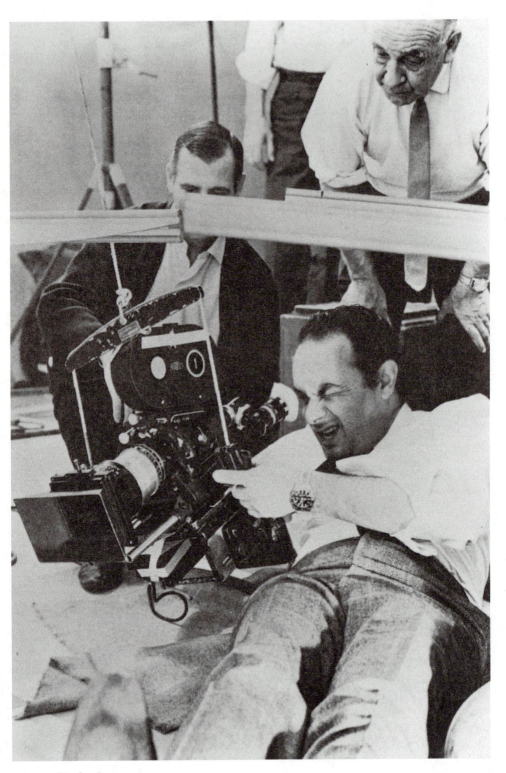

Stanley Donen.

6 Following Your Feelings

Stanley Donen interviewed by Kevin Macdonald

Introduction

Last year (1995) the Edinburgh Film Festival mounted the most complete retrospective ever of Stanley Donen's films. Donen himself was scheduled to attend, but was forced to pull out at the last minute due to commitments on an (ultimately unrealized) film project. Consequently, I conducted the following interview in New York for BBC Scotland's programme *Edinburgh Nights* and relevant excerpts from it were video-projected before each film in the retrospective.

What first struck me about Donen as he walked into our low-rent studio was the lightness of his step and his *youth*. This man simply did not look old enough to have directed *On the Town* with Gene Kelly all the way back in 1949, let alone the miraculous alter-ego number in *Cover Girl* in 1944. It's easy to forget that next to Stanley Donen, Orson Welles was a bit of a slouch. He started directing when he was just nineteen, and had made *Singin' in the Rain*, to my mind the most pleasurable movie ever made, when he was all of twenty-six.

Donen's precocity is more than a matter of 'first-ism'; its consequences permeate his work. Because he started so young, he literally grew up *through* the movies. Coinciding with one of the most optimistic periods in American history, his early musicals, up to and including *Seven Brides for Seven Brothers*, are bursting with youthful energy, iconoclasm, inventiveness and innocence. The later movies, while showing no let-up in Donen's remarkable visual inventiveness, grow progressively more cynical, more aware of the flaws in human nature and the difficulties of love.

Considering that he is the last major survivor of the golden age of the Hollywood musical and that many of his films have attained classic stature, Donen's current reputation is surprisingly muted. Perhaps it's because the sheer fun of *The Pajama Game* or *Charade*, the unadulterated glamour of Fred Astaire dancing on the Champs-Elysées in *Funny Face* and the wit of Jean Hagen's performance – 'bringing a little pleasure into our hum-drum lives' – in

67

Singin' in the Rain, are out of step with modern ironic tastes. More than likely it also has something to do with the perception of Donen as somehow the minor partner in the partnership with Gene Kelly. The question always posed is: exactly who was responsible for what? Donen goes some way towards answering this in the interview, but also makes it clear why he thinks the question is irrelevant. Donen felt that he was one part of a team; a team that included producer Arthur Freed, writers Comden and Green, the lead actors and, of course, Kelly himself. *Singin' in the Rain* and *On the Town*, in particular, come as close as anything in Hollywood to being genuine collaborations. And in retrospect I realize that the quality that I respond to in these films, the thing that makes them unique cinematic achievements, is exactly that: their tremendous sense of generosity.

Kevin Macdonald: Can you tell me a little bit about your upbringing and what brought you into the movies, and specifically musicals?
Stanley Donen: I was born in South Carolina and my family had nothing to do with theatre, music, movies, showbusiness or anything. My father ran a group of ladies' dress stores. I had a perfectly ordinary childhood but I saw Fred Astaire in *Flying down to Rio*. It may not have been the first time I'd seen him because *Dancing Lady* had already come out, but it was *Flying down to Rio* that made this enormous impression on me. I didn't know what I wanted to do, or be, or be around, or be with, or relate to or anything. I just knew that there was something about the magic of movies and in particular Fred Astaire and music that galvanized me. I was nine years old. And I decided I wanted to study dancing. It seemed a ludicrous ambition for a young man in South Carolina. I don't know what they thought of me – homosexual probably! – because it was completely outside the normal young boy's interests. However, my family must not have thought it was peculiar because they said, 'Go ahead and study dancing' and I did.

My father used to spend a month or two in New York every summer on business and my mother and I would go with him. So I saw all the Broadway shows from around 1933, or even before. And even during school time in Columbia, South Carolina, I went to the movie theatres almost every day after school.

KM: Your first professional job as a dancer was in *Pal Joey*. Was that a revelatory experience?
SD: I was sixteen years old and knew less than nothing. I just knew I wanted to get out of South Carolina. I graduated from high school and told my family I wanted a job on Broadway – because New York was much closer to South Carolina than Los Angeles. They indulged me again and said go ahead. My father didn't have a lot of money, but he gave me enough to get to New York and see if I could get a job. I read about an audition for *Pal Joey* in the *Daily Variety* and I turned up and got the job. So, there I was, barely sixteen years old, completely ignorant and in a show. I think I probably wouldn't have been hired had they known my age.

KM: How did you originally get together with Gene Kelly? What impression did he make on you?

SD: I got together with him because he *was* Pal Joey in *Pal Joey*. I was in the chorus and he was the star. So what did I think of him? He is this remarkable, talented, incredibly winning, Irish-American extrovert personality with a fantastic gift for dance and athletic movement and enormous enthusiasm, energy and drive. I thought he was splendid, although we didn't really know each other extremely well on *Pal Joey*.

Then George Abbott, who had produced and directed *Pal Joey*, announced that he was doing a show about young people called *Best Foot Forward* set in a boy's military school, and they asked me if I'd like to be in it. So I left *Pal Joey* and went immediately into rehearsals for *Best Foot Forward* and after only a couple of days Abbott decided the choreographer he'd hired couldn't do the job and he asked Gene Kelly if he'd choreograph it while he was appearing in *Pal Joey* at night. So Gene started work and because he knew me he asked me to assist him in the staging of the show. So we got to know each other a little better. Then he went to Hollywood and I stayed in New York and did that show and another show. And eventually I saved enough money to go to Hollywood too.

I arrived in Los Angeles in early 1942 and auditioned again for jobs. MGM was making a lot of musicals at the time and they offered me a job and put me under contract.

KM: How would you characterize what film musicals were like when you first arrived in Hollywood?

SD: Well, film musicals were a lot of things. At that time there were a considerable number of Astaire and Rogers musicals, a number of 20th Century Fox musicals – which you either like or dislike, but they were a genre of their own – then there were RKO musicals which were another kind of thing. And then we had all the European musicals: we had the René Clairs etc. So musicals didn't necessarily stick to one little category.

KM: What kinds of musicals did you like best?

SD: I liked the Astaire–Rogers films. They had all the great composers and lyricists – Gershwin, Kern, Porter – and their stories were simple, romantic and personal. I preferred that enormously to the Busby Berkeley musicals which at that time I thought were ludicrous, stupid, outrageous and dumb. I had a very negative attitude to that kind of geometrical extravaganza. I steered away from them when I started to make pictures and towards the Astaire and Rogers pictures. Also, I am particularly interested in cinematography, and I thought then – and still think – that musicals liberate the possibility to be bigger than life. On the screen you can do things you can't do in ordinary life. I used to joke about 'renewing my musical comedy licence' because music gives you a licence to do things which are beyond what you consider reality. People don't sing and dance on the street or in their homes in real life. The orchestra doesn't swell up. Music gives you the opportunity to be imaginative.

KM: Presumably musicals also allow a degree of technical and stylistic innovation.

SD: I think they do. I *still* think they do. When one watches a musical and you hear music, you accept that it's going to be unlike true, real documentary life, and it's exciting to be imaginative in that way. Of course, the camera is the greatest invention for recording reality, but it is also wonderful for going beyond reality. Here we are, and you are photographing me – God only knows what it's going to look like – but it is close to the reality of what I'm feeling and showing. So the camera is the most remarkable piece of magical, mechanical process – although I don't know if we can call it mechanical much longer, it's now getting to be digital and computerized, and what have you.

KM: How old were you when you first directed and how did it come about?

SD: The first thing I ever directed – that is to say set up, shot and so on – was one sequence on *Cover Girl*, which is referred to as Gene Kelly's 'alter ego dance', a number where he dances with an image of himself. That was around 1943 when I was eighteen.

KM: Could you talk me through that number and what you did?

SD: The idea was to make it appear that Gene was dancing with himself by double-exposing the film. The problem was to repeat the camera movements – the pans, tracks and the tilts – at precisely the same moment both times without the aid of a computer, which is what they'd use today. The front office said that it was impossible to do because there is no way to time it. In my naiveté I told them that there was a way to time it because we were shooting to a pre-recorded sound-track and since Gene was such a precise dancer he'd land at exactly the right position at the right moment in sync. with the music. From that I could chart out the camera moves and shoot it the first time in the real setting and then we'd black out the set with black velvets and repeat the camera moves precisely. The director of the picture [Charles Vidor] said, 'That's ludicrous, it can't be done and I'm not going to be a part of it!' But Harry Cohn, who ran Columbia Studios, said to Gene, 'Do you think this young man knows what he's talking about?' And Gene said, 'I'm sure he does.' So Cohn let me direct it myself.

KM: The result was a really wonderful, unusual number. Who or what was the biggest influence on you as a choreographer?

SD: Fred Astaire, without any doubt. But I'm also a great admirer of Charlie Chaplin. You know, he had a choreographer's imagination. Two of the greatest musical numbers are the dance of the rolls in *The Gold Rush* and the dance with the globe that he does dressed as Hitler in *The Great Dictator*. There's another great number in that movie when he's playing the barber and he shaves a man in time to the Hungarian Rhapsody with the shaving soap and the razor and lots of little bits of business. He wasn't a trained dancer, but he did some things that are the equal of what anyone has ever done.

KM: Did you pick up on this wider idea of what choreography could be – not just grand-scale musical numbers – from Chaplin? Your films often make use of choreographed movement in the widest sense.

SD: You know, I don't know where anything comes from. You can't, or at least I can't, have a theoretical approach to anything. I can't say 'This is the way you do it : ABCDE . . . now I have to think of something which is movement and not dancing, and now I have to think of something which is dancing and now I have to think of something which is singing or whatever.' It just comes from heaven knows where, from the combination of all the experiences one has had, and things you liked and things you hated. Out of it all come these ideas which you never really succeed in achieving. You have these wonderful moments of euphoria where you say, 'God what a terrific idea!' and then when you're doing it, it seems to be back to the banality of what's been done before and you feel like you haven't really gotten it. I don't know where it comes from, but certainly not from a theoretical approach.

KM: Do you strive consciously though to do something that's different than what's been done before?

SD: No, no, you can't. You do strive consciously to say: 'I'm not going to do that, they did that, so that's old hat.' You reject what's been done, what you've done and what anybody else has done, because that's not an homage, that's plagiarism. You have to come up with something new. The joke the second time told is not funny.

KM: To go back to *Cover Girl* briefly, how do you think, aged eighteen, you had the know-how to be able to say that you could do this. Or was it just naiveté?

SD: I think it was both. I was certain I knew what I was talking about. My father gave me a camera at the age of six or seven and I used to make 8mm films at home, and I had still cameras and I'd always been fascinated by photography. I had a little 8mm projector and then later a 16mm projector and I'd buy short rolls of film and run them over and over, studying how they were made. So I knew the rudiments of photography, and I obviously knew what I was talking about because it worked. I just felt, 'What have I got to lose?' When you're eighteen years old you think, 'So what if it doesn't work?'

KM: Around 1945 you undertook another piece of virtuoso film-making in *Anchors Aweigh*, when you blended live action and animation for what was – I believe – the very first time.

SD: Yes, I had Gene Kelly dancing with a mouse. We were always trying to think of new ways to do musical numbers and one night at two o'clock in the morning – I'll never forget it – I sat up and I thought, 'Why don't we have him dance with Mickey Mouse?' There and then I called Gene and woke him up and I said, 'I have this fantastic idea.' And he said, 'Well, Christ, it better be good, it's three o'clock in the morning and I have to shoot tomorrow!' So I told him: 'You're going to dance with Mickey Mouse.' And he thought it was a great idea.

The next morning we went to the studio. Joe Pasternak was the producer and he went to L.B. Mayer and they said: 'Terrific! Get Mickey Mouse. Gene will dance with Mickey Mouse!' So an interview was arranged for Gene and me with Walt Disney. We went into this very simple office there at Disney Studios and explained that we were going to do this live-action cartoon

Anchors Aweigh: Kelly dancing with the mouse.

sequence and we'd like to have Gene dance with Mickey Mouse.

Disney just looked at us. 'Let me get this straight,' he said. 'You want Mickey Mouse to be in an MGM picture?' And we said, 'Yes.' And he said, 'Mickey Mouse will never be in an MGM picture!' So Jerry Mouse – who was MGM's mouse – got the job.

I'd never worked with animation before and so I had to learn everything from scratch. We worked everything out in the tiniest detail and then went and shot Gene doing his part. Then I spent almost a year in the MGM cartoon department putting the mouse in, while the studio went bananas because they had a completed picture with Kelly and Sinatra which they couldn't release! I was known as 'the mouse' around the studio in those days.

A funny little memory: at the beginning of that sequence Gene is in a children's kindergarten and the kids ask him how he got his medal and he makes up this story about the mouse. And the adorable, curly-headed little boy who he tells the story to is Dean Stockwell, who's probably now a grandfather! You can recognize him. He looks exactly the same – except now he's old and smokes cigars.

KM: After directing these sequences in other people's movies, how did it come about that you and Kelly got the chance to co-direct *On the Town*?

SD: Well, during the war Gene had gone into the navy and when he came back the studio said they wanted to make another Kelly/Sinatra picture but they didn't have a story. So in about two afternoons Gene and I wrote the outline for *Take Me Out to the Ballgame*, about American baseball players. It went down reasonably well and Arthur Freed and Roger Edens, both of whom I'd worked with quite a lot, and who owned the rights to the Broadway musical *On the Town*, asked Gene if he and I would like to direct it. It was a real leap of faith – from Freed, Edens and, I guess, Mayer too.

KM: Arthur Freed is often cited as the most important influence on the development

of the musical during the 1940s: he's often said to have made the musical more intelligent and more narrative. Would you agree?

SD: Well, I don't know that they were more intelligent and often they were less narrative than what had come before. He did musicals which had no plot whatsoever, like *Ziegfeld Follies*. What Arthur Freed had was an enormous admiration and great feel for what was good in a musical. Remember, he himself had been a very good lyricist. He fostered the people and the things that he believed in. He gave people chances – and those chances often paid off for him. Look at the list of names: Vincente Minnelli, me and Gene, Charles Walters, Roger Edens, Comden and Green, Alan Lerner – he even had Gian-Carlo Menotti there writing, although nothing ever came of it. Freed just appreciated talent.

KM: So you wouldn't agree that musicals became more narrative through the 1940s with films like *Meet Me in St Louis* and *On the Town*?

SD: I know people say that, but I don't know that it's necessarily true. The Astaire/Rogers pictures and the René Clair pictures, and the Mamoulians and Lubitsch's *The Smiling Lieutenant* were narrative. I don't know that I agree that the music became more integrated with the pictures. I'm not sure that that's a correct image of what happened.

KM: But you and Gene and the others in the Freed unit certainly moved away from the traditional backstage musical which had dominated the 1930s.

SD: I did backstage musicals. Gene did backstage musicals. *Singin' in the Rain* is sort of a backstage musical.

KM: In a way, but you didn't make the kind of films where people only dance and sing when they're on stage – like Busby Berkeley did.

SD: Yeah. They weren't like that, but you're leaving out Fred Astaire. Fred and Ginger didn't only dance on the stage. In René Clair's films he has the whole city of Paris singing. You see, I don't think we invented it. I wish I could take credit for it, but I can't. We simply used it.

KM: In *On the Town* and several of your other musicals, you focus on working-class characters in a working-class setting at a time when most musicals were about aristocrats or the idle rich. Why?

SD: I don't know. I seem to be a meat and potatoes sort of fella. That's what I understand. That's what I know. There's no reason that sailors can't sing and dance. I'm reminded of a sketch that Sid Caesar did on *Your Show of Shows* after we'd done *Anchors Aweigh* and *On the Town*, in both of which Kelly and Sinatra play American sailors. Everyone was dressed up in sailor suits and they were theoretically on board a big navy ship and Sid says to the collected sailors, 'Men, as you know, it's traditional before we go into battle, we always do a big musical number!'

You know, Fred Astaire was immortalized by Irving Berlin in black tie, top hat and tails. But there are no laws. Gene is a guy from the real world, from the streets and the bars and the working class. And even in *Singin' in the Rain*, his origins are a little boy dancing for pennies in a pool room. It just happened like that and it seemed right. I don't think any of us said, 'No, no, no, we're not going to do white tie and tails!' We made a few jokes about it in *Singin' in the Rain* though.

KM: Not only are many of your characters working class, but they're often rebellious and anti-establishment. Was that a reflection of your own temperament?

SD: Well, young people are rebellious and, sure, I think that's part of it. Also, you know, movie stories are about conflict. You can't make a movie which praises people. It's very hard to make a movie where everything's OK all the way and you like everything. There has to be something that you're fighting against. A movie audience is waiting for trouble. That's what you make movies about, some problem which you then try to overcome. In most cases you do, or if you don't it becomes a tragedy. So, yes we were young and we were rebellious and that's what stories are about – rebelling.

KM: Your characters also seem more robust and earthy than characters in other musicals. They even seem to be relatively open about sex.

SD: Well, they were not very open. We couldn't be very open about sex or about a lot of things.

KM: But you were much more so than other people.

SD: I guess. I guess. But I'm not sure that we've made great strides. It seems to me that pictures had more romance and sexuality when you knew that certain things were forbidden – couldn't be shown. People went inside of a door and closed the door and you knew what was happening. You didn't have to see the image of humping. As Oscar Wilde said after his one physical time with a woman: 'The position is grotesque, the pleasure is momentary and the cost is enormous.' Humping is not a musical number. It's more romantic imagining screwing than showing it. So while they're earthy people, there are boundaries. It seems to me that once you can say everything in a movie – when you can say 'Fuck' and 'Shit' and everything it was impossible to say back in the 1930s and the 1940s – nothing has any power. To say 'Fuck you' has no power any more. Whereas in, say, *Gone with the Wind*, when Clark Gable said, 'Frankly my dear, I don't give a damn,' the word 'damn' carried so much power because it was forbidden.

It's harder and harder to make a big impact so film-makers blow up bigger and bigger buildings – but even those have now lost their impact. And now we're blowing up outer space and pretty soon there'll be nothing left. So restraint is better. It gives you a wonderful tension in a movie or in a story. When you take away all the restraints, nothing's left. If everything is possible, nothing is satisfactory.

KM: It's like the famous Lubitsch touch . . .

SD: That's right.

KM: To go back to the subject of sexuality in the musicals you did with Kelly. One thing those films have in common is a woman character who is sexually aggressive and makes the first move on a man – like the Betty Garrett character in *On the Town* and the Cyd Charisse figure in *It's Always Fair Weather*. Can you say something about that?

SD: Well, in both those instances a lot of things came from Comden and Green.

A sweet naive girl is not amusing, is not fresh. And we could certainly relate to that. However, there is something in *On the Town* which embarrasses me enormously, now that we're talking about it. It's the way we treated the character that's played by Alice Pearce. She's a physically unattractive-looking woman and we made jokes about her appearance which, when I see the movie today, make me ashamed. I shudder to think that I had to let this woman stand and be humiliated to make the audience laugh. We were all so unfeeling, not only the film-makers but the audiences too. No one ever said, 'This is horrible what you're doing to that woman.' She had played the same part in the original show and she was wonderful, a very gifted and remarkably talented person, but what we did to her is not human.

KM: *On the Town* **was one of the first musicals that was – in part at least – filmed on location. Did MGM encourage that or did they consider it rebellious?**

SD: MGM thought it was rebellious, but it just seemed to Gene and me that this is a story about three sailors and twenty-four hours in New York and New York is a city you can't do on a sound stage. So we have to do it in New York. But it took a lot of doing to persuade MGM of that. You see, when sound movies first arrived in 1929, or whatever, the studio bosses thought, 'In order to show how wonderful our new sound pictures are we're going to make a lot of musicals!' and in those days you couldn't record sound on location because the equipment was massive and bulky and so all musicals were, as a matter of course, shot on the stage. By the time we came along this was a deeply ingrained habit, and nobody had stuck their head up to say, 'We don't need to

On the Town: One of the first musicals shot on location
(Jules Munshin, Frank Sinatra and Gene Kelly).

do this any more – the sound systems have changed, we can record or play back sound wherever we like now.' Remember that even in 1949, the majority of the staff at MGM had been there since the silent days and their resistance came from experience – except that that experience was no longer valid because technically things had moved on.

Anyway, after a long fight MGM let us film for two weeks in New York, which wasn't nearly enough. What we tried to do was use the short time we had to give the picture the flavour of the city, so most of it is at the beginning, during the 'New York, New York' number. You get shots of Chinatown, Little Italy, the Statue of Liberty and the occasional shots of taxis and so on throughout the film.

KM: Would you say that you are much more interested in the visual aspects of film-making than the verbal ones?

SD: Well, you know Alfred Hitchcock's famous line: somebody asked him if he had enjoyed seeing a particular movie and he said, 'No I don't go to the movies.' And they said, 'Why not?' And he said, 'I don't like to see photographs of people talking.' I agree with that, but on the other hand, there are wonderful movies about people talking. I miss the great talk of the early sound films, when they often filmed plays, which were written by people from a certain literary, erudite background. People spoke wonderful lines then. But today, I fear, we don't have such good talk in films.

KM: When film-makers discuss your movies, they often enthuse about the wonderful camera movements you employed. Did you consciously keep the camera moving?

SD: I certainly didn't move the camera just for the sake of moving it. I'm reminded of this ridiculous comment that a new director made to me. He showed me his picture and I said, 'Yes it's nice but tell me, why do you move the camera so much?' And he said, 'Well if I don't move the camera, how will they know I'm directing?' Moving the camera is not a clue to being a great director. And anyway, few people understand that movement on the screen is not necessarily camera movement. I'm thinking of a John Ford movie called *The Long Voyage Home* where the camera never moved. Not one shot. Occasionally a minor pan. That's all. The camera was always on a tripod. But it's a wonderful picture. On the other hand, so is *Bullitt* where the camera never stops moving.

KM: So you were trying to get movement into the frame, not necessarily camera movement?

SD: I try to get movement in the movie. Movement means all kinds of things: story movement, physical movement of the actors or the dancers and camera movement. It's a funny thing about dancing for example: if a dancer moves across the screen the effect is the same as if the camera were moving. If, on the other hand, the camera travels with a character walking down the street, the movement is less. Today the camera can do anything – in a helicopter, on a rocket – but it's how you use that movement that's important. It's like a pencil: anybody can write a book, but it's very hard to write a good one.

KM: When you and Kelly directed together, how did you divide the responsibilities?

SD: We didn't. We didn't divide them up. We just did the best we could. We didn't say: you do this and I'll do that. Having said that, there are certain obvious ways in which our roles differed. He was standing in front of the camera and I was standing behind it – so I was more concerned with what the camera was doing. But apart from that, we didn't divide things up. We did whatever we thought was best and we disagreed a lot and tried to come to some agreement and perhaps – although it's a terrible word – compromise.

You know, in the movies I've worked on there's been no such thing as improvisation. The improvising goes on before you get to photographing it. You plan it down to the tiniest detail. I only improvise when I'm rehearsing or thinking or writing or planning, but when the moment comes to shoot it's all fixed, and planned and detailed. So Gene and I would fight it out until we'd worked out what we were going to do and he would have thoughts and I would have thoughts and we would put them together. We rehearsed together in the rehearsal halls and we spent endless hours working together.

KM: You were both involved in choreography, camera set-ups and everything?

SD: Yes, we both worked at it. We were true collaborators.

KM: Can collaboration really work in cinema?

SD: It can work in anything, if the collaborators can work together. Look at Powell and Pressburger, they put both their names on everything and it worked out OK. People often think of playwrights as a single person but many of the best American plays were written by teams like Hecht and MacArthur. So collaboration can work. Comden and Green are a perfect example, they write the screenplay and the lyrics together.

Film-making is all about collaboration, about finding out what people do best and taking advantage of it. Like in *It's Always Fair Weather* we got Gene to do a roller-skating number purely because we knew what a good roller-skater he was. Or in *Singin' in the Rain*, we went into the rehearsal hall with Donald O'Connor for the 'Make 'em Laugh' number and said 'What can you do that's funny?' And we put together a series of things which he did better than anyone else.

I once said to Bob Fosse, 'What do you think is the most important quality a choreographer should have?' He didn't think very long and he said, 'A good memory.' You see, you just have to remember what people are good at and then use it in a way that's fresh.

KM: Back to Comden and Green. They wrote two of the three films you did with Kelly – *Singin' in the Rain* and *It's Always Fair Weather* – and contributed to the third – *On the Town*. What qualities did they bring to those films?

SD: They brought a very funny, very fresh satirical approach to things. Both of them are very educated people and they bring an enormous wealth of culture to whatever they write. To this day if I can't remember something, or who did this, or what a piece of music is like, I simply get on the phone and call Adolph Green and say, 'Adolph, who wrote this?' And bang! he tells you. Did you know that in the original stage version of *On the Town* Comden and Green

Singin' in the Rain: The fun of being childish.

played the parts that Anne Miller and Jules Munchen took in the film?

KM: Their sense of humour can be quite acerbic – laughing at human foibles.

SD: And crying at human foibles, in the case of *It's Always Fair Weather*, a film which is really about failed ambitions and aspirations, and has a certain amount of pain in it.

KM: Yes, I find *It's Always Fair Weather* very moving. Can we talk a little more about *Singin' in the Rain*? It is still many people's favourite musical and has a great cult following. Why do you think it was so successful?

SD: For lots of reasons, but mainly because it has an irresistible energy. Almost everyone who worked on it was young and at the peak of enthusiasm – Kelly, O'Connor, Debbie Reynolds, me, Jean Hagen – and the movie just explodes with physical energy. Also, although it's very funny, it's also a fairly accurate look at what actually went on in the movies when sound arrived. There were many stars like the character played by Jean Hagen, whose careers were ruined because they didn't have a good voice. Another thing is that all the numbers worked out to be good numbers and it has more musical numbers in it than any other movie of its kind. I once timed it and there's more time spent on the musical numbers than on the story.

KM: But one never feels the numbers are being dragged out.

SD: Yes, the picture is full of energy and it never lets you down.

KM: I'm sure you've done it a million times, but could you briefly talk me through the inception of that film, where the idea came from?

SD: The idea came from Arthur Freed who was probably the most powerful producer at MGM at the time. He said to Gene and me and to Comden and Green, 'Why don't you do a movie using the songs that Nacio Herb Brown and I wrote together?' So we played all those songs and it was clear that they were written in the early, early years of the talkies. So it seemed obvious that we should do a movie about movies and the early talkies. Arthur said, 'We'll call it *Singin' in the Rain*.' And we said, 'Why? It's not about singing in the rain, it's about Hollywood, it's about talking pictures.' But he told us that we should call it *Singin' in the Rain* because that had been their biggest hit – and that's the only reason it has that title, just like *Easter Parade* was called *Easter Parade* because it was Irving Berlin's big song and the same with *White Christmas*. Then Arthur asked us, 'So what are you going to do with this number, "Singin' in the Rain"?' And we said, 'Well, Arthur, we re going to have Gene sing in the rain!' How else could you use that number?!

KM: Can you talk me through that number – how you put it together?

SD: The number comes out of the plot situation: he and Debbie Reynolds have finally admitted to each other that they're in love and he goes out and it's raining and he signals his car to go home – he doesn't want to get in. He puts his umbrella down and he lets it rain on him and he's singing in the rain because he's in love and the girl he loves loves him. He's a happy man, being a child, dancing in puddles and getting soaking wet and being so euphoric about this sensation that he's feeling. The whole number's about the joy of suddenly realizing you love someone who loves you back. And it's expressed through the silliness of a child, you know, stamping around in the puddles on the street, jumping up and down off the kerb and scraping his umbrella down the picket fence. That's it, it's just the fun of being childish.

KM: There is a very famous moment in that number when the camera moves right in over Gene Kelly's face. It's a moment of tremendous euphoria. Can you remember how that came about?

SD: It just seemed like the right thing to do. I don't know why I did it, I just said, 'Let's make the camera do that now.' It was just a feeling. That moment when the camera comes to him and he says 'Come on with the rain, there's a smile on my face' and you see him looking up and the rain pouring on him and the camera rises up and goes over his face – that seems to get some sort of emotional response.

KM: Can you tell me about my other great favourite, the 'Make 'em Laugh' number?

SD: Well, Gene is miserable because he's in love and he can't find the girl and his great buddy Donald O'Connor wants to cheer him up. So the whole idea of the number is to make Gene laugh. We didn't have a song for that and it was the one new song that Brown and Freed wrote especially for the movie. So when they'd written the song we went into the rehearsal hall and said, 'Donald, what do you do that's funny?' And he did all the things that are in the film: walking into walls, prat falls and that wonderful moment when the dummy flirts with him and he rejects it. We just had a lot of props brought into the rehearsal hall by the prop man and one of them was this funny old dummy and Donald saw it and did this gag with it. We thought it was hilarious but would be even better if the dummy was dressed like a person. So we asked them to fix the dummy up and put a head on it and we dressed it up. And the end result was that it wasn't funny any more. So we threw out the new dummy and went back to the limp, broken-down dummy which was one of those dummies they have as dead bodies lying around a battlefield or whatever.

KM: Your last collaboration with Gene Kelly was on *It's Always Fair Weather* and as you said before, it's got a more melancholy feeling about it. Did you have any difficulty persuading MGM to make it?

SD: Well, I don't know that we persuaded them. Arthur Freed took the idea to them. It turned out to be one of the last musicals MGM made.

The original idea was that it would be Sinatra, Gene and Dan Dailey, because it had been ten years since we did *On the Town* and it seemed a good idea for Comden and Green to write a story about three guys who'd been separated for ten years and come back together again only to find that they don't have much in common any more, that they've grown up and been disappointed by life. I think it related quite strongly to what was going on in our own lives at the time. We had gone our separate ways – Kelly, me, Comden and Green, Sinatra – and we were brought back together to do this picture. But Sinatra pretty soon said that he didn't want to be in it – we cast Michael Kidd instead – and by the time we were shooting, I don't think the studio really wanted to do it either.

It's Always Fair Weather: A farewell (Michael Kidd, Gene Kelly and Dan Dailey).

KM: For a musical it's very downbeat, and, I suppose, adult.

SD: Yeah. I don't know if it's downbeat, although it is a surprise that the three leads really don't like each other when they meet up after ten years. But in the end they do like each other. It's certainly very different in tone to *Singin' in the Rain* and *On the Town*.

KM: In retrospect it seems like a valediction to the optimistic, golden age of the musical? Did you have any sense of that at the time?

SD: I didn't think of it as a farewell to musicals, maybe a farewell to Kelly and the movies he and I did together. But I didn't think it was the end of the road for musicals, nor do I think it is now. There's no reason there shouldn't be musicals. You just accept that the spiral has gone down, and it's hard to send it up again. But I don't think musicals are over. I hope not.

KM: All three movies you did with Gene Kelly centre on a threesome – there's the romantic lead, played by Gene in each case, a clown figure and one other undefined. What do you find attractive about this kind of grouping?

SD: I really don't know the answer to that. It's not two guys, a buddy-buddy kind of thing . . . I don't know. It just happened. The idea of the Trinity seems to be satisfying. A triangle is a very nice shape . . . I have no theoretical reason for it. I just like three.

KM: I suppose that if you have two people you have romance, but if you have three you have camaraderie.

SD: You have all kinds of things with a triangle. It's unusual. It's symmetrical, but it's odd.

KM: Why did your partnership with Gene Kelly come to an end?

SD: I don't know. The partnership was over, that's all. I'd gone my own way. I wanted to go and do things without him. Partnerships usually break up, the best of them: Rodgers and Hart, Hecht and MacArthur, Gilbert and Sullivan. I think you get fed up with each other. Collaboration is a very trying situation.

KM: Did you argue?

Seven Brides for Seven Brothers:
'You can't make a musical about seven backwoodsmen dancers!'

Seven Brides for Seven Brothers: Guys lonely for girls.

SD: We tried not to argue on the set. We tried very hard only to argue off the set, or in the privacy of some office or something, but it was a struggle. It was not a great romp.

KM: To move onto the musicals that you made on your own. *Seven Brides for Seven Brothers* **– set in the Wild West, with a group of relatively uneducated, unsophisticated characters – is very different to the kind of thing you were doing in** *Singin' in the Rain* **or** *On the Town*. **The script doesn't have that satirical edge. What attracted you to it?**

SD: Everything. I loved the idea of making a musical set in Northern Oregon, about people who raise sheep and were sort of crude backwoodsmen who were brought culture by women. It was just a wonderfully fresh way of making a musical. Nobody had done anything like it before – remember *Oklahoma* hadn't been done yet. I also loved the idea of having fourteen lead characters who were all musical performers. It was thrilling to work with so many characters. Of course, the studio thought I had gone completely bananas. They said, 'You can't make a musical about seven backwoodsmen dancers! We'll be a laughing stock!' I tried to explain to them that dancing could be a very physical way of expressing yourself and it didn't have to be balletic in its inception. I wanted these guys to be very masculine, able to handle an axe and ride a horse. But the studio didn't see it like that. They wanted to use all old country songs like 'Turkey in the Straw'. I wanted to commission a complete score. Fortunately, I prevailed almost entirely. The picture is not shot in real locations enough to satisfy me and it showed then and it shows now – the fake painted backings and things. But again, there's so much energy in it, so much physical live energy, especially in Michael Kidd's terrific choreography, that it comes off.

83

KM: The film goes so far in being artificial and painted that it almost seems deliberately stylized.

SD: Well, I didn't intend it to be. It was meant to represent reality, but you just can't do it with painted backings. No, I hated that aspect of it. I wanted to shoot it all in Oregon, but the cost would have been enormous because we needed to be there in the winter for the snow and in the spring. It would have meant an expensive extended shooting schedule and we really had very little money for the picture. The studio didn't think very much of the idea and so they gave me a very small budget. They were making *Brigadoon* at the same time and spending a fortune on it because they thought it was going to be the big hit movie. The good thing was that because it was inexpensive they just left me to get on with it and didn't interfere.

Last night I remembered – because I knew we were going to talk about it today – a newspaper clipping someone sent me about ten years ago from one of the British tabloids, with a headline: 'BARMIE BERT' and a picture of this porcine, smiling man's face. And underneath it said that every day when Barmie Bert comes home from work he puts on a cassette of *Seven Brides for Seven Brothers* and his wife says he's run it over six hundred times now and she's going to leave him if he runs it again. And there was this big, smiling, goofy guy who sat looking at *Seven Brides* every night of his life and I guess his wife left him. That's the best review I ever got!

KM: Can you tell me how you developed the 'Lonesome Polecat' number which I think is one of the most effective in the film?

SD: It's the guys being lonely for the girls. It's an image of these masculine men in the snow, doing male, physical, athletic moves and showing their loneliness and longing for the girls who had locked them out of the house. A curious thing is that it's all done in one shot, all one camera set-up. I don't do that very often. I just did it to please Michael Kidd who wanted to do it like that. I said to him, 'We'll sacrifice a lot doing it like that and nobody will even notice. If we do it right and cut in the right places nobody will ever notice the cuts.' But he said, 'Please, do it in one shot.' So I agreed. There are two problems about doing a number like that. In the first place, it takes a long time to rehearse and organize and secondly, if anything goes wrong you can't cut around it, you've got to settle for the one take where the least goes wrong – because inevitably, one thing is not going to be exactly right.

KM: It's a very subtle number.

SD: Yeah, and Matt Mattox is very good in it, and the guy sitting on the log. And the lines of the song are just so wicked: 'A man can't sleep if he sleeps with sheep!'

KM: Can we talk a little about *Funny Face* and *The Pyjama Game*? One thing they have in common with many of your films is a striking use of colour. In *Funny Face* there are some very stylized sets which use colour in a very bold way – like the magazine office set with its outrageous pink doorways – but I was particularly struck by Audrey Hepburn's dance in the bookshop. The shop is dusty and grey and she brings out this bright yellow hat with a long piece of silk trailing from it . . .

SD: Well, that's what it's about. It's about realizing there's something emotional, enlightening and joyful which can't be expressed in the sombre reality of deep literary, philosophical thoughts and expressions. And also she's fallen in love. He's kissed her and she sings 'How long's this been going on, what have I been missing?' This bright yellow hat in this sombre place with the flowing trail expresses what she has suddenly become aware of.

KM: How much do you think about colour when you're choreographing a film? How involved are you in the over-all design of the film?

SD: You don't do anything theoretically, you just do what comes into your mind, what works. She was in this musty bookshop, she's fallen in love and just seen all these beautiful photographic models in gorgeous, colourful clothes and to do the song and dance like that just seemed obvious.

KM: You worked with Hepburn on three films – was she a favourite of yours?

SD: I loved Audrey Hepburn, yes.

KM: What did she have that was special?

SD: God knows. I wish I had said this, but Billy Wilder said it and I always quote it: 'What Audrey had you can't teach, you can't learn, God kissed her on the cheek and there she was.' She had every kind of magical, mystical, feminine, ethereal thing and she was the most attractive, irresistible creature. On the first day of every movie she did, within three minutes of walking on set, everybody was in love with her, male and female. A lot of it was in the way she sounded, her voice was honey, and the way she looked, and the way she moved and her elegance, her stature, the way she sat, the way she stood, the way she was wonderfully unique.

KM: In 1958 you made your first film in London and subsequently moved there. Why?

SD: I came to make *Indiscreet*. I just came because I had this play which had originally been set in Washington and New York and for some – completely untheoretical – reason I said, 'Wouldn't it be fun to set it in London?' So we set it in London, I liked it there and I stayed.

KM: *Indiscreet* signalled a change in the kind of films you were making. You pretty much stopped making musicals until *The Little Prince* in 1973. Was that because the studios didn't want them?

SD: I remember feeling, 'I don't just want to be the Alfred Hitchcock of musicals. I want to do other sorts of movies.' I had made musicals and made musicals and I wanted a rest. I had nothing against them, but I wanted to do other types of movies, and I had to become a film producer to do it.

KM: That feeling of yours coincided almost exactly with the decline of the musical.

SD: It was just luck for me that that I happened to step away when they were fading as a genre.

KM: Did your films become more personal when you became your own producer?

SD: Probably, yes.

KM: It seems to me that your films also became darker, and more adult in their concerns. *Indiscreet* is a love story – but it's about mature, experienced people, not idealistic, fresh-faced teenagers.

Two for the Road: Audrey Hepburn
and Albert Finney.

Below:
Two for the Road: On the road.

SD: I wouldn't agree that it's darker. It's very light.

KM: Maybe it's not dark – but it is very adult. One of its themes is the difficulty of finding and sustaining love.

SD: No! It's a romantic story about a man who doesn't want to marry and how the woman he loves eventually captures him.

KM: But wouldn't you agree that in *Indiscreet* and later in *Two for the Road* and *Bedazzled*, love is seen as a far more complex and difficult thing than in your earlier films where it's all pretty straightforward and idealized? At one time or another all the characters in those later movies have been disappointed by love.

SD: Well, *Two for the Road* is a story about what it's really like in a long-term marriage, partnership or relationship: it comes with pain. Love at first sight is easy, love after twenty-five years of looking at the same face is very difficult and *Two for the Road* is about what we do to each other through a long-term relationship. It's a hard look at marriage. Audrey and I and Freddie Raphael, who wrote the wonderful script – we were all older than we had been and

that's reflected in the movie. *Bedazzled* was about the same thing, but it's also about selling out, about what we are prepared to do to gain the things that we want and what that costs you in terms of humanity. It's a funny look at that serious subject and it's full of really broad jokes about what you'd put up with to get the woman you love.

KM: Were you interested in these themes just because you were getting older or was there a more profound disillusion – with America perhaps?

SD: No, I certainly never became disillusioned with America. We were just older, I guess. It came out of our unconscious feelings. Yes, I was going through that in my personal life, I was going through a difficult marriage and Audrey was too and it was what was interesting to me at the time. It wasn't exactly euphoric. Many people think that *Two for the Road* is a very romantic, lovely sort of movie. I personally think it's a very painful look at a marriage which they managed to keep together in the end.

KM: It doesn't pull any punches.

SD: No, it really says that it's tough going.

KM: Structurally, *Two for the Road* is fascinating – the way it jumps around through time showing a relationship changing and evolving. I particularly like the way you have the honeymooning couple having a conversation on the side of a road, a car goes by and you cut inside the car and it's the same couple several years later, when the relationship has completely changed. Did you find this kind of temporal trick liberating?

SD: Yes, but I don't think you can do it over and over. We decided that we'd only see this couple on holiday, when they went back to the same part of France every year. You never see them at work or at home and therefore to see the pain and the change Freddie came up with this remarkable idea which is a sort of literary, novelistic notion, of going back and forth in time. It's a structure which suggests that you carry the past with you all the time, and so the past has as much weight in the movie as the present does. In fact, you never know where the present is, the present is wherever you're seeing it. So it doesn't really feel like flashbacks.

KM: At the end of *Bedazzled* Peter Cook, who plays the devil and who has been disappointed by God, makes a very vitriolic, bitter speech in which he says that in revenge he's going to turn the world into a horrific place, filled with rubbish and advertising and fast food and all that is cheap, nasty and commercial. It's a striking moment because suddenly the film – which is generally very light hearted – becomes very serious and almost nasty. Is that because those sentiments were your own?

SD: I felt it, Peter Cook felt it and Dudley Moore felt it and I still feel it. *Bedazzled* was made in 1967 and they *were* filling the world with noise and supermarkets and Wimpy bars and fast food and jet sounds, ruining it for everybody. That's what the devil says he's going to do and God laughs and that's the note it ends on. And it *has* happened, the world is noisier, uglier and less pleasant and it's just going to get worse.

KM: Over a long period of time you had an association with Morris Bender, who did

many brilliant title sequences for you. Can you tell me what a good title sequence should do and what made him so good?

SD: Again, I don't have any pre-set notions. One movie is not like another. I met Bender because I took an ad out many years ago in *Variety* which he designed for me. So when I did *Indiscreet* I asked him to do the titles. He'd never done them before, but he came up with something very clever and very much about the movie: peering through a keyhole and seeing a rose on the other side and so on. The titles in the *The Grass is Greener* are very funny. You see a group of little babies over the credits and you get the idea that the people involved in making the movie are these babies. The credits for *Two for the Road* are terrifically imaginative. He was a very gifted man.

KM: I particularly like the titles for *Bedazzled*, so simple and clever.

SD: We had no money, that's why they were so simple. The movies are like that; there are so many controlling factors: when you shoot, who's in it, the money and how fast you have to do it. All these things get in your way.

KM: In 1973 you made *The Little Prince*, your last complete musical to date. At the time musicals were very much out of fashion – Bob Fosse was really the only one making them successfully with *Cabaret*. Why did you decide to return to musicals?

SD: Paramount sent me the book of *The Little Prince* and asked if I'd like to make it into a film. I said yes because it touched me a great deal. It's a tiny little thing, it must be thirty pages if that and rightly or wrongly I thought it was a most remarkable piece of imagination and says a lot of true things. However, I don't think the finished movie lives up to Saint-Exupéry's original. The execution was not totally successful. It has some very good things in it: a couple

The Little Prince: Bob Fosse and Steven Warner.

of good songs by Lerner and Lowe, a wonderful number by Bob Fosse and a good sequence with Gene Wilder as a fox. So while I'm very glad I made it, I don't think it's completely fulfilled and it should have been better than it is.

KM: Do you think it's harder to make musicals today because the audience is more knowing?

SD: No, I don't think there are any laws. If you have the right idea and the feeling, the emotional hit, then it will work. It has to really hit you, you can't fake it. That's true of musicals and non-musicals. You can only do what comes right out of you in a very powerful, strong way, because first of all the energy, the time, the commitment to make a movie – a year is not even it, it's more like two years of total, absolute monk-like commitment to a picture. Making a movie is suffering, pain, anxiety, pressure, tension, argument and conflict – most of it. That's what making movies is. It's not fun. It's hell. And in order to get through it, you have to have such a tremendous fascination and desire and energetic commitment to that subject or idea and really want to carry it through, otherwise you're just going to fake it and give up and the result will just be flaccid and dead and empty. You have to love it with all your might and that doesn't come easy.

KM: Bearing that in mind, can you tell me a little bit about the movie you are working on at the moment?

SD: It's an unrequited love story about a man and a woman who want each other and love each other, yet something keeps them apart. They're absolutely passionately in love from the age of seven until she dies and there's something extremely moving about it. Like we were talking about earlier, it's got conflict. Movies are about conflict. This is about a love affair that doesn't ever come to fruition.

KM: In recent years you've found it difficult to raise funding for your projects. If you were given an endless supply of money would you make movies all the time?

SD: Well, I would make a lot of movies. Money is the controlling factor. Money makes the world go round.

7 To and from Fiction

Shohei Imamura interviewed by Toichi Nakata

Shohei Imamura's reputation in Japan has long been secure: he is acknowledged as one of the most important directors of the post-war period. In the West, however, few of his films were distributed until *The Ballad of Narayama* (*Narayama Bushi-Ko*) won the Palme D'Or at the 1983 Cannes Film Festival. In 1994, the Drambuie Edinburgh Film Festival mounted Britain's most comprehensive retrospective of his work, spanning more than thirty years of filmmaking. I was attending the festival to present my own film *Osaka Story – a documentary*, and had the pleasure of spending a lot of time with Imamura and his wife. This interview was recorded during their week in Scotland.

My first contact with Imamura dates back to the short time I attended his film school in Japan. This was launched in 1974 as the Yokohama School of Broadcasting and Films; it moved to its present base in Shin-Yurigaoka (out-

Shohei Imamura.

side Tokyo) in 1986, and is now known as the Japanese Academy of Visual Arts. Imamura remains its president and director. The films I now make are documentaries, and my interest in Imamura springs from the fact that he (unlike most feature directors anywhere) has given equal emphasis to fiction and non-fiction films in his own career. Indeed, several of his films play on the impossibility of knowing where 'reality' ends and fiction begins. But whether he starts from a fictional story or a factual situation, his work consistently tries to uncover fundamental truths about lower-class people, many of them outcasts from mainstream society.

Unlike his sometime mentor Yasujiro Ozu, often cited in the West as 'the most Japanese of all Japanese directors', Imamura has never been seen as offering stereotypical representations of Japan or Japanese people. Imamura's characters, both real and fictional, tend to be loners and misfits. The way he looks at them is severe, but never without an underlying affection. As I am Japanese myself, I find that his films attain a deep understanding of the people who appear in them – people he knows well and loves dearly. In this sense, I find his films both very personal and immutably Japanese.

Shohei Imamura was born in downtown Tokyo in 1926, the third son in the family of a private doctor. Seeing Akira Kurosawa's *Drunken Angel* (*Yoidore Tenshi*, 1948) while he was a student made him determined to become a filmmaker. After majoring in Western History at Waseda University, he joined the Shochiku company in 1951 and was assigned to work as an assistant director at its studios in Ofuna. The directors he worked under included Yasujiro Ozu, Masaki Kobayashi, Yoshitaro Nomura and Yuzo Kawashima. The Ozu films he worked on were *Early Summer* (*Bakushu*, 1951), *The Flavour of Green Tea Over Rice* (*Ochazuke no Aji*, 1952) and the masterpiece *Tokyo Story* (*Tokyo Monogatari*, 1953), but it's impossible to trace direct influences from Ozu in his work. The director he apparently learned most from in his days as an assistant was the anarchic Yuzo Kawashima; he edited a book of essays about Kawashima after the latter's premature death in 1963.

Imamura moved from Shochiku to the newly re-established Nikkatsu company in 1954. The revived company was recruiting young talent from all the other production companies at the time. Yuzo Kawashima also moved to Nikkatsu, and Imamura worked for him again. They co-wrote the film now considered Kawashima's best, *Sun Legend of the End of the Tokugawa Era* (*Bakumatsu Taiyo-den*, 1957, also known in English as *Shinagawa Path*); this was the first screenplay that Imamura worked on to be produced.

Imamura himself began directing in 1958. His first four films, inevitably, were company assignments made quickly and on low budgets. The fourth was *My Second Brother* (*Nian-chan*, 1959), based on the best-selling diary of a ten-year-old Korean girl living in Japan and describing her family's struggles. This film was a critical and commercial success, but Imamura himself balked at its sentimentality and resolved to stop accepting assigned projects.

Ever since, he has followed his own path. In *Pigs and Battleships* (*Buta to*

Gunkan, 1961) he dealt with the low-life gangsters and prostitutes operating around a US naval base. In *The Insect Woman* (*Nippon Konchu-ki*, 1963) and *Intentions of Murder* (*Akai Satsui*, 1964), he focused on strong-willed women battling against their apparently bleak destinies. He left Nikkatsu in 1966 and established his own company, Imamura Productions. His first independent production was an adaptation of Akiyuki Nosaka's sardonic novel *The Pornographers*, which he retitled *Introduction to Anthropology* (*Jinruigaku Nyumon*, 1966). He went on to make the extraordinary *A Man Vanishes* (*Ningen Johatsu*, 1967), which starts as a documentary account of a search for a missing person and turns into a blend of fact and fiction unprecedented in world cinema. After spending nearly three years working on one of his greatest films, *Profound Desire of the Gods* (*Kamigami no Fukaki Yokubo*, 1968, also known in English as *Kuragejima: Tales from a Southern Island*), he moved into making documentaries.

From *The History of Post-War Japan as Told by a Bar Hostess* (*Nippon Sengoshi: Madamu Omboro no Seikatsu*, 1970) to *Karayuki-san: the Making of a Prostitute* (*Karayuki-san*, 1975), Imamura's documentaries all centre on real-life people who in many ways parallel the heroines and heroes of his fictions. Many of them are soldiers and 'comfort women' who were forced to go to South-East Asian countries during the war and who have chosen to remain abroad. Through their personal histories and present-day plights, Imamura opens up many issues that have been ignored or covered up since the end of the Pacific War. It was while working on this series that Imamura founded his film school, the first of its kind in Japan.

Imamura's return to fiction with *Vengeance is Mine* (*Fukushu Suru wa Ware ni Ari*, 1979), a film about a serial killer who hates his father, began to bring his work to wider international attention. His subsequent films have won him increasing acclaim: *Eijanaika* (*Eejanaika*, 1981) on Japan's opening to the outside world in the nineteenth century, the Cannes prizewinner *The Ballad of Narayama*, the provocative film about a trafficker in women, *Zegen* (1987), and *Black Rain* (*Kuroi Ame*, 1989), based on Masuji Ibuse's novel about the bombing of Hiroshima. At the time we spoke he was in pre-production for a new film, which he hopes to shoot in 1996.

Most of the following interview was recorded in two long sessions on 16 and 19 August 1994. The English critic and film-maker Tony Rayns took part in the first of these sessions. I have also used some material from the Imamura Masterclass at the Edinburgh Film Festival, which was chaired by Rayns on 15 August. Imamura spoke in Japanese throughout, and this is my own translation of what he said.

Toichi Nakata: Can you sketch your beginnings in the Japanese film industry?
Shohei Imamura: My eldest brother – he was twelve years older than me – was a stage actor. My father used to take me to see him at the famous Tsukiji Sho-Gekijo in Tokyo. Among the plays I remember seeing was the adaptation of

Shunsaku Iwashita's novel *The Rickshaw Man* [*Muhomatsu no Issho*], which was later filmed twice by Hiroshi Inagaki; I also recall seeing some German expressionist plays. My brother died in China during the war, but I think those childhood experiences of the theatre stayed with me. When I was in high school, my dream was to write plays and become a stage director.

I was eighteen when Japan lost the war in 1945. I won a place in Waseda University to read Western History, but I wasn't a diligent attender of classes; I spent most of my time working with a student theatre group and getting involved with the communist movement. I was strongly against the continuation of the imperial system, and had many discussions with my friends about Hirohito's responsibility for the war. But my greatest obsession was individual freedom – the condition that the state had denied us absolutely during the war years – and I became fascinated by existentialism. At the time I was making a living from the black market: I bought illicit liquor and cigarettes from soldiers of the American occupation forces and sold them to my professors. That was the only time in my whole life when I was well off, although I spent all I made on drink. [*Laughter.*] My parents had been evacuated from Tokyo to Hokkaido and hadn't yet returned, and so I was on my own and totally free. I was surrounded by prostitutes and other low-life types, who had a great influence on me. I thoroughly enjoyed those times.

I also saw quite a number of films around that time. At first, most of them were French or German. Then there was the tide of American films that flooded into Japan after the war. But the film that shocked and moved me most was Akira Kurosawa's *Drunken Angel*. I found the gangster played by Toshiro Mifune incredibly real; he reminded me of people I'd met on the black market. I thought that Kurosawa must be a truly great director if he could make an actor as bad as Mifune look so real. And so when I graduated from the university in 1951, I was set on becoming an assistant to Kurosawa. Many of my friends meanwhile went into theatre work.

But Kurosawa worked for the Toho company, which was then in the throes of a prolonged strike. Consequently the company held no admission examination that year, and so I sat (and passed) the exam for the Shochiku company instead. Seven of us were taken on as assistant directors, and we drew lots to decide which director's crew we'd be assigned to. However, only six directors were working in the studio itself, and I was left the odd one out among the new recruits. I was told to wait around for Yasujiro Ozu, who was then filming on location in Nara.

TN: What are your memories of working for Ozu?

SI: I was an assistant on three of his films. There were five assistants in all, and I was the fifth and least of them. I was basically just a clapper boy, and Ozu barely acknowledged my existence. The first time he called me by name was towards the end of the filming of *Early Summer*.

My mother died of a cerebral haemorrhage while I was working on Ozu's *Tokyo Story*. When I got back from her funeral, I found Ozu in the sound studio, dubbing the scene in which the grandmother [played by Chieko Higashiyama] is dying, also from a cerebral haemorrhage. I could not stand watching the scene over and over again – it reminded me so vividly of my mother's death – and so I ran out of the dubbing theatre and into the toilet, almost in tears. But Ozu followed me and came to urinate next to me. 'Mr Imamura,' he asked, 'is that what a cerebral haemorrhage looks like? Have I got it right?' At the time I thought him incredibly cruel, but I later realized that a great film-maker sometimes has to behave like that.

Obviously, Ozu was very different from Kurosawa. He was always calm, placid and well dressed. But I can't say I ever cared for his style of film-making. Many years later, on *Black Rain*, I was working with the cinematographer Takashi Kawamata, who had been an assistant cameraman on Ozu films. We had to keep telling each other not to shoot *Black Rain* like an Ozu film. On the other hand, after working on three films I came away with the conviction that Ozu was a great director. It was while working for him that I learned most of the basics of film-making, and I'm sure that everything I learned is reflected in the films I've made.

TN: Why did you move from Shochiku to Nikkatsu?

SI: Nikkatsu was newly re-established, and they approached me. I turned for advice to both Ozu and Yoshitaro Nomura, another Shochiku director I'd worked for, and both of them encouraged me to take up Nikkatsu's offer. They probably thought that I would have more of a chance at a go-ahead new studio than in Shochiku. One other factor that triggered my desire to move was the fact that I was dating the company administrator, who was the only woman working with sixty male assistant directors. I felt it would be easier to marry her if I left the company myself. She is now my wife.

Compared with Shochiku, which was still a highly feudalistic company, Nikkatsu was remarkably free and energetic. It brought together young people from all the other major companies – Toho, Shin-Toho, Daiei, Toei and Shochiku – all of them looking to do something new and fresh. I felt more at ease in Nikkatsu.

TN: That was when you teamed up with Yuzo Kawashima?

SI: Yes, he came to Nikkatsu from Shochiku soon after me. I had worked for him in Shochiku, while he was making a completely worthless film. I couldn't restrain myself from asking him why he was making such a stupid comedy. He looked me straight in the eyes and said: 'For a living.'

Kawashima shared my interest in society's 'lower dregs', but he had his own idiosyncratic way of looking at people and a strong sense of black comedy. He had a reputation for profligacy in his personal life. Between films, he would take off for Kyoto and spend weeks at a time drinking with young geisha girls. He'd then return to Tokyo with empty pockets and make another film to finance his next excursion. He was an outrageous man, and an extremely interesting one.

Kawashima wasn't interested in the conventional grammar of film-making and he often used jump-cuts. I wrote *The Sun Legend of the End of the Tokugawa Era* for him and left many things in the script deliberately ambiguous, but he never paid any attention to the details anyway. That's the kind of man he was. The film's lead actor Frankie Sakai came to Kawashima and me separately to ask whether his character was really suffering from cancer or not, and we gave him different answers. Kawashima made a handful of masterpieces and plenty of flops. He died very suddenly in 1963, at the age of forty-five, but I remember him very clearly to this day.

TN: Why did Nikkatsu let you become a director so soon after you joined the company?

SI: One day three other assistant directors and I were called in by the studio head and told to write scripts for our first features. I was still in my sixth year as an assistant, and I'd always expected it would take ten years to be promoted. But this was obviously a fantastic opportunity, and so I began work on a script that very evening. I decided to do something about prostitutes in the old red-light district Yoshiwara. I thought this would definitely be right for me, since I knew a lot of prostitutes from my black market days. But when I gave my outline to the studio head, he found it banal and uninteresting. I couldn't disagree with him, and so I abandoned the idea.

Then a producer recommended me to read a story called *Tent Theatre* by Toko Kon. It was about a university drop-out who joined a travelling theatre troupe. My own student experiences made me identify with this character, and so I wrote a script based on the story. And that became *Stolen Desire* [*Nusumareta Yokujo*, 1958], my first film as director.

TN: Looking back, your fifth film for Nikkatsu [*Pigs and Battleships*, 1961] seems like the first 'authentic' Imamura film.

SI: That's a film about dumb gangsters in Yokosuka, which was an important US naval base. These guys buy a herd of pigs from the GIs and fatten them up to sell them for a profit. I did a lot of research for the film, and got to know the world of these gangsters rather well. They were greedy and capable of every dirty trick in the book. As I got to know them, it struck me that although they always lived for the moment they had their own kind of pride and enjoyed a kind of freedom all their own. They were pretty much like pigs, but at the same time very human. I ended up empathizing with them quite a lot.

One gangster once harangued me. 'Hey, Imamura,' he said, 'you work pretty hard, but you don't seem very comfortable on it. You can't even afford a decent suit, can you? Look at my new shoes. Better than yours, aren't they?' The same guy said to me, 'It's hard enough making ends meet when you work, Imamura, but it's much harder not to work and still be well-off.' I got very annoyed when he said it, but I couldn't deny that he had a point. I ended up using his words in the film.

I originally wanted 1,500 pigs for the climactic sequence of the gang fight in the middle of the red-light district, but we ran out of money. The head of Nikkatsu was furious with me. In the event I had to make do with only 400 pigs, including a lot of piglets. I had to do the best I could within the financial constraints.

After that, Nikkatsu wouldn't let me direct again for three years. They thought that I would disobey their orders, and that I'd overspend. And so I had to bide time writing scripts for other directors, including *The Street with the Cupola* [*Kyupora no Aru Machi*, 1962] for Kirio Urayama. During that period I also wrote the play *Paraji*, which later became the basis for *Profound Desire of the Gods*.

I was friendly with the writer Shinji Fujiwara; my third film *Endless Desire* [*Hateshinaki Yokubo*, 1958] was based on one of his stories. One night Fujiwara invited me for a drink and told me that he'd liked *Pigs and Battleships* but felt that it was somehow like a Kurosawa film – 'large-scale and full of dramatic action scenes'. I told him I couldn't see anything wrong with that. 'I got into film-making because I wanted to be like Kurosawa,' I said, 'and so I'm not sorry to hear that you think I'm getting there!' But Fujiwara went on to say that he was more interested in seeing an Imamura film than in finding 'the new Kurosawa'. Thanks to conversations like that, my ideas about film-making changed a lot during those three years when I wasn't allowed to direct.

TN: You mention your research quite often. Your approach reminds me of the way that documentary film-makers need to research their projects before they begin. Can you say something about the way you do your research?

SI: I'm interested in people: strong, greedy, humorous, deceitful people who are very human in their qualities and their failings. It may be that some of my fiction films look a bit like documentaries because I base my characters on research into real people. It was when I began to write scripts that I realized how much I needed to understand people. That's why I began spending time in the university library (for the first time in my life!) at the age of thirty. I first tried to gain a sociological perspective and set out to analyse 'reality' through social structures. It didn't take me long to realize that this was very limiting, and so I turned my attention to social anthropology – which took me a lot further in my understanding of human beings. My films *The Insect Woman* and *Intentions of Murder* were founded on those researches.

TN: But aren't you also sceptical about social anthropology?

SI: Of course, social anthropology doesn't provide all the answers. A sociological perspective can be useful too, but that's not enough in itself either. All scientific approaches have their limits. Above and beyond anything else, working as an artist means having a limitless curiosity about human beings. I have no interest in films made by directors who don't care about people. At my film school, I often tell the students that it's a place where they can learn about human beings. I'm happy if they graduate with an interest in knowing more about people. I tell them: 'You could be a bartender or a prostitute. Whatever you do, though, be an interesting person.' Some of the students think I'm crazy.

TN: The heroines of your films all counter the Western stereotype of the submissive Asian woman. Like Tome in *The Insect Woman*, all of your female characters are strong and determined . . .

SI: In my opinion, Japanese women generally are like that. Women generally

The Insect Woman.

outlive men, which means amongst other things that they're stronger than men. I certainly find them more interesting than men. The women who have marked me most in life are the lower-class women I met during my black market days. They weren't educated and they were vulgar and lusty, but they were also strongly affectionate and they instinctively confronted all their own sufferings. I grew to admire them enormously. My wife is a bold, strong woman, too, and I respect her a great deal.

TN: But you are from an upper middle-class background. Your father was a private doctor. What gave you such an empathy with working-class people?

SI: I went to an élite junior high school, and some of my classmates went on to become government ministers. Many of them looked down on people in the medical profession (like my father), and even then they thought of themselves as being somehow above the law – or rather, as members of the social class that controlled the police force. I despised them, and remember thinking that they were the kind of people who would never get close to the fundamental truths of life. Knowing them made me want to identify myself with working-class people who were true to their own human natures. At that age, though, I probably still thought of myself as being innately superior to working-class people.

When Japan lost the war, I had to face personal hardship for the first time. In my black market days, I was basically looked after by prostitutes and bar hostesses and came to depend on them heavily. I also came to know everything that was good and bad about them, and realized how honest and instinctual they were – especially in comparison with my former classmates at school. I found myself feeling more and more at ease with them, and losing any sense of superiority.

TN: The first of your films to blur the line between fiction and fact was *A Man Vanishes* [*Ningen Johatsu*], which you made independently in 1967.

SI: I made it for Imamura Productions, which I'd founded in 1965. The film was partly funded by the ATG [Art Theatre Guild], a small organization which invested in and distributed low-budget independent features. My original intention was to investigate twenty-six cases of men who had disappeared, but it soon became clear that one case alone would be quite complicated enough to deal with. I centred the film on the case of Tadashi Oshima, who disappeared in 1965 while on a business trip. I learned about him through meeting his fiancée Yoshie Hayakawa, and I soon guessed that Oshima had vanished because he wanted to get out of his obligation to marry her.

TN: How did you go about researching it?

SI: I always try to talk to people myself as much as I can. That can get boring, but sometimes I can sense that there's something that needs to be explored further behind what they're saying. While making *A Man Vanishes*, my crew and I stayed in the room next door to Yoshie Hayakawa for a whole year. She had every imaginable bad quality, and none of us could really stand her. And yet I wanted to understand why I found her so disturbing, and that was enough to keep me going.

TN: Did you ever think twice about using hidden cameras and exposing her and other people's private feelings in public?

SI: Yoshie Hayakawa gave her explicit consent to being filmed. She took leave from her job to be in the film, and we paid her a salary. In other words, she approached the project as a job and she took on the role of an actress in front of the camera. She used the camera as much as we used her as subject. Of course, there are serious ethical questions involved. Hayakawa didn't know what the film's outcome would be, but we behind the camera didn't know where reality was going to lead us either. I'm not sure myself if the use of hidden cameras was justified, and I have to admit that the finished film did hurt Hayakawa's feelings. These are difficult areas, and I have no glib answers. As a film-maker though, I did what I had to do to see the film through completion. I put the needs of the film first. I had no other choice, really.

TN: After *A Man Vanishes,* you made one more fiction feature [*Profound Desire of the Gods*, 1968] and then switched to making documentaries for the next nine years. What happened?

SI: The filming of *Profound Desire of the Gods* took place on Ishigaki Island in the Okinawan archipelago, and it was originally scheduled to last for six months. But six months got dragged out to one year, and then eighteen months. I had a great time on this remote island and got on very well with the local people. I immersed myself in Okinawan folklore and tradition. But my actors and actresses couldn't stand the protracted filming and began complaining about being stuck on the island for so long. I'd never had any problems working with actors before, but on this occasion their complaints made me really fed up. Funnily enough, I was so fed up that I lost all desire to make fiction films for many years.

Also, I came out of *A Man Vanishes* with a feeling that fiction – no matter how close to reality – could never be as truthful as unmediated documentary. And documentary seemed a better vehicle for my unending desire to get close to people's true natures. I started with *The History of Post-War Japan as Told by a Bar Hostess* in 1970, and then devoted myself to documentaries for some nine years. No actors to worry about. I simply travelled around with a skeleton crew; often just one cameraman and one sound recordist.

In Search of Unreturned Soldiers [*Mikkan-hei o Otte*, 1971] was about former soldiers of the Japanese army who chose not to return to Japan after the war. I found several of them who had remained in Thailand. Two years later, I invited one of them to make his first return visit to Japan and documented it in *Private Fujita Comes Home* [*Muhomatsu Kokyo ni Kaeru*, 1974]. During the filming, my subject Fujita asked me to buy him a cleaver so that he could kill his 'vicious brother'. I was shocked, and asked him to wait for a day so that I could plan how to film the scene. By the next morning, to my relief, Fujita had calmed down and changed his mind about killing his brother. But I couldn't have had a sharper insight into the ethical questions provoked by this kind of documentary film-making.

In 1975 I went to Malaysia to look for Japanese women who had been sent to South-East Asia during the war to serve as prostitutes for the Japanese troops. These women were known as Karayuki-san. While researching the project, I met around twenty old ladies who had been Karayuki-san, but none of them seemed right for a film. And then I met Kikuyo Zendo, a gentle old lady of seventy, who came from the family of a poor farmer in the Hiroshima area, and she became the focus of *Karayuki-san, the Making of a Prostitute* [1975]. She was very open with us from the start, but I had to ask her a series of shockingly direct questions: 'How many men did you have to sleep with every night?', 'Did you enjoy sex with your clients?', and so on. Despite everything, she remained astonishingly kind and tolerant towards us.

For my part, though, I was less and less sure that I could justify asking her such questions. I had to ask myself whether or not I was exploiting her, whether or not I had good enough reasons to expose her past in public, and whether or not I really understood her feelings. I also found myself wondering whether documentary was really the best way to approach these matters. I came to realize the presence of the camera could materially change people's lives. Did I have the right to effect such changes? Was I playing God in trying

Profound Desire of the Gods.

to control the lives of others? I'm in no way a sentimental humanist, but thoughts like these scared me and made me acutely aware of the limitations of documentary film-making.

During the nine years I made documentaries, I was basically supported by my wife, who ran a company producing artwork for animation films. No one can make a living directing documentaries for Japanese television. In fact, it's impossible to make documentaries at all unless you are ready to sacrifice many things in your personal life.

TN: So those were the considerations that led you back to fiction film-making with *Vengeance is Mine* in 1979?

SI: It grew out of an increasing frustration: there were many things I wanted to express that were beyond the reach of a documentary. A film-maker named Azuma Fujisaki drew my attention to a novel by Ryuzo Saki based on the real-life story of a serial killer. I read it and found it very provocative, but I couldn't immediately see any way of turning it into a dramatic film. Then I started researching the facts of the case for myself. That took me a year, and I came up with some details that had escaped Saki and the police. By the time I'd finished, I was confident that I could write a script that would incorporate a lot of documentary elements in the story. Making *Vengeance is Mine*, I particularly enjoyed the freedom I had to tell the actors what I wanted from them – a freedom that doesn't exist in documentary film-making. The film went on to be a critical and commercial success, and it enabled me to get the ownership of my house back from the bank.

TN: Shichiro Fukazawa's story *The Ballad of Narayama* was first filmed by Keisuke Kinoshita in 1958. He used stage conventions and colour schemes from the kabuki theatre. Why did you decide to remake the story in a more realistic way?

SI: I saw Kinoshita's version when I was still working an an assistant director and I was impressed by the way he used stylized sets and traditional music. But I always had the feeling that this story could be told in another way. In my version, I wanted to focus on the day-to-day lives of these mountain villagers, and particularly on the hard, physical work they have to do, and on their sex lives.

TN: Is it true that you originally planned to open the film with a present-day sequence?

SI: While I was working on the script, I had the idea of starting with a scene in modern Japan. There's an upper middle-class family with an elderly grandmother, who is to be taken to an old people's home up a mountain. We see the father driving her in his Mercedes Benz and arriving at this expensive, high-tech institution. The other family members say goodbye to Grandma, promising to visit her again soon, and she waves them goodbye. As the car drives away, another old woman, a long-term resident, asks Grandma if the family said they'd be back to see her soon. 'Of course,' says Grandma. The old woman laughs and says: 'No, they never come back.' And then the title *The Ballad of Narayama* comes up.

TN: Why did you drop the idea?

SI: I was very attached to that idea, but I was afraid that peole would see the film as some kind of polemic if I used it. Of course, I did want to imply that this kind of abandonment of the elderly is a fact of life in present-day Japan, but I wanted the film to have other dimensions too. On balance, I think I was right to drop it.

TN: Was there a connection between the success of *Narayama* and the relaunch of your film school as The Japan Academy of Visual Arts?

SI: Yes, the income from the film's distribution enabled us to move from the old premises in Yokohama to the custom-built premises in Shin-Yurigaoka, which opened in 1986. We began offering a three-year course, which gave us a better status in the eyes of the government. I founded the school in the first place because my father always taught me that I should do something for young people when I reached the age of fifty. Because the old studio system of entrance examinations and apprenticeships broke down in the 1970s, it was important to give young people an alternative way to learn the skills necessary to become film-makers.

TN: Would your own career have been different if you had been to a film school rather than trained in a film company's studio?

SI: The old studio training system had both good and bad sides. The Shochiku studios in particular were very conservative and had a very rigid pecking order. Once you were assigned to one director's crew, it was impossible to move to another's. The system there actively discouraged innovation and initiative. But I learned a huge amount, both consciously and unconsciously, by working under Ozu for three years. If I'd started as an independent film-maker or gone to a film school, very probably my approach to cinema would have been different. At that time, though, the film studio route was the only option open to me.

TN: Is there any difference in approach when you work from your own original screenplay rather than adapting a literary source?

SI: It usually takes me around ten years to get from an original idea to a finished film. And it takes between twelve and eighteen months to write a script, whether it's an original or an adaptation. Before writing any script, I spend a lot of time doing research, and that process modifies the original idea, especially if it's from someone else's work. And so it actually makes little difference whether I start from my own idea or from a novel or story. One exception to that general rule is *Black Rain*, which I based on two books by Masuji Ibuse: *Kuroi Ame* and *Yohai Taicho*. I've always admired Ibuse's writing, and I liked those books so much that I changed very little when writing the script.

TN: Does that explain why *Black Rain* seems different from your other films?

SI: Everyone tells me that *Black Rain* is so calm and restrained compared with my previous films, but I think I'm just making films that are suitable for a man of my age.

TN: What's the project you're working on now?

SI: It's called *Doctor Akagi* [*Kanzo Sensei*]. Towards the end of the Pacific War, there's an old doctor nicknamed Kanzo Sensei who diagnoses everyone suffering from hepatitis. The Japanese army accuses him of squandering precious

resources when he prescribes glucose injections for all his patients, believing all of them to be malnourished. It tells the story of his exploits in those chaotic months when Japan was losing the war. I've been working on the script with my son Daisuke Imamura [who writes and directs films himself under the name Daisuke Tengan], and I hope to start shooting soon. But I haven't yet raised all the money I'll need.

TN: Isn't it easier to raise money now that your films have an international audience?
SI: No, the strength of the Japanese yen makes it particularly hard to attract foreign investors.

TN: What advice do you give to young film-makers like me and your own son?
SI: The same advice I always give to my students at the school: stick with human beings. Be curious about them and interested in what they can reveal to you. All people are complex and strange and hard to fathom. But until you really examine them closely, it's impossible to find out what really makes them tick. For instance, you may think you know your parents well from having lived with them for most of your life. But try changing your angle of perception: try seeing them as a struggling middle-aged couple. When you watch them carefully, you start to see how complicated they are. That's your starting point. And once you begin to see people's hidden depths, you can probably begin to sense how interesting all of us are.

Translated by Toichi Nakata
Edited by Tony Rayns

Scene by Scene

(in association with the
Drambuie Edinburgh Film Festival)

Introduction

The Edinburgh Film Festival was born in 1947. It was predated by a similar event in Venice, but that had been hijacked by Mussolini. The relaxed Provencal town of Cannes had hosted its first festival proper the year before, and the world was just getting used to the idea of festivals of movies.

The world was getting used to other ideas too. The United Nations came into existence in 1947 and that was also the year of the birth of the Committee of Un-American Activities. These two institutions, one dreaming of a bright future, the other plagued by dark prejudices, prefigured the post-war period with prescient ambiguity. 1947 was the UK release year of such optimistic films as Danny Kaye's *The Secret Life of Walter Mitty*, MGM's *Ziegfeld Follies* and René Clair's *Le Silence est D'Or*: it was also the year of the more troubled visions of *Gilda*, *Out of the Past* and *Odd Man Out*.

Edinburgh's first few years were documentary festivals. John Grierson's Caledonian seriousness hovered over the selections. The festival purposefully turned its face away from the bikini Mediterranean beach festivals and film-makers flocked. John Huston and Vittorio de Sica were Honorary Presidents in 1954 and 1955 respectively; in the sixties Marlene Dietrich, Fred Zinneman, Carol Reed and Sam Fuller visited and were given retrospectives and awards; the seventies explored American cinema with influential books and retros of Corman, Sirk, Tashlin, Raoul Walsh, Jacques Tourneur, Scorsese and Max Ophuls, as well as conferences on Brecht, psychoanalysis, feminism and the avant garde; the eighties looked eastward with major events on Japan and perestroika cinema.

In the nineties, the Scottish liqueur Drambuie helped bail the festival out of financial problems and in 1995 the remaned Drambuie Edinburgh Film Festival was able to renew its artistic direction. It presented a retrospective, *Stanley Donen: Paradise Lost* and argued in a series of essays that the unifying theme in his work is the loss of the kind of innocence typified in the title song in *Singin' in the Rain* (the Donen interview in this edition was given especially for Edinburgh's retrospective). The festival launched new thematic sections, and for the first time showed films in every cinema in the city. The festival's films also played in the underground War Cinema Apollo at the invitation of the Obala Art Centre in Sarajevo.

Another new event at the festival was Scene by Scene, of which the following are some edited transcripts (the Scene by Scenes on acting appear in the next *Projections*). In an attempt to move beyond the shallow question-and-answer format of many masterclass sessions with film-makers, Edinburgh committed its peak evening times in its main theatres (Filmhouse 1, MGM, etc.) to live events in which film-makers would describe their methodology, assisted by an on-stage edit controller hooked up to a high-powered video projector. The edit controller would fast-forward through the film, at certain points slowing down and playing through a scene or freezing sound and image to illustrate the point the film-maker was making. House lights were on faders and mike and screen sound were mixed to keep the speaking audible throughout. The audience was a mix of film-makers and the general public; the average house was 280.

Scene by Scene worked best when the discussion related most minutely to the sound and pictures the audience were experiencing. For example, the Coen brothers were able to show exactly how the Capraesque opening sequence of *The Hudsucker Proxy* was constructed out of layers of model and real-size live action and computerized moves and effects shots. Other film-makers, such as Suso Cecchi D'Amico, who wrote some of Visconti's most rounded work, took a more directly discursive approach. These, paradoxically, work better on the page.

Scene by Scene brought to audiences the intriguing situation of having a film-maker in the same visual field as their film, for two hours or more. The format went some way towards eliminating the potential vagueness in such meet-the-film-maker sessions. It combined some elements of education and drama (the latter is lost in transcription) and most of the film-makers commented that they found the closeness to their work stimulating.

The events in Edinburgh were managed by great technical teams in the festival and the cinemas. Channel Four and Scottish Television provided tapes and telecine. BBC 2 Acquisitions (Steve Jenkins, Nick Jones, Alan Howden and Michael Jackson) helped with funds and films, STV sponsored Scene by Scene Training and Faber and Faber sponsored the Robert Towne event. Festival staff excelled themselves.

1996 is Edinburgh's 50th festival. Exciting Scene by Scenes are already booked.

Mark Cousins
Director, Drambuie Edinburgh Film Festival

8 Robert Towne

On Writing

Subject: Screenwriting *Chinatown*
Interviewer: Mark Cousins

Robert Towne: As we go through *Chinatown* I'm hoping that I myself can find out something because I think that ideally every effort either to write a movie or deal with a movie is in some sense an act of discovery. Even when you think you know where you are going when you start a script, if you are lucky or if you have done your job well, then you will be surprised, if not by where you end up then by many things along the way. Did you ever read those comic books where they have about fifty numbers and you connect the numbers and it creates a face? That's all you really have to do. One of the problems with trying to analyse something is that you want to be sure that people don't feel that this was all foretold. Movies and scripts are a little bit like wars in that you can prepare for them, and then all you can do is just hold on to survive; it's only after the fact that somebody can describe what happened. Being a participant in the battle, you really don't often know exactly what happened. I think it was Wellington who said a war was like a ball, that you didn't dance every dance and you couldn't possibly be in all parts of the ballroom at once, so your view was necessarily limited. That's the way it was with *Chinatown,* both in the writing and in the production.

This afternoon, something oddly appropriate happened. I was having my photograph taken outside the Sheraton Hotel, and there was a lone piper playing by the fountain. This is not because I'm in Edinburgh, but I have always been dramatically affected by the sound of the bagpipes. I think it's one of the most compelling sounds in the world. I think it's because it is hard to analyse something like that, but you sure know why people would go into battle behind it. It is both very rousing and very sad. I mention this because when I was working on *Chinatown* at a point of unusual difficulty for me I was, for a variety of reasons, exiled from the mainland of California. I went to Catalina Island, which is a little island off the coast of Los Angeles, existing very much even today as the mainland did fifty or sixty years ago at the time of *China-town*, with its climate and landscape. Catalina is shaped sort of like an eight and I was working at the isthmus, which is a little eighth of a mile of land that separates the windward side of the island from the leeward side. I had a cottage that was overlooking this place and it was there that I was writing. One afternoon I was struggling with a scene and I heard the sound of a bagpipe, a lone bagpiper right in the centre of the isthmus. I walked outside and looked down and about a hundred feet below there was a lone bagpiper playing. I don't know how or why he ended up on Catalina Island, but he would play about three times a week and you could hear that pipe for probably five miles out to sea. So, a lot of this film was written hearing that piper and when I heard that piper today, it brought me back to the time that I was working on it.

The genesis of the film came about partly because I was unable to get a movie going called *The Last Detail*. The screenplay was written for Columbia Pictures at a time when we had just been given a kind of freedom in Hollywood to use language we hadn't been able to use: explicit treatment of sex and violence that hadn't been permitted before.

I don't know how many people have seen the film, but it makes very explicit use of language and at that point David Beagleman, who was the then head of Columbia, called me and said, 'Robert, we'd like to make this movie but let me ask you something candidly. Wouldn't it be better if you used twenty "mother-fuckers" in this film rather than forty? Wouldn't it be more dramatic?' and I said, 'Yes David, it would be more dramatic, but it's kind of the point that the use of this language is because these fellows can't do anything else but swear. They are essentially impotent, under the thumb of an authority that will make them whine and wail and swear, but do nothing other than their job and so it would be immoral in that sense: to cut the language because it would suggest that they were actually going to do something,' – and that killed the film for a while.

At that time there had been a variety of things going on in Los Angeles. The kind of destruction and despoilation of the city that had continued unabated since *Chinatown*, and that, combined with a photo-essay in a local magazine, made me realize that there was still enough left of the city actually, judiciously to photograph and suggest the past which I had missed. At that time, fortuitously, I happened upon a book called *Southern California Country: An Island on the Land* by a man who is now dead called Kerry McWilliams. He wrote what I think still is the single finest book on Southern California ever written and maybe ever will be written. It's just extraordinary and in it there is a chapter called 'Water Water Water' about the destruction of the Owens Valley and how water from the Owens Valley was siphoned off from the valley 225 miles down from Central California – bypassing Los Angeles – to the San Fernando Valley. The San Fernando Valley was arid sheep-farming country which the land speculators bought up quietly, secretly, and then caused panic in the city of Los Angeles by fomenting a drought. They then made millions and millions of dollars as a result and the Owens Valley was destroyed. There are many books on the subject, but it was actually rather new to me. The fallout of this episode was, oddly enough, that water could have been used in both places, but in order to speculate they had to do it quietly which meant that the water had to come down, and not be used in the city on the way down. What's more they had to have the dams at the terminus, not the origin. Terminus dams were then dirt-banked and inadequate to hold the flow of water, and as a result the San Frasceto – or possibly the San Norman – dam broke.

Living in that area were five hundred Mexicans who did not speak English and when the County Sheriffs went out there to warn them to leave, they thought they were just being hassled by a bunch of Gringos and so they stayed and were drowned. There is an echo of this in the expanded version of the script when Mulwray expresses a refusal to build another dam, and Escobar, a Mexican character who is police chief and who had relatives drowned in that dam, has no sympathy or regret for the death of Mulwray. In any case, that fascinated me and I hoped to dramatize the formation of a city on a basis which was deeply destructive both for the city that was destroyed and the city that would gradually grow like a cancer. That was really the beginning of it for me, and I thought I would couch it as a detective movie because I didn't feel that a polemic on water and power would really sell very well. I thought that a mystery just following water – you turn on a water faucet and water comes out – wasn't very mysterious but you could make it into a mystery, and it would be a real crime, although not a crime as in most detective stories where it involves something more ostensibly exotic like a jewel-encrusted bird. Whatever it was, I wanted a real crime, and then I wanted a real detective. While still wanting to use the traditional genre of the detective story, I wanted to inform it with the reality I remembered – if not from the 1930s then the 1940s which was close enough – what detectives were *really* like then. As much as I admire Philip Marlowe and loved Chandler's evocation of the city, successful private detectives were not tarnished knights who refused to take divorce work and dressed shabbily. They were peepers, hired to catch people *in flagrante delicto*, and have photographs taken and do all the correspondence stuff that is made fun of in divorce cases. There were several models for Gittes in the past of whom I knew, so I made my detective a dapper guy who would basically take only divorce work and that – plus having worked with Jack Nicholson for years in acting class watching him work and using what I knew of him – was the beginning of *Chinatown*.

It may seem strange, but one of the basic structural problems that I had to deal with first – although it is embarrassingly obvious after the fact – was what scandal do you deal with first, the water-and-power scandal or the incest? The more serious, the more important one is the water-and-power, but the more dramatic one is the incest. I got it right finally because one led rather nicely into the other and the underlying notion and horror that most people can identify with of a man violating his own child, awful as that is, is not nearly as significant as the larger crime of a man who is willing to violate everyone's child, namely the future, and ruin a place that was probably arguably one of the nicest places to live on earth. So that really was the beginning. At a certain point I had to leave my home, partly because I was broke and it was cheaper to work on Catalina, and there was the piper. So with that, I more or less completed the film, except for the last little bit. A friend of mine who had an apartment loaned it to me – I was moving around and had no real home at that point. This was Curtis Hanson, who has just directed *River Wild* and has done some wonderful other things, and he told me it had been inhabited years ago by John O'Hara when he was doing *Pal Joey* in LA. So I completed it. I have been asked several times today if I thought the film was going to end up being whatever it was. I can only say that after both the writing of it and the production of it, up until the very day that I saw the answer print, I was just hoping that I had a career left. I really thought it was a fucking mess and I was just hoping that I wasn't going to get killed. It started off very ambitiously, but once you get embroiled in the thicket of a melodrama you just think, 'Oh Jesus Christ, I hope this is more fun for people to see than it is to write'. That's pretty much the beginning.

My wife said to me the other day that she thought that the movie was really about Noah Cross, and I think she's right, and we can use that as an organizing principle to see the kind of shadow that Cross casts even in scenes where he isn't seen. Maybe we can go through it and also discuss incidental things that related to Roman with whom I worked on the shooting script after having done two drafts and who was, and is for that matter, my collaborator. As much as we infuriated one another, he was inextricably a part of the process, and probably the best collaborator I ever worked with, as infuriating as the little fart is! But he would say the same about me too . . . it was a funny time.

CLIP: OPENING SCENE OF *CHINATOWN*

A couple of things here. One of the things that Roman Polanski would say, and it's always important, is that you really cannot or should not introduce a character or even a location without repeating it, almost like a refrain in music, because it loses its significance if you just have the character show up and never recur. Sometimes one does it by instinct which I did in this case, and I tried to take it out but Roman said, 'No, no, it's important.' I think movies are most effective in the use of the refrain and I think it's what sets them apart from novels and even the stage. You can take a movie, for example, like *Angels with Dirty Faces*, where James Cagney is a child and says to his pal Pat O'Brien, 'What do you hear, what do you say?' – cocky kid – and then as a young tough on the way up when things are going great for him he says, 'What do you hear, what do you say?' Then when he is about to be executed in the electric chair and Pat O'Brien is there to hear his confession he says, 'What do you hear, what do you say?' and the simple repetition of that line of dialogue in three different places with the same characters brings home the dramatically changed circumstances much more than any extensive diatribe would. You understand automatically the irony inherent in this same kind of buoyant statement under the changed circumstances, and that is also true even in the repetition of a scene.

Chinatown: Gittes and Seabiscuit.

If you go forward a little bit in the film – this is just an odd piece of history – he talks about Los Angeles being a desert and thematically that is terribly important. The other thing that is important is something that never really got there. Gittes is a sort of dapper pimp and he is holding a racing form there with the horse Seabiscuit on it, and if you listen in the morgue scene you will hear Joe Hernandez calling a race with Seabiscuit in it, but it never again made the film. The intent was to suggest that Gittes's affection for this little horse – who was so much smaller than other racehorses and who broke down and came back – was a kind of early warning suggestion that he was not immune to class. It was an attempt to suggest that when he became convinced that Mrs Mulwray was classy, he would begin to feel the same way about her. It didn't work out, but that's one of those things.

If you go forward through the surveillance scene to the point where we see the stills of Mulwray with John Huston – Huston's first entrance. He is a villain and everything that is going on in the movie that Gittes does not know about is related to this man here and the bond issue; everything you've seen – the way the city council is behaving, passing the ordinance – all of this is being controlled by this man here who is the villain. Detective movies have certain things in common with dreams and with Oedipus Rex. As far as dreams are concerned, there is nothing extraneous in a dream. It is all your own story, your creation; you observe yourself going through a dream, even though while you are dreaming you may not know where the story is going. To be really effective in a detective movie, which is most like a dream with puns and visual repetitions, there can be nothing extraneous because unlike life, its reality is that everything fits, everything has a meaning, everything has a pattern – just as in your dreams. As far as Oedipus goes, Oedipus determines to find the killer of the king and he has the killer in front of his eyes – basically himself – from the very beginning, though he doesn't see it. Similarly, most detective movies

Chinatown: **The villain's first appearance.**

that are satisfying, generally speaking, have the villain appearing almost from the beginning, and only the detective doesn't see it. He is blind to what is right in front of his face. Mary Astor as Brigid in *The Maltese Falcon* is, after all, the villain and she's the one who shows up in the beginning in Sam Spade's office. Lauren Bacall's sister is almost the first person you see in *The Big Sleep* and she is the murderer of Shaun Regan and the origin of everything that set him on his adventure. This is also the case here. It is so striking it is unavoidable. Poe's *Purloined Letter* is almost a paradigm of a detective movie. There is a letter in plain sight on the wall for Dupin, but he only finds it at the end. It's almost as if there are rules for a detective movie that can be extrapolated, and that's one of them – whether you come by it through instinct or you come to realize it.

MC: You say that you shouldn't find anything extraneous in a detective movie but is there not a case where a detective, in the process of investigation, might be led up a blind alley and is actually on the wrong lead?

RT: That's true, but you are talking more about an investigation as in *French Connection* where you might go up a blind alley. In a classic detective movie, generally speaking, the hero, like Oedipus, shares to some extent the responsibility for the crime, by either a failure to see it or hubris of some kind that he can solve a problem. In attempting to solve it, he becomes part of the problem, and this is the case in *Chinatown*. I got the notion for the title from a Hungarian vice cop who actually sold me a dog who ended up getting a credit on *Greystoke* and who was for many years the love of my life; I've always felt a little guilty for stiffing him with that credit for *Greystoke*. But I asked the vice cop where he was working and he said Chinatown, and I said, 'How do you like it?' and he said, 'It's terrible. You go down there and you have no real idea of what is going on, so the best thing to do is nothing because you don't know what the hell is happening.' That's sort of emblematic for the whole city, with the manipulation going underneath with Cross and in a larger sense, it stands for the futility of good intentions. With the best will in the world, Gittes tries to make things right and screws it up. As I said, in a classic detective movie I think that – and I don't mean every movie that involves detection is like that – where the detective is the kind of central figure involved in an investigation, he is really investigating his own limits to act in a way that is meaningful and positive.

CLIP: GITTES TELLS CHINAMAN JOKE IN HIS OFFICE

I would probably have been roasted today for the Chinaman joke, but aside from its intrinsic entertainment value and because I like racist jokes, it was emblematic of the time: a kind of naked racism that was rampant in the thirties that was not disguised. It's like the attitude to women, which was 'Sophie, go to the ladies' room, you can't hear this'. Those are attitudes that did exist and I think it's important in doing any period piece really to try not to revisit that time and kind of clean it up and make it as it is now with our allegedly enlightened attitudes. The other side of it was that people were not nearly so much victims; they could call someone a name and they wouldn't sue you for it. They would either punch you out or do something else. So, it sets up the time, and it also sets the crudeness of the man. It's an attempt really to suggest what this pimp in his suit is like when he is involved with a woman of some substance and elegance. A nice piece of casting on Roman's part with that lawyer who is nervous and sweating about being in the room with a guy like Gittes. It was nicely done.

Let's go to the scene with John Hillerman. Gittes goes to Hillerman's office, the Department Head, and investigates the room. You see here who works his way into Mulwray's office – who is not there – and Gittes sees that it says '7 Channels Used'. In other words, when we saw him following Mulwray from the water bed to the ocean to various places – confused a bit by the scene in Echo Park with them rowing around with water everywhere – this is a clue, saying that seven channels were used when emptying water out of the reservoir. He

Chinatown: Gittes and Evelyn Mulwray.

doesn't know what that means now; again this is the first scene in the Water Department and it's nicely reprised later. It's important to say that in a complex story, a secondary character like the one that Hillerman plays increases your understanding so much by the fact that you are dealing with the same character in the same location. It makes it that much easier for you to absorb the information that comes your way.

CLIP: SCENE IN WATER DEPT. YELBURTON ENTERS

He [Nicholson] very carefully takes some of Mulwray's cards when he goes, running into that guy there, Mulvihill, who he knows is a hood working for the Water Department. This scene is interesting for the use of the chammy there. You hear this squeaking on the car and this is the third time he turns to hear this. Roman is wonderful at taking his time. It was written that way, but he actually did it that way, which is unusual. It was a time when you could hear the sound of a chammy. You could hear sounds that you cannot hear now: leaf-blowers and everything else are all going.

Now we get to the pond. The solution to the crime is right here – Mulwray's glasses in the salt-water fountain which he sees a glint of. The potential solution is constantly before his eyes.

Now you are going to see Evelyn Mulwray. It is an interesting scene. She says she will drop the lawsuit and Gittes is confused and says he can't afford to do that because, in effect, it will ruin his reputation. He says he has been made to look like a jackass and somebody was out to make her look bad. It actually occurs to her that he is right, but there is not much to do about it. We go on from here to the reservoir where he very nicely uses the card that he had taken from Yelburton and there he meets his old nemesis.

CLIP: GITTES GOES TO RESERVOIR AFTER THE DISCOVERY OF THE CORPSE. CONFRONTATION BETWEEN PERRY LOPEZ AND JACK NICHOLSON

Anthea Sylbert did a superb job with the costumes. You can almost see on the big screen the difference in fabric between Perry's clothes and Jack's – the hang of the shirt, that kind of starchy look on Perry's shirt and that soft, fuller thing on the soft collar and the colour of Jack's suggests somebody who has done well for himself without it being glaring.

There's a gag about the Chinese spinning in the laundry here, just to remind you that this is a constant and ongoing leitmotif.

CLIP: MULWRAY'S BODY IS DISCOVERED

There is another major change in the plot, where Evelyn Mulwray, confronted with the choice between going further with something she wants to say nothing about, lies and hopes that Gittes will back her up, which he does. That thereby begins the complicity on which their relationship is built. I think it is plausible because she certainly doesn't want to get into the fact that she is dealing with her daughter.

Chinatown: Clothes make the man: Perry Lopez and Jack Nicholson.

MC: Coming back to two things you mentioned in these two scenes: the use of the business cards and also the growing complicity between the two central characters. How much of that was mapped out in detail right at the beginning of the script and how much of it fell as you were doing it?

RT: I remember the complicity happened as I was writing it. Confronted by that inquest or preliminary, I realized that that's probably what would have happened. It just came out of the character's mouth as I was writing it. The card . . . I don't know. When I was doing the scene it didn't develop in the same way as this did which was quite a surprise. I may have thought of it just prior to writing the scene. The guy is routinely looking for any target of opportunity to get something that he can subsequently exploit.

MC: When Jack Nicholson goes to the office that Hollis Mulwray used to work at and he opens the book and finds the '7 Channels Used', he walks away and leaves the book open. Is that supposed to imply that he has in some way had an effect in the killing of Mulwray, because he has actually left this evidence that Mulwray is onto them?

RT: Mulwray is already dead by this point, although Gittes doesn't know it. This is ten in the morning. He goes to the house at eleven and at noon the body is discovered. He goes and she says he is attending lunch, so the man is already dead. We obviously don't know this.

CLIP: NOSE-SLITTING SCENE

I've been asked a number of times about that little piece of violence. It just came out of nowhere, really. I remember thinking about something really horrible, something that would appeal to your imagination, and I thought of all kinds of things like slitting cheeks, or ears, but there is something about the nose that for a detective is irresistible. Just slitting a nostril seemed to be horrible and I guess I was right because other people reacted in the same way. For a movie with such little actual violence in it, it had a huge impact. At the time people said it

Chinatown: **The nose-slitting scene.**

was so violent they couldn't look at it. When you think about movies over the last twenty years it is really nothing by comparison and yet it still has its effectiveness because most of the time when you are seeing the kind of violence displayed now it is so grand that it loses its reality completely. You are lost in wondering about all the special effects associated with it, and the buckets of blood and the body parts that go flying around the screen. That sort of takes you out of it, whereas here it doesn't take you out of it because it is so brief and because you actually think it could happen: just a little nose slit, and you start thinking, 'God, I wouldn't like that happening to me.' It really informs the potential for violence throughout the rest of the movie and it scares you and continues to scare you because it appeals to your imagination and you think, 'God that must really hurt.' Then the other thing one should say is that from this point most directors would try to get rid of this Band Aid that Nicholson wears as soon as possible. Roman, to his everlasting credit said, 'No, it would be a mess, and we are going to keep it on him.' Jack agreed and so he is one of the few leading men who goes through a movie with a Band Aid patch across his face. It actually gives ballast to the reality of the thing and it makes you fear a little bit more for the potential violence that you are afraid is coming. It has, in the parlance of our time, a resonance.

MC: **Was Polanski already on the film when you were doing this little act, because Polanski is obsessed with knives, right from his first shorts through all Polanski's life. He must have loved that part.**

RT: I guess he did, but frankly, no, he was not. It was before. The nostril antedated Roman. It doesn't seem as if it did, but it was certainly made for him. The length of the knife, however, was Roman's choice.

MC: *How about the 'midget' line?*

RT: We put it in during a rewrite, and Roman didn't seem to object. I remember years ago a friend, Jay Siebring, who was a hairdresser and not a very tall man –

one of the people murdered at Sharon Tate's house – was talking to Roman one day and Jay said, 'Hey man, do you think you're too short?' and Roman said, 'No, but if I was any shorter . . .'

CLIP: ENVELOPE SCENE

This scene here is critical because Noah Cross begins to cast his shadow again here; you see that Evelyn Mulwray starts coming unglued over the envelope with the name 'Cross' on it.

CLIP: GITTES DISCOVERS CROSS AND MULWRAY WERE PARTNERS

We go into this second scene with Hillerman which again repeats the location and setting, and that's the scene where Jack accuses Hillerman of complicity. Hillerman, in covering up a conspiracy to dump water in an LA river, owns up to the fact that they've been supposedly irrigating property. There is an extraordinary amount of information conveyed in here: that Mulwray and Cross were partners, and that the entire history of the Water Department is done contrapuntal to the marvellous secretary who is absolutely infuriated with Gittes's fussiness. She enables us to get through what is a mouthful of information, and Roman's willingness to play that out over the photographs allows you to take enjoyment from the scene and at the same time be given what is absolutely vital information. In terms of a writing problem and a directing problem, this scene is pivotal. While it may not seem as dramatic or flash as other scenes, it is one of the more important scenes in the movie in terms of solving a problem.

We go to Gittes's office where Evelyn Mulwray again speaks about her father. She lights two cigarettes and in doing so offers to hire him. By this time Gittes knows who Cross is because he has seen the photograph in the office, and he has seen the photographs that Walsh has taken. He knows that it is Noah Cross and in going to meet him he now knows that he has seen him. This is a critical scene.

CLIP: GITTES MEETS CROSS (HE IS EATING A FISH WITH ITS HEAD ON WHICH GITTES COMMENTS ON)

Cross's entrapment by Gittes with the photographs by Gittes was not something I planned in the beginning of writing the scene, it just evolved and you realized he would know. He had the pictures and so he sort of let Cross go down the garden path. 'When was the last time you saw him?' – a natural question – then, 'You lied to me because it was five days ago!' I didn't know that's how it was going to come out, I was just writing it and that seemed the natural way to do it. One of the problems in writing a melodrama – for me at least – and trying to have the scenes organic is that you know you have to accomplish certain things, but you don't know how you are going to do it. You have to let the scenes run, and you stumble across that place where the story point is made most natural and work it into the fabric of the structure.

Gittes then goes up to the hall of records, not a scene that most detectives end up doing terribly dramatically.

Chinatown: Gittes meets Noah Cross (John Huston and Jack Nicholson).

CLIP: GITTES LOOKING INTO THE HALL OF RECORDS (WITH ALAN WARNICK) USING A RULER TO SCAN DOWN PAGES ACCURATELY

We got to the old folks' home where Roman has that wonderful old man goosing the nurse. Most people miss it. Then Gittes asks the man that he has come to see about the fact that his father needs to be admitted to a home. He says, 'Do you accept people of Jewish persuasion?' Evelyn Mulwray is of course shocked – and he says, 'Well, don't feel bad about it, neither does Dad.' Again, it is one of those times in the history of LA where there were things like 'No Dogs or Jews Allowed' written on country club signs. It was pretty blatant and being about virtually the only Jew growing up in San Pedro I became aware of this at a fairly early age. It is an attempt to let people know what the times were like. That was part of it, part of the prejudices that were accepted without thinking and were useful to use.

There is an echo of that gunshot here and she touches her eye then we get to the bathroom scene. He evades her question about what happened in Chinatown and she says if this kind of thing happens to you in the course of a day, in the afternoon or evening, it's amazing that you are able to get through a day.

CLIP: EVELYN MULWRAY SAYS TO GITTES, 'THAT'S A NASTY CUT' LEADING TO LOVE SCENE.

In this scene we have a deliberate use of something that I had seen in someone's eye to suggest, in a sense, her vulnerability and a tainted family. Of course she is eventually shot through the eye, although that was a complete accident because I didn't write it with her being shot initially.

I always thought the boldness of Roman starting a love scene in light from a bathroom was very good. It was written that way, but he lit it like a bathroom, not like a love scene.

Chinatown: 'That's a nasty cut' (Faye Dunaway and Jack Nicholson).

CLIP: FILM SPINS FORWARD (GITTES KNOCKS OUT EVELYN'S TAIL LIGHT TO MAKE HER CAR MORE IDENTIFIABLE AND EASIER TO FOLLOW)

He knocks out the tail light to follow her in the car and that is again a technique that was used at that time by detectives.

CLIP: FILM SPINS FORWARD

This is the confrontation scene where Evelyn says, 'It's my sister, my daughter . . .' and there are a couple of things to point out here. There is again an identical repetition of a setting and a scene – you saw through water darkly the glasses at the very beginning, and here he picks them up; he could actually have picked them up all along. Now Gittes is convinced that as he was murdered at the house, then she did it.

CLIP: 'SHE'S MY SISTER, MY DAUGHTER . . .' SCENE

I always felt on reflection that in the playing of this scene there was a couple of moments more over-the-top than I would have liked. It's really saved by her reading of 'Or is it too tough for you?' For me, it takes the edge off it. It is a critical line-reading at a critical point, probably the most critical line-reading in the movie. If we go on to where she gets to the glass, this is an absolutely diabolical moment in terms of plotting, because nobody had a fucking idea how to deal with this.

CLIP: AUDIENCE DISCOVERS THAT MULWRAY 'DIDN'T WEAR BIFOCALS . . .'

To establish a smoking gun it's not enough to get the glasses in there, it had very clearly to be John Huston's glasses, so one guy wearing bifocals and one not was something we arrived at in trying to get that scene to work.

CLIP: GITTES DISCOVERS THE TRUTH ABOUT THE DIFFERENT SPECTACLES

And now you know that Gittes knows . . .

CLIP: ACCUSATION SCENE: 'YOU KILLED HOLLIS MULWRAY IN THAT POND.'

That's basically the heart of the story right there. Renoir once said, 'Everyone has their reasons,' which is probably the single smartest thing anybody ever said about anything. You see it every day, that kind of infinite capacity for people to rationalize their behaviour. In the course of my life I have found it particularly true of people who long for power and who want to rationalize; they have a need from time to time to rationalize how they've gone about getting it. It's the same thing here, and to me this is a story that was set before the Second World War with a detective who is used to all kinds of cynical chicken-shit things, but incest, this kind of infinite desire for power, these are things beyond his ken. It would have been beyond the ken of most of us prior to the Second World War and prior to all the monstrosities we were exposed to after it. In that context he is rather naive even though he thinks he is a wise guy. That capacity for evil is something he doesn't have in him and he doesn't have the ability to imagine that kind of grand design in someone else. Generally, people who scheme at that level can't be punished, so society ends up rewarding them, putting their names on streets and buildings as great founders of the city. Basically, Gittes is being had and from that point on he can't control what happens, as indeed he couldn't from the very beginning, and the story unwinds. We go now to Chinatown and her death.

MC: You key in at some point in the film what the horn of the car she is driving sounds like, and right at the end the thing that tells me she has died is the horn. Had you worked all that out beforehand?

RT: Yes. At the time when I did the rewrite for the ending I did do that. She puts her head on the horn in the earlier scene so that you know.

MC: It's a very memorable effect.

RT: I think we are inundated by the use of sound like that all through the film, from the chammy to the horn to the fly buzzing and all of those things. What's that George Lucas effect where they absolutely deafen you before the start of the movie by advertising the sound system? It deafens you and desensitizes you to little things that are significant. Sound in a movie is hugely undervalued in the sense that it is the great common denominator. You watch a movie and you are in all parts of the theatre and nobody will see the picture in quite the same way: you'll get distracted, you'll drop your popcorn, you'll be looking at your girlfriend. Whatever it is, you might not see something but everybody will hear the same thing at the same time. That was the power of radio and it's the power of sound in film. It gives you that extra little distance if properly used, and it's underappreciated really.

CLIP: SHOOTING SCENE AT END OF FILM.

That's the end of the picture.

On Directing

Subject: Directing *Personal Best*
Interviewer: Ginnie Atkinson

***Personal Best*:**
Mariel Hemingway.

Robert Towne: *Personal Best* was actually shot by three directors of photography so there is a little inconsistency in the interiors. The exteriors are pretty much the same. To begin with, I'll talk a little bit about the way the film was shot. I spent a lot of time looking at the way athletic footage had been shot. Years ago, when ABC television really began assuming the dominant role in sports broadcasting, they would do these little segments for the Olympics, up close and personal, and it was Robert Reagar who first used very, very slow motion, extreme slow motion, 1,500 frames a minute, which is what I used in *Personal Best*. He did some swimming sequences that I thought were extraordinary. So I was affected by him, and of course Leni Riefenstahl's *Olympia*. For example, when I was shooting the shot putt sequence – which is sort of a montage going from one athlete to the other – I did the reverse of what she did in that film, which was that I had the highest speed, which is the slowest motion, on the camera at the beginning. I slowed it down even more when the athlete is slow, that contemplative moment where they are gathering their strength. I gradually went from 120 to normal speed at the moment of the explosion. To emulate the movement itself – the preparation, the glide, the spin, the release – it went from 120 to 92, 72, 48 and then to explosion. The shot putt had not been done that way, but it was an attempt actually to underscore the way in which the athlete himself moved. I paid a good deal of attention to trying to convey character, because I think film does this, through movement rather than the traditional thing where character is revealed through action. In film, the character is as often as not in movement. It's so distinctive when you look at the way Henry Fonda or James Cagney or Gary Cooper moved; in older films, the directors would actually shoot the entire body of the actor rather than shoot him like a perfume bottle, which is what a lot of contemporary directors do. For example, commercials tend to isolate parts of the actor within the frame and don't allow him to act with his body. This is a pity because movement within film conveys character as much as anything else.

Ginnie Atkinson: What factors do you use to determine the scenes which deal with personal development as opposed to the scenes which deal with physical development?

RT: By guess and by God. Part of what I am saying is that I saw, literally, the development of character in motion. The main character's girlfriend, Tori, was the embodiment of the title and the way that the actress, Olympic athlete Patrice Donnelly, moved was an embodiment of that. You hear these guys on the BBC talking about Wimbledon players playing well within themselves, and that's the kind of athlete that she was. She had a kind of perfection as far as she could go, which was limited, but she realized everything she had – much in the way that Ken Rosewall, as a tennis player, was a kind of perfect player. He realized about everything he could as against Lew Hoad, who had limitless power to explode. The title character here was somebody who realized everything, as against the black girl, Jody, who is more like Hoad in that she is very explosive; she is a great athlete. Mariel Hemingway, who plays the main character, is meant to be somebody who hasn't quite got her feet underneath her sets but is on the way there. In a way, that moment in the hurdle race at the end where you cut from one to the other of the three athletes going over the hurdles as well as they can was probably the most personally satisfying moment to be had. You see the way that they move – Mariel actually looks as though she can move – two world class athletes, and cut from them to Mariel and sell that point. The way that they move right there, to me was delineation of character. I did not see a distinction between athletic action and character, and so much of the point of it was about the nature of competing and about the nature of how you square that with yourself in terms of someone you really care about, either defeating them, or going ahead and trying to realize yourself the best way you can. These are two fundamentally different approaches to competition. That was the point of the film.

GA: How did you prepare for the first film as a director?

RT: Your whole work career is preparation – as a writer and having been on sets from almost the time I started writing. Specifically, I think that when you write it, you've sort of prepared it. A screenplay is really an attempt, ideally, to describe a movie that has already been shot, only it hasn't been shot. I think that has an awful lot to do with the preparation of it. In the case of *Personal Best,* I determined (because of what I've said) that it was terribly important for me that the actors were convincing athletes and that the athletes were convincing actors. Unless they were really effective, it would be like doing a movie about racehorses using men in sacks. I've always been disturbed by films when I didn't believe the action. A lot of the preparation involved working with Patrice Donnelly. She had

Personal Best:
Prelude to
love-making (Patrice
Donnelly and Mariel
Hemingway).

never acted before, and I had to get her ready to do a role that would be demanding under any circumstances. Every film is different, and so much of this was trying to get athletes to be comfortable actors. Sometimes, in very intimate situations which would be taxing for anybody, it was interesting how those scenes were prepared, and what happened in the course of production to make them feel comfortable. For example, I had a very good sound man who got little hearing aids for Patrice and Mariel so that in that long arm-wrestling scene that leads to the love-making, I was able to talk to them all during the sequence. It was multipurpose because on the one hand you could say, 'Hey, you're getting near the frame line, just watch it,' but I also felt, and this is applicable to more than just amateurs, that if you tell good actors, who are naturally rebellious, to concentrate, then the opposite thing is going to happen. The tendency is for them to say, 'I'll be the judge of that, go fuck yourself!' Whatever it is, they are going to be rebellious and so, because of the sensitive nature of this, I kind of teased them by talking to them and interrupting them while they were acting. So, their tendency was to say, 'Shut up and let me act!' and that distracted them from being self-conscious because they had this idiot who was talking in their ears. That also helped the sense of being stoned in the scene because there was this distraction of a voice in their ear telling a silly joke or something that would keep them from worrying about anything and make them spontaneous. I think it was actually very effective and that sequence was done very quickly.

GA: What inspired you to write it in the first place?

RT: At that time I was doing a lot of swimming at UCLA and I was working out a little bit in the weights room before I would go over to the pool. I had an incident not dissimilar to the one that happens to Kenny Moore in the movie. It's really kind of appalling to see a girl who is 50 lbs lighter than you are lifting 50 lbs more than you – it's kind of amazing and fascinating, that combination of power and grace. Track was then, and in some ways still is, an amateur sport and these athletes were the most beleaguered and the most disadvantaged, yet

the most passionately drawn to what they were doing because they were really doing it in spite of all kinds of terrible conditions. I've always been fascinated by people who love what they do. I don't think I've ever been able to do a movie in which somebody's profession wasn't critical to it. I've thought about everything I've done in almost every movie, whether it's *Chinatown*, or *Shampoo* or *Personal Best* or *Tequila Sunrise*. What people do, their profession, seems to me critical and central to what interests me.

GA: Was the Moscow boycott in your own script or did you have to revise the script?
RT: The Moscow boycott came just right in the middle of it, but that happened all the time. It's like when we were shooting in Eugene, Oregon; there was not supposed to be bad weather, and there I was shooting the Olympic trials and the weather went from rain to sun, so I was constantly getting them to change the board.

GA: Does that devalue the last scene in any way, the fact that they are competing for something in which they can't participate?

RT: I don't know. I worried about that, but as I reflected on it it struck me as very much the plight of the athletes themselves. I don't think so. That was the Games for them; it was a bad, bad year for athletes generally and it was a terrible mistake to boycott the Games.

GA: How difficult was it, having nobody to collaborate with as writer, director or producer?

RT: I actually felt that I had everybody to collaborate with. The athletes were wonderful collaborators. You put an individual in a situation that they are used to every day of their lives and they just sort of fall into it naturally, and if you do something that violates their sense of what would happen, they let you know in a hurry. I felt that I had collaborators virtually everywhere I turned and at a certain point there was always somebody who stepped in and helped with critical decisions. My editor did this in terms of camera, and would say at certain points that the camera needed changing. My sound man did the same thing, and when people are willing to do that – and this is not always the case on a movie – you pay attention to them. I felt that I had wonderful collaborators. It's theoretically possible to have a really great producer to help, but all you are talking about is another creative sounding board and they are likely to be anywhere and, given the current state of American movies, you are not necessarily going to find that from a producer. There are very few producers like that now, and have been very few for some time. Most producers, the good ones, are 'packagers' who put things together.

GA: When you wrote *Personal Best* was the idea of directing it yourself always in your mind?

RT: I had written a script which was the basis of a movie that caused me to want to do *Personal Best* first, and that movie was *Greystoke*. As I wrote it, at least seventy minutes or so would have been silent with apes and a child. The problems of trying to delineate character through movement without much dialogue interested me. But I never got that far because of all kinds of things that happened. Somebody else ended up doing it and I ended up using a pseudonym on *Greystoke*, which I've never seen. What really interested me the most, which I gather they never did with the film, was dealing with the idea of storytelling with no dialogue. I was actually going to work with apes, and did for a time, but I never got to do it.

GA: Did you want to direct yourself because as a writer you felt that you were losing control at a certain stage?

RT: I don't think anybody has control in a movie. The one thing that you know when you are finally in that position – I had final cut and I was the writer and, out of necessity, became the producer and director – is that moment when you theoretically have control is the moment when you realize that you have *no* control. Anything can happen. Control is a loose term. Intention, now that's a different matter. What always surprises you is that no matter how carefully you write something, if you are not in constant communication with the director, the number of ways in which every single moment and every single shot can be misinterpreted is just amazing. In writing *Greystoke* and realizing that I would hand over a script to somebody, eighty, ninety or a hundred pages of which had no dialogue but were screen directions, it would be kind of grim to say, 'Hey, you really screwed this up, man.' At that point you pretty much realize that you have to do it yourself because the amount of time you would take explaining to someone what you had in mind means it's just easier to do it yourself. What you realize then is that there is no turning back. Sometimes you don't necessarily want control, sometimes you want a strong collaborator. Thank God for Roman on *Chinatown*! In spite of all our fighting, *Chinatown* would have been a disaster without him. I think finally you do have to recognize that if you are going to do anything remotely personal, you pretty much have to do it yourself, particularly with the way films are now.

GA: I would like to know what you do when you are asked to do drafts for directors and producers in Hollywood. What do they ask for once they've taken the job out of another writer's hands and passed it over to you to do a draft?

RT: This is an area where it's almost impossible to say what anybody asks for at any given moment. I think that generally speaking, the course of rewriting on a script is all downhill. They go to fix it, and the more they fix it, the more they mess it up. For example, I think it's very hard to learn much of anything from unsuccessful films that you've worked on. The only occasion where you can get a notion of the way things work is when the film works and you are able to look back and get some idea of how it all came together. Francis Coppola on *The Godfather* had no scene between Marlon Brando and Al Pacino. There were no scenes in the book and he got to a certain point and he realized that the two central characters never had a scene together. He called me and asked me to come in and read it and the result was that scene in the garden between Al and Marlon, which is probably the longest scene in the movie, where you see the transfer of power from one to the other. That was a case which was successful because Francis had done wonderful work, he knew what he wanted, but he didn't really know at that point, for a variety of reasons, how to do it. He was exhausted, he wasn't sure what to do, he was about to lose Marlon, and so in the course of a couple of meetings between Marlon and Francis, that worked. There really is no one thing that people ask for in a rewrite. Generally speaking I'm asked, 'What do you think?' and 'How do you think it should be?' I did a little work on *Mission Impossible* which had to be rewritten for Tom Cruise and that was the approach, 'Well, what do you think?' and it goes from there. It's so variable. In rewriting *The Firm* for Sydney Pollack, again there were problems about how to deal with this book. People had gone through a number of drafts on it and I had never really read them and the last third of that book just goes on and on and on. The fascinating thing is that situations rarely duplicate themselves, so there is no one thing that anybody asks you. I suppose that's what makes it so interesting, the problems are never quite the same.

GA: On average, how long does it take to write a screenplay for a film such as *Tequila Sunrise*, *Chinatown* or *Personal Best*?

RT: *Personal Best* didn't take long, about a month. *Chinatown* took about ten months. John Le Carré's film, *The Night Manager*, took about nine or ten months. Movies that involve heavy plotting and melodrama take a lot of time to do properly because you want to have scenes that appear natural within a very unnatural framework. That takes extra effort. I turned in a draft of about one hundred and fifty pages which is long for a first draft but, if you know the work, it's not that long. You cannot pre-censor your work without the scenes losing their flow, and yet you have to fulfil certain very specific requirements in a spy novel where there are wheels within wheels and subplots etc. In order to make scenes natural, you have to write an awful lot of them and see what works, what sequences will naturally tell the story, and to do that you must just keep writing.

GA: You said that when you wrote *Personal Best* you used personal experiences. Did many of the characters that you wrote into the script come out of people you knew personally?

RT: Yes. They were combinations of characters, but most definitely they did. In casting certain people, the minor characters, the athletes themselves became the characters. But the coach and the girls were all based on certain characters or combinations of them.

GA: Did you put a microphone in some women's locker rooms and listen in to get some of these jokes?

RT: It was an intimate production in that sense. For example, in the steam room sequences, we built an actual steam room for the actors, rather than poison them with smoke, and just got them to talk. We were talking earlier about collaborators, and a lot of those jokes belonged to Martha Watson, the black girl, who just told them. She told two or three of the jokes and even the jokes told by other people were probably her jokes.

GA: Rumour has it that you've written a brilliant screenplay for John Fante's *Ask the Dust*. Is that ever going to get made?

RT: I don't know. I think it is a good screenplay. It's indicative of what's happening in Hollywood today. It's the first screenplay that I've written that I haven't been able to get made straight away. If you haven't read *Ask the Dust*, John Fante was an irascible little man, about four foot eleven and a half in high heels, and a wonderful writer. One of his novels, *Full of Life*, was done as a film. He did several novels, but didn't have any particular successes and I read *Ask the Dust* when I was doing research for *Chinatown* because it was a novel written in the 1930s set in the 1930s. It's the story of a young Italian kid who comes to Los Angeles determined to make his name and his fortune as a writer and marry a beautiful blonde girl. It was during the Depression where everybody had this passion to be assimilated, to be American, and your background was a source of deep embarrassment if you were any kind of minority. He falls in love, not with a blonde girl, but with a Mexican waitress who is in love with a blond, tubercular bartender. It is actually very funny, very touching, a sort of 'blue collar' *Wuthering Heights* on

Bunker Hill. Bunker Hill was a place of mansions which became boarding houses and which were then torn down as part of an urban redevelopment programme about twenty years ago. You'll see some of them in these old *noir* movies, *Kiss of Death* and Alan Ladd's first movie, *This Gun for Hire*. This guy is in love with her and naturally calls her a 'spick' and she calls him a 'wop'. He's really crazy about her and it's his version of dipping her pigtail in an inkwell. Every studio executive has said that it's terribly racist and it's become a kind of a victim of political correctness which is a shame because it is oddly relevant. In the end, it has the opposite effect and he's deeply ashamed of everything he's done, and everything he's felt and everything he's been made to feel. It's also a shame because in a country that increasingly sees itself as a nation of victims, whatever you say about those two people in that book, they really wailed away at each other like one long Apache dance – that routine that Frenchmen used to do with the girl in the beret and the tights, where they would throw her around the room; they stood up for themselves, and if somebody called you a name you didn't collapse. They were admirable people in that way. In any case, I think it will get made. I reflected on it afterwards and found that most of the movies that I had written would not have been made had there not been movie stars wanting to do them. *Chinatown* would probably not have been made, almost definitely; *The Last Detail* almost didn't get made for the same reason; *Shampoo* had a hard time getting made because people said that nobody would want to see a movie about a hairdresser. Part of the problem with *Ask the Dust* is that the hero is so young and you can't find the right movie star. Johnny Depp wanted to do it, but he still wasn't big enough for them to commit that kind of money for a period piece, which is a shame. I don't even know if *Personal Best* could be made today as far as that goes.

GA: How difficult was it to raise the money for *Personal Best*?

RT: It was not difficult at all. They were quite willing to make it. That was during those days at Warner Brothers when John Calley ran it and people were quite willing to try movies of all different kinds; *Taxi Driver* was being made, and they were quite used to it. That isn't the case now.

GA: Is that because of the 'packaging system' you were talking about?

RT: The 'packaging system': the fellow who is probably responsible for the way movies have been put together, Mike Ovitz, has now gone to run a studio. I think in the course of doing that what happened was that in putting the so-called elements of a movie together, as an agent and an agency he was emphasizing the director and the star. Rather than saying, 'This is an interesting piece of material, I would love to see this as a movie,' it was, 'Well, I think Barry can do this, and I think Tom can do this, we'll get someone to rewrite it . . .' He would get them together, then he would get people rewriting it and that's how the movie would come about, rather than coming from an idea. That also has driven up the cost of movies, because in order to get these people to commit, part of what he was doing was escalating their prices. I think he did that very much at the expense of story and of material, and that had a damaging effect, certainly on movies made in America.

GA: What other contrasts do you see between American cinema and British cinema?

RT: The most interesting English-speaking films that I've seen have been Australian or British. I just saw *The Madness of King George* which I thought was a wonderful film. You haven't been as victimized by it as we have because we have more money to spend and that's actually been a bad thing. One of the more interesting American movies of the past few years was *One False Move* by Carl Franklin. It has probably the most extraordinary treatment of violence in a movie; it scares the shit out of you. There is a hair-raising opening sequence where people are killed and it's fascinating because when you don't have recognizable stars in it: you get about half through the movie and you have no idea who the protagonist is. Who the good guy is emerges slowly and that development has a force of revelation as you come to know that this silly cracker is actually the hero, as you come to realize that it's *his* dramatic dilemma. You have no idea up to this point and it reminds you how limiting the use of stars can be because they sometimes give you too much information that could be discovered to much greater dramatic effect if they weren't so recognizable, and you didn't have certain expectations of them which are fulfilled.

GA: Because *One False Move* is a black film with black characters, is that why it wasn't successful in the market-place?

RT: I don't know. I think that a lot of that had to do with the marketing of the film. I don't think they knew what they had. It's just a bold movie and Carl Franklin is a bold director. It's a little dangerous to say that it's a black movie: I could say *Beverly Hills Cop* is a black movie, but of course it's not. What's interesting about the movie is that one of the villains in it is black and gives a fascinating performance, but have you ever heard anything about that actor since then? He was brilliant. American films, certainly through the 1980s, have been about superheroes who can commit any kind of action regardless of consequences. It started with *Superman* and relates to a country that feels that it needs superheroes because everybody feels so ineffective that they can't do it themselves; they have to have Sly Stallone or Arnie or Robocop do it for them.

GA: You seem slightly cynical about the industry. Why do you stay in the game; what's in it for you? Is this just a job for you now?

RT: I'm tempted to say, 'Hey look, it was ever thus.' What's 'in it' is the desire and the hope of still doing really good work, which is what I'm trying to do. I think there are signs that it may be changing. I like good movies and I still want to see if I can be involved in making them. It's been a difficult period, but what makes me keep going is a desire to make good movies. My ambition is to do a few things decently.

GA: Do you have a list of ideas, of projects you still want to make?

RT: Yes. I'm about to do a film right now which I hope to write and direct about another track athlete, called Steve Prufontaine. There are a number of things I want to do. I've finished a screenplay of *The Night Manager*, for Sydney Pollack.

I'm certainly not sorry I did that and I have every hope that it will turn out to be an interesting movie. I've about given up on the idea of trying to write for anybody else anymore. I think that it's a dead end for me. The state of things is such right now that for me it's impossible to be satisfied working for someone else. I want to direct from now on. I was unable to direct for a number of years for personal reasons so I had to write, but that's no longer the case – so I can do both now.

9 Joel and Ethan Coen

Subject: Writing, directing and producing *The Hudsucker Proxy*
Interviewer: Mark Cousins

Mark Cousins: The aim of this session is to get under the skin of *The Hudsucker Proxy.* Joel Coen: We have three or four clips here that we'll roll through and Ethan and I will talk a little bit about how they were shot, and how we made them, and then we'll be happy to answer questions.

CLIP: OPENING MONOLOGUE, CAMERA PANS THROUGH CITY IN THE SNOW, BUILD- INGS, CLOCK THEN DOWN TO TIM ROBBINS. SHOT COMBINES MATT-PAINTING, LIVE ACTION AND MINIATURES.

JC: The intention of that opening was to create a scene where we were moving into a building through a landscape that didn't look real. We wanted it to have a slightly fantastical quality to it. We weren't interested in taking a helicopter out and doing aerial shots and that sort of thing. For that reason, the whole thing was done with miniatures on a stage. The miniatures in this case were actually not so miniature; how big were those buildings?
Ethan Coen: The tallest buildings were getting towards twenty feet, it's actually our biggest set. It was a sound stage about 100 feet by 60 feet and we pretty much filled it with those models. They're 1:24 scale.
JC: The first shots you see in the movie are all of the models clustered together, and then we flooded the floor of the stage to make it look like we were look- ing across water. The camera was on a crane that moved through the minia- tures. The biggest problem was trying to figure out how to do the snow. Since we were doing it in real time, on miniatures, we essentially needed miniature snow: miniature snow that fell at the right speed. We ended up using little mini-fibres – they're tiny, tiny paper fibres that were cross-lit from the sides and after a lot of experimentation we got it to fall at a slow rate that looked like snow. The last shot in this sequence is actually a combination. We got off the miniatures and we shot Tim coming out on to a full-scale set.

CLIP: FILM RUNS IN SILENCE AND COENS DESCRIBE THE SET.

EC: One problem right around here is when you get off the miniature and are

entirely and exclusively inside the live set and get close to Tim. We snowed him live, so we had to get out of this previous snow and seamlessly get to real snow.
JC: This is mini-fibre snow in the foreground, dissolving into real snow over his head.
EC: We sort of papered over the difference with a little computer-generated snow to smooth the seam between the two.
JC: The two snows are different in that they fall at different rates which is what we were worried about. More than you've ever cared to wonder about the problems of shooting miniature snow! We can now go through the falling sequence and take some questions about that.

CLIP: FALLING SEQUENCE

JC: Essentially the falling sequence was done on a long miniature of the building that was lying on the floor of the studio and we would shoot plates of tracking down the length of the building and we composited that on a computer with shots of the actors who were suspended from wires with huge air guns hitting them.
MC: He's not falling, he's just lying on his face.
EC: He's suspended with wires that get removed later.

CLIP: FILM ROLLS FORWARD AND THE COENS DESCRIBE MORE OF THE SET FROM FALLING SEQUENCE

The Hudsucker Proxy: Falling (Charles Durning).

EC: These are obviously real people! There are miniature buildings at the top and bottom, but the cars in the street in the middle there are real.

JC: So that's a real street with miniature buildings going down to meet the sidewalk.

MC: When you watch old optical-type films you can almost see them hovering. How come this is so perfect?

JC: Essentially, it's the difference between optical matting and matting on the computer.

EC: The photo-chemical way of extracting this guy from the blue screen that he's in front of is just cruder than using a computer. We put both images into the computer and composite them there.

MC: How do you imagine this stuff? How does it go from script or conception to execution? What kind of technical background do you have, how did you get so involved in computers and matting?

EC: That's an interesting question because the answer is 'none' in terms of our technical background. We wrote this script largely eight or nine years ago with a friend of ours, Sam Raimi, before most of the technology that we availed ourselves of here existed. We don't really think of how we are going to do it in a technical sense while we're writing it, we were just lucky that we could *not* get the money to do the movie when we wrote it which was the reason we set it aside, because sequences like this would have been a lot cruder if we were doing them eight or nine years ago.

MC: In other words, if someone sees your script and likes it, you have access to the best technicians and they are going to help you realize this.

JC: Yes. One of the most interesting things about making this movie from our point of view was the opportunity to learn about this sort of stuff because we really hadn't done any of it in our previous movies, and probably won't do it again! We worked with a guy named Mike McAllister who was a very experienced visual effects supervisor whose job it was, after we had designed the shots, to help us figure out ways to accomplish them. So it was a learning process for us and the making of this movie was an introduction into a whole new world.

Q: From your first movie, *Blood Simple*, you have always been interested in camera movement – what is the leap from that to this?

JC: Well, it's moving a camera very fast down the outside of a building! It was just a different technical challenge from our point of view. We've always been interested in problem-solving, whether it's visual effects or other kinds of effects in movies. This was just a different kind of problem-solving. A different challenge in this movie than we had had before, a different area.

MC: When you are doing the matts, how much attention do you pay to the lighting and so on, because I noticed with the matt coming into the window that the colouring of the frame around – which was a model – and the real window was extremely good, and the lighting was all perfect. Then when you see the chap falling down, he doesn't quite light so well; it's a little bit more obvious that he has been placed on the background.

JC: You're right. The hardest thing to do is make the elements in any composite marry in terms of the lighting because that's what really makes your eye accept them as being part of the same scene more than anything else. Whether you are aware of it or not, you can have no idea really what is wrong if the composited human element doesn't feel as if it's in the same environment in terms of lighting as the background element. It doesn't look quite right, and it's a very difficult thing to do, especially since these things are generally lit by different crews. For instance, while someone was shooting the miniatures, another crew were hanging actors up on wires and lighting them to the best approximation of what they thought the miniature was going to look like. Sometimes they are done in reverse order, so it is one of the most difficult parts of this kind of work.

Q: How did you get the newspaper to follow Tim Robbins?

JC: The newspaper was on a wire. It was done by the same guy, the same mechanical effects person, Peter Chesney, who did the scene at the beginning of *Miller's Crossing* where a hat floats away.

EC: Another wire just pulled it into Tim, and again there were air movers on the thing to agitate it and give it a natural windy action.

MC: From the beginning of the scene we just saw, the camera seems to move all the time; I don't think I saw a single stationary shot. Was that purposely to enhance the feel that this is 'a tale', or is there another factor that made you feel that the camera had to be moving constantly?

JC: I don't know why we moved the camera so much! We did want it to flow.

EC: There's also supposed to be this feeling at the beginning of the movie that these two characters are going to meet, or almost meet, or just miss each other. Somehow the moving camera makes you feel like they are being drawn towards something. Also, in the most obvious way, if you have a guy falling down a building, you're going to have to move the camera.

Q: I have a question regarding the watch he pulls out and he takes all that time to set, and he sets it for midnight. Every time we see a clock in that movie it is somewhere towards noon or midnight. What was your decision in writing that made you choose that time consistently throughout your film?

JC: We sort of goofed actually, if that's how you read that! He's supposed to be winding his pocket watch, not setting the time, and in fact that is just the time it happens to be, twelve noon.

EC: We worked backwards. It came from the fact that there is this New Year's Eve stroke of midnight thing at the end of the movie and for the sake of symmetry we made the clock twelve noon at the beginning. The jumps and falls in this movie kind of 'book end' the movie and feel very similar: one is at night, one is in the day, but they both happen right around twelve.

JC: Since the story is framed as a flashback, we are saying at the beginning of the movie that there is this horrible thing that is going to happen and we are giving it a very specific and easy-to-remember point to which the story is going to return at the end.

CLIP: PRODUCTION SCENE (HULA HOOPS) AND 'SUCCESS OF PRODUCT' MONTAGE.

JC: There's a lot of stuff in there that was shot by Sam Raimi who was doing second unit for us on the movie and some of the shots of the newsreel were his also, but of course we wrote the movie with Sam. This was an attempt to do an old-style montage that told in shorthand what happened. We wanted to tell a little story basically using an old-style montage.

EC: The hula hoop image. There's nothing more tedious than sitting in an alley and the prop guy is throwing hula hoops over the camera and you are waiting for all of them to fall except the red one which has to go to the mouth of the alley. We spent about half a day there. The red hula hoop that rolls by itself had water inside so it was more stable, and there was also a ramp release contraption to make its movement sort of predictable and sort of repeatable.

JC: There were all sorts of theories that the special effects guys had about how to make the hula hoops behave. At the end of the day it was kind of hit or miss.

EC: Arthur Bridges, the kid, was a real artist. We had a lot of kids come in and audition with the company hula hoop that we provided, but Arthur brought his own! He had a lot of charisma, but I never actually heard him say a word on the set.

MC: We have talked about technical matters and precise film-making matters, but also there is a lot of content to this picture. Even the opening scene seems to show the city as a very romantic place, a very beautiful place, but at the same time it's the sort of place, as the voice-over says, that has a rat race which forces people to commit suicide for whatever reason. Here you have the woman reading Russian literature while America is doing its thing. I'm not suggesting this is a critique of capitalism, but to what extent did you want to take the piss out of America and the idea of city living?

EC: To be specific again for a moment and the Russian literature thing – we come back to the advertising guys trying to think of the name of the hula hoop three times, and we thought, 'Wouldn't it be funny if the first time we see the woman she is reading *War and Peace*?', then when we come back to her she is still at it, she is reading *War and Peace Volume 2*, and the third time we come back she is reading *Anna Karenina*. But you can't really see it, so there goes that joke.

We weren't really thinking of it as a parody or critique of capitalism. That didn't mean much to us.

JC: As a world to set the movie in and to invent or create completely, that was what was interesting to us. Taking this monolithic corporation – you never really find out what it is that they do – and make that a world unto itself. Obviously, there is a certain amount of parody about corporate culture, but it wasn't intended so much as a comment on capitalistic society as it was just an opportunity for us to take something very specific and lampoon it.

MC: To push this point a bit further, it seems to me that one of the pleasures of this film is that the cynic, the real hard-bitten character, Jennifer Jason Leigh, when she bumps into this man from wherever he comes from – and this is a theme in Capra movies – the

The Hudsucker Proxy: Tim Robbins and Jennifer Jason Leigh — playing with elements . . .

pleasure is to see him triumphing over her. In some way you must have really enjoyed that theme of the hard-bitten urbanite being won over by the heart of gold.

JC: Yes, the theme does come from those old Capra movies, the idea of the tough-talking Jean Arthur or Barbara Stanwyck type. To take those elements and play with them ourselves was definitely of interest to us.

MC: I believe Roger Deakins has been your cinematographer for your last few films. I wonder if you could describe your working relationship with him?

JC: We just shot our third film with Roger. We collaborate very closely with our cinematographer, it's not very different from the way we worked with Barry Sonnenfeld who shot our first three movies. What happens especially in a movie like this is after we have written the script and Roger comes on, we usually do our own thumbnail version of the storyboards. We go through and break the scenes down into shots and at that point we bring Roger in and essentially do a

. . . from old movies (Gary Cooper and Jean Arthur in *Mr Deeds Goes to Town*).

second draft of the storyboards where we get Roger's ideas about the scenes after he has heard what we want to do. He puts his two cents in and lots of things change and we do a second draft of the storyboard. Not so much for these scenes, but for the special effects scenes it is absolutely necessary to have them storyboarded because you are dealing with so many elements that have been shot in different little pieces, and they all have to agree with each other.

EC: Logistically, for Roger, this movie was even more of a nightmare for him than it was for us in terms of keeping track of everything. In all of our movies previous to that, and in the one we have shot since [*Fargo*], we have had one unit working. It is us and Roger on the same set from day to day. On this movie we had the first unit working, plus the miniature unit, plus the blue screen unit shooting the actor in front of the blue screen, plus, frequently, Sam Raimi's second unit overlapping, and sometimes all shooting at the same time. In terms of co-ordinating all of that, that fell largely on to Roger's shoulders. He had to make sure all of the disparate pieces would work.

JC: It is like any other collaboration. We've just discovered that we work really well with Roger, that he understands what we are trying to do and we understand what he is trying to do without there being a lot of fuss involved. That's why the collaboration has worked out over the years.

MC: Can you talk about the early stages of writing the script. What did you actually start with and do you bounce your development ideas across each other?

EC: We do just talk ideas back and forth between the two of us or, in the case of this movie, the three of us including Sam. What we don't do is separate stuff up and each do scenes individually. We talk stuff through and do it pretty much from beginning to end in script order without an outline. We start at the beginning; in this movie it was the idea of the guy on the ledge, starting the movie with this imminent situation and telling the rest of the story in flash-back. Then we just talk it through, scene by scene, trying the dialogue out on each other.

JC: It is frequently the case that we just paint ourselves into corners without really knowing where we are going. We then try to figure a way out of the corner.

EC: It was an especially egregious problem with this movie because you have your main character out on a ledge and it's going to be a cheat to just have him crawl back inside the window, so he has got to fall forty-four storeys. On the other hand, you can't kill him, so that kind of defines how we paint ourselves into a corner. We had to resort to the ridiculous extremity of stopping time in order to save him, but that's what happens when you work that way.

JC: I must say that we did put the script aside for eight years without really wanting to do it before we finally came back to it.

Since we have been talking about Sam Raimi, you saw him in that last scene. There are three guys trying to come up with the name for hula hoops; one of them is Sam, one of them is the Assistant Director of the movie, John Cameron, and the third is a local person. We shot the movie in North Carolina because Dino De Laurentiis built a big sound stage complex there.

MC: I'm interested in the music for the sequence we just saw. I think the music throughout the movie is particularly exquisite and in my imagination I assume the way it works is that you have a storyboard, then you shoot, then you get a rough edit, and then the music begins to get laid down. The music and the final edit have then got to meet up with each other.

JC: It is very interesting in this case because it evolved on this movie in a way that it never had before on any of our other movies. Just as you say, we shot the movie, did a preliminary edit and then we did a temp track. The music editor did a temp track for a preliminary screening and he was the one who first married up the Katachurian themes with the action. We essentially liked the temp track a lot and we asked Carter Burwell, who has done the music for all of our movies, to arrange those musical themes from Katachurian and score it for the particular action in the movie.

EC: You are asking how the picture and the music dovetail. With rare exceptions, very occasionally you make a picture cut to accommodate something you want to do with music, but generally you cut the picture to however you want it. Ultimately, it is the responsibility of the composer, who in this case was acting as more of an arranger, to arrange the music and shape it around the picture. It gets very specific because it needs to hit in specific places and you don't use an existing recording; you have to re-record everything. All of the musicians have a click track so that time values can change in the course of the cue so that the hits will happen in the appropriate places. It's all very precise work by the composer to make the music fit the picture; it doesn't often happen the other way round.

JC: Occasionally it does. We have just finished mixing a movie where we discovered that during the mix, once we saw it with the score, the pacing of certain scenes felt different. When you are looking at something on a silent cam, it feels a lot different in terms of pace than when you are looking at it with a musical track next to it. In that case, we actually went back in a few places and made picture changes, and stretched the scenes a little bit to accommodate the fact that pace-wise they were playing faster than we imagined they would when we were cutting the movie without that track. As Ethan said, that's the exception rather than the rule. Generally, you work the opposite way: you cut it so it feels right and then you give it to the composer.

MC: You are often portrayed as technophiles. What kind of responses do you try to achieve in audiences?

EC: I'll plead guilty to that. We are technophiles to the extent that we have to be, and in the case of this movie we had to be to a very, very large extent, more than usual. But it is all in the service of telling a story. We did not learn about all of this stuff – the compositing and effects work – for the sake of learning about it. Although what is interesting about making movies are the new technological problems that each one poses.

JC: Here's one way of looking at it. When we write a script, technical considerations very rarely enter into the mix. We are just thinking about the story. All the technical questions come afterwards when you start to break it down. That's the interesting part of making movies: once you have written something that you are happy with and that you want to make, your focus changes and it becomes something you have to make real. The actual process of making it real often involves figuring out things that are fairly technical, or learning about things that are fairly technical.

Q: Do you get a kick out of people laughing at your movies?

JC: Sure!

EC: At the point where the movie is done we are certainly not laughing at it anymore. We are well sick of it, so that is the only pleasure remaining.

CLIP: 'I'M GETTING OFF THIS MERRY-GO-ROUND!' FOLLOWED BY GUY HITTING THE FLEXI-GLASS.

EC: His actually hitting the glass was shot in reverse. When you want to do something which you know you want to have play in reverse then you actually turn the camera upside down so that you can take the piece of negative of that action and flip it head to tail so that the image will be right side up and the action will be reversed. So we had him pressed against the glass, rolled the camera, then yanked him away from the glass to play for his hit.

JC: Interestingly enough, the biggest technical problem in shooting that way is that if you start with someone pressed against the glass and then yank them away, they leave a smudge on the glass which is there before they hit it when you play it the right way round. He has to be really powdered down in order to avoid a smudge.

The Hudsucker Proxy: 'I'm getting off this merry-go-round' — wide-shot . . .

The Hudsucker Proxy:
... and close-up.

EC: Hobsie is sitting on a bicycle seat which we are jerking away from the edge.

JC: He is on a sort of catapult that brings him back, but you can't see it because it's behind his back.

EC: In the preceding shot, that is a stuntman who is running towards and will punch through an open window; there is no glass there. Paul Newman promised that he would nail us a Royal Command Performance Screening of the movie and he never did. They showed *Age of Innocence* which his wife was in and I suspect they sold us down the river.

CLIP: SECOND FALLING SCENE, FOLLOWED BY 'COMING ROUND THE MOUNTAIN'

JC: The problems in doing this were essentially the same as the first scene only they were compounded by the element that we were talking about before which was that there was snow on everything. The elements in the scenes where the actors, the background miniatures, and all the snow elements – which in some scenes had to fall down through the frame and in some scenes had to fall up through the frame and in some scenes we are receding away from the camera and in some scenes we are falling towards the camera – all of those different snow elements were shot to combine with the appropriate sequence, depending on what the camera was doing, where it was positioned, and what it was looking at. There was another scene in here which we shot which was cut out of the movie because we felt it was holding things up. It cut with that shot of Paul Newman being very still, and the ball-bearings frozen in time. We had the camera floating to various scenes in the city as if time had stopped all over the city; we did it with mimes. Everything was frozen except for the snow falling. We had scenes where someone had just popped open a champagne bottle and the cork was stopped in mid-air, and all the mimes were stopped and looking up in the air, but the snow was falling down.

EC: Somebody had a bright idea. We had a cop on horseback pointing a nightstick at a drunk, all of them frozen, so we had to find a stuffed horse!

JC: It worked out very nicely, but it just took too long: 'OK, we get the idea that time has stopped, now get on with the story!'

Q: When you are developing these stories and you paint yourself into a corner and

The Hudsucker Proxy: Angel Scene.

you have to find a ridiculous way out of it like stopping time, does it ever bother you that the audience wouldn't buy it?

EC: Yeah. In this case we try to buy it off with a joke. We figure that anything you confront and acknowledge as a ridiculous problem, the audience will then cut you a little slack because at least you are not ignoring them. It gets a laugh, so the moment goes . . . theoretically.

Q: In your films you have little things that get the audience going. In *Miller's Crossing* you have the hat and people don't know why it keeps blowing across the screen. In *Barton Fink* there is the contents of the box, and in this film you have things like the twelve o'clock idea, and the things that chase people like the hula hoop that goes after the boy, and the paper that goes after Norville. Are you doing that to tease us?

JC: People do become fixated with certain elements in scripts or movies that we have made that remain intentionally ambiguous. It is certainly not our intention to wind people up. It's a little bit different in each case. With *Barton Fink*, we felt when writing it that it would be pretty obvious to the audience what was in the box. But we felt it didn't buy us anything to make it explicit – to show or mention it – and take it a step beyond what we'd led people to believe in the movie set-up. There was no percentage to be made in saying, 'Well, the head is in the box.' Leaving it a little bit ambiguous made it more effective.

EC: You were talking about things across movies, the hat, the newspaper etc. We don't think of our movies as being connected in any way. In each case, similar effects served different purposes. The hat set the mood at the beginning of *Miller's Crossing*, the newspaper here pushes the idea that Tim Robbins's character is fated to go to this place and has been pushed to this building, this company: it is just to answer that need. He sets down the coffee cup on the ad and the newspaper sort of finds him; things are a little fated. Similar effects, but to different ends.

MC: There seems to be a large cartoon element in this film and in *Raising Arizona*. Have you been influenced by cartoons and does that relate to storyboards?

JC: There is definitely a cartoon element to this, in particular. The whole Road Runner idea that you can fall off a cliff and not hurt yourself is an element here. To a certain extent that's also true in *Raising Arizona*. I'm not sure if it's an element in anything else that we have done.

Q: I was struck by the almost choreographed movement of the actors and sequences. Was this deliberate? Had you thought of it in conception or was it just something that happened?

JC: It's hard to generalize, but there are certain instances where we have a very strong idea while we are writing something about what we want the blocking to be and how we want the actors to move. In other cases, we really have no idea at all and it comes out of rehearsal with the actors. I think in this movie it was a combination of the two. It was clear what we wanted the jumping sequences (where Tim falls off the building) to be like. The whole idea of Charles is an interesting case. We cast him on the idea that a fat person falling forty floors is a lot funnier than a thin person falling forty floors. Charles actually used to be a dancer, that's how he started, and all that stuff he does at the beginning where he gets up and digs his heel and shakes the tension out of his body was all Charles. A lot of the vamping that he did when he was up on the wires to shoot the blue screen stuff, the wiping the bug off his eyeglasses, was all Charles. It is sort of choreographed, but in that case it was Charles who was choreographing it, so it depends.

MC: When Tim first arrives in the office, isn't there some very stylized movement that he does?

JC: You mean the scene where he comes into the room with the clock throwing the shadow across the floor?

MC: And also when he runs around trying to put out the fire.

JC: That grew more out of rehearsing the scenes with him before we started shooting. We had a clear idea of what the sets were going to be like, and the distance he had to cover, what the action was in terms of the fire, in a rough way. The specifics of how he moved and what he was doing with the water jug came out of rehearsal. Tim is also a great improviser, so if you give him a prop or a situation he goes off on his own.

EC: There is another strange technical thing involving Tim: this end here when he hurtles towards the camera and stops, frozen. We had to shoot that in reverse as well for safety reasons. It was safer to yank him away from the stop position than to drop him towards the camera. So he actually had to do his acting in reverse. We roll film and he started by looking about with a stupid look on his face, then he has to start screaming as he got yanked away.

The Hudsucker Proxy: Putting out the fire (Paul Newman and Tim Robbins).

CLIP: TIM ROBBINS ACTING BACKWARDS. TIM HURTLES TOWARDS CAMERA THEN STOPS, FROZEN

JC: He started the scene with his face composed, and as the camera rolled he gave himself that little whiplash effect to cue the hoisting away. He is being pulled rapidly away from camera against a blue screen.

MC: When you talked about writing the film, you mentioned that the three of you wrote it simultaneously. I was wondering how long it takes you to do that? Does one person go away and have a go at the scene and the other two comment on it, or do you literally go through it line by line, and if so doesn't it take a long time?

EC: Yes, and yes. We do go at it together line by line. It probably took two or three months.

MC: Did you watch some of the old pictures immediately before?

EC: No, but we all knew them. We didn't specifically revisit them.

MC: How did you manage to synchronize a camera moving from real action to miniature?

EC: It has to be scaled down. If you have a 1:6 miniature, the camera move has to be a sixth of the speed. It's that simple really. We did very little motion control which is the rule in doing this sort of thing where a computer strictly governs camera movement and makes it absolutely repeatable and gives it a very defined speed. There is more latitude, since you can do this computer compositing as opposed to the old photo-chemical compositing, for when one image is swinging against the other one. You can frame by frame compensate and make the two images go together by blowing up or reducing it a little.

JC: Your computer allows you to use less motion control than previously.

MC: Are any of the hula hoops digitally generated?

EC: No. But there is one matt painting. There is a big warehouse full of hula hoops, and forklifts are moving bails of them down the centre aisle. The forklifts and operators are shot live against a concrete background and a matt painting supplies the warehouse stacked with hula hoops.

MC: Your films seem almost unique in American cinema in having a strong mystical and spiritual sense informing all of them. They deal with intuition, dream, predestination, higher forces. How much of your own personal experience or belief systems are at play here and are you consciously trying to communicate that?

EC: Well, this isn't autobiographical!

JC: We've just finished a movie which is the first one we've done without a dream sequence!

EC: It is also a movie which we shot in Minnesota which is where we are from, and so the setting is what we are used to in real life as opposed to these very consciously fictitious and artificial worlds.

Q: If you read Frank Capra's autobiography, he talks about a spiritual experience that he had fairly early on in his career which changed his movie-making from that point on, and a film like *It's a Wonderful Life* came from that. Your films seem to have a similar sort of content, like this one, *Raising Arizona*, where there is a strong sense of higher forces, and the same with *Miller's Crossing*, and I just wondered if this is something coming through because it is fun to do or, like Capra, it is something you strongly believe in?

EC: This movie *is* in some sense about higher forces, but that's just the nature of the kind of story we chose to do.

JC: There is another way of looking at it which is closer to the way we approach these sort of things. It's less a question of higher forces as it is a case of, as with *Miller's Crossing* or *Raising Arizona*, the movie attempting to talk about the inner life of a character and give it an expression on film. In *Raising Arizona* we spend a lot of time in Nic Cage's head, the dreams that he has, what he is thinking about, what his fears are, the idea that he is willing this villain who dogs him throughout the movie into being, springing from his own fears. In the case of *Miller's Crossing*, we ask what exactly is happening with the Gabriel Byrne character, what is his inner life about? That's more the way we look at it when we have written the scripts as opposed to thinking consciously about higher forces. It is trying to give expression to that idea. To a certain extent that's true in this movie too.

MC: Was Paul Newman your first choice and did he mind being topless in it?

JC: He was more concerned about showing his legs. In one scene where he is being fitted by the tailor, he is standing there in his boxer shorts and he thought he had knobbly knees. But he was definitely first choice for the part.

EC: Even though we didn't get a royal screening, Paul got us into the White House which was a bit of a come down. It was a horrible screening and we really died there. There were all these economists there . . .

MC: The film is fairly close to two hours and you have already mentioned one scene that you have cut out. Are there any other scenes you omitted for time or plot reasons?

JC: There was a scene in the elevator between Paul and Tim. It was short and interrupted the flow of the movie.

EC: There was one we talked about but never shot. The first time Tim meets Paul he confronts the secretaries in Paul's outer office first, and there's a screaming secretary whom we track into as she is reacting to this blue letter that Tim is holding. At one point we talked about continuing the track into her mouth, past her uvula, plunging down her oesophagus and zipping through her intestines. But you know, we only had so much money.

MC: How do you collaborate as director–producer? How do you divide the work?

JC: The work is not divided at all. We are both on the set the whole time. We really co-direct and co-produce the movies. We are both involved in all of the decisions.

MC: Since *Miller's Crossing* you seem to be preoccupied with older styles of film-making: 1940s and 1950s gangster-style old Hollywood films. Are you ever going to make anything in the present?

JC: We have just done something that is a fact-based crime story which we just finished shooting. It takes place in the mid-1980s, but for all intents and purposes it is a contemporary, reality-based story. One of the nice things about doing period movies is that it lets you create the world yourself. That's one of the attractions. This particular story was interesting to us from a stylistic point of view because it was different from what we had been doing.

MC: In your movies you seem to dip into many different genres; is there any style of movie you wouldn't make?

JC: I don't know if we would do an outer space movie. Or a dog movie!

MC: Because you co-direct and co-produce, do you disagree very often, and if so, how do you settle it?

EC: Because previous to co-producing and co-directing we have co-written the movie, we tend to see the movie on the same terms. There are no fundamental disagreements of what we are dealing with since we created it together.

JC: We share the same fundamental point of view towards the material. We may disagree about detailed stuff, but it's just a case of one person convincing the other that their point of view is truer to the final objective. It gets talked out and decided through discussion. Also, by that point we are also collaborating with a lot of other people.

MC: One last question. Could you possibly explain the end of *Barton Fink*?

JC: Boy that's a tough one!

EC: No!

JC: That's a really funny question!

EC: There's a guy on the beach with a head in a box. What do you say beyond that?

Q: Your films are all very enigmatic, but did you try to leave a deliberate enigma at the end for the audience to think about?

EC: This is the kind of movie that's very resolved in that it is that kind of story. *Barton Fink* was a movie that we wanted to leave a little unresolved.

JC: It's really just trying to find the right terms to put it in. The end was intentionally ambiguous in certain ways. Often when you are trying to come up with an ending – and *Barton Fink* was one of these occasions – what seemed important to us when we were writing it was not a literal tying-up of loose ends in the story or laying out and explaining where everyone stood and what everything meant, as trying to come up with sequences and images that evoke something that feels like an ending to you.

10 Walter Murch

Subject: Designing sound for *Apocalypse Now*
Interviewer: Mark Cousins

Mark Cousins: We will discuss briefly the early stages of Walter Murch's career and he will talk us through the sound design elements of *Apocalypse Now*. Could we start briefly at film school? Who were you at film school with? What was your outlook on life?

Walter Murch: I remember very clearly the bewildered expression on the instructor's face when our class assembled for the first time in 1965. All throughout the 1940s and 1950s and into the early part of the 1960s every class at film school would consist of thirty-two people coming in every year, and they could almost rely on this as a religious principle. Suddenly in 1965 it shot up to eighty and that was actually the first lip of a tidal wave that was about to escalate beyond anyone's conception. I think the admissions to film schools now are on the order of three or four hundred in graduate studies. Why were people coming to film school when there was no guarantee that they could do anything with it? The truth is that none of us knew either. We were being pushed by something and I'm still wondering what it exactly was. It may have had something to do with the fact that we were the first generation of people – I was born in 1943 – who had been raised with television in the home, and so the image was more friendly to us in the sense that it was an intimate companion that we associated with everyday life and therefore, we thought why not go to film school? You go to school for other things, why not film school?

It's also just the simple fact of demographics. We were the baby boom generation and there were not that many people in all the generations prior to us. So, even if the percentages didn't increase, the absolute number had to rise. It's obvious in retrospect that film was and has become an obsession in the second half of the twentieth century, but this was not evident in the mid-1960s. The general mood in Los Angeles, which is where I was going to school, was that everything was winding down, and it was reasonable to expect that there would be no film industry within the next fifteen years and that nobody knew what was going to happen. But it was the interim between the old dinosaurs: Louis B. Mayer was still alive, a number of the heads of other studios were still active and whatever was going to come next?

In that mix of people coming to film school was George Lucas, John Milius, Francis Coppola, Carroll Ballard, Caleb Deschanel, a number of other people and me. The strange thing was none of us had any connection through family or any other history with the film business, which was also unusual because it was a tradition in the film industry that you got your children some kind of job within the industry. It was a self-perpetuating, slightly nepotistic situation. Suddenly, to see all these people coming who had no connection and prospects and in such numbers!

MC: So, Francis Coppola was the first of this group to make a film. He went to Hollywood, he had a bad experience on _Finian's Rainbow_. How did that affect you and what did it make you determined to do?

WM: Francis was across town at UCLA, which was the rival school to USC. There was a kind of hot-cold, warm-cool, soulless-soulful division between the two schools. We would go to all their screenings and throw things at the screen and they would reciprocate. So Francis was part of UCLA, along with Carroll Ballard who was in his class; he was not only a couple of years older than us but, unlike us, he had a very clear vision in the largest possible sense of where he was going. It didn't percolate down into specifics, but he knew that this was it for him.

Francis, whom I didn't know by sight at the time because he was over there at UCLA, was already this kind of mythic figure in 1966 which was when he first began to emerge from film school and started to make an impact on the industry at the age of twenty-five or twenty-six. So Francis was then, and has continued to be for thirty years, a kind of ice-breaker in many ways, somebody who was going into areas that nobody else had even thought of, or if they had thought of it they didn't think they could do it. Francis charges ahead and does it and he pulls with sort of a suction action and some of us follow along behind. He linked up with George Lucas who got a scholarship to be at Warner Bros. and hang out for six months. At that time, Francis was shooting _Finian's Rainbow_. They immediately bonded to each other because they were the only two people there who had beards and a collaboration emerged out of that which continued with some ups and downs for the next twenty-five or thirty years. The experiences that Francis had had within the industry at the time were stifling and his heart was really set on making low-budget films that allowed a certain degree of personal expression. Also, one of his other passions was technological innovation and its impact on film. At absolute levels, things that were technically innovative then seem like child's play now, but you have to adjust the scale of values appropriately to the time. All of this lead to Francis, George and a convoy of six mobile homes travelling across country making a film that was also writing itself in the process, depending on the nature of the locations they found. It was called _The Rain People_ and starred Shirley Knight and James Caan. They wound up shooting the last four weeks of the film in a small town in Nebraska, and they used an old shoe shop that had been abandoned several years earlier as their command headquarters. The realization hit them sometime in the middle of all this that if they could be making a film in Ogalala, Nebraska, out of a shoe shop, 15,500 miles from Los Angeles, then there was no reason that they had to be in Los Angeles. After the filming was over, and with that thought in the back of their minds, they drove back to LA, passing through San Francisco, and encountered another film-maker who was doing similar things, but based in San Francisco, named John Kordy. That really made the situation crystallize and from that moment the decision was made to start a company, lift it out of LA, infuse it with all of the newest technology that a modest budget could buy, and make personal films, each of them budgeted at $777,777.77 – seven being Francis's lucky number.

It was shortly after that decision was made that I got a phone call from George Lucas asking if I wanted to be a part of this experiment. Nobody knew how it was going to turn out; all of these leaps into the unknown are thrilling, but you don't quite know where you are going to land. I said great, I didn't plan on spending the rest of my life in LA, and the conditions in LA at the time, especially for a young person, were depressingly narrow – particularly so for film school graduates who had this mark on their foreheads which said 'Knows Too Much'. So, we all decamped and Aggy, my wife, and I and our six-month-old drove a van with all of Zoetrope's equipment up from Los Angeles to San Francisco. Aggy did most of the driving since I was exhausted after working on the soundtrack and doing the post-production sound for *The Rain People*. The goal that we miraculously managed to achieve was to mix the soundtrack for this film in the as-yet-unfinished basement studio of what was to become Zoetrope Studios, based in a warehouse in San Francisco.

MC: Had there been such a thing as a sound designer before? Who thought up the idea, what did it mean . . . ?

WM: From the very beginning of movie sound in Los Angeles there had been something called Director of Sound or Sound Director. This was generally the one person at the studio who oversaw all of the sound for a film. If you actually look back at the records of who was nominated for Oscars throughout the 1930s, you'll see the same names coming up suspiciously dozens of times. Well, what happened then was the Oscar nomination was given to the studio that did the best sound, and the person who went up to collect it was this Director of Sound. In the very earliest days, he had a creative role but as time went on and the success of Hollywood in the 1930s became more vast than anyone had anticipated, the role became more and more administrative. It was symptomatic of what happened to sound during this period. There was so much work to be done, and it was such an evolving technology that depended on cumbersome pieces of vacuum tube equipment and large microphones and large cables, that specialization was the key. People found themselves stuck in very small niches within the terrain of film sound.

What had happened from the beginning of the 1960s – really the end of the 1950s – was the fresh breeze of the transistor began to blow through the landscape. Under its impact, equipment that had been very big was now very small. Of course, this has continued with the microprocessor – now it's all smaller than I could hold between my fingers – but even that first condensation was enough to raise the prospect that you could actually buy this equipment yourself, because along with the size, the cost had come down. It was portable and you could move it about – you could even use it in Ogalala, Nebraska. With this condensation of equipment came the possibility of one person overseeing the whole situation again.

That's what was also in our baggage when we left Los Angeles: this dream of setting up a situation where the sound of a film was under as unified a control as the picture. Just as there is a Director of Photography who is practically and theoretically responsible for the look of the film's photography, we didn't see any reason why there couldn't again be the same situation as regards sound. The experience of Francis and myself, limited though it was, was of great departmentalization. This had a practical aspect in that it was always easy to point the finger of blame somewhere else, but one of our other goals was to find a way to condense it so that if there was something wrong, there was one person responsible for it – just as if it turned out right, that same person would get the credit. So, there was a real desire not only to be on our own – we were young film students, ex-film students, ready to show the world – but also to somehow latch on to something that seemed to be happening in the world in general, a process which has obviously continued to this day; the shrinking of technology and the lowering of the cost of work.

MC: Let's move on to the first clip.

WM: What I'd like to do is have you think of sound – just because I was comparing it to photography – in terms of light. Think of a spectrum of sounds as you would think of a spectrum in a rainbow. At one end of the rainbow you have red, at the other end you have blue. There is, at least conceptually, a kind of equivalent of that in sound where you have at one end of the spectrum sound that has a high degree of meaning in it. The most obvious example of this is dialogue. When you have dialogue in a film it is being conveyed by sound, but what is being conveyed is a code, and in order to understand what film-makers are talking about you have to understand that language. So the shell which is put in your hands is sound, and you, through your ability to understand language, crack open that shell and consume what is inside which is the meaning of the words. Let's say that that is at the blue end, the ultraviolet end. At the far end, equally opposed to that is infrared – music – which has very little code, very little language, very little specific meaning, but tons of emotion, tons of manner, and an unrivalled ability to communicate mood to the audience.

That gives us two ends to the rainbow, but obviously it's never quite as clear cut as that. There are elements of code that work their way into music, and by the same token, how somebody says something is very strongly influenced by the audience in that they decide about the meaning of what is said, so there is an element of music in any form of speech. But in between is this rather vague area of just pure sound: it's not dialogue any more, but it's not really music. It's what would be conventionally thought of in terms of sound effects, but it can float rather independently from one end to the other. Sometimes sound can become almost pure music; it doesn't declare itself as music which is actually one of its advantages because it can have a musical effect on you without you realizing it, but at the other end it can sometimes deliver very discreet packets of meaning.

What I'm going to talk about this evening is mostly that middle section, and when I say sound, that's what I'm talking about. I may sometimes slip and say sound effects, but for the purposes of what we are talking about tonight, it's not the infrared, it's not the ultraviolet, it's this middle, yellow part which is sound effects. Why do you put them in a film and if you do put them in a film, how many do you put in and what kind and all of those other qualitative and quantitative questions?

I'm going to sidestep the 'why' for a moment and just talk a little bit about the 'how', and make one further observation before I push the button here, which is that sound has a most remarkable ability to superimpose upon itself. In fact, there's an almost endless ability to create a sandwich of sound. You can have a layer of sound that is nothing but traffic background, but then you can add a layer that's nothing but horns of the automobiles, and then you can add a layer that's nothing but seagulls crying in the background, and then you can add a layer of people talking, and then a layer of people's footsteps and on and on and on. You can actually look at any single frame in a film and, realizing that you don't have to restrict yourself to what is in the frame, you can imagine things beyond the corner of the frame. If there is a 'beyond the corner', then there is certainly a 'beyond the beyond', so in fact you can end up with a sound-track which included the sound for the entire world on a single frame of film. It wouldn't be understandable, but at least it would be conceptually something that you would have to grapple with. The problem is that if you did that it would sound like the sound in between radio stations, something called white noise, which is just all spectrums and all amplitudes of all sound simultaneously. The problem with that, like white light, is that there is not a lot of meaning in it, so we have to find a balance point in there where there is enough sound to add to the meaning of the film, but not so much that it overwhelms the equal-ity of the picture.

In the end it's a dance between the amount of content that is presented visu-ally and the amount of content that is presented as far as sound goes. I have here a section from *Apocalypse Now* with seven layers, one after the other. Visually you are seeing the same thing over and over, but what you will hear on the soundtrack is one layer after the other which in the end all come together and, in an almost geological sense, give you the sound landscape of this particular scene. I broke it down this way because this was the way I was working, partly because I was simply overwhelmed with the amount of sound that I was dealing with, but it's not a bad way to work because it's the equivalent of having to paint a mural. The problem that confronts you is that you are overwhelmed by the imbalance in scale of painting something that's sixty feet by forty feet, and looking at your own height which is somewhere between five and six feet. How do you possibly do this without it turning out all crazy with the perspectives all wrong? What you do is break it down into squares and deal with small squares at a time. What I'm going to show you here is kind of the equivalent to that.

The first clip is the odd bits and pieces that had to be fitted in somewhere. I'm going to show this to you in the opposite way to how I mixed it, for dramatic reasons. When in any one scene I decide what is the dominant sound for the scene, I mix just that. In this case it happened to be helicopters. Then I say to myself, 'What could be the next most dominant sound?' It happened to be gunshots, and the next most dominant was the music, and the next were the explosions. So I work my way down from the violins which in an orchestral sense are carrying all the melody and the main harmonic lines, down through the various instrument groupings until at the very end you are hearing just the little triangle. I'll begin with the triangle.

[Each clip is from same section of the film where the US troops arrive in helicopters in the middle of a battle to the sound of gunfire, explosions and a Wagner concerto. Descriptions of clips relate to sound effects, not visuals.]

CLIP 1: WIND, FOOTSTEPS, ODD BACKGROUND NOISE

WM: That was mostly footsteps, some occasional explosions and wind and some other odd bits and pieces that I couldn't find anywhere else to put. This next clip I think is explosions only, which doubled up on some of the other explosions.

Apocalypse Now.

CLIP 2: ODD GUNSHOTS AND EXPLOSIONS

WM: I should have added that in most of *Apocalypse Now* there was no production sound so that nothing of what you are hearing was recorded at the time. It was all done later.

CLIP 3: HEAVY GUNFIRE

MC: Did you go out into a field and shoot guns?
WM: Yes. We had a two- or three-day session where we recorded nothing but all of those sounds. At that time there were no stereo recordings or any of this.

CLIP 4: MUSIC, PLANES AND HELICOPTERS

WM: This next one is just called 'crowd background', which is something that we improvised as a group with some students from one of the state universities in California.

CLIP 5: CROWD NOISE

WM: The dialogue you heard was all added later. The dilemma that confronts me when you have that dense a soundtrack is that when you put all of that together it simply has a danger of collapsing into a ball of white noise. There is a lot of sound and it's very loud, but you can't extract meaning out of it. What I'd like to do is show you the end result of this and then just say a few words about how I got to that. Then we'll show it again. The original soundtrack for this film was mixed in what I guess you would call quintaphonic sound. It had three soundtracks coming from behind the screen and then two in the back. You could also think of it as a quadraphonic set up: sound coming from each corner of the room and then one soundtrack, mostly the dialogue, coming out from centre from behind the screen.

CLIP 6: FINAL VERSION. MUSIC, SHOUTING, GUNSHOTS, HELICOPTERS, EXPLOSIONS, DIALOGUE.

[*Applause from audience*]

WM: One of the first jobs I had was on a film that George Lucas and I made together called *THX 1138*, and because of production limitations the amount of sync-sound we could get was limited. It was also a science fiction film, so frequently the sound that you did get was at odds with the illusion that you wanted to create. One of the illusions we were after was the sound made by some policemen who were ostensibly robots made out of six hundred pounds of steel and chrome, clad in leather, who roamed the street of this underground city. During the filming these were people in costumes who made the normal sound that anyone would make, but I wanted to get the idea that these people were machines, that they weighed six hundred pounds, which meant that I had to concoct all of their steps myself. Also because of production limitations I

THX 1138:
The Policemen

couldn't record this in what's called the 'Footsteps Theatre' in England (in Los Angeles it's called the 'Foley Stage'), where you are looking at the picture and recording something simultaneously. At any rate, I built a machine that gave me the kind of footsteps that I wanted and went to the Museum of Natural History at three o'clock in the morning in San Francisco and recorded it all, one footstep at a time. When I was done doing the recording for that session I suddenly had to confront the obvious fact that now I had to put all these foot-steps in, which meant that, laboriously, item by item, I had to sync up each of these footsteps. Just as I was beginning to go down for the third time a principle came to me. I won't say that I thought of it, it just came to my rescue like a rope thrown from above. What I discovered was that if you had one robot walking, the footsteps for that robot had to be in sync, and you had to do all of the work yourself. This also applied to situations where there were two robots walking side by side. But, if there were three robots, or four or five as there frequently were because most often in the film it was in multiples that these people occurred, I found that you could have anything you wanted. It didn't have to be one or two or three, and it didn't have to be in sync. Something that sounded roughly about the right speed, and roughly sounded about the right number of people, in some mysterious way satisfied one's mind look-ing at the film.

I began to be sensitive towards this strange twilight zone between the numbers two and three – that up until two you had to pay very specific attention to the elements out of which you were constructing something. When you got to three or more, it became almost immaterial how many elements you were composing the thing out of – which, in a practical sense, saved me a lot of work. I became curious about this, and on subsequent films I started to examine this because the more I thought about it, the more it seemed to be a recurrent pattern. As one thinks about these things one's mind gets full and starts to spill over and I began to see this principle applying to other areas of life as well.

The clearest example is the Chinese ideogram for tree and forest which is suitable because the metaphor for this is kind of the problem of seeing the forest for the trees and vice versa. If you want to draw the image for tree in Chinese you draw something that, thankfully, looks quite like a tree – sort of a pine tree with drooping limbs. If you want to convey the idea of a forest, you draw three trees. Now, it was obviously up to the Chinese how many trees they drew, but two trees did not seem to be enough to convey forest, and on the other hand sixteen trees would just create a welter of marks on the page which would not be readily decipherable. You might get away with four trees as being understandably a forest, but if every time you have to draw a forest you have to draw four trees and you can get away with drawing three, why not? So after thousands of years of daily experience writing Chinese, they came up with a solution which was very akin to my dilemma doing the footsteps for this film. That somewhere between two and three is that borderline where you go from individual things to group. In fact, the three footsteps of the robots are in sync, it's just that the question of what is in sync had been kicked up a level and we are now talking about the sound of a group of people in sync with a group of people, and it satisfies the question.

We are no longer talking about the minutiae of each foot being in sync. The mind is simply overwhelmed with feet hitting the floor so it abdicates and says, 'Yes, I see a group of people and what I hear sounds like a group of people walking.' This is akin to what Monet wrote when he was talking about Impressionism which was 'Don't count the grapes.' One of his students was drawing a bunch of grapes and drawing every single grape, and he knocked the brush out of her hand and said, 'Don't do that. What I want you to put on the canvas is what that group of grapes feels like to you. What is the colour and the light hitting the grape? That is the important thing.' Even in real life when you see a bunch of grapes and say how beautiful they are, you don't stop to count the grapes first.

So this is something akin, some other principle going on there and I've since made a notebook, a kind of collection of these things. There is Bach who thought the human mind could not follow three melodic lines simultaneously; he always had somebody drop out right at the crucial moment. He would have three together at some time, if that was the effect he wanted to have, but a sustained three melodic lines in full song happening for a long period of time he felt was outside of what people could sustain in a musical sense. The principle here is that when you have a large number of sounds and you play them all together, they simply collapse – like those footsteps of the robots – into one new thing which is a bunch of noise.

You are no longer able to hear the individual things which comprise this sound, and because we were trying to make the point of music in *Apocalypse*

Now – the music coming out of these helicopters, the sound of the helicopters themselves, the voices of the people, the explosions, the fact that they were leaving the helicopters into a hail of gunfire – we wanted people to experience all these things and we built them as if they were continuous but the paradox was that if we played them all simultaneously, nobody would take anything away from it. It would just be a bunch of noise and they would put their hands over their ears and ask the projectionist to turn the sound down. So, in mixing, you are playing the mixing board the way you would play a piano so that there were only two dominant sounds happening at the same time – helicopters and music, maybe a little bit of voice, but that's it: no footsteps, no gunfire. Now, if you want to make the point of gunfire, you have to get rid of something, get rid of maybe a little bit of that voice and add a bit of gunfire in its place, or get rid of all the music completely. For example, when the boy says, 'I'm not going, I'm not going,' there is no music at all. On a certain logical level that is not reasonable because he is actually in the helicopter that is producing the music, so if anything it should be louder there than anywhere else. The problem is, if you played it at that level, you wouldn't get the benefit of either. You are watching the film and you are involved in the story dramatically. Your impression when the scene is over is that everything has been played at full volume all the time. In fact, that is not true.

MC: Is that what you call the 'Law of Two-and-a-Half'?

WM: It's cumbersome, but that's what I call it.

MC: We are listening here for how other sounds disappear when two main sounds are up.

WM: The music is probably the most consistent while it's on, but even that goes away at some point. It's like watching things come up from the bottom of a lake and you see maybe two or three things, or two-and-a-half things, at any one time, but you are certainly not seeing four or five at the same time.

CLIP 6: FINAL VERSION

WM: I'm going to roll back to the beginning of the film and talk about the opening scene, but are there any questions?

Q: Do you let a random element filter in to how you are mixing a film, or are you really precise on your two that are coming up from the bottom?

WM: I'm probably over-articulating the point for the purpose of making it. It's similar to playing a musical instrument and that's generally the principle. You are going to sacrifice the principle when it still works for some mysterious reason, even if you stopped and counted the grapes and saw that you have three levels going in, it still seems to work.

Q: There is a really beautiful wind-fire sound effect that seemed to get lost in the final version.

WM: Yes that's true. There are some wonderful sounds in the premixes for this film that, when you put it all together, weren't there. But I'm sure if you had anyone up here who has an orchestral background, when they listen to the final performance of their work there are things going on that are simply inaudible, but you try to do what you can do.

Q: How long did it take to mix that section?

WM: Probably a day. The whole film took three months to mix, and then it was premièred at Cannes and we made some changes after that and some of the music was replaced. I was in and out of the mixing studio with the film for probably six months or so.

Q: Do you archive these prints and use them again?

WM: Yes, to some degree. I don't have any of them. I think they are in the basement of American Zoetrope, so if you want them just call up Zoetrope and ask for them.

Q: Whose idea was the Wagner?

WM: That was John Milius's idea. That was present in the story right from the beginning of the script and it's actually not far from the truth of some these situations. You may recall something called Operation Just Cause in Panama where they were trying to flush Noriega out of the Vatican Consulate and they played rock 'n' roll and they thought he would kind of run out of the consulate because he couldn't stand the music any more. This film came out before that happened so, in some weird way, reality might have been influenced by the film. Certainly the film was influenced by things that actually happened like this, not only in Vietnam but in other wars as well. When you boil it right down, just the idea of having bugles and drums which goes way back to the Egyptians, Greeks and maybe beyond is a form of this – that somehow organized sound that is very rhythmic and strident has a terrifying effect upon the opposition.

MC: Did you know you were doing something radically different when you were doing this? Did Francis Coppola expect such a complex soundtrack?

WM: Francis really didn't come to the mix at all. He saw it at Cannes, and he had some notes when we showed it there, and we incorporated those notes and showed it again at a theatre in San Francisco, and he had some more notes. But in terms of film-makers getting highly involved in every single brush stroke of what his collaborators do, Francis tends to join up with people like John Huston who try to partake of the audience's point of view on things rather than the film-maker's.

When I started the film he said he wanted three things. First, he wanted it to be quintaphonic, he wanted the sound to fill the room, to seem to come from all sections of the room which had never been done before in a dramatic film. *Tommy*, which was mixed at EMI in London, had a quintaphonic soundtrack, but it was primarily a musical film which didn't have very many sound effects in it. So, he wanted it to be quintaphonic. Second, he wanted it to be authentic, by which he meant the weaponry had to sound like it really sounded in Vietnam. He had very much in mind the veterans who had been in battle in the war who would be looking at the film. He wanted them to feel that the film was an accurate portrayal of what they went through just simply on the level of the hardware – the helicopters and the boats and the gunfire and all of those things. He wanted it to be real, so we found ways to get AK-47s and real ammunition and we did a three-day recording session in the hills behind San Francisco where we just shot all of these things off and recorded them. The final thing he wanted was the film soundtrack to partake of the psychedelic haze in which the war had been fought, not only in terms of the music for the soundtrack – The Doors and what kids listened to on the radio – but in general, kind of far-out juxtaposition of imagery and sound; for the soundtrack not to be just a literal imitation of what you saw on the screen but at times to depart from it. Those were the three things in my packet when I set out on this adventure and it never got down to any specific observations about any of the work that was done.

In an overall sense we have talked a little bit about the 'how' or the 'how much' aspects. Now we can talk about the 'why'. Why do you add sound to a film, what are you trying to achieve? In the earliest days of film the goal was to show in a theatre an illusion of reality that had escaped the theatre until that time. So you recorded sound effects and you recorded them live at the time of filming, so doors had to sound really like doors when you operated them. At its simplest it worked like an amusement park ride; it gave the audience a thrill because they had never seen anything like this before. You can see this very clearly in some of the early Disney cartoons where sound itself – the idea of syncing up a bell sound with a bell, or a squishy sound when you milk a cow – the nature of it was wonderful. That lasts only so long and people get used to that fairly quickly, and after three or four years you didn't do it quite so obviously. By that time the technology of sound had started to improve and it was now possible to record sound in one location and marry it up to the picture in another, as we did with the gunshots in this film. You didn't have to record the sound at the same time as you shot the picture.

There is a limit to that, not only a technical limit, but also a conceptual limit. Yes, if you add sound to a film it increases the reality of the scene, but film exists in several dimensions simultaneously and the relentless addition of real sound to film has, eventually, the negative side-effect of crushing the very reality that it is trying to observe. In the end the audience looks at the film and says, 'OK, it's great but there is no place for me, I don't know why I'm looking at this.' It begins to raise up the possibility of adding sound that is divergent from what you are looking at. Effectively, there is no reason why what you are looking at should be producing the sound that you are hearing.

This next section is the very beginning of the film. The dilemma of the main character is that he is a soldier without a mission, stuck in an overheated hotel room in Saigon waiting to be told what to do. He has been back to the United States and discovered that he couldn't go back, there was nothing there for him, so he is back in the only place that has any meaning for him – which is Vietnam – and he is frustrated because they won't give him a mission. In terms of both the picture and the sound, we were trying to get into this person's head.

Look at the second section of this piece. You are looking at Saigon, you are in a hotel room, but you begin to hear the sounds of the jungle. One by one the elements of the street turn into jungle sounds: a policeman's whistle turns into a bird, the two-stroke motorcycles going back and forth turn into insects, and item by item each thread of one reality is pulled out of the tapestry and replaced by another one. You are looking at something very improbable which is a man sitting in a hotel room – and you are listening to the soundtrack that you would hear if he were in the jungle – which is the point. Although his body is in Saigon, his mind is somewhere else.

CLIP: OPENING SCENE WITH MARTIN SHEEN IN HOTEL ROOM. SOUNDTRACK SEAMLESSLY MOVES FROM EVERYDAY NOISES IN A TOWN INTO THE SOUNDS OF A JUNGLE

[*Applause from audience*]

Q: Where did your interest in sound come from?

WM: I wish I had an answer . . . my ears stick out a little bit, maybe I hear the world slightly different to other people. When I was six years old I used to go to the newsreels which were still showing in cinemas at that time. My mother would take me on Friday afternoons and they always showed cartoons and there is a freedom of association of imagery and sound in cartoons that could have had a slightly determining aspect on things. Maybe I'll find out someday. Although I'm interested in sound, the other thing that fascinates me is silence. There is a famous quote from Versjon where he said that the soundtrack invented silence. It is true that prior to the invention of a soundtrack, there was never such a thing as a silent film. There was always sound that went along with images, but it was music. Even in some of the largest cinemas they had people doing rudimentary sound effects off-screen for some sequences. The paradox is that in the days of silent films, there was sound from beginning to end, there was never a moment when it got quiet. So the invention of sound on the film where you could have people talk, paradoxically, allowed the invention of no sound – this is to say sequences where for various dramatic reasons you pull the sound away from the image. I'm fascinated with this because it gives the minds of the individual people in the audience an opportunity for their imagination to plunge into the film and they can hear whatever they want to hear. It's not that the sound stops, it just stops coming out of the speakers and begins to be the sound that any one person hears in their head. In any film, I like the opportunity to show a scene with just silence, to get to a point where there is nothing but silence. In this next scene, the Dorlong Bridge scene, there is a point when all of the sound you have been hearing – which is of a chaotic battle going on off-screen – item by item disappears until all you are hearing is the voice of this wounded Vietcong calling out into the jungle. The dramatic reason for this is that a character called Roach has been called upon to kill this straggler who is taunting the soldiers from the barbed wire. Roach is a kind of human bat in that he doesn't need to see anything, he can echo-locate very precisely. At least for this brief period in the film, you are hearing the world the way Roach hears it, which is focusing in with a sublime subjectivity on just what he needs to hear.

CLIP: BATTLE SOUNDS GO DEAD AND ROACH KILLS STRAGGLING VIETCONG BY INSTINCT. IMPRESSION CREATED IS THAT WE ARE HEARING WHAT ROACH HEARS, BLOCKING OUT ALL EXTRANEOUS SOUND TO LEAVE NOTHING BUT THE VIETCONG'S VOICE

[*Applause from audience*]

11 Suso Cecchi D'Amico

Subject: Writing *Rocco and his Brothers*
Interviewer: Mark Shivas (BBC Films)
Also Present: Katerina D'Amico (Suso's daughter, helping with explanations)

CLIP: INTRO SCENE TO *ROCCO AND HIS BROTHERS*

Suso Cecchi D'Amico: I'm here to tell you the story about the writing of this film which I love very much indeed. The idea of talking through it and talking about the writing of the script came to me when I learned that last year *Raging Bull* by Martin Scorsese had been shown and discussed. Martin Scorsese – who is my good friend – had always told me how much he thought of *Rocco* in making *Raging Bull* and I was so surprised because we never thought *Rocco and his Brothers* as a story about boxing. I thought that maybe I should show it and explain what kind of story we wanted to make. Also, some critics wrote about it as a magnificent love story. It wasn't a love story, so I thought I should explain what we really wanted to do and maybe failed to do. We are living on a success which is really a personal 'unsuccess'. It's worth remembering that

Rocco and His Brothers: Alain Delon in the ring.

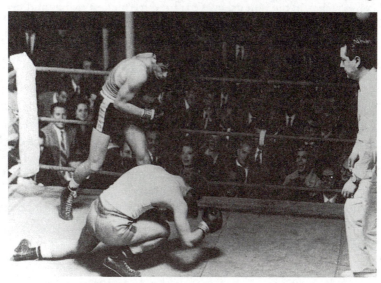

this film was realized in 1958, when we had already had experience of what was called the 'neo-realism' and what I think I prefer to call neo-realism: 'everyday facts'. With neo-realism chronicles we always thought of improvisation, and we didn't even use professional actors, we always prefered to take what we call actors from the streets as in *Bicycle Thieves*. This time, we said we should write a real novel with epic ambition about contemporary problems in Italy that completely changed society: emigration from South to North. Visconti had already told this story with the *La Terra Trema* which was a story about poor fishermen in Sicily. The first idea was to write a novel – not a short story or a chronicle, a novel – and this time it was to be played by professional actors with an execution which should be quite close to the writing: no improvisation.

To deal with this problem of poor people emigrating from the South to the North and what happens to them, Visconti's first idea was a story of five brothers, five like the fingers of one hand, with their mother, a widow. We discussed five, then started to say maybe three, maybe four, maybe two. It ended as five and it was never changed. I insisted because it's part of the story which has a consequence in the film itself. We started to think of stories and began with the mother. Visconti always used mothers in his pictures.

Katrina D'Amico: His idea was of mothers in some way taking advantage of their children and living through their children, using their children to succeed in life.

SCD: She wanted a success of her own. She wanted to obtain it through her sons: that is his idea of a mother. We wanted to have two of the brothers very close to one another and little by little the story started to develop. At this point, I must confess that, as usual, we had stolen a lot of things from books. We stole from Dostoevsky, for instance, and for the character of Rocco we had in mind Dostoevsky's Idiot. That gave us the idea of having a female character like Nastasza Fila Pauvna. We were pretty happy with our story which was written by Visconti and myself, but at this point, in order to be really sure of

having the breadth of a novel we asked a very good Italian writer, Vasco Pra-
tolini, to join with us in a final construction of the story. The idea to use boxing for one of the brothers came as we discussed which work could give him
quick success; as we discovered, because we had spent a lot of time in Milan
among people who had emigrated from the South, a young man, in order to
gain a small amount of money, often went into boxing. The poor used it for
amusement, so they had fights among very young boxers who were not professional at all; they'd do it for a few lira in a small dirty place. All they got was
a broken jaw. We never gave much emphasis to the boxing element that Martin Scorsese thought was so important. It was just one job like any other.

**Mark Shivas: It seems to us here that having five or six screenwriters on a film was
unusual. How do they work together?**

SCD: From what I know of American pictures, when they only have one name,
it isn't at all true that it's only one writer. I know very well how many there
really are. We are more generous, we put their names up on screen. When we
had finished with our treatment, and started to write the real screenplay, we
accepted a writer from the South because we wanted to deal also with the
dialects there. One of the points of the story was that these people coming
from the South to Milan didn't understand the language absolutely. Neither
could the Milanese understand what they were saying. It was one of the problems, so we asked this southern Italian writer . . .

KD: There were two because they worked as a team.

SCD: But, in the end, the problem was that when the script was finished we
decided that it was impossible to deal with the problem of language because it
made for a *lot* of wasted time. So we had everybody speak Italian with a sort
of slight accent – it was one of the big changes. Also, the acceptance of this
solution came from the fact that television was coming up. We had television
for the first time in Italy in the 1950s and we were in 1958, but in the first year
no one in the South had television as they couldn't afford to buy one. I must
say, to my despair, in Italy they speak a language which is not Italian: it is 'tele-
language', something in Italian with a very, very poor vocabulary with special
accent on words that are ridiculous. At that time, it was only killing the
dialects, it was not yet a language in itself. We had this nice fellow to work on
a southern accent and a southern character because they were useful for the
story that we wanted to stress. We did use it, but the result was not very clear.
For instance, a widow in the South amongst poor people has the same respect
for her first born son as she did for his father. The first born son becomes a sort
of chief of the house. At this point it had been necessary for Simone to be the
eldest, but Visconti wanted there to be brothers so we kept Vincenza as the
eldest, and I must say that it is not quite right that he sort of disappears from
the film because it weakens the drama between the two brothers, Simone and
Rocco, fighting for the same woman.

KD: The point is that the age of the brothers is very important. You have a first
born who, after the death of the father, becomes the head of the family, and so

all the respect and all the power is due to him, but the first son – who is the one sent North to Milan to prepare for the coming of all the brothers – meets a girl, gets engaged to her and therefore in a way leaves the family because he starts a family on his own. This is a reason for great resentment on the mother's part. This is something that may sound tribal but it was absolutely true then, thirty years ago. So, Simone, the second son, becomes the new head of the family and therefore whatever is done against him by the youngest brother is seen, even by himself, as a reason for great guilt. When the third brother finds himself courting the woman that was once the older brother's fiancée and is attacked for this, he realizes that he is guilty and that the older one is completely within his rights. It's a very complex relationship that is quite clear to us because it belongs to the tradition of the South and the peasant families of the South.

SCD: It is something that the girl can't understand.

KD: It is probably not understood nowadays, even in Italy, because the reality has changed, but it was like that at the time.

SCD: When Rocco wants the girl to go back to Simone, the girl feels a sort of vengeance because she doesn't really understand.

MS: Shall we look at a second clip?

CLIP: SIMONE AND NADIA

SCD: I chose this clip with Simone and Nadia because I would like to explain it. First, our idea was to tell the story of poor, ignorant emigrants from the South who boxed to get small amounts of everyday money. We wanted someone to suggest that you could get real money through boxing. The suggestion was made by the girl, the young prostitute, to Simone. From this moment, Simone starts to box not for a few hundred lira but in order to gain real money, with no passion for the sport. After the first really disastrous fight he is afraid.

Rocco and His Brothers: **Simone and Nadia.**

Our idea was to show the different ways those brothers lived their lives in Milan and how they changed. There is Ciro, the only one who decides that it is necessary to study and who goes to school, gets a degree and then a proper job in town while Simone stays, and goes on boxing and stealing. However, we didn't follow much of Ciro going to school; we know it but we never show the school or follow it step by step. He is becoming a man about town but little by little, step by step, the love story between Simone and Nadia and Rocco becomes stronger. I don't know how it happened, but the love scenes grew in meaning. Visconti himself has always been a man of theatrical melodrama and grand passions. He loved the idea of making a social novel about what was happening in Italy with the emigration from South to North but little by little the love story took over the screen. It also happened that Renato Salvatori, the actor who plays Simone, and Annie Girardot, the girl who played Nadia, fell desperately in love on the very first day they started to play together. It was a passion that became part of the story. A work, at a certain point, starts to take on a life of its own and it happened a little like that with this picture. We always wanted Simone to be attracted to the girl and in his way to be in love, but not so much. It is true that there was this tribal reaction to the fact that Nadia was in love with his brother but it was not intended to be as much of a story of jealousy and passion as actually came out in the film. What is funny is that if you read the screenplay you'll find a perfectly respectable story which wanted to put the accent on how people from a city ruined and corrupted people who were more tribal, more pure.

MS: Suso, you did say to me that the first scene of the film, which we just saw, was not originally going to be the first scene.

SCD: We started from the place where they lived to stress their poverty and to show the mother's decision to leave the country.

KD: The story started with the death of the father who we never see in the picture and the funeral was so poor that the body was thrown into the sea. That was something that was allowed and legal for people who could not afford a funeral with a coffin. This was to give the idea of how poor these people were and then the mother makes the decision to leave the countryside and go North and emigrate and sends the first son.

MS: Why did you cut that first scene?

SCD: Because it was long and dealt very much with dialect. We couldn't have them in this region speaking Italian. It was never actually shot, it was cut from the screenplay. It was absolutely impossible to see and hear them talking in Italian.

MS: When you finished the film, did you know that it was no longer about social issues, no longer about the move from South to North. Did you realize that this was a film that would go on and still be popular today, thirty years later, a film about more human issues?

SCD: Not much. I followed the picture, so I lived with it day by day. I am more concerned with what happens now at the moment. Things have changed very much since then. Just imagine, for instance, the scene where Simone kills Nadia. It was to be shot in a place where prostitutes went at the time in Milan. You had to have permission to shoot in the streets or regular places where you had to bring lights etc., and we had not got permission because they thought it was an offence to Milan to show a murder in this place. As Visconti was very well known and his work on this particular film was well followed, there was scandal in the papers but there was nothing we could do. We found a place near Rome which looked like this place, but we did not get permission for this either. You have no idea how many murders we had in this place.

KD: This film has been under several trials in Italy for different reasons. There was a judge that was called Pafundi, and the family name in the film was Pafundi and the whole film was shot with the Pafundi name. It was a real name from the South and this judge sued the film and had the family name in the film changed to Parondi. They changed it on the negatives and Parondi was the only name they figured you could change it to by closing the 'f' and 'u' to make 'r' and 'o'. It's ridiculous that he felt offended by this story being so harsh and so violent and so against proper feelings. Even socially, it was considered a dangerous film. Not because it showed violence, but because it showed a city corrupting the people who emigrated there.

MS: When it came out, there was a scandal about the sort of things shown in the film, the whole idea of the film.

SCD: There was a scandal, for instance, about the violent scene between the girl and Simone: the rape.

KD: You couldn't cut it. We proved that it was essential to the story and the judges decided that the scene had to be printed black so that you could just hear what was going on but not see it.

MS: You mentioned changes. Could you please tell me, thirty years ago when you were writing this film, after you finished it and the director and producers took over, did you notice many changes that they made? Nowadays when you finish a script, they say, 'Forget it, it's not your script any more?' It becomes the producer's film and the producer can completely change the ending or anything.

SCD: Not in Italy and not with a director like Visconti. Absolutely not. Many times I have worked on a script where there have been changes during the realization. This time, no.

CLIP: FAMILY SCENE

MS: Was that Alain Delon's first film?

SCD: He had done something not very commercial, a small part in France. We wanted to make this with professional actors and they were chosen before we wrote. We wrote with Salvatori and Delon in mind.

MS: From the beginning was it always *Rocco and his Brothers*? You said you chose five brothers, but was the original perception always around Rocco?

SCD: It was the better title. When you start to look for a title, the choice comes out for a special reason sometimes.

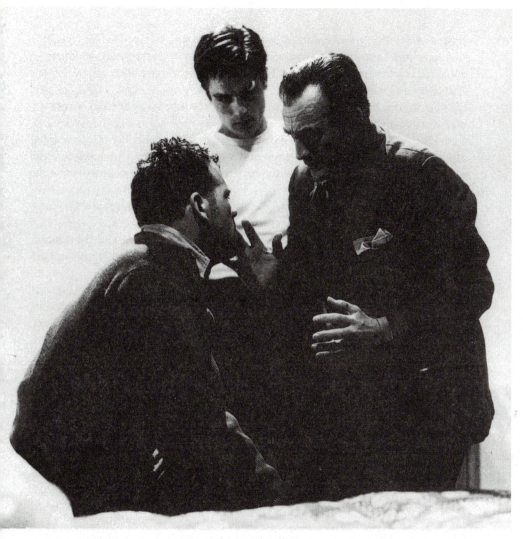

Rocco and His Brothers: Visconti directing Renato Salvatori and Alain Delon.

MS: You said that you based Rocco's character in some sense on the Idiot in Dostoevsky, so Rocco was always going to be a pivotal character in the drama.

SCD: It was a choice we made because it is a book I love very much indeed and in Dostoevsky you find characters who are very close to Italian characters – which is a good excuse to steal them. They could never be Scots or Londoners, but they could be Italian.

MS: Can you say something more about the structure of the film. It's divided into segments which deal with the oldest brother down to the youngest. Was that always planned and how did the writing of each segment work in practice? Is it true that you each wrote a separate segment?

SCD: The naming of each chapter came pretty late. We did write different segments but then we all changed because I had all the women to deal with. We took a section and then we changed and changed and changed. Of course, I defended a character like Nadia because I was the only woman so I said, 'Leave me in peace, I know better.' With Vincenza, for instance, it's an example of southern habits disappearing. In the South, when you are very poor, the way to have a wedding is to run away.

KD: When you meet a girl, and you like a girl, but the girl is poor and can't afford to pay for the wedding – there are major expenses in a wedding in Italy – they run away together. They still do this in the South; they come back saying, 'So what?'

SCD: We have this situation with Vincenza but there is not much stress on it.

KD: Who was the writer for Vincenza in the first place?

SCD: Francosa, who was the least important of the team. He had the task of dealing with the chapter on Vincenza and then we all exchanged. Then we had Dico Medioli, who was just learning his profession.

KD: He was somebody who wanted to be a screenwriter. He had just arrived from Parma and had the ambition of becoming a screenwriter so he worked in the team to learn how to do it. It was his apprenticeship, but then he stayed on.

MS: Could you tell us a bit more about how you worked with Visconti, not just on this film but others too, and why you think you worked so well together?

SCD: That is something you should have asked him, because he always called me. He thought I was a good help to him. The first script I wrote with him was a screenplay which was not realized. It was a film that Renoir made afterwards but not with our script, *The Golden Coach*, and that's why we made *Bellissima* afterwards because he had promised Anna Magnani. Magnani had long hoped to make a film with Visconti. She arrived on the set of *Ossessione*, but was sent away because she was five months pregnant. I made a big mistake with *Senso*. The screenplay was too long and we had to cut a lot before shooting. I didn't know how Visconti would shoot certain scenes, but from that time I was never mistaken.

KD: She didn't realize, up to that time, that once Visconti was confronted with interior decoration he would just shoot forever. So all the sequences on paper that were meant to be two or three minutes long became ten or twelve minutes.

SCD: In *Senso*, for instance, when the officer and the lover go into the country villa, I couldn't imagine that she was going to take the jewel through *fifteen* drawing rooms!

MS: How long did you think the ball and party scene at the end of *The Leopard* would be?

SCD: We knew it was going to be long because when the decision was made to cut the last two chapters of the book and give the sense of death at the ball, we knew we had all those pages of the description of the prince's death in the book.

MS: Is it true that 20th Century Fox, who put money into *The Leopard*, assumed that because it starred Burt Lancaster it was going to be made in English and they were

The Leopard: The ball (Claudia Cardinale and Burt Lancaster).

shocked and horrified when they found it wasn't?

KD: Lancaster had a contract that said the film was going to be shot in English and, to be fair, he was the one who said forget it. He had it in his contract, but he realized immediately that the other actors were very down about it because virtually none of the others were English apart from Leslie French. The others were acting in English; Cardinale spoke English decently, Delon so-so, and the others just learnt the lines. So Lancaster was the one who said let them speak whatever language they speak, and we should mix languages. So each was acting in his own language.

MS: Can I ask about neo-realism? Did you feel that you were part of this ground-breaking movement?

KD: The adjective neo-realistic comes from a private letter sent by the editor, Marius Sedandri, who was a very cultured man who edited lots of films in Italy after the Second World War. Visconti never even saw his own rushes. He had the cinematographer watch them and tell him if it was correct lightwise. The rushes were sent directly to the editor who was practically the first person outside the set to see them. Once Sedandri saw the first material of *Ossessione*, he wrote a letter – *Ossessione* was not shot in Rome, it was shot in Ferrara – to

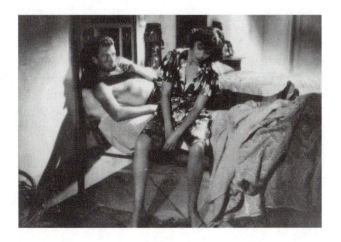

Ossessione: The birth of 'neo-realism'.

Visconti saying, 'I liked the material very much and I think it is great and it has a very new flavour which I do not know how to describe. It seems very new, maybe neo-realistic.' So the word was first employed there, and then it became used by the critics much later, in fact, after Rossellini's films. *Ossessione* was shot in 1941, so the first neo-realistic films are in 1945 – *Open City*, *Bicycle Thieves*, *Paisa*.

SCD: It was just our way of recounting our experiences of the war and of Fascism. I always say that maybe if we had as many papers and magazines as we actually have today in Italy, many of us would have become journalists instead of working in film. For instance, there is a good writer of the time called Pavesi. In Italy we do not have the same tradition of the novel as you have in Britain or America. English-speaking countries have a great tradition of story-telling, but less so in Italy. The cinema taught the writers how to write stories, and Pavesi wrote that the best writer at that moment was De Sica with *Bicycle Thieves* and then Visconti.

MS: There was one scene in *Rocco* which left me a little confused. It's where Simone goes to the character who is going to give him money and they fight and there is a shot of a television with some images. Could you explain the point of that?

SCD: It's one of the things we wanted to say about the influence of television, that it existed. You have this character from the very beginning and you ask why does Simone choose boxing with the help of this man? This of course is the history of corruption; the man fixes matches so that Simone will win. The first time Simone loses he does not like it at all and we find that he is a coward, not a sportsman.

MS: But when the television was switched on, it had these Renaissance images which were very unusual for TV. So why did you write it and what is the meaning of this?

SCD: Those are images that Visconti chose to make a contrast. It was to draw your attention to television's existence.

MS: A number of Visconti's films were released in versions cut from his original intention. How did you feel when a film went out which was substantially shorter than what you had written, and was there any danger of that happening with *Rocco*?

SCD: I have seen very few versions abroad of Visconti's pictures and I have always seen them in festivals where they were not cut; they were cut afterwards. We had a shock when *Il Gattopardo* [*The Leopard*] was released in the States because the dubbing was unbearable. It was dubbed like a Western! The worst thing was that they printed the whole dance scene in a very high, light colour to avoid the sense of death which has dark colours. It was not at all successful and Visconti refused to write to the papers in the States but instead wrote to *The Times* in London because they hadn't seen the picture at all. He sent a letter to *The Times* saying that he hoped that they were not going to see this version of the film, showing the respect he had for England and not the States.

12 Terence Davies

Subject: Directing *The Neon Bible*
Interviewer: Mark Cousins

Terence Davies: The film is based on a book called *The Neon Bible* by John Kennedy Toole who is famous for *The Confederacy of Dunces*. This book was actually found by Elizabeth Karlsen who produced the film and, very roughly, it's about a poor white family growing up in the Southern part of the United States. Into the family comes Aunt May who represents everything that is glamorous, and this young boy just basically falls in love with her. She is wonderful and full of life. It's about his relationship with her and how the relationship with his mother and father gradually decays as she becomes the dominant person in his life. The Second World War breaks out and the father goes off to fight and gets killed in Italy and the mother slowly declines into a kind of madness. Then at the end he is deserted. That's what it's about; sounds fun doesn't it? It's not nearly as dreary, honestly. There are some great underwater routines in there. They are out-takes from *Waterworld*, how do you think we got finance? So that's roughly the story. I've chosen some clips that have a lot of camera movement, some with just conventional cutting, and some which are conventional cutting and camera movement and song as well. You know me and song!

CLIP: 'WE GOTTA EAT, WE NEED MONEY'. LONG CLIP THAT ENDS IN SINGING SCENE.

Mark Cousins: What was your idea behind the scene where the boy grows up?
TD: Because in the book the fight we've just seen and his father going out and not coming back for hours and hours is the moment where he actually grows up emotionally, I wanted to see him physically grow up in front of us. I didn't know how it was done and when they said 'morphing' I said, 'It's going to cost a fortune.' Why didn't I think in terms of Polaroid, but you don't. What I wanted was for the scene to carry on even though he has grown up and six years have elapsed. Many people don't get that and say, 'This beating must have gone on for a long time,' which was not the intention. Because I know the material well, I've read the novel forty-seven times, you get to the point where you can't read it again, this is the only way you can think of doing that particular bit, and eliding two or three chapters together at a time. You can't film a novel, you just

can't; you have to capture the essence of the book as well as its literal narrative. That's what I was trying to say.

MC: Was there any idea behind your making of the film having seen *Night of the Hunter* with Charles Laughton? He did a cross shot that goes out of the window and up to the stars which seems to suggest mind over matter.

TD: Yes, I adore that film and think it's such a masterpiece. I'm afraid I haven't done it as well as Laughton did. *Night of the Hunter* is one of those films I absolutely adore. People who say they don't like it, I want them killed, but that's awful and you can't do that can you? But I'm the same with *Carry on Sergeant*, so what can you do? What's wonderful about *Night of the Hunter* is it is a fairy tale for adults shot through a German Expressionism. There is that wonderful way children have: there is black, there is white, there is evil, there is good. That sequence on the river, it's just one of the greatest sequences ever filmed. A well-known writer, who shall not be named, said to me recently that it is a flawed masterpiece. I said, 'Well could you do as good, even half as good?' The answer is no, none of us could, it's such a great, great masterpiece.

MC: Were you attempting to reach for that effect?

TD: No, this is not in the same class as *Night of the Hunter* and also it is not about the same thing. It would be like making a musical. The touchstone is *Singin' in the Rain* which I saw when I was seven. Nothing is as good. No matter how hard you try, you can't do it. It is very much one of my big touchstones, one of the most important films in my life, but so is the American musical which is what influenced me most of all. *Singin' in the Rain* was my first film at seven; at eleven I discovered Doris Day in *Young at Heart*. That was it, I was lost to her forever. When I grow up I want to be Doris Day, what I lack in freckles and blond hair I more than make up for in willpower, I assure you.

MC: You were going to say something about memory there.

TD: Sorry, I forgot. The way the nature of memory works is you feel and remember the intensity of the moment, the quintessence of the moment and you don't remember what went before or after. You remember it in a sequence of intense moments, and children feel intensely. In the book he goes out onto the veranda and looks at the stars. How do you make that magical? You make him go out and see nothing but stars, because that's what a child would do. We know that's not true, you would see the landscape, you would see the blackness of the shrubbery, then the sky and then the line of the horizon but that's not what you see in memory. You only remember its intensity and how it burned into you. I was trying to get that because I do think that memory has such a hold on us in the way that Eliot describes it at the beginning of *The Four Quartets*. It is ever present, it is not time gone by, it is now; we can oscillate between what happened twenty years ago, what is happening now and what we will be doing next week. In a film, you have to set it up in a way where it's not going to be conventional narrative; it's not going to cut from this to this, because that implies that events follow each other. If you dissolve, it always

Young at Heart: Doris Day and Frank Sinatra.

indicates time passing. No one has ever told us that, but we all read it as that. It can be time passing forward or backward, but it's time passing. What interested me in this was actually to have a scene that was happening now, dissolve, cut within that sequence, and dissolve back. Now what does that mean? Is that parallel time, is it real time within the memory, or what is it? It is Eliot: 'Time present and time past / Are both perhaps present in time future, / And time future contained in time past. / If all time is eternally present / All time is unredeemable.' It is what memory also does; it fixes on the tiny, never the big. 'Then a cloud passed, and the pool was empty' – that's what you remember, and that's what I wanted to try to capture, that essence of the book. John Kennedy Toole wrote it when he was sixteen and there is a lot of weak writing in it: him being bullied by Mrs Watkins at school is not interesting, the fact that Aunt May can't cook is not interesting. What *is* interesting is how you feel when you are with someone you intensely love. I drew a little bit on autobiography. I used to mind my sister's children when I was growing up, and very often I would be allowed to stay and very often I went to bed with them and we'd look out of the window if it was a hot night and talk, then go to sleep. That brought back a whole lot of memories for me and I knew it was right to have him in the bed and to have her say, 'We'll pray tonight,' and he just says, 'Amen.' He does that in the book, and then we go into the sequence in the revival tent; I'm interested in the poetry of the ordinary which is why I love Chekhov because he is too. At big moments, people say the banal thing, they don't say the dramatic thing – unless it is *All About Eve*, when you forgive it!

MC: Would you talk about casting Gena Rowlands and also about working with an actor who is so much a part of the collaboration.

TD: When I read the book and Elizabeth said to me, 'Who do you want to play Aunt May?' I said, 'Gena Rowlands,' thinking we'd never get her. She said, 'I'll ring her agent.' She did, and a month later we were in Los Angeles in the Le Torc restaurant on Sunset Boulevard sitting opposite Gena Rowlands. I thought, 'God, it's Gena Rowlands and I'm sitting here. I better say something or she'll think I'm an idiot.' We then sent her a VHS of *Distant Voices, Still Lives* and the *South Bank Show* and she loved them and she liked me and we got on. I told her how I wanted to do the story, but the script wasn't written and she agreed to do it. Her agent said that in twenty-two years she had never ever done that, which was a great compliment. The old ego went sky high and she was a joy to work with. The only slight disagreement we had was that long speech she has at the window. She wanted to play it in a certain way and I said, 'No, I find that a little bit sentimental, but could you just think about it.' It required her to cry and she said, 'I can't cry, I've never cried in a film.' I said, 'Can you imply tears in the voice?' and she said, 'Yes.' Give an idea like that to an American actor and they do wonders with it. That was the first take and I could feel the tears rising up in my throat. This is absurd, I'm supposed to be their fearless leader.

Before we did the scene in the bed, I told her it was summed up by a poem by Philip Larkin – I read her quite a lot of poetry actually – *An Arundel Tomb*, 'What will survive of us is love.' I thought that she would think I was an idiot. She did think I was a bit strange at first because I don't do a lot of coverage, but after two days they saw the rushes and liked them and were absolutely dedicated.

The way she uses her eyes in that long sequence: 'When I was young I could wear clothes and I could always carry a tune. But you get older honey. You get old' – it was so moving.

CLIP: SEQUENCE INCLUDING 'THE OLD RUGGED CROSS' SONG. TIME PASSES, FATHER KILLED IN WAR, AUNT MAY GOES TO WORK IN A FACTORY

MC: Did you write your scenes with certain camera movements in mind? It reminded me of some scenes in *Distant Voices, Still Lives*.

TD: I write the way I feel, and I see it in that way. I see what's in the mise en scène. I see if the camera is tracking or panning down, that's how I see it, so it's very difficult to extrapolate and say, 'Well, I did it because of that.' I was try-ing to conflate a number of things that happened in the book. Dad had hit her, he's gone out, he's not come back, the war breaks out, he goes away, nothing is resolved and then he is killed. By this time Aunt May has gone into a factory and has made friends there. How do you do that interestingly? You deny geog-raphy, that's what you do. You can, as you move in and out of blackness, go somewhere else. If any of you know Bruckner's music, there are rolling crescendi and then you end on a cadence and start again. If that doesn't sound horribly pretentious, that was the feeling behind it, that these sequences are conceived over a long stretch like a long tune in a symphony.

MC: Why did you choose that particular hymn for that sequence?

TD: The hymn that is quoted in the book is not terribly interesting and I did-n't know the tune. I needed to get across immediately the idea that you know it's a hymn. 'The Old Rugged Cross' I just happened to like and I thought it was that kind of fundamentalist hymn that they would sing. With a piece of music you're trying to say something more than just its function in the narra-tive. It's got to be a hymn, but it should be one that has a true ambiguity like in the next sequence where she sings in the factory. In the book she sings a blues song and it was not right. I wanted something that summed up her emo-tions. She wants to get a man, and she never succeeds. The man she goes away with is not right, but that's never resolved. Also, she's got to sing for herself and for those women. Their menfolk have gone away to war and a lot of them will not be coming back. So, because I love Rodgers and Hart, I chose 'My Romance' because that sums up everything; all that romance about wanting someone – 'My romance doesn't need a thing but you' – and how you want those people that you love that have gone away. Even the people that you don't love that have gone away; you still want them. It was a way of trying to get all of those things within a single song. It has all those resonances for me.

When we finished the film someone said, 'How about a score?' I said, 'No, the music that's in it, that's all there needs to be. We don't need someone putting in "Aunt May's Theme" or something like that.' This I *didn't* want, and they just looked at me as if I'd just landed from the planet Thorg, and I had. I got terribly kind of 'poker-up-the-arse' about it: if I had wanted a score, I would have asked for one. At the end of the day, you can only really follow your instinct. This is going to sound terribly arrogant, but you can only make it for yourself because you can't go out to please other people. A film is either liked or it's not; there is no way of knowing which. So, if you pass me on Princes Street, please be generous.

CLIP: SINGING SEQUENCE

MC: You were saying that people don't make musicals anymore, but you do, don't you?

TD: Sort of, but it's not *Pajama Game*, it's not *I'll Never be Jealous Again*, it's not even Betty Grable in *Mother Wore Tights*. I wish it were. There is too much

The Neon Bible: Gena Rowlands.

angst in my films. Musicals have got to be jolly, ending on a bright note so that you go out on to the street thinking 'Isn't life wonderful.' You don't go out of my films thinking life is wonderful.

MC: Maybe not the mood of the musicals, but if you compare the camera moves in the title number of *Singin' in the Rain* with some of your camera moves, there is still a sense of epic sweep.

TD: That's a huge compliment, thank you. That film is so seminal to me. It's one of the films which literally did change my life and I weep almost all the way through it if I watch it now, because I can remember the happiness it gave me when I sat in the Odeon Cinema in 1953 with my elder sister. I'll never forget it as long as I live, never. When you love something as much as that you can't have any kind of distance on it. When I look at my own films I think that they are very poor compared to that, because those were the great days of Hollywood. You went to the cinema, queued, and saw these films, and it created the land of magic. I can remember shortly after *Singin' in the Rain* was released and my sister took me to see it. In those days, if a girl had an American for a boyfriend it was just so swish. She had an American boyfriend and he came down the street in the middle of this Liverpool slum in a white suit. Everybody came out to look at him and they knocked on the door just to hear his voice, the accent. He brought us six pairs of nylons, a big thing of Wriggley's Spearmint chewing-gum, some peanut butter and a percolator. We didn't know what a percolator was, so we used it for paint. There's sophistication for you. When I see those films, it's not just the films that come back. I can remember being taken to see *Young at Heart* and we got the last two seats in the Liverpool Forum. I went with my older sister Helen. We slightly missed the opening credits. It was a very hot Sunday afternoon and we went to the early performance and we came out and walked up the road because we couldn't get a tram. She went faint, and she was wearing a little black costume suit with a little blouse with a frilly collar. I can still see it now. It's so vivid, so when I see those films I know where I saw them, which route I took and who I saw them with. But when I see my own, I don't think they will ever have that effect on anybody.

MC: There are a number of things connecting there. You are talking about the precise memory of things, yet it seems to me, say, the last shot in *Young at Heart* where the camera goes through the window to see Frank Sinatra on the piano: you've done the camera through the window so many times in your films it seems that in some way you are borrowing the perfect form of these films, using them to express something much darker and more serious.

TD: I think there must be, because once you are exposed to something you can't then 'un-know' it. No matter how much you think you haven't borrowed, you do, and that can be a good thing or a bad thing. The film begins by going into the window and it comes out at the end. It's like a perfect arc. But that wonderful track of Judy Garland's when she sings 'The Boy Next Door' at the window, just sublime. I'd have done anything to do that, anything. Even in *Mother Wore Tights* with Betty Grable – and it's not a good musical – there is one wonderful moment when she sings 'Cocomo Indiana' with Dan Dailey. These are wonderful tracks and it is as smooth as silk – 'Gee I'd like to be back home again, in Cocomo In-di-ana' – it's just gorgeous! But, alas, we don't make musicals in England. What have we got? Musicals by 'Andrew Rice-Pudding', 'Don't Queue for me, I'm the Cleaner'. Wonderful!

MC: You are speaking of your influences and they are all pre-Cinemascope. In this film were you trying to evoke the Cinemascope feelings of the 1950s, and were you trying to comment on the shape of the screen by having frame within frame, and sometimes screen within screen? Later in the film you have washing hanging up which acts as a Cinemascope screen – or am I reading into this too much?

TD: The first Cinemascope film I actually saw was *The Robe*, again in 1953, and it was the first Cinemascope film ever made. I can remember going to see it at a packed cinema, the curtains went back and the audience gasped. You just saw this huge, epic thing. There was a wonderful performance by a man called Jay Robinson who played Caligula which made me want to be an actor because he had all the best lines. He was terribly camp, but just wonderful.

The Neon Bible: While the menfolk are away at war.

There is a wonderful bit with Jean Simmons in it where he says, 'Ahh, the Lady
Diana. As beautiful as ever . . . and as cold.' I thought, 'Isn't this dramatic?'
When I went out to see Gena, the casting director said, 'Is there anyone you
would like to see?' and I said, 'Yes, I want to see Jay Robinson. Is he still alive,
because he had such an important impact on my life?' He was alive and living
in Los Angeles and we had tea together. I said, 'I can repeat all your dialogue
now,' and I did. He was so lovely. He didn't make many films – *The Robe*,
Demetrius and the Gladiators, the remake of *My Man Godfrey* and *The Virgin
Queen* – but he's still got this wonderfully rich, bump-it-with-a-trumpet voice,
like those wonderful strippers in *Gypsy* who sing 'If you wanna make it, twin-
kle while you shake it. If you wanna grind it, wait till you've refined it. If you
wanna bump it, bump it with a trumpet!'

So the influence was actually that film. When you want people in the middle
of the frame, how do you make it alive? What you do is make the texture
behind them alive. But I used much more asymmetry than I ever used before
because the beginning of that second sequence with the people walking down
the street was originally supposed to be them walking this way and we are
tracking that way. Dull, so dull. So we just moved the camera round – not a lot
– and the scene came alive because you have got interest all down the frame for
the length of time it takes for that track. It was interesting how you can create
that epic quality. It's very easy to make it epic, you have just got to put a lot of
extras in. To make it intimate, and feel intimate rather than big – that's different. In this film I had three hundred extras, more than I've ever had in my
entire life. When they said you have got three hundred I wondered what I
would do with them. My crew were wonderful. I said that I really needed help
with the extras because I'd only ever had half a dozen up to now – coming
from the Third World! – and they were fantastic.

The frames within frames, I think that's an unconscious thing. I just do it. In

The Long Day Closes it's the carpet; in *The Neon Bible* it's the sheet, and in the next one it's going to be cutlery.

MC: How do you get shadows in colour? I always thought that once you get colour in film, you negate all shadow.

TD: What I did was I looked at a lot of photographs that were taken at the beginning of the war by Eudora Welty, Dorothea Lange and Walker Evans. Now, they are all in black and white, but with the sunlight being very strong, you get very deep shadow, but you also get detail in the shadow. I said to my cinematographer, Mick Coulter, 'I want a reproduction of this, but in colour, like three-strip Technicolor, where you can get very deep but very detailed shadows.' Look at Douglas Sirk, for instance: you can always see detail in the shadows. I don't know technically how he did it; I just said this is what I want and he gave it to me. It's a question that only he could really answer. They were based on black and white photographs, not colour ones.

MC: I know with *Distant Voices, Still Lives* you said you didn't rehearse very much. Did you have to rehearse more for this one?

TD: It was almost exactly the same. The only thing that we did differently was that we read through the script to begin with, just for the accent, rather than for the performance, because I needed to attune my ear to that accent. We based it actually on Diana Scarwid's accent because she is actually from Savanna which is very gentle. We finished reading it and I then read them the opening of *The Four Quartets* by Eliot which is really foot-tapping. Then I told them to go away and read the script; don't read it too often, but read the scenes the night before. Then we rehearsed them. Sometimes I read them poetry, sometimes I didn't. With Diana I usually quoted music rather than poetry. They give the performance so quickly. I remember the first day we were working with Diana and all she had was one line – it was a sequence of pans and it ends on her saying 'Who do you think the murderer is, David?' By this point she has started to slide into madness. While we were going through it, with Gena first and then Jacob, then her, she just sat in the chair and you could see her literally becoming this woman. It was breathtaking. We came to do it and it was just fabulous. She had to say hardly anything, just this one line, and even *I* felt moved . . . and I wrote the thing!

There was another moment when we had been doing pick-up shots all day which are very boring – people going in and out of doors, very dull – and you just can't make them come alive. We had two shots with her at the end of the day and it was a very hot day and everyone was very tired and these shots were last. She came on and she electrified that crew. In the first take you could feel this electricity go through you; it was so moving. When people do things like that I want to adopt them legally, I get so excited. But by the same token when it doesn't go well I get really depressed. Unfortunately, when you are the director that communicates itself to other people. In America the director is God, literally, but I don't believe in all that and think it's a lot of nonsense and I become terribly like Thora Hird.

MC: You were talking about music and said that there were certain songs in the book that didn't appeal to you. Do the alternatives suggest themselves while you are reading the book?

TD: It depends. Sometimes you know the sort of song you want, but you're not sure which one. I have quite a lot of knowledge about American popular song-writing up until the rise of Elvis Presley because I don't really like rock 'n' roll and that's when my interest in pop music really did cease. I know that great tradition which is now, alas, no more. Songwriters now aren't writing anything that's got any wit in it. Can you imagine a Cole Porter now? You can't because nobody is writing like that. The sheer wit of the man. One song begins 'Ravel is chasing Debussy, The aphid is chasing the pea. The gander is chasing the goosey, but nobody is chasing me,' which has become my theme song because it is alas all too true. When I was writing the whole of the ending sequence, I was listening to Radio Three and one night they had a programme of Stephen Foster songs and the only ones that I knew were 'Camptown Races' and 'The Old Folks at Home'. I thought I would listen to it anyway, sung by Thomas Hamson who has now become a very big opera star and lead singer, and he sang the song 'Hard Times Come Again No More', and I thought that's it, that's what I need. Those things have always been serendipity. I've always managed to hear them just when I needed them, and I dashed out to the music discount store on The Strand and I got the last copy, and I thought I'm destined to have this. So it depends, sometimes you know what you want, sometimes it occurs to you, sometimes someone suggests something to you and you say 'It's not that but it's this.' The film opens and closes with a hymn called 'Oh Lord How Long'. A friend of Elizabeth Karlsen got me this old Baptist manual from America, a hymnal, and he played the song and sang it. The words were not that interesting, but the tune was wonderful. I thought, it's got to be a solo instrument, so I said, 'Can we record it on a cor anglais and an oboe?' When I heard it played back it had that wonderful, open American sound like Copland, and you could see how he had got his influence from American folk song and American hymnals. You have to be open to things like that, they come to you and find you. I love music and when it's right it gives me such pleasure. Can you imagine *Psycho* without that wonderful score? You can't. As soon as you hear that *moto perpetuo* you are frightened, and on edge, and when she goes into the house, and it's all played with strings with the mutes on, it's just Fabbo! I get terribly worked up about that, which shows you how boring my private life is.

MC: How do explain the contrast between the sobriety there is on screen and the jollity of you in person?

TD: I'm actually very miserable. No, I don't say that as a joke, I really am. I get very depressed, very easily. I've poured my life into making films at the expense of a private life and if there are any film-makers amongst you, it is not worth it. There's nothing more depressing than going back to a hotel room after people have said they like what you do, or were very responsive, and you end up going into a hotel room alone. There is no one to put their arms round you and say well done or never mind. That's depressing. You get sick of getting on and off planes on your own. There are times when you cannot bring yourself to go to another festival, but you go because you don't want to let anyone down. I want to be entertaining, I don't want to be miserable, and I don't want to let anybody down who is connected with the film. But at home I get very low indeed. In the last year two members of my family have died, and that's very hard to cope with because I loved them very much. I wish I was intrinsically happy but I'm intrinsically miserable. You try to compensate for it by trying to be funny but there is something unseemly about that, because what you are actually doing is saying 'Love me, love me, love me', and at forty-nine that's really rather unseemly. I've stopped biting the furniture though, so that's one thing I've achieved over the last few years. Actually, I'm really terribly miserable.

MC: Why not give up film-making then?

TD: Well, I don't know what else I'd do. I need to make films, but I don't like all the crap that surrounds it. Cannes was very damaging. I came back feeling completely worthless and completely talentless and that will take a long time to get over. People were unbelievably nasty: there was someone who, after a screening of *The Long Day Closes*, sent me a letter which was two pages of complete viciousness, I mean, unbelievably vicious. So I wrote back and said 'Please take your bile out on somebody else.' This was a friend, which was very hurtful. There was some booing at the press-showing, but not at the evening showing where we got a standing ovation. I got back and there was a letter from the same gentleman saying 'I'm sorry it went badly.' I mean, it's gloating, and you think, 'Aahh, why do people do it?' Life is too short, and so am I.

MC: They booed the Antonioni film *L'Eclisse* at Cannes.

TD: But when you're on the receiving end of it it's very hard. Especially when you've poured everything into it. The work means more than it should. I think the best thing is to be married, or if you are gay have a partner, and what should be of secondary importance is your work. It's the other way round with me, and it's a mug's game. I'm sick of doing things alone, really so fed up with it. You think, 'Oh well, I want to help the film' and all that, and then you come to something like this – and you all laughed at the first joke and I can't tell you what balm it is, truly, truly, I really am grateful – but you don't want to let the film down, so I try to be jolly.

MC: You recite poetry so much I just want to ask you, do you think there are similarities between film-editing and the way poetry gets written – the condensation, the elliptical things – because you seem to like it a lot, and also music?

TD: Yes I do. I think music is the closest of all the art forms to film because notes on their own don't mean anything. They only mean something when they are juxtaposed with other chords and notes.

A great composer latches on to our inner harmonic so that when something is resolved, either in the minor or the major, we recognize it and therefore are moved. Poetry is the same but not quite as powerful, it's still the same. You know the way Eliot constantly elides but repeats; he will always repeat something: 'Do I dare?' and, 'Do I dare?' So it is like hearing a trill at the end of a cadence in a Mozart symphony, and you can hear that trill in Mahler but played on double basses: it's still a trill but the difference is huge, it's huge. You read a sonnet by Shakespeare and it can have the bleakness of 'Prufrock' but its form is utterly perfect. I can read something like 'Like as the waves make towards the pebbled shore' and have exactly the same kind of terror that I do when I read 'Prufrock' – 'I grow old . . . I grow old . . . I shall wear the bottoms of my trousers rolled. Shall I part my hair behind, do I dare eat a peach?' All that terror of being alive. Film can create that same terror of being alive, but over small things.

MC: What are your opinions about the essence of being a director?

TD: Arrogance is the wrong word, but I think you have to be driven by something you need, a need to make films. Although I try to make the films as co-operative as possible, because it is a co-operative effort, there has to be a central vision, and that vision has to be the director's. It couldn't be anybody else's. You cannot make a film by committee. So you have got to have that, and you've got to have the willpower to carry on doing it when people have said horrible things about what you've done. When you begin a new film all those terrors come back and you've got to try to control them because they are terrors. You walk out on to a set and there are seventy people, and they are looking to you and you've got to do it, you've got to pull it out of the bag every time; that's your job. There is something terribly exciting about that. You think, I want to pull this big sequence off, I hope I can, and then somehow you do. I think the essence is that you've got to have a vision, and that vision can be great or small, but it has got to be there, and more than anything else you've got to be true to it, you can't compromise it. If you compromise it, there's no point in doing it. I would rather not work than compromise something I believed in, that's why I would never survive in Hollywood, never. An actor would only have to say, 'I want an extra close-up,' and I'd say, 'You'll get the close-up you deserve, and no more.' And I would say that but, of course, I would be sacked. If it's Tom Cruise or Keanu Reeves or Christian Slater they've got the power because everyone wants to go and see them, they don't go and see it for the director. So I wouldn't survive there, and anyway it's so grim out there I don't know how people do. Those that go out and survive and make a success of it deserve knighthoods because it's awful. I had a tiny taste of it – very, very unpleasant. I didn't like it at all, I couldn't wait to get back. But I think you've got to have a great deal of tenacity. It's no good if you are thin-skinned, and I am very thin-skinned. So it's a question of tenacity, vision, needing to do it. More than wanting it, you've got to need it.

13 Steve Martin & Gillies MacKinnon

Subject: Acting, writing and directing *A Simple Twist of Fate*
Interviewer: Ginnie Atkinson

Ginnie Atkinson: Perhaps you could tell us why you wanted to do the film and wanted to write it yourself, because it's based on the book *Silas Marner*.

Steve Martin: Do we have to? I'd rather start with the Disney Logo. No. I had read *Silas Marner* recently and thought it was a beautiful story and I had this crazy idea that plot worked in movies. I thought this had a beautiful plot, very emotional, and it had a similar feeling to *Roxanne* where the story was so compelling that comedy would naturally evolve from the story and I could write it in a funny way. It actually turned out to be more serious than I expected. Sometimes you don't know what a thing will be like until it's done, and sometimes you have to let it tell you what it is. I started analysing the book, writing it, and made one significant structural change for the movie which we'll talk about at some point – maybe tomorrow, depending on how long we go! I could keep my microphone on all night and I could broadcast from the hotel, because once I start talking, I really don't stop.

So that was that, and I think I've answered it pretty satisfactorily. I'm actually quite pleased with myself.

GA: It's Gillies's turn now to tell us why he wanted to do the movie.

Gillies MacKinnon: I though it was a great idea and it is a very intriguing combination: George Eliot and Steve Martin.

SM: I loved working with George by the way!

GM: I didn't actually meet him myself.

SM: I saw him in the shower.

GM: When Steve first told me about this, I thought it was a really strange combination. Steve is somebody who really explores in different directions and I thought this direction he is going in sounded really interesting. I read the script and I liked it, we talked for an hour on the phone and I remember trying to be a bit humorous and crack a few jokes . . . but Steve didn't laugh.

SM: It was stifling!

GM: So we talked for an hour, and at the end of it I basically thought that we had the same movie in mind, and that was very exciting. All of sudden I was in Los Angeles starting to make the film.

SM: I was excited because I thought Gillies looked like me. Am I wrong?

GM: You kept saying that.

SM: Well, it was late.

GA: So what kind of character was the character you played in the film? Was it written with you playing it in mind?

SM: When I write something, even if it is for myself, I don't think of myself as playing it. It's strange. I remember when I wrote *Roxanne* we were about three days from shooting and I said to the producer, 'I've been writing this thing and worrying about it. I have no idea how I am going to play it.' This was much the same: you try to get it to work as a screenplay and as a character and then blunder your way through it, wake up really early and be tired.

GM: Let's see some clips. If you fast-forward it, we'll shout stop.

CLIP: FILM FAST-FORWARDS.

SM: We can talk about the wavy lines. I think I am being hypnotized.
  (*Describes scene.*)

GM: There were four children in the film playing the little girl. We had one just over one, one who was about three, one who was about eight and one who was about eleven. When we auditioned the eleven-year-old, she had a little sister, so we told her to bring her sister in. She was really shy and never said a word. After the audition was over and she said nothing, I said, 'It was very nice to meet you,' and I put my hand out and she nearly ripped my arm off, gave me this cheeky wee smile and I thought, there's a character here.

SM: Did you just say 'cheeky wee smile'? I guess the Italian part of my vacation is over.

GM: That lady on the screen there was actually her mother and it's a feature of working with children in Hollywood, different to working with children here, that they get into a type of business. The mother and father become managers and everything becomes rationalized.

CLIP: PAIR OF HANDS SPINNING GOLD COINS.

SM: That's me. Those are my hands! That is a misspent youth. OK, you can roll forward now.

CLIP: FILM SPINS FORWARD THROUGH SCENES FROM A POLO GAME.

GM: Oh God, the polo scenes. We had a second unit there, and it was the first time I had seriously used a second unit, and we had to shoot some polo shots. There is about fifteen seconds of polo in here, but the producer, Rick Kidney, went off and shot about two days' worth of polo. Every time I looked to the end of the pitch, for two days I could see these polo players shooting this documentary. That's how it is in Hollywood compared to Britain, you get much more of everything. That is the essential difference to me: if you want polo, then they just keep on shooting polo.

GM: This is a scene with Gabriel Byrne and Stephen Baldwin. It was the first real scene between the two brothers and everyone was nervous because when actors have got to do something like two brothers arguing and it's the first time they've worked together and everyone's a little bit nervous, you want to protect them. I made sure that nobody from the crew was in the room. We had silence and we rehearsed the scene for about half an hour. I then said to Stephen, 'OK, we'll bring the crew in now.' The moment I said it, windows and doors burst open all around me and people just piled in the room and fell all around me. They had been up against the walls and doors!

CLIP: STEPHEN BALDWIN AND GABRIEL BYRNE CONFRONTATION.

GM: This shot here is just the trim-end of a very elaborate shot we did where the camera started off in the house. Stephen jumped over a railing, ran up to the car, got in the car and the camera tracked through the lights of the car. But typically, it just takes too long and you end up cutting out all this amazing work that you've done. If anyone is familiar with *The Grass Arena*, this is the same shot I used in that and because I liked it so much I had to use it again.

CLIP: STRAIGHT AFTER BYRNE/BALDWIN CONFRONTATION, ONE OF THEM LEAVES IN A CAR: 'PENNIES FROM HEAVEN'.

SM: I'll make a point and you can decide if it's interesting. What I loved about the story is that there are these cinematic revelations that advance the plot. This one is a good example: we don't know what is happening, we know Stephen Baldwin is bringing Amy some money, but we don't know why. We understand that there is a child, we see the mother start to inject herself with heroin, and then the camera pans over and reveals this child sitting there. To me, this is a plot point because suddenly you feel all this emotion for the child because of her circumstances and it is told without dialogue just by the move of the camera. It's something I think movies do really well.

CLIP: STEPHEN BALDWIN BREAKS INTO STEVE MARTIN'S HOUSE BECAUSE HE HAS HEARD A RUMOUR THAT THERE IS GOLD THERE.

GM: Stephen is an interesting kind of actor. He's one of these 'up for anything' type of actors, he's always got an idea and always wants to try something different. Sometimes you don't want him to do it, but you've just got to let him try. It's quite exciting to work with an actor like that who is always active.
SM: This moment is actually quite tricky because the movie is kind of split in two. There is this elaborate plotting in the first half, and then in the second half the movie becomes about a relationship. In a way that's the risky part of the movie because audiences tend to like it to be one thing. But I believed that the plot in the first half of the movie was very interesting, and I also believed that the relationship in the second half was as well so I had to trust that and let you be the judge of its success. I knew that it was going to be a problem, but I thought that it would be an interesting problem.

GM: This next scene is the snow sequence which dominated our lives for about a week and a half and nearly drove everyone crazy, working all through the night. It was a mixture of synthetic snow being shot through hoses and freezing ice coming down through hoses; we worked all through the night doing this stuff and you constantly had a layer of frozen snow under your clothes. People were trudging around in a total white-out and everybody was white. It was a nightmare.

CLIP: SNOW STORM LEADING UP TO CAR CRASH.

SM: This is another one of those moments where the action completely changes the story around. In the final shot of this scene, the point of it was that a new life begins for someone.
GM: This is a complete turning point in the film. The high shot here seemed really appropriate, to have the car slide in and stop here. It was very late at night and everyone was really tired and exhausted and covered with snow. I always associate this shot with River Phoenix having died because the news came out that night.

CLIP: BABY WALKS FROM THE CAR IN THE SNOW.

GM: This is a shot that I was particularly happy with and felt it seemed to open out what was going to happen in the story, and I love what this guy did with the music: it was a mixture of human voice and pan pipes. This close-up of the child was shot in the studio, we just couldn't get it on the night so it's a mixture of studio and location here. I argued with my editor about this because he said it was the worst cut he had ever seen where that child starts walking off and we cut half way, but I absolutely feel it's right.
SM: There's very delicate cutting and writing between the tragic elements of this scene and the comic elements, because the mother is dead in the snow, and we save the revelation that she is dead until after the comedy happens inside.

CLIP: STEVE MARTIN FINDING CHILD IN HIS BED.

SM: Of course, there's a timing question here of how long I lay in the bed before I realize that there is a person in it with me.
GM: Getting this child to say 'Mummy' here was very hard, it was a major thing.
SM: Let's go down to the old pram scene, that's kinda fun. We've got a long list here and you know what, we are only on item three! This was a scene we essentially ad libbed. We made up the shots as we were out there.

CLIP: PRAM SCENE WITH 'LOCH LOMOND' SONG.

GM: There is a sequence with the child in the pram and I remember rushing around shooting it. I just set the camera up against a street with houses and we brought Steve down and asked him just to go from left to right with the pram.

I love this because you did something different every time and we had so much to choose from.

SM: Did we use the Perambulator song?

GM: No, we used 'Loch Lomond' instead.

GA: Why did you use 'Loch Lomond'?

GM: I went into Steve's trailer one day and he was just playing all this Scottish and Irish music.

I have to say that I was very homesick in Atlanta, Georgia. Things had been going on for a long time and I was a way from home. Putting this piece of music in actually meant quite a lot to me.

SM: It's a song I used to play on the banjo.

CLIP: BABY-FEEDING SCENE WITH RELUCTANT CHILD.

SM: This is the feeding scene. This is where the child was so reluctant to act and it worked so well for us. We wanted her not to open her mouth and that's exactly what she did. This is a moment when a man is transformed. He used to walk down the street with a sour look on his face every day and now he's doing this. This is why I find so much emotion in the scene; it's so great to be able to do comedy when you have a naturally emotional scene.

There's a moment there where the baby looks right into the camera! Let's go down to the balloon rescue. When I was a kid, I had this *Life Magazine* and there were pictures of people attaching weather balloons to themselves and running and leaping in the air, as a sport, like it was going to be a big thing. It looked like so much fun and I always remembered that image and finally got it into a movie. Once, I was doing the *Tonight Show* with Johnny Carson and he had just done an impression of Goofy the cartoon character. We go to the commercial and he leans over and says to me, 'You'll use everything you ever knew,'

A Simple Twist of Fate:
Steve Martin –
a man transformed.

and it was the wisest thing anyone ever said in show business because anything you learn now, if you're in show business, you'll use it.

GM: It is incredibly difficult to shoot a sequence with balloons. You can do a wide shot and see the balloon in the distance, or you can get a close-up, but on mid-shot it is not very interesting. You run out of ways of doing it, especially when you've got a steadicam operator running along and tripping over the turf.

CLIP: BALLOON SCENE.

GM: This was an idea of the storyboard artist. One day he did this drawing for me of a dusk shot with the house and the gold balloon with the light which I thought was a lovely idea.

SM: Beautiful shot and a lovely actress, Laura Linney.

GM: That hospital scene where she is crying – it was very late at night in this hospital, everyone was very tired and I forgot my golden rule of 'protect the actor'. A focus-puller, who we had had to sack because the focus was a problem, turned up this night very cheerily talking about post office workers. This was relevant because a post office worker who had recently been sacked turned up with a gun in his old post office and shot people. It was a slightly spooky atmosphere, everybody was making a lot of noise and I looked in the corner and I saw Laura. She was sitting there preparing herself for this terrible scene. I had broken my golden rule of protecting actors when they are preparing for a part, but when we turned over, she just turned on the waterworks. She is such a good actress.

This scene comes from *Silas Marner*, the idea of tying the child to the table with a piece of string so the child couldn't escape while he was working.

SM: In the book he has to figure out how to punish her for cutting the ribbon and he locks her in a dark coal bin, which doesn't quite work today, so I had to come up with something new.

CLIP: THE CHILD HAS ESCAPED AND ENDS UP ON LEDGE OF CLIFF AND STEVE MARTIN RESCUES HER WITH THE BALLOON.

SM: This child sitting on the ledge was never in any danger, she wasn't even near the ledge but the illusion that she is six inches from falling over this cliff is so effective. How did you get the shot of her, over her back into the lake? It looks like she is sitting on the ledge and what I said never happened.

GM: Recceing this scene became a really major operation; we must have done it ten times. It seems so simple when you look at it, you don't think it's very complex. However, it was very complex, almost every shot had to be designed; we had to work out how to do it. For example, the real cliff had about a 140-foot drop to the water in the quarry. What we did was to build a separate platform so that as you shoot down you don't see the true edge of the cliff. It was a false ledge with a space of about four or five feet where all these stunt guys were standing by. She was sitting on the false ledge and the shot coming towards her was a crane shot operated with a manual device which swoops the camera down towards her. When Steve grabs the child and swoops out of camera shot, that's done in a totally different place with just some rocks. We must have swung you in on a crane?

SM: Yes, I was strapped into something.

GM: We swung him in on a crane, he grabbed the child, there was a mattress below and the whole swing was only about five or six feet altogether. You rehearse these things over and over again with stunt people until you are confident that you can do them. The child was on pulleys. We were working with Touchstone and they could do some wonderful things with Paintbox [computer software package]; so we painted out all the bits of string all over the place. If we had problems, we brought these people in with the Paintbox techniques and got them to paint something out or paint something in. Where you see her feet walking across the ground, the ground there is not actually white, but we brought in lots of chalk dust and put it on to the rock. I always like to use repetitions in films and we put this chalk dust on the ground so that people would hopefully remember the feet walking in the snow as they walked towards the house.

CLIP: BALLOON RISES BEHIND THE GIRL ON THE CLIFF.

GM: The rising sun image was something that I really liked; the way the balloon comes up like the rising sun. The girl is strapped up of course and that is a false rock. The light on the water is supposed to plug into the idea of shining gold on everything. As the balloon descends, there is a kind of gold shining circle on the water. That is there because when we did the test with the balloons,

A Simple Twist of Fate: The rising sun image.

A Simple Twist of Fate: The balloon scene.

there was beautiful sunlight which reflected the balloon as it descended, like going into a gold coin, but on the day the sun didn't do the right things so Disney painted it in for us.

We should say a few things about something that I am very, very conscious of. When you make a film you get so excited about what you are doing and it becomes so important to you and everything has to be done right. You are always under pressure and it is very easy to make mistakes. You try to be as safe as you can. You have stunt organizers who test everything and tell you if it's safe. What I am going to tell you about was re-awakened on my new film, *Small Faces* when somebody leant on a window and glass fell down towards the young actor and the stuntman who got some glass in his hair. We shouted down, 'Are you all right?' but there was no reply for thirty seconds and I thought, 'I can't believe this has happened.' It is so easy for an accident to happen in a film and you have got to keep remembering that. In this case, the stunt guys tested and tested and tested this balloon and I was absolutely sure it was OK; not only that but the guy had a parachute which would break his fall. I was on a boat and there were frogmen standing by and we were watching the first take and the balloon came down to the water fine. It wasn't great, but it was acceptable so we said let's have a second take. It took half an hour to get the balloon in a damn vehicle and back up to the top. The second take occurred, but just before I had been talking to the stunt guy and saying 'Don't kick your legs about, just let yourself drop down.' The balloon came out and I heard on the walkie-talkie, 'I'm drifting back to the cliff' – wind had hit the balloon – then another walkie-talkie said, 'Oh my God he's got weights on.' That meant they had put weights on his body to bring him down. Not only that, and I didn't know this, but the stunt organizer had told him to do the second take without a parachute on, he was so confident it was OK. All of this happens and I watch this balloon floating back towards the cliff – it's a one hundred and forty foot drop to the water – and then pop, the balloon bursts, the guy falls and he hits two ledges on the way down. It was like a dream. We were helpless. The guy hit the water and the balloon flattened out on top of him and then everything was very still. It seemed like minutes while we were watching and waiting for the rescue boat. I didn't realize the frogmen were literally under the water, and when we looked at the rushes it was such an incredibly short amount of time it took for them to get the guy out of the water. I thought this man was dead but we got news saying he was conscious but he had hurt his back. It's something that's very hard to forget. The guy had damaged his back and went to hospital, but he will eventually be all right. It was very dramatic and something that makes you think very hard and remember that you are only making a film.

CLIP: FILM SPINS FORWARD.

SM: Let's look at the Gabriel Byrne/Laura Linney scene because they performed it so beautifully. The point of this scene is that this is where Gabriel reveals to Laura that the child is actually his and he had hidden it from her all these years. What had to happen was that Laura had to get from her anger to her resolution in the course of this two-minute scene. She did it so beautifully and some of the lines in the scene are directly from the book.

How does this compare to other Scene-by-Scenes that you've seen? You can do this at home you know. Find a celebrity and a film-maker, your own little VCR, bring them home and have your very own Scene-by-Scene – the Scene-by-Scene Home Game.

CLIP: GABRIEL–LAURA SCENE REVEALING CHILD'S PARENTHOOD.

GM: In a way these two are going to be the ones you hope don't get the child, but I like the way this was written. For me, working with actors creates an opportunity to make them sympathetic. I think you can understand what is going on with these two people, I feel you can understand that they have a problem too.

SM: The intent of the screenplay was not to present these two people as evil because they did have a legitimate reason. The power of drama is leaving that little bit of room for the bad guy to be understood.

GM: Every actor has a different way of working, a different sensitivity, and from my point of view as director what I have to do is understand that as best as I can. Each actor I go to, I have a certain amount of information and way of approaching them; you have to understand the actors who like a lot of takes and actors who only like one or two. Laura was somebody who could have gone on forever and ever, but I felt that in the scene in the hallway here when she was trying to speak to Gabriel, she got it in the first take and I knew she wasn't going to get any better than that. Even though we did three takes I knew that the first one was right. Previously, when they were in the house and she confronts him and says, 'You're the father of the child,' we must have gone to six or seven takes and each time all I did with her was say, 'OK Laura, I'd like you to try it in a more defeated way this time, or try it sad, or try it angry.' That seemed to be the best way of working with Laura because she did it one way and then she would switch her emotions up to another gear and in the end we chose the one where she was more angry. We just let her go through a whole range of ways of doing it.

Q: I have a small question. You have had a really diverse career, you have had comedy, you are a producer and a writer and I'm sure at some point you will be a director. Is there anything else that you want to do?

SM: I am writing plays now, but I don't want to be a director.

Q: Why are British directors so popular in Hollywood?

SM: We like to think of UK directors as artists, and that's what we want to be more than anything. There is a certain cachet to having a European or UK film director and we like their work.

GA: What's the difference in cultures in terms of directing?

SM: In general, I think that there is an artistry to film-making across the Atlantic. If you imagine this film made by a Hollywood director – not to put them down because they do great work – it would just be a different movie. This is the feel I wanted for it.

GA: What work of Gillies had you seen before?

SM: I saw *The Playboys* and *The Grass Arena*.

Q: When you wrote the script, how important did you feel it was to adhere to the book?

SM: I made one major structural change. I liked the tone of the book and I used a lot of the book. The structural change that I made was that in the book the discovery of the gold and the skeleton happens in the middle and then the rest of the book deals with the parents coming and asking if they can have the child back and the child deliberates and decides she would rather stay. I thought, for dramatic purposes and for film-making purposes, if I could somehow get that discovery of the gold and the skeleton at the end of the movie and have the plot turn on that, then I would have its solution.

GM: I'm going to show you something that again is to do with the facilities we have. This quarry was full of water and we needed to have the quarry empty. What's complicated about this isn't just the fact that we painted out the water and painted in an evacuated quarry, but the figures are also moving in the foreground. If the figures were not moving it would be easy to do, but they have to separate it and paint around the figures moving. It was quite a complicated job, but it was the kind of thing that by just being there on the lot at Disney you have these fantastic facilities. They take it away and when they bring it back a few days later, there is no water anymore, just an empty quarry.

CLIP: QUARRY.

GM: Those figures here actually overlap on to the paint job. This shot here was on top of a very high crane; as we came down, we made the camera mounted on top of the crane dissolve. It's the shot where the skeleton is revealed and the problem was this quarry in winter time had this incredibly freezing, blasting wind going through it and every time we did the shot with the crane, the camera shuddered. It would come up, go through the coins, go over the skull and as it came up my heart was in my mouth because every single time, the wind would hit it and it shuddered again. We must have gone to over thirty takes and this take is the best we have. Even this version is actually not as good as it could have been, but you put music on it and it's dramatic and people don't necessarily notice. If you look at it critically, it is not working the way it should work and the reason is we just couldn't beat the ferocity of the wind.

CLIP: CAMERA REVEALING COINS, SKELETON.

SM: I'll tell you one last thing about the writing process. I was working on the script and the movie ended with the discovery of the body. I gave the script to my now ex-wife to read and she read it and said, 'She should find her mother at the end.' I just said, 'Of course,' because it made such sense, and that's how writing is done because somebody will just go 'Hey, how about that . . .'

A Simple Twist of Fate: The skeleton.

Cinematography

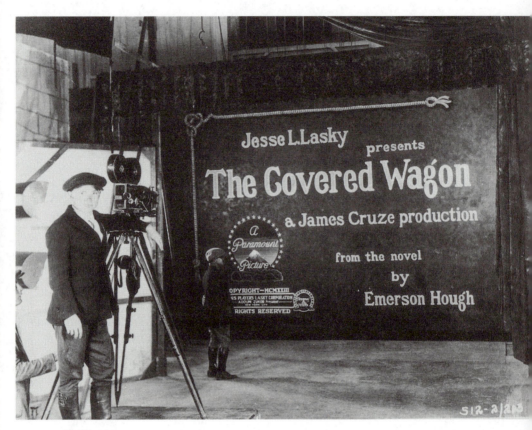

Karl Brown.

14 Karl Brown

Westward the Course of Empire

Surely there can't be anybody in the world who does not know all about covered wagons and what happens to the people on the long trek across the burning deserts and freezing mountains. The story has been told and retold so many hundreds of times that there is nothing left to add to what has become a cliché-infested narration, a tired and limping worn-out horse on its last legs.

But it must be remembered that *The Covered Wagon* was the great grand-daddy of all these swarms of imitators and that when it was produced all the old familiar places were new and fresh and vitally alive. And how many told and retold scenes there are: dumping precious old furniture to decrease the load to save the worn-out oxen; burying a dead pioneer and running the entire train over the grave to hide all traces from the Indians; the arrival of the news of gold in California, with half of the train going north towards Oregon, the other half south towards California which gave us a wonderful shot of the formerly straight wagon train splitting into a Y as every other wagon fell into line at the back of one train or the other. And of course, we had to have an attack by the Indians, partly because it was an expected necessity and partly because the damn fool – pardon me – the misguided heroine was just about to marry the dirty villain when an arrow caught her right above her right shoulder. It was a proverbial arrow, too, because otherwise our ill-starred love story would have ended right then and there.

Not that it would have mattered. By the time the wagon train had run into this Indian fight all attention had been captured by our two character men: Ernie Torrence as Jackson and Tully Marshall as Jim Bridger. Ah, but what performances those two men gave. I'd known Tully since he played a plotting villain in Griffith's *Intolerance*, and I didn't think he had it in him to be so authentic a Jim Bridger. Nor did I suspect that Ernie Torrence, who had played the part of a psychotic killer in *Tol'able David*, could be so utterly charming in his portrayal of Jackson, an old-time plainsman.

I first became aware of Ernie one day when I heard wonderful music coming from the tiny old upright piano in director Jim Cruze's tent. I went in to see who had turned that battered old wreck of a piano into a concert grand, and who should I see at the keyboard than the rough-bearded, mad-eyed Ernie Torrence. I watched his inspired hands caress the keyboard for a moment before I asked, 'What in the world are you playing?'

'This?' he asked. 'Oh, nothing. Just improvising. I do that sometimes. Relaxing.'

'Why in the world don't you publish some of this improvising, as you call it. It's wonderful.'

He nodded. 'Yes, I know. But the publishers don't. All they want is Amy Woodford Finden and they won't listen to anything else.' He stopped playing to explain, 'I spent years studying piano, harmony, theory and composition, and now look at me. A *movie* actor. But then, it's a living.'

'What have you written? I mean really, on paper?'

'Well, I set most of Shakespeare's sonnets to music. Know the eighteenth?'

'Sure. "Shall I compare thee to a summer's day . . ."'

'That's it. Here's how it goes.'

The way that man made the piano speak brings shivers to me whenever I recall it. I could have learned the sonnet word for word from his wonderfully expressive melodic line, supported by the northern harmonies of his native Scotland. Ernie was no longer a bearded, insane-eyed monster but an exquisite artist in every fibre of his being. No wonder he could play any part assigned to him, and no wonder that he proved to the hilt the old saying that there are no bad parts but only bad actors.

I would have been more than pleased to have heard Ernie's treatment of the rest of the sonnets, but Cruze came weaving in, followed by Baby Egan and her all-girl band with their accordians, which they insisted on calling stomach-Steinways, and when they began to cavort around the big round poker table in the middle of the tent, blaring out Cruze's current favourite song, 'On the Erie Canawl', I knew that my own little private concert was over. I looked at Ernie, questioningly. He shook his head. Pearls before swine . . .

I got to know the real Tully Marshall in quite another way. Tully wore steel-rimmed glasses with bows that went over his ears. For some reason a trade-rat had set its heart on owning those glasses. Not that it would steal them; being an honourable tradesman he would leave a few buttons or seeds or acorns in payment, hence the name, trade-rat.

Tully was in bed, half asleep, when he heard a scratching sound somewhere in his tent. He grabbed his flashlight and shot the beam towards the source of the sound only to catch the trade-rat in the very act of stealing his one and only pair of glasses from his table. He let out a yell and grabbed the glasses while the trade-rat prudently fled.

It was a close call. Tully would have been half blind without those glasses, so from then on he wore them to bed, only to be awakened by small claws creeping up his cheek. It was that damned trade-rat again, and this time Tully grabbed and all but caught the little rodent. Somehow this aroused the hunter instinct in him, and he schemed and he schemed until he finally hit upon using the glasses as bait. Tully placed his glasses out in the open and then hid behind his cot, a lethal shoe in hand, poised to destroy the trade-rat with one well-aimed fling.

He waited, shivering in the cold. But his patience was rewarded, for there was the trade-rat, creeping cautiously towards those coveted glasses. Just as he was about to grab the prize Tully threw his shoe with all his might. The trade-rat leaped to one side while the shoe hit the glasses, destroying one lens and both bows. Henceforth, Tully went around peering through one lens with the frame held in place by loops of white string tied around both ears, to the great merriment of our Indians, who promptly named him Chief One-Eye.

These Indians lived in their own lodges set in a double row near our replica of Fort Bridger. Each morning and evening a sort of town crier walked up and down the rows delivering all the news of the day, in Indian language, of course.

Our northern Indians, mostly Arapahos, had their own peculiar set of guide-lines by which they lived. The women did all the slaughtering and dressing of their own on-the-hoof beef supplies. All of our Indians were especially fond of the raw intestines, which they stripped reasonably clean of contents by drawing them between thumb and forefinger, after which they would take one end into their mouths and chew contentedly as they worked and no doubt pitying us poor whites because we had no appreciation of so delicious a delicacy.

As a result of this habit, the real Westerners customarily referred to the Indians as 'them gut-eating bastards'. This was all right with the Indians, because they did indeed love a meal of raw guts, while any child born into the tribe, regardless of paternity, increased the strength of the tribe, so the paternity of

The Covered Wagon: James Cruze examining a medal worn by the Indian Chief while Tim McCoy looks on.

the new arrival was never questioned, much less condemned. All was clear sailing until one disgusted old-timer of our own race made the mistake of calling them gut-eating savages.

Well, to be called savages was more than any Indian could accept, so the next thing we knew war-drums were banging and war-dances were being performed with all the wild yipping anyone could be so unfortunate as to hear. Our men loaded their .45s and their deer-guns and prepared to get themselves a few Indians if they made good their threat to a general massacre.

In the end, the Indians eventually quieted down, probably at the orders of Yellow Calf, their chief. Yellow Calf was a wise old man. He knew all about what had happened to Geronimo and he wanted nothing of that. In order to make further disturbances impossible, he sent for Cruze and offered to make him an honorary member of the tribe. Cruze accepted, made up his face with solid diagonal paint of red and yellow divided by a white line. The ceremony was enacted and Cruze became Chief Standing Bear, together with an eagle-feather war bonnet, and now the tribe could not possibly run afoul of a brother.

Yellow Calf came in for some unexpected publicity some time later. I made a close-up still of him, in profile, which came out very well indeed. This still went to the publicity department and from there to the artist who used it as a model for designing the Indian head of the buffalo nickel. So you never know, do you?

Another thing that I didn't know until it was too late was that the power wagons, designed by Frank Garbutt back in the Vine Street studio, had been fitted with a gas-saving device that fed all the unburned gas back from the crankcase into the carburettor. When the time came to take the night shots of the pioneers' camp, we lined up our sun-arcs and then started the power wagons, which promptly blew up when the accumulated gas in the crankcase exploded and shattered the oil-pan without which no internal combustion engine can run.

Fortunately, I had been trained in the use of magnesium flares for night shots by the great Billy Bitzer during my years with D.W. Griffith. So I stripped the big thirty-inch parabolic mirrors from the sun-arcs and instructed the grips how to feed the hot white flame of the burning magnesium into the focal point of the mirror. One try-out showed that it would work, but that it would be an awfully long throw from the camera to the encircled wagon train in an establishing long shot. Idea: why not hide the flares and the mirrors from the camera view behind or close to the many campfires? This was tried. It worked. The shot was a beauty, thanks to the imparted wisdom of my old master, Billy Bitzer himself.

Another case of instant improvisation came when we set up to cover the sequence of the cattle and wagons crossing the wide part of the lake which doubled for the River Platte. The oxen absolutely refused to enter the water. Here we were, with all three cameras on a barge, all set to be towed by a rope from the opposite shore to follow the crossing in close shots, but the steers went on strike and absolutely refused to budge one inch despite all the yelling and yipping of our stockhands.

Above and below:
The crossing.

Then, for no reason at all, the leading ox began to sniff and nudge the water with his nose. Impelled by a sudden hunch, I yelled 'Camera!' and all three of us, Lyman Broening, Doc Willat and myself, began to turn. The lead ox walked slowly and deliberately into the water, with all the others following. It was an exciting and thrilling sight to see all those ox-drawn wagons enter the water and to swim like so many water buffalo, with only their noses and eyes showing as they drew the wagons slowly across that stretch of water.

All of our lenses were set at infinity so there could be no reason to stop to focus. I nailed my camera and my attention to the lead wagon, piloted by Charlie Ogle and his picture-character wife, Ethel Wales. Charlie was cracking his whip and yelling, 'Keep swimming, you long-horned bastards! Keep swimming!' while Ethel chimed in with 'Amen, brother, Amen!'

Lyman and Willat were covering the rest of the wagons, sometimes flipping over six-inch lenses for close-up shots of the rocking wagons and the struggling oxen. Cruze was on the raft with us, but he might as well have been on the other side of the moon for all the influence he could have. The picture had taken the bit in its teeth and was running away with itself.

It's amazing how quickly you can run out of film on an all-important scene such as this. My new assistant, Bobby Pittack, a chunky blond from the northwest, was standing by with a fresh magazine with the film pulled out to the exact length for a loop. The second the film ran out I snatched open the door, slipped the film out of the gate, whipped the handle around to run the film into the uptake magazine and unscrewed the lock. Bobby grabbed the used magazine from the camera and handed me the new one. I seated it, slid the film into the gate and locked the sprockets while Bobby was screwing down the magazine lock on top. I slammed the door shut and began to turn. Elapsed time, not more than fifteen seconds at the outside, about as much time as it takes the trained mechanics at an auto race to change a wheel.

The oxen reached the other side of the lake and began to struggle painfully up the steep, slippery clay bank. They could get themselves up but they could not pull the heavy wagons out of the water. Cruze yelled, 'Cut!' and all cameras stopped. Cruze was grimly triumphant. The last big obstacle had been cleared and he could now do the rest of the picture with his left hand.

Scenarist Walter Woods* was similarly elated. He had been watching from the bank we had just reached and his corn-cob was puffing at accelerated speed as he pictured in his mind exactly which cut in which to get the smooth flow that his mind and his instinct demanded.

It took only moments to hitch teams of mules to the wagon-tongues to add power, out of camera range, to the exhausted oxen. Separate side-shots showed the wagons being pulled, rocking and threatening to turn over, up to the dry

---

* Karl Brown may well have seen Walter Woods at work in the cutting room. In those days, people could do a variety of jobs and he may well have been involved in the editing. However, the official editor on the film was Dorothy Arzner, who later became a director herself.

land. The crossing was completed and now we could go on to easier things.

Among these easier things was the meeting of Jackson (Ernie Torrence) and Jim Bridger (Tully Marshall) at Fort Bridger, an old and weather-cracked stockaded fort, thanks to the timbers brought from the Milhouse mine. Bridger had two Indian wives named Dang Yore Eyes and Dang Yore Hide. They were both fat and sloppy and lazy and very, very happy.

I made the mistake of referring to Indian women as squaws, only to be caught up instantly by Jim Cruze, who advised me earnestly, 'Don't you ever call any Indian woman a squaw. It's the most insulting thing you can do.'

'But why? That's what everybody else calls them, even in the books.'

He explained. In the Indian language the term squaw refers strictly to their characteristic female parts and it is as insultingly vulgar as it would be to call a white woman by the same term in the lowest of vulgar slang. The Indians put up with it because they think of the whites as the lowest of the low whose boorishness is abundantly proved by their refusal to eat raw guts and live grasshoppers, which are a crispy crunchy delicacy. The lesson sank in, mostly because Cruze's dark skin and extreme fondness for booze seemed to point to a certain amount of Indian blood in his veins, the same as in Will Rogers, who made no secret of his part-Cherokee ancestry.

Anyway, these two old cronies, Torrence and Marshall, had a glorious time boozing it up, to be topped by a shooting match in which these two boon companions endeavoured to prove their loyalty for one another by shooting a tin cup filled with whiskey from one another's heads.

And they did it, too, with a certain amount of help from old Pardner Jones, who sat beside the camera with Old Betsy across his lap, and who raised the heavy .50 calibre buffalo gun to his shoulder and shot immediately, without the slightest hesitation, tearing a hole through the tin cup, drilling dead centre with the whiskey flowing down the man's face.

When the shooting was over, and each had shot a tin cup from his friend's head, these two reeling drunks literally fell into one another's arms, to proclaim to all the world how great it was when a friend could trust a friend.

Another sequence showed our villain, played by Alan Hale, running his horse hell-bent across a deceptively green stretch of grassy land which contained a hidden bog. Into the bog they went and down went the horse, throwing Hale over its head and face down into the bog which began to sink under him like quicksand.

Jackson (Ernie Torrence) saw this from a distance. He did not recognize either the man or the horse so he spurred at a dead gallop to the edge of the bog, waded in, and grabbed the man by the hair. He turned the head around and wiped off enough muck to see who he was. He recognized Hale as the villain, made a wry face of disgust and thrust Hale back into the muck.

Jim Cruze laughed his cackling little laugh at the scene while Walter Woods's face was bright with smiles. Both of these men knew their audiences inside and out and they knew a winner when they saw it. But expert as they were at judging audience reactions, they could not forsee that the trivial little love story would be lost in the shuffle and that these two lovable scoundrels would steal the show, to be outdone only by the huge sweep of all those wagons rolling on towards destiny. That was what really counted; the sight of living history right before their eyes exactly as old grandpa had told it, years and years ago.

The final scene to be shot was a good old melodrama gimmick of the off-stage shot. Here we have Our Hero panning for gold and finding it in splendid quantities. And here we have that same villain, played by Alan Hale, sneaking up on Our Hero from behind, creeping from rock to rock to lift his rifle and take dead aim at Our Hero's back. His finger turns around the trigger, his eyes are filled with a fiendish lust for r-r-revenge, and it seems to be all up to Our Hero when bang!, the villain gets it right through the head as he staggers back to die all over the place, while we cut to good old lovable Ernie Torrence, with his wild eyes and his exploding whiskers, nestling his cheek against the butt of a still-smoking rifle.

Kerrigan, aroused by the shot, drops his pan with all its gold to rush up to Ernie to berate him for shooting a man in cold blood. Ernie hangs his head sheepishly and explains that he had been eating bacon and his finger got all greasy and sort of slipped. Everybody knew it was a lie, but they knew also that it was the whitest of lies, so he could never be blamed. And so, with the villain dead, we had no more story to tell, because when the villain dies, so does the story, although there have been examples of films running on and on after they've nothing to say, like a gossiping visitor hanging onto the doorknob to rattle on interminably while taking leave.

But we did no such thing. That was it, the end of the picture. We returned to Hollywood, where Cruze went into retirement while Walter Woods buried himself in the cutting room to assemble the picture exactly the way his ceiling told him it should be. I saw him there often, seated at the rewind with its twin reels, with lengths of film draped around his neck to be examined piece by piece and fitted, jigsaw fashion, into a flawless whole. Walter did not do the cementing. He fastened the cuts together with paper clips and wound them into the take-up reel, which would be joined later with the new Bell and Howell machine which did the job with flawless mechanical accuracy, almost without human hands – except for clamping the film into the pilot pins – drawing the knife which cut a clean diagonal cut to expose the film base (instead of trying to scrape the sticky gelatine off by hand, as before) and which welded the cut ends together with the help of a little solvent, usually amylacetate.

The finished first cut was wonderful. We shipped it to New York. The teletype clattered. The film was not finished at all. Take another hundred thousand and show what happened to the Oregon-bound people who split off from the train.

So we did. We took off, bag, baggage and oxen and wagons for Oregon, where everything was covered by a thick blanket of snow. A logging train, pulled by a Shay engine that had all its works on the outside, dragged us up the mountainside where we stopped at a clear open meadow with unbroken snow, which would pick up any and all tracks, and then we waited. And waited. And waited still more for the sun to come out. I kept watching the sky for any sign of a break. At last a patch of blue appeared, moving straight for the sun. I motioned to Cruze, who yelled through a megaphone, 'All right. Bring 'em on!'

And here came our wagon train, from out of the dark depths of the pine forest into the clear open land of Oregon, beginning with a clean sheet if ever I saw one. Just as the lead wagons were halfway across the open meadow the sun hit the wagons. Cruze yelled to tough old Elmer Ellsworth, who was playing the preacher, black hat, black frock coat and all, to get out and give thanks for arriving safe at journey's end.

Elmer got down, raised his hands imploringly to the heavens and cried out to the sun in his loudest voice, 'Keep shining, you son of a bitch! Keep shining!'

'Kneel!' yelled Cruze. 'Everybody kneel!' And they did, pouring out of their wagons to kneel with bowed heads, while Elmer Ellsworth, also kneeling, called back to his flock, 'Any of you bastards laugh and spoils this scene and I'll break your goddamn neck!'

And just at this moment, by the purest fluke of luck, a faint haze of fine snowflakes fell to pick up that ray of sunlight falling upon the praying people and their covered wagons like a benediction from heaven itself, a totally unlooked-for effect that was of heart-rending beauty. And with that we faded out, for the final ending of the picture.

(Extract taken from Karl Brown's *The Paramount Adventure* [unpublished], courtesy of Kevin Brownlow)

The wagons covered in snow.

Freddie Young with David Lean.

15 An Interest in Photography

Freddie Young interviewed by Frank Mannion

Freddie Young's career began almost eighty years ago in the seemingly primitive era of silent movies. By the time sound was introduced he was a cameraman of considerable experience, and by 1937 he had already used colour for the first time for the last reel of *Victoria the Great*. He has worked with Carol Reed, George Cukor, Michael Powell and John Ford. But his greatest collaboration was with David Lean for whom he shot *Lawrence of Arabia* (1962), *Doctor Zhivago* (1965) and *Ryan's Daughter* (1970), each wining him an Oscar for Best Cinematography. He was friends with some of the great innovative cameraman of the century, including Charlie Rosher (who co-photographed Murnau's *Sunrise*) and Gregg Toland (who photographed *Citizen Kane*).

As a young film lawyer working in London, I can only dream of producing or working on a movie of the scale and quality of *Lawrence of Arabia*. By reading everything I can about the making of that film one name recurs time and again – Freddie Young. I discover that he lives in retirement near Richmond and arrange to meet him.

I arrive at his home and his wife shows me into a sunny room decorated with Freddie's watercolours. Now in his nineties, he is in great health, is as mentally agile as ever and paints almost every day. He shows me letters written to him by David Lean as he leads me into his study where his OBE and his portrait by Snowdon hang on the wall. In a corner of another room his three Oscars and other awards stand discreetly. Out on the balcony Freddie sits down on one of those old movie deckchairs with his name on the back and I begin the interview . . .

Frank Mannion: When did you start in the film industry?
Freddie Young: I started in the film industry in 1917 at the Gaumont Studio in Shepherd's Bush. It was a big glass house so that the daylight could get in, because the film and the lenses were slow in those days. We had some lamps on the floor to help the daylight. It was a nuisance when the sun came in and out, because suddenly the set would go dark when a cloud came over. We

painted the glass black eventually and used more lights. But that's where I started in 1917. 'Course, the war was on. I was there for ten years. Then I went from the laboratory into the studio as an assistant cameraman. At the end of ten years I was taking second camera, projecting the rushes at the end of the day, driving the studio camera cars, taking the stills and developing and printing them, and editing the film at the end of it – editing and cutting the negative to match the print. So I was a pretty good all-rounder by that time. It really was quite a different sort of life in those days.

FM: I think you worked on H. G. Wells's *The First Man on the Moon*.

FY: Yes, I developed and printed that one in my first year in the film industry. I went to the length of toning and tinting parts of that for the première – the trade show, not for the general release. I had even coloured some frames. I had an engineer chap with an Emery wheel. Sparks would come from the Emery wheel and I tinted those sparks red and yellow and so on, you know, by hand with a little paintbrush, with dye. So I was always having a go at something around then.

FM: What inspired you to go into the film industry?

FY: Films were marvellous. I had a brother about eighteen months older than me. We would go to the cinema on Saturday morning and it was tuppence. In those days there were 240 pennies to the pound, so for two pennies we would see two films, three for three halfpennies or tuppence each, and we'd sit through two programmes – unless we were thrown out – which was a full-length feature, with a cartoon, a newsreel and a travelogue. A two-hour programme at least. I used to go to a swimming bath which was right opposite the glass house, the Gaumont Studio in Shepherd's Bush. It doesn't exist any more – it's been pulled down. One day I said it would be marvellous to get a job in films. So I went across and there was a little house right next to the studio, I knocked on the door, a chap opened it wearing a white coat and said, 'What can I do for you, young man?' I said I'd like a job in film. He asked what I was interested in. In those days I had one of those little Kodak Brownies, so I said, 'Well, I'm interested in photography,' and he said, 'Well, you can start tomorrow,' because the 1914–18 war was on and they were short of labour. So I started the next day, developing and printing. That's where I started in Gaumont.

FM: Do you remember your first day at work?

FY: Oh yes. I was terribly happy. I stayed there for ten years. It was very interesting. Developing baths – you had all these chemicals in a forty-gallon wooden tank and a frame to wind the film around, 180 feet of film. Then you'd stick it with a drawing pin, put it into the bath, wiggle it up and down and, with a red light, bring it out and look at it until you thought it was enough. Then you'd take it out, put it in a bath of hypo and fix it. Later on, of course, everything was done by time and temperature. In those days it was all done by judgement. This was 1917, and developing and printing was done by red light and amber light for positive, red light for negative, and it went on like this for quite a few years. Then at the end of ten years, a producer–director came to me and said, 'Freddie, I'd like you to photograph my next picture.'

FM: Was that Herbert Wilcox?

FY: No. It was another chap called Weatherall – F. A. Weatherall (whose previous job had been working in a laundry). So I said, 'Oh well, you know, I've
got a good job here. I've been here for five years,' and I was earning £5 a week,
which was good money in those days. '£5 a week?' he said, 'I'll pay you £20 a
week.' So I said, 'OK, you're on.' So I went to the boss who was Colonel
Broughhead and I gave him a week's notice. And he said, 'You're a bloody
fool, Freddie, because you'll be crawling back here for a job. This is the biggest
studio in England.' I never did go back there. So I did a picture called *Victory
– The Battle of the Somme* and it went very well, then I did two or three two-
reelers, then Herbert Wilcox signed me up. He had built a new studio in
Elstree. It was called the British Dominion Film Corporation and I was with
him for ten years, during which we had actors like Jack Buchanan, Ivor Nov-
ello and Anna Neagle. She was a chorus girl and he married her, made her a
film star.

**FM: During that time, sound and then colour was introduced. How much of a differ-
ence did the introduction of sound have from the point of view of the cameraman?**

FY: Do you remember a picture called *Blackmail* which Hitchcock did? He
was doing that film and another company was doing a picture called *White
Cargo* when sound came in. So after Hitchcock had completed *Blackmail*, he
decided to turn it into a talkie. So he reshot all the close-ups for sound and we
did the same with *White Cargo*. A German cameraman photographed it, but
he had gone back to Germany so they hired me to do the sound part of it. We
did it at British International Pictures at Elstree, a little corrugated-iron studio
lined with blankets and things; we went in with *White Cargo* and in about five
days we did all the close-ups for sound. For that reason we had these new
incandescent lights with bulbs instead of arc lights. It was very, very hot – all
the studio was padded with blankets; no doors or windows open. So it got very
hot. The last two days of shooting we shot all day and all night and all the next
day, because Hitchcock was coming to do *Blackmail* on the Monday morning
and we had to be out by then. The actors were lying about on the floor, sleep-
ing in between their takes, while I had to carry on. I was like a zombie.

FM: I think you had to put cameras in blimps.

FY: Oh yes, booths to start off with – a big box on wheels with a glass window,
all padded. You shut the door, it was soundproof and airproof! You'd shoot
1,000 feet and come out gasping for air. We'd shoot with five cameras in
booths for a whole 1,000 feet of film, with one microphone swinging about on
a long boom. Whoever was speaking, the mike went swinging to that person.
The mike was just out of the top of the picture, and you had to light for long
shots, medium shots and close ups all at the same time. All these five cameras
had a different lens to get all the long, medium and close shots. It was very
tricky to light all the different angles, so the lighting was rather flat. It was a
forerunner of television. I mean, television started off like that, using a lot of

cameras. They were only taking over from where we had left off. Eventually, they silenced the cameras. The blimps which we made were very heavy. They would weigh more than a hundredweight. They were insulated inside with cotton wool, rubber and lead.

FM: What impact did colour have?

FY: For instance, when Cinemascope came in with the wide screen, Panavision came out with a superior camera which was noiseless, had better lenses and so on. So when colour came in, you had three-strip Technicolor and it still seemed that, for a week or two, you would have to battle for a new technique for sound, or lighting for colour and so on. But they were all gradual developments that you took in your stride, really.

FM: Some of the early Technicolor films look a bit garish now.

FY: I prefer Eastmancolor. A lot of people thought Technicolor was good in its time. But it was a dye process and it's a bit garish compared to what you get on Eastmancolor.

FM: What is the difference?

FY: Eastmancolor is a single strip of film. It's more natural. Technicolor was three films, each dyed a different colour, then all blended together. It's still a dye process and therefore it hasn't got that natural colour that a single film has, whether it's AGFA or Fuji. Now, they're all good colour film.

FM: I think the last reel of *Victoria the Great* with Anna Neagle is in colour.

FY: We were nearly finished shooting the film when colour came in: Technicolor three-strip. You had three films running in your camera: one was the red record, one was the blue record, one was the yellow record. It was a very big camera and extremely heavy. Herbert Wilcox, a very go-ahead chap, decided to make the last reel in colour. At the end of ten years of working with me, Herbert said, 'The next film, Freddie, we're going to Hollywood.' So I said, 'Oh, they won't let me work there.' 'Oh yes they will. No problem, Freddie.' So we went to Hollywood.

FM: To do *Goodbye Mr Chips*?

FY: No, I did *Goodbye Mr Chips* in 1937. I went to Hollywood to do *Nurse Edith Cavell*. But for *Goodbye Mr Chips*, Herbert lent me to MGM because they had a studio here. They had just bought a new studio in Borehamwood. To do the film in Hollywood I had to leave America, then come back in on a work permit because I only had a visitor's permit. So I had to go to Mexico to a place called Collexico, a little town on the border. Well, I went back to Hollywood and started shooting the next day, and we did *Nurse Cavell* in, I think, about twelve weeks. At the end of that time the war was about to start and so I returned to England. When I got back I tried to get into the army. They said I was too old – I was about forty – so I did a picture with Carol Reed, *The Young Mr Pitt*. Then I went to Canada to do *49th Parallel*. We were there four months and we travelled all over Canada. I quite enjoyed it.

FM: It was a propaganda movie.

FY: Yes it was. Funnily enough, I owned a little hand camera called an IMO which was wound up by clockwork and took 100 feet of film. I took it with me and used it an awful lot, as Mickey Powell was always asking me to shoot something.

FM: What was the advantage of that camera?

FY: You could grab shots with it quickly. We weren't being paid out there. We were allowed a dollar a day which bought a packet of cigarettes and a glass of beer. The production manager was called 'Dollar-a-day Brown'.

FM: Did you admire Michael Powell as a director?

FY: Yes, he was all right. He was a cold-blooded chap, a very clever director, really, but he prided himself on his physical prowess, you know. When we were in Canada we went to Baffin Island which is off the Hudson Bay. It was a bare little island with no trees because it was winter – no trees, just rocks. One day we had a submarine which the art director had built in Canada in three sections; made of wood and canvas, you know. We had the Canadian Air Force come over and bomb it. To shoot this submarine being bombed we climbed a rocky hill. Mickey Powell had iron studs on his boots, like mountaineer's boots, and he went charging up there. We were staggering up carrying cameras and gear, you know, and every time Mickey would disappear around the corner, we'd get up there huffing and puffing, and he'd be further up saying, 'Come on.' I got fed up with this and said, 'Come back here, Mickey, we're shooting from here.' So he stared at me and then came down, because he knew I wouldn't go any further. So we shot it from there. That's the sort of thing I mean. Another scene we had to shoot involved the Nazis trying to escape over the border in a stolen plane. They are flying over Canada and run out of petrol over a lake. Our plane was made of canvas. One of the actors, Niall MacGinnis, cut a hole in the cabin and they all got out to swim to shore. The one who was flying 'the plane' was a rather fat actor named Raymond Lowell who couldn't swim much. He was almost drowning when Niall MacGinnis helped him to get ashore. I left my camera and went in to help. We got him on the shore and were pumping out water from him. He was in very bad condition and Mickey Powell stormed around saying, 'Don't forget we're English, chaps. Don't get too excited.' So the principal actor, the principal Nazi – I can't remember his name – said, 'You bloody bastard, Mickey. Here's a man nearly dying and you're telling us not to get excited.' Anyway, next day we got to Montreal and were shown the rushes. We had left the camera and sound running so we all saw this, 'You bloody bastard,' and so on. Mickey just sat there. We were all rolling around with laughter. Well, that's just to give you a feeling about Mickey Powell. I quite liked him. We did have our squabbles now and then.

FM: You did *The Young Mr Pitt* with Carol Reed. Did you respect him as a director?

FY: Oh yes. I have reservations about a lot of directors. I mean, Carol was a very good director. But on one film that he did – not the one I photographed – the cameraman told me they did twenty-two takes of a shot of a little boy running down the stairs.

FM: *The Fallen Idol*?

FY: Yes. Each time the little boy ran down the stairs, Carol would say, 'OK, let's do it again.' By the time he got to take twenty-two, the kid was fed up and exhausted, and ran his fingers down the banister like this, and Carol said, 'That's it. Print it.' I maintain that he would have been a much cleverer man if he had told the kid to do that in the first place and not wait until the kid did it voluntarily, you know what I mean? But I loved Carol, he was a nice chap. Of course he was an actor, you see. For instance, there's a story about Carol when we were shooting *The Young Mr Pitt*. After about a week shooting, George Black, the producer, came to me and said, 'Freddie, the rushes are lovely, we're very pleased with them, but, you know, we're three or four days behind schedule.' So I said, 'That's not my fault. You go and have a talk to Carol Reed about that. He's the one who controls the speed of shooting. He walks on down with Robert Donat yapping, yapping, yapping about how he's going to play the scene, with nothing happening for half an hour at a time.' So next day Carol said to me, 'George Black told me he was worried that we were getting behind schedule,' and I said, 'Yeah, I told him to see you. You're the bloke who controls the speed of the picture.' 'That's quite right, Freddie. Don't you worry, you carry on as you are. I'm very happy, Freddie. I have an infallible method with these blokes.' I said, 'What do you mean, "an infallible method"?' 'Oh, well, I burst into tears and say, "I can't sleep at night, I'm terribly worried about it,"' and the producer would pat him on the shoulder and say, 'Look, Carol, don't worry. Let me do the worrying,' because he was an actor before he became a director. So that was his infallible method. David Lean was just the same. He would completely ignore the producer who was saying we were behind schedule. We were two years on *Lawrence*.

FM: From what I have read about Sam Spiegel, he was an extraordinary character.

FY: Yes. He was a nice bloke, actually. They had a love/hate relationship, David and Sam. We were six months in the desert under canvas in Jordan and at the end of that time, Sam cabled David to tell him that he had to pull out of Jordan and move to Spain, which David was furious about. But Sam had run out of the money he had in Jordan. He had used it all up; he had a lot of frozen money and money you got on a film you couldn't take out of the country. So we had to go to Spain. I mean, David was absolutely furious about it. We were, I suppose, over a year in Spain, more than a year, and then finished up in Morocco. Sam had very good reasons. I mean, do you remember the blowing-up-of-the-train sequence? We wouldn't have been able to do that in Jordan. We had to lay two miles of railway track. We did that in Almeria on the sand dunes. We transported engines and carriages across Spain. You couldn't have done that in Jordan, you see. One of the reasons why we were slow in Jordan was because we had all these Bedouins who were there at the request of King Hussein. Of course, they didn't speak English and we didn't speak their language. So to get a scene with them on 2 or 300 camels, it took all morning to get them organized for one shot. And just when you were ready, one of them would get up to do a pee, another would get off to pray to Mecca. And you

Lawrence of Arabia: Peter O'Toole and the wrecked train.

couldn't tick them off because they weren't getting paid anything; they were just there at King Hussein's request. Anyway, all these sorts of things happened in making the film. Of course, some directors like David Lean, being so successful, spend a lot of money. A young director would have to make a picture in six weeks on a very limited budget with limited amounts of money to pay actors and that sort of thing, until they prove themselves.

FM: You did two pictures with Sam Spiegel: *Lawrence of Arabia* **and** *Nicholas and Alexandra*. **But David Lean wouldn't work with him again after** *Lawrence*. **He went straight to Carlo Ponti for** *Dr Zhivago*. **Did you have many dealings with Ponti?**

FY: Oh, we never saw him. He owned the rights and that's how he got the producer's credit. He had nothing to do with it. He never came to the set.

FM: And *Ryan's Daughter*?

FY: Anthony Havelock-Allen produced it. He had no control over David. With some directors like John Ford or David, the producer is at their mercy. He has no control at all. If there is a powerful producer with a young director making his first picture, the boot's on the other foot, you know. I remember doing a film with John Ford in England at Elstree. I think it was *Mogambo*. The producer's name was Sam Zimbalist, if I remember rightly, an American producer. Quite a nice chap. Of course, he came in one day when we were shooting and while he was on set, John Ford just sat in his chair. He had a patch over one eye and Sam Zimbalist said, 'John, you know, I'm very worried, we're about six days behind schedule.' John Ford looked up at him with one eye and stared at him for quite a long time – very embarrassing for the producer. John got hold of the script and he tore out six pages and said, 'Now we're ahead of schedule.' Obviously, he knew what he was doing. He probably knew he wasn't going to use those pages.

FM: Did John Ford ever look through the camera?

FY: John Ford would never look through a camera. Neither would George Cukor.

FM: What effect does that have?

FY: Well, directors like George Cukor would natter, natter, natter to the actors all the time. He would completely leave the photography to the cameraman. He wasn't interested in photography.

FM: What do you make of that?

FY: Look, would you hire a cameraman, a director of photography, who is not an expert? So why would the director want to query what he was doing? You might as well say the cameraman could query what the director is doing. 'George – you know, I don't really like the way you directed that scene.' You might just as well have it that way around. You see, a lot of directors, when they first come in, they want to assume all credit for the picture and the press tend to give the director most of the credit. In fact, making a film is a team effort. On *Lawrence of Arabia* we had about 200 people working on it, all of whom contributed in some way or another to making the film. What would the director do without them? You see, some of them behave like gods once they become directors.

FM: Did you come across any who behaved like gods?

FY: Well, I worked with a lot of first-time directors. I showed them how to do it. By the end of the film they thought they knew it all.

FM: You'd worked with David Lean before *Lawrence of Arabia*.

FY: He edited some of my pictures before he became a director.

FM: What about *Major Barbara*?

FY: I did about ten days' work on *Major Barbara* to help him out because he was in trouble with the camera. I was already engaged to do another film, so I had to leave him and I recommended Ronnie Neame to continue.

FM: How did you get to work on *Lawrence of Arabia*?

FY: Oh, Sam Spiegel rang me up and said, 'David Lean would like you to photograph *Lawrence of Arabia*.' So I did. I had to go out to Jordan and do a recce with him – go over all the places we were going to photograph. From there I had to go to Hollywood to choose all the Panavision equipment. It was going to be shot in 70mm. Robert Gottschalk, a very brilliant man, was President of Panavision. I chose the equipment knowing we were going to be hundreds of miles from anywhere in the desert. I had to have plenty of lenses, plenty of tracking equipment, plenty of dollies, cranes, everything you could think of, because once we were in the desert I knew I wouldn't be able to suddenly get extra equipment. When I was leaving for Hollywood David said, 'Freddie, I'd like to get a mirage in this film. I don't know how the hell we're going do it, but I want you to give it a bit of thought.' When I got to Hollywood, I went around with Gottschalk looking at all their equipment and I saw a long lens on the desk. I said, 'What lens is that, Robert?' And he said, 'Well, it's a 450mm or something.' So I said, 'Stick that in my bag.' 'I'm only too glad, Freddie – nobody uses it.' I had immediately got the idea that with that telephoto lens I'd get a close-up of the mirage. I mean, a mirage is always a mile away as you walk towards it. It's always the same distance away. But by putting on a long-focus

lens, you got right into all that wiggly stuff. So that's how we did the mirage.

FM: What a brilliant piece of thinking.

FY: It was a great introduction for Omar Sharif!

FM: When Spiegel called you up, did you realize what you were letting yourself in for?

FY: Oh no. I didn't know it was going to take two years. That's the way it went. Once a film is started, when you spend 1 or 2 million pounds, you can't just sack the director. You have to put up with it, don't you?

FM: What were the living conditions like in the desert?

FY: Oh, very nice. We had lovely tents – double-clad tents. We had baths in the evening. We had a servant, you know, who'd fill a hip bath with hot water, and have soap and a towel there ready for you at the end of the day. We had a big refrigeration truck for food which I stuck my film into at night to keep it cold. We had umbrellas for the cameras with wet towels over them. It was very healthy. It was about 110 degrees, but dry heat – you didn't sweat; it evaporated on you. It was a very healthy life, actually. No problem, except now and then we'd get a sandstorm. All you could do was cover yourself up and wait for the sand to disappear. To do a sandstorm (which we did in the film) you had to make it yourself with wind machines. In a real sandstorm you can't see anything; it's just like a thick fog.

FM: I think Nicolas Roeg did some second-unit work on *Lawrence of Arabia*.

FY: He did what we called the bloodbath, when Lawrence's men chase the Turkish army. We did the majority of it and left Nic Roeg to do a few more days because we went on to do something else. That often happened with David. Like on the storm sequence in *Ryan's Daughter*; we left Roy Stevens to complete it. In fact, David Lean put on the titles 'Roy "Storm Sequence" Stevens' and resented it afterwards. Yeah, he was sorry he did it because he had given Roy a bit of credit. It was sad, really.

FM: What were the hazards of shooting in the desert from a cameraman's point of view?

FY: We didn't see the rushes. We had a little plane, a twenty-seater plane, which would fly the rushes out to Aqaba, then a bigger plane would fly them to England where they all went back to Technicolor. And then we'd get a cable or a telephone call the following day to say the rushes were OK. So we didn't see any rushes at all for months.

FM: Were you worried?

FY: No. We were worried a couple of times when there was mottling on the rushes. They must have been affected by some radar in the air – you know, by a plane – but then they washed the negative again and it had just been a dirty bath. It hadn't been washed decently, so we didn't have to do any retakes at all. We had another scare when Technicolor called us to say there were fingerprints in the middle of the roll. You know, a 1,000-foot roll. So it must have been the clapper-loader loading the film. So I said, 'Don't be bloody ridiculous. The clapper-loader can't put his fingers in the middle of a 1,000-foot roll.' The manager at Technicolor stayed up all night, everyone wore white cotton gloves, and the next day there were still fingerprints on the rushes, just the same. So they thought it must have been the Kodak. The film was coming from Rochester in New York. They stayed up all night and it still had fingerprints on it. In the end they took the fingerprints of everybody connected with the process and it turned out to be the chap who did the perforating. The perforating was done in pitch blackness and, now and then, this fellow was simply touching it to see if the film was still travelling through all right in the darkness. It didn't cause any retakes. It didn't affect the film when it was edited.

FM: How many takes of the mirage scene did you do?

FY: Just one. That's a funny thing about David. In those days MGM, United Artists and Warner Bros. – all those people would demand what they called coverage. So when we were shooting in England we would make two prints: one for ourselves and one would go to Hollywood. The next day we would get a cable from Hollywood asking for more coverage, more close-ups. The reason for that was so they could edit the film after the director had had his cut; so the company could recut it the way they wanted. For instance, when *Lawrence* was finished it ran about four hours. The exhibitors don't like a picture that runs four hours; they want to have three showings, so they don't like a film to run longer than two hours. Sam Spiegel had certain bits cut out which were later put back in the restored version. David Lean and John Ford were the same. I worked with John Ford on a couple of pictures. They would shoot only what they wanted; no coverage at all. They would do a shot, then cut where they were going to edit it. I know that Herbert Wilcox engaged Merrill White, an American. He was called 'the Doctor' and if a film was not very good they would call Merrill White in and he would re-edit it. He would ask for some inserts to be done – some letters, close-ups – and he would reconstruct the whole film with little bits of extra film.

FM: You worked with Vincente Minnelli on *Lust for Life*. Did you have any discussions with him as to how the picture should look?

FY: No, no. The chief cameraman at MGM in Hollywood insisted that I use Ansco film because he said the yellows were better. The idea was to capture Van Gogh's yellow paint, to focus on the yellows. But Ansco was slower and, in my opinion, no better with yellows than Eastmancolor, but that was what we used because of the chief cameraman in Hollywood. Vincente didn't have a problem with that. MGM made wonderful transparencies of all Van Gogh's paintings which we were going to use on canvas. We were doing a scene in a wheat field in France and the crop was ripe. So MGM had to buy the field from the farmer because, you know, we had to run a bulldozer through the middle of the wheat field to make a road the same as it was in the painting; also we planted a big cherry tree in the foreground which weighed about two tonnes. We lined up with Kirk Douglas in the foreground with his canvas, and on each side we had property men with crows and they were all circling around Van Gogh's head as it was in the picture. So we got it all lined up exactly the same as the painting, Vince looked through the camera and said, 'Ah no, no, Freddie. No good. We have got to move the tree three feet to the right.' So I said, 'Don't be silly, Vince. For God's sake, we move the camera three inches to the left and it's exactly the same thing.' 'No, no. I want it moved.' 'Well,' I said, 'you won't get the shot today.' They had dug a big hole and with a crane lowered this two-tonne tree into it, using piano wires all around to hold the tree upright. So they had to dig another hole three feet to the right, pull the tree up with a crane and, of course, it fell over and broke a lot of the branches. A hell of a kerfuffle. All because silly Vince decided he wanted it moved three feet to the right. I was the cameraman and I knew much more about angles and things than he did; I knew that my moving the cameras three inches one way would have exactly the same effect. Those were the sorts of things you come across at various times with directors.

FM: In light of that, do you think that it's better if the director has some idea about the technique involved?

FY: No. David Lean was fine to work with because he would pat me on the back and support me in every possible way. He would look through the camera plenty of times, yes, but he wouldn't interfere. David would listen to everybody. I mean, he would ask the operator his opinion about a tracking shot or the focus puller about the focus. Sometimes he might say to a stagehand, 'What do you think, Joe?' Joe would say, 'I don't know, guv.' He was very affable in that way. He wrote me an eleven-page letter once. He was a very bad correspondent normally, but he wrote me an eleven-page letter begging me, pleading with me to do *Ryan's Daughter*. 'Will you do battle with me again, Freddie?' He also said, 'I'm afraid you're a marvellous cameraman, but maybe we'll get too complacent. Maybe we ought to think of some new ideas. So I'd like you to get much more involved in the writing of the script,' and it went on like this for eleven pages.

FM: *Dr Zhivago* was probably the most challenging of the three films you did with David.

FY: That's right. The four seasons are represented. I mean, when you consider that we shot it all in Spain and a lot of it in the summer, and with all that snow and ice you had to make it look cold. A lot of that was owing to my photography. I mean, we had people on the train wearing greatcoats with rock salt on their shoulders, and things like that, when it was boiling hot. The only thing we couldn't do was make their breath show.

FM: You have photographed some of the most beautiful actresses of our time . . .

FY: I don't have a method. Whatever I did, I did automatically. I mean, people ask, 'What is your method?' I don't have any method. I just do what I think is right at the time. In the old days a lot of actors used to say, 'This is the best side of my face, Freddie.'

FM: Is that rubbish?

FY: Of course it's rubbish. I mean, people have got to move about. You can't have the left side of their face towards the camera all the time. David was keen on photography himself and we would go around with a loaded truck full of autumn leaves so that if suddenly we were doing an autumn scene, he'd have all those leaves and we'd have a wind machine blowing them about. We would have snow machines and so on; everything was well thought out. We'd do things like, for instance, in the hospital scene, we had a plant in the foreground and blossoms falling off the tree – one would fall, then another one and, with the music, it sort of blended together, giving it a sad tone. I did several things in *Zhivago* which David praised me for – though not to anybody else. For instance, there's one scene where a doctor and an assistant doctor, played by Omar Sharif, prepare to operate on a woman. As the doctor is about to operate on the naked woman he sends Omar out; Omar goes down into what we called the machine room, because it was a dressmaker's establishment, he walks into this room and everything is trembling because there are trains running underneath. I mean, who would go to the trouble of having everything vibrating but David Lean? There is a window there and Omar can see one light showing a hand on the side of a chair. That was my idea, you see. As Omar sees it he moves towards it, looking at the hand. Suddenly the door opens at the other end of the room, Rod Steiger comes in with a lamp, and you see that it's Lara sitting in the chair and she's crying because her mother is being operated on upstairs. Rod Steiger is in love with Lara and he tries to seduce her, you remember, in the film. You see the door open, Rod Steiger coming in with a lamp and he stares at Omar Sharif, Omar sees him, they stare at each other, and Lara gets up weeping and throws her arms around Rod's neck. He takes her out and the door shuts and it goes dark again. Well, all that's a lighting effect and it was all my idea. David praised me for doing it. He wrote in a letter once: 'I always remember that lovely effect you did showing Lara's hand. I give you full credit for that.'

FM: It's a beautiful scene.

FY: There were lots of things like that. We planted daffodils in a greenhouse. We did that scene in Seria, the coldest part of Spain; we grew these daffodils and when they were coming to flower we took them out and planted them in a field and we iced up the windows. When Omar rubs the ice away you see a

Dr Zhivago: Rod Steiger.

Dr Zhivago: The crystallized window (Omar Sharif and Julie Christie).

flood of daffodils which had been planted that morning. That sort of thing. And then, for instance, we painted some of the windows with Epsom salt which crystallizes when it dries. But with the window that Omar looks through, we took the pane of glass out and put it in an ice-box until it was all frosted over, then stuck it back in. When Omar rubs the window, I've got a hair dryer over his hand, the ice melts and you see the daffodils. Every little thing like that, you see.

FM: You worked with Omar Sharif again on *The Tamarind Seed*, directed by Blake Edwards.

FY: Quite an enjoyable film. I had my wife and son out there with me in Barbados. Blake told me a funny story. We were talking one day about John Ford and he asked, 'Did you ever work with John Ford, Freddie?' I told him I'd made two pictures with John. He said, 'The first time I met John Ford I had just got out of the army and I got a job as a crowd-control man on a picture he was making in the Pacific. We were shooting on an island.' At the end of the day they were leaving the island to go back to the mainland and were making their way to the boats – they had a number of motor boats and things. John Ford was sitting under a palm tree and Blake went over to him and said, 'Excuse me, Mr Ford, for talking to you, but I've just come out of the army and I'm very fit. If you want any stunts done, I'm your man.' So John Ford, with his patch on his eye, stares at him a bit as he was inclined to do, then said, 'Climb this tree.' He was sitting under a palm tree about fifty feet high and Blake had just a pair of shorts on and nothing else. So he got on to the tree and climbed up; it was a rough bark so that by the time he got to the top his legs were all bleeding. He was puffing and blowing, he looked down and saw John Ford getting into a boat heading for the mainland. So he had to come down the tree – more scraping – and then he found they had left a little rowing boat for him. That's all that was left. Everybody had gone. In the blazing sun. He says, 'I always remember John Ford. He taught me a lesson.' Blake was telling this story about himself. Very Funny. Typical of John Ford. Sort of thing he would do.

FM: You were an innovative DP. For the storm scenes in *Ryan's Daughter* you invented the clear screen.

FY: I didn't invent it, I borrowed it. It was a ship's clear screen. They have a glass revolving at tremendous speed so that when a wave or rain hits it, it becomes like a sheet of water, like glass. I got my camera mechanic to put plastic around it and fit it about the camera.

FM: But it was your idea.

FY: Oh yes, but it was actually made by my camera mechanic.

FM: Did Samuelsons patent it?

FY: No, it wasn't patented. Nothing is patented. Everything is borrowed, really. You don't invent it – you just adapt it.

FM: Those storm scenes are spectacular.

FY: Yes, it had never been done before. You couldn't have done it without that clear screen, because the waves and the rain were pouring into the camera. We

Ryan's Daughter: The storm.

were all in wet suits and we had to chain the cameras to the rocks. That part of the coast was the nearest part of Ireland to America. So we would get a storm warning, it was a two-hour drive from Dingle, so we would get there at about eight o'clock in the morning, the storm would be raging and it would rage for about two hours and then die away. Then you would have to leave until the next storm warning. We went on like this for months and months. In fact, we went to South Africa in the end and left the second unit to continue with the storms.

FM: So are the storm scenes shot in Ireland or South Africa?

FY: All Ireland. But the main unit, David Lean and myself went to South Africa because by December it was pouring with rain in Ireland, we still had to complete the summer beach scenes and we had to find somewhere that was sunny. We went to South Africa and the rocks were so white we had to paint them black, so they'd look like the granite rocks in Ireland.

FM: Do you remember the bluebell scenes?

FY: That was the last scene we did in Ireland. We had to wait two or three days to get that sunny day with the bluebells and the horse. Sarah Miles and Christopher Jones came in on horseback, dismounted, and then it started to rain and the weather deteriorated. There was a little village house with a corrugated-iron roof and we put them in there, covered it with moss and put a sky backing all away around the wall, blue sky, and we had heating with arc lamps and so on, we had birds come in and the trees did very well because the atmosphere was warm and damp, you know, and we did the entire love scene in that village house.

FM: Is there any truth to the story that David Lean spent months filming cloud configurations?

FY: Well, that's rubbish. We might wait sometimes for an hour or two to get an

effect with the clouds scudding across and shadows of the clouds on the ground – things like that. Well, I was delighted to go along with that. But on other accounts I would say, 'David, we can shoot this – it's just as good as sunlight.' In fact, in Hollywood they are constantly putting gauzes on the sun to try to minimize the strong sunlight. It's boring, strong sunlight generally, but in Ireland it's very good because the sun is never very high; it's always lowish and you have lovely skies and lovely quality of light. If you go abroad like to South Africa, the sun is always dead overhead. For that reason, for an actress you shade the sunlight out and put an arc light on her.

FM: Do you remember shooting the beach scene with Robert Mitchum and Sarah Miles walking without any close-ups at all?

FY: Yes. I was in a box with a piece of plain glass in the front and I had Vaseline on the glass and rubbed it to get a diffused effect all around the figures. It's like a dream sequence. Remember, he's thinking he can see the captain walking along, they look in the water and they find this shell, and that triggers his imagination. So for that reason I used the glass with Vaseline.

FM: The film was not well received by the critics.

FY: No, it was just the critics. I think they take delight in doing this; in fact, they did the same on *Zhivago*.

FM: I remember you saying that *Ryan's Daughter* was shot on 70mm, but it could have been shot on 35mm. Why was that?

FY: The point was we did *Lawrence* in 70mm. We did *Zhivago* in 35mm and MGM blew the negative up to 70. I couldn't see the difference, myself – I thought the 35mm was just as good as the 70mm. The point was that *Ryan's Daughter*, for instance, was supposed to be a modest little film, but David Lean spent a year shooting it in Ireland and about five weeks in South Africa. One of the reasons why I think the critics slated *Ryan's Daughter* was that it was a very bad year in England for films. There was a tremendous number of people out of work and here was David Lean spending a year in Ireland on one picture. There was a lot of resentment about that. That was probably part of the reason why the critics gave it a slating, although they also gave a slating to *Zhivago* which, I think, made more money for David than all his other films put together.

FM: David Lean was going to film *Mutiny on the Bounty* in two parts. Were you involved in that?

FY: No. I might have been if he had made it. All that time he was having a lovely time travelling around, staying in Bora Bora– he sent me postcards. He used to take a long time in between films. I mean in his whole life he shot fifteen films. I've shot about 150–200 films.

FM: Were there any cinematographers whose work you admired in the 1930s or '40s?

FY: Oh yes. Gregg Toland, Lee Garmes and George Barnes. They were my heroes.

FM: Did you ever meet them?

FY: Oh yes, I met them. I became a member of the ASC. Charlie Rosher was the first Englishman to go to Hollywood and become a cameraman. He was a stills photographer in Bond Street, and he went to Hollywood and got a job there way back in the Mary Pickford picture days. That was Charlie Rosher and he finished up in his eighties. I met him when I went out. I went out there many times, you know, besides going out there in 1939. I went out there a number of times for MGM to have cameras converted to 3D or Cinemascope – things like that. I went out there for Cubby Broccoli when I did the James Bond picture *You Only Live Twice*. Cubby sent me out there with my wife and son, and we spent about three weeks in Hollywood. We had a lovely time just to see that the prints which came into the laboratory in Hollywood matched up with the Technicolor prints here.

FM: What films of Gregg Toland did you admire?

FY: Besides *Citizen Kane,* there were a number of others. He was a great photographer. In those days, black and white was beautiful, you know, before colour came in. I mean, a lot of my late pictures were comparable to Hollywood. I had Spencer Tracy in *Edward My Son*. I did a lot of films for MGM with famous actors and directors. I did about four pictures with Elizabeth Taylor – the first one when she was sixteen and the last one was in Russia, *The Blue Bird*, which was a rotten picture. George Cukor made some fine pictures in his time and that one wasn't his cup of tea at all.

FM: Were you constantly watching the work of Lee Garmes and Toland to see what they were up to and getting ideas from their films?

FY: Oh yes, but they had better lights, better equipment and they had regular jobs. They would be with a studio for years under contract – steady jobs. They all had motor cars in those days; we had to get to the studios by train and bus.

FM: There was a big celebration in your honour at Shepperton Studios for your ninetieth birthday. Jan de Bont, the director of *Speed* and cinematographer for Paul Verhoeven, said that you were the greatest influence on his work.

FY: Yes. I did a picture called *The Deadly Affair* with Sidney Lumet. It was for Warner Bros., I think. I can't remember which company it was now, but they

The Deadly Affair: Freddie Young with Sidney Lumet
(in patterned sweater) and James Mason (lower right corner).

wouldn't allow another picture to be made in black and white. Sidney Lumet rang me up from New York and said, 'Freddie, what can we do? You know the picture should be in black and white. It's a picture with criminals and colour will glamorize it. What can you do?' So I said that I would think about it. I exposed some film on a white card and gave it about 10 per cent exposure, then 15 per cent exposure, then 20 per cent exposure so that it veiled the film. It muted the colour, you see. It took the vividness out of the colour and that's the way we shot the film. Fox and Kodak were horrified about fogging all the film before photography, but they praised me at the end. There was a cameraman in Hollywood, a famous cameraman with several Oscars, who told me, 'I owe all my Oscars to you, Freddie, because I have pre-fogged all my pictures since that time.' This was several years ago.

FM: About fifteen years ago you said there was more artistry than ever before in photography. Do you still think so?

FY: Not right now, not at present. But in recent years we've had a lot more artistry. Nowadays they are doing fantastic things with computers. I mean, they can put another actor's head on somebody else's body. So if they use a street with television aerials they can edit out all the TV aerials after they have shot the scene. That's simple – they have been able to do that for years. They can do all sorts of things. If the road is macadamed, they can make it gravel. All sorts of things. I mean, you can photograph a film, but then they can alter a lot of what you've done. So, in a way, a lot of creativity has been taken away from the cameraman. Now looking back, and with the centenary of cinema arriving, I think I worked during the best years of the film industry.

Dr Zhivago.

16 From Vigo to the *Nouvelle Vague*: A Cameraman's Career

Michel Kelber interviewed by Kevin Macdonald

Michel Kelber.

Introduction

Michel Kelber's film career spanned sixty years, from the late 1920s to the late 1980s. During that period he was lighting cameraman on more than 140 features, mainly in France, but also in Spain and Germany. His working life spans the golden age of French cinema and his credits include many of the classics of that era. Over the years he has known and worked with nearly every major French director: Renoir, Vigo, Claire, Feyder, Duvivier and Cocteau, to name just the most obvious. Among the foreign or émigré directors he has collaborated with are Siodmak, Ophüls, Lumet, Parrish, Ray, Bardem and Pabst.

Born in Kiev in 1908, Kelber's family fled the Bolshevik Revolution in 1920 and settled in Paris. I met Michel Kelber at his apartment in Boulogne, just outside Paris, close to the recently closed Billancourt Studios. Our conversation ranged widely over his career, though there was obviously no way we could discuss all the directors he has worked with, let alone all the films.

Kevin Macdonald: You studied Architecture at the Beaux-Arts. How did you get involved in cinema?
Michel Kelber: I had wanted to be a painter but my mother disapproved and architecture seemed to be the next best thing. While I was at the Beaux-Arts I became interested in motion pictures. I had a couple of Russian friends who introduced me to a young cameraman from the same town as them, a place called Bialystok, which is now in Poland. This fellow's name was Boris Kaufman* and he was the younger brother of the famous film-maker Dziga Vertov. Boris already had a camera, which, as I recall, the French Communist Party had lent him at Vertov's request, so that he could shoot newsreel footage for the Russians. It was a little bit mysterious and I never quite knew what was going on.

Boris, my friends and I spent a lot of time talking together about the philosophy and theory of motion pictures. Then Boris showed me how to load his camera and how to stop; at the time they didn't have photo-electric cells and you had to set the exposure by eye. That was practically all he taught me, but it was enough! Shortly afterwards he shot a documentary for the Belgian director Henri Storck and he asked me to assist him, which I really found thrilling. Then one day Boris called me up and asked me to come round and meet his brother Vertov, who was in Paris visiting. Unfortunately, I don't remember much about him; I didn't realize how important he was. To me he was just Boris's elder brother! We spent the day visiting various French film people and then in the evening he showed us *The Man with the Movie Camera*. It was wonderful! Vertov's idea was to capture everyday life on film. He

---

* Boris Kaufman (1906–80) was the younger brother of Denis Kaufman (a.k.a. Dziga Vertov) and Mikhail Kaufman. He photographed all of Jean Vigo's films, and in later years in America worked predominantly with Elia Kazan and Sidney Lumet. He won an Oscar in 1954 for *On the Waterfront*, his first American feature.

thought that at every moment around us there are interesting things going on and the cameraman's talent is to get there at the right moment and shoot it. After seeing *The Man with the Movie Camera* I decided that being a cameraman was the best job in the world! It really influenced me.

KM: Did you continue to assist Boris?

MK: Yes, every now and then. I spent most of my time with him and when he was busy I sometimes used to replace him. So, for instance, I shot a documentary short for Henri Storck about a train line in the Pyrenees, on the Spanish border – a kind of publicity film for a new train line.

KM: Some time in 1929, Boris met Jean Vigo and they made *A Propos de Nice* together.

MK: Yes, they met through a well-known Communist film critic called Moussinac.* Vigo wanted to make a film and had an idea, Boris had a camera, and so they got together. Over the next few years I got to know Vigo quite well – he was a marvellous fellow, very funny. You never knew if he was being serious or whether he was joking.

KM: *A Propos de Nice* seems to have been very influenced by Vertov.

MK: Certainly – but at that time very few people had seen Vertov's work and so *A Propos de Nice* seemed highly original and was a big success. All the avant-garde people loved it, and Boris and Vigo became quite famous among cinephiles. It really seemed a wonderful film at the time and I admired Boris a lot. It was socialistic – about the rich people who do nothing but sit in the sun all day – but it was also very humorous.

KM: Do you think they were trying to be the French Vertovs?

MK: No, because right from the beginning what Vigo really wanted to do was feature films.

KM: Did you do any work on *A Propos de Nice*?

MK: No, I think I went into the cutting room a few times to help, that was all. But a year or so later, Vigo wanted to make a short documentary about Cochet,† a famous tennis player at the time, and he asked me to shoot it – I guess Boris must have been busy. There was a script, we went to see Cochet play and talked a lot about how we were going to do it, but in the end he couldn't raise the money. I tried to help him get finance from Paramount, where I was working at the time, but they didn't want it either. I still remember that the opening was to be a wide shot of a tennis court covered with hundreds of little naked babies – I think we calculated that we needed eight hundred babies to cover the court. This was the way Vigo's imagination worked: you have to be *born* a great tennis player! A few months later, Vigo managed to get the money to make a forty-five minute film called *Zéro de*

* Léon Moussinac (1890–1964) was a noted novelist and film critic. He was director of studies at the Film Institute of the University of Paris and administrator of the Cinémathèque Française. Among his books were a biography of Sergei Eisenstein and an early (1928) history of Soviet cinema.

† The project was known as *Cochet (ou Le Tennis)*, scenario by Jean Vigo and Charles Goldblatt, and was written in November/December 1931.

Conduite and I shot two or three days on that, when Boris was ill.

KM: Vigo's films seem to be bursting with original ideas and have an amazing energy about them. Was that obvious when you were working with him?

MK: Yes, he was very talented – you could feel it! He had ideas, personal ideas! By the time he made *Zéro de Conduite* I had spent some time working at the French Paramount Studios and I had seen all the directors there do the same thing: long shot, close-up, long shot, close-up . . . and we were always supposed to show the actors from the front – not in profile; not from the back – because the management wanted to show the public how the sound was perfectly synchronized with the lip movement. But Vigo – he was inventing a personal style, he really was – he broke all the rules and didn't feel obliged to follow anybody's advice.

Zéro de Conduite:
Michel Kelber's brother
Constantine.

KM: The most famous scene in *Zéro de Conduite* is the pillow fight in the dormitory, when the pillows burst open and there are feathers everywhere, and the film moves into slow motion. It has an unforgettable sense of joy and magic about it. Were you around when that was shot?

MK: No, I only shot some exteriors, but my half-brother, Constantine, had a part in the film as an actor – he's the little boy Bruel, with the Joan of Arc haircut. He was an impossible young fellow at the time and I took him to meet Vigo who liked him a lot and gave him a good part in the picture.*

KM: Did Boris collaborate very closely with Vigo? Do you think that he was largely responsible for the images?

MK: Yes, many of the visual ideas were Boris's. Vigo was much more interested in directing the actors; he left the technical stuff to Boris. Vigo might have had the basic idea of what he wanted, like in the feathers scene, but Boris knew how to achieve it. But what you have to realize about Boris is that he was always trying to justify philosophically every shot he made. He was theoretical about motion pictures – perhaps he got it from his brother – and he was always analysing the scene. I thought he overdid it a little. Sometimes you have to light things just to be correct, you can't always justify your lighting theoretically.

KM: *Zéro de Conduite* was hardly shown at the time because the censor banned it as 'revolutionary'. Do you think it was?

MK: A little bit. Vigo wanted to show that you ought to leave children alone and give them freedom instead of disciplining them. Vigo disliked authority intensely and the film was interpreted as anti-capitalistic – I guess he inherited those views from his father.† He never mentioned his father to me, but he told Boris, who later told me the whole story. But you know, he wasn't so radical. I remember that when he first earned some decent money, when he made *L'Atalante*, he rented an apartment in a nice part of town – on the rue Gazan, overlooking a park – a nice bourgeois neighbourhood! I think that if he lived longer he would've been as great a director as Renoir – maybe even better than Renoir.

KM: Let's get back to your career. You said earlier that at the time you worked on *Zéro de Conduite*, you were under contract to Paramount. How did this come about?

MK: An American camera-operator friend of mine got me a job for two or three days on a silent film, around 1929. My responsibility was to wind up a gramophone to provide the background music for a ballet scene. Anyway, that same friend – his name was Bill Willmart – called me a month or two later and told me that, if I wanted, he could get me a job in the camera department of a new American company that was opening up in France to produce sound films. Bill himself had decided that in this new era the place to be was the

---

* Kelber's half-brother was called Constantine Goldstein-Kelber and was known as Coco. He received a screen credit as Coco Goldstein.

† The Anarchist Miguel Almereyda, who died in mysterious circumstances while in police custody.

sound department and he had already got himself a job as a soundman with the same company. So I went to see them and they hired me immediately – at what seemed an enormous salary. I started to assist an American cameraman called Harry Stradling,* who later became very well known, but at the time was very inexperienced – which was good because I learned with him. I owe most of what I know to Harry and Boris.

Before long Paramount bought the company to produce foreign-language versions of its films. It was a real production line and the films were terrible – really terrible! We made each film in about twelve days. First everyone was shown the 'master' American version, then we would produce versions in five or six different languages: Swedish, Danish, German, French, Czech . . . There was a different cast and crew for each version, but of course there was only one set and it was used in shifts, twenty-four hours a day. For a long time I worked nights with Harry doing the Spanish versions. The sets never got aired and we'd arrive on a stuffy, hot stage and reset the lights for the way Harry wanted to light it.

KM: Was it your experience that in the early days of sound everything was subjugated to the microphone?

MK: Yes, for the first year or two the camera hardly moved. We had very primitive old Bell and Howell cameras which made an incredible racket and they built booths to put them in with a bit of optical glass at the front. There would be two cameramen and two cameras on each set – one for long shots, and one for medium shots and close-ups. The medium-shot/close-up booth had wheels on it, but they didn't usually move it – for the close-ups they just stuck on a long lens. You can imagine what it was like with two people – the assistant and the cameraman – stuck inside this little box. I was bent over double and there was hardly room to focus. And then, of course, nothing was ever right for sound! There was always a fly or something on the set!

KM: How many films did you do with Stradling?

MK: I really couldn't tell you. Working at Paramount we shot each picture in two weeks and moved straight on to another one. It was an assembly line. From time to time, when Harry wasn't working, I tried to get jobs with other cameramen – I believe you can learn something from everyone, even if they are not very good. I assisted Rudy Maté† for a while – who taught me a lot of little tricks, and also demonstrated how important it is to be diplomatically

---

* Harry Stradling (1902–70) first gained prominence for Jacques Feyder's *La Kermesse Héroïque* (1935) and subsequently photographed numerous important European and American productions, including: *Knight without Armour* (1937), *Pygmalion* (1938), *A Streetcar Named Desire* (1951), *Johnny Guitar* (1952), *My Fair Lady* (1964) and *Who's Afraid of Virginia Woolf?* (1966).

† Rudolph Maté (1898–1964) began his career as an assistant cameraman to Alexander Korda in Hungary and then apprenticed himself to the great German cameraman Karl Freund in Berlin. His films as director of photography include Carl Dreyer's *The Passion of Joan of Arc* (1928) and *Vampyr* (1932), Fritz Lang's *Liliom* (1935) and Lubitsch's *To Be or Not to Be*(1942). In the late 1940s he turned to direction, the most notable of his films being *D.O.A.*(1950).

Paramount Studio, France, 1931/2: Boris Kaufman is behind the camera
and Harry Stradling is to the right of the camera.

clever with the director and the stars – with Franz Planer,* Otto Heller,† and
with all the other American cameramen who worked at Paramount. In this
way I also met Eisenstein when he came to Paris. I turned up at his hotel to ask
if I could assist Tisse, his famous cameraman, and Eisenstein was very nice to
me. I was about twenty at the time and he was going to make a picture in
France. He had to go to Versailles so he took me with him in the car, we chat-
ted all the way there and all the way back! But he never made the film – I think
[Grigori] Alexandrov‡ did it instead.

I was really keen. I rented a small flat near the studio and made myself
available to work at any time. I never turned anything down. I ended up shooting most of the screen tests because the cameramen were too tired by the end

---

* Franz Planer (1894–1963) was a Czech portrait photographer who turned to cinema in the early 1920s. His
fluid camerawork was seen to best effect in the work of Max Ophüls, on films such as *Liebelei* (1932) and
Letter from an Unknown Woman (1948).
† Czech-born Otto Heller (1896–1970) worked in his native country, Germany and France before fleeing the
Continent for Britain in 1940. His films include Max Ophüls's *De Mayerling à Sarajevo* (1940), Alberto Cav-
alcanti's *They Made Me a Fugitive* (1947), Alexander McKendrick's *The Ladykillers* (1955) and Lewis
Gilbert's *Alfie* (1966).
‡ Initially Eisenstein's chief assistant, Grigori Alexandrov (1903–83). His first film as a director was *Romance
Sentimentale* (1930), made in France. He went on to direct a number of highly regarded features in Russia.

of the day and just wanted to go home. After a while I also got the opportunity – thanks to a young director called Claude Autant-Lara,* with whom I later made many features – to shoot a couple of shorts, which really gave me my first chance to play with lights.

KM: Are you still in contact with Autant-Lara? His reputation has suffered a lot in recent years.

MK: Yes, he is ninety-two or ninety-three now and he lives in the South of France, but every month we have a long telephone conversation. But you know, he used to be a socialist, a very radical, anti-militaristic man, and suddenly he became a fascist! He even made some anti-Semitic declarations in the press a few years ago.

KM: But you are still able to remain friends?

MK: Well, he really gave me my first chance so I couldn't get cross with him. I've told him what I think – he supports Le Pen now. He has always been a very excessive and passionate person, but when his wife was alive she calmed him down. Since her death he's just been surrounded by Le Pen people. He doesn't realize how silly it is. He's spoiling his career with his political declarations. They stripped him of his *Légion d'honneur*; he was member of the French Academy, but he's been sacked from there too. He wrote three volumes of memoirs in which he writes awfully about everyone – excluding me! I am the only person who he is nice about! – and they couldn't publish the last volume because both he and the publisher were sued several times over the first two.

KM: Apart from Autant-Lara, did you work with any other notable directors during your time at Paramount?

MK: It was really lousy work – the bottom of the rung, but obviously a lot of people got their first chance doing this sort of thing. Everyone working there was either on the way up or the way down. Paramount in America used to send us all the people they didn't want, but who they had on long contracts. It was a kind of penance. In this way I met Alexander Korda in about 1931. He was considered a bit of a has-been, and the Americans sent him over to do the French and German versions of a film by Harry D'Arast called *Laughter*. Harry Stradling and I worked on the French version. It was a kind of operetta and the lead was a very disagreeable actor called Henri Garad. Korda and Garad disliked each other terribly and one day Garad, who earned more money than anybody else, brought in a pile of old neckties which he wanted to sell for ten francs each. I bought a couple, but only had a 100-franc note on

---

* Claude Autant-Lara (b. 1903) spent many years working as an assistant and set decorator for René Clair and Marcel L'Herbier, and in 1930 went to Hollywood to direct French versions of films by Harry Langdon and Buster Keaton. He directed a few films before the Second World War, but his career as a front-rank director started in 1942 with *Le Mariage de Chiffron*. In 1946 he gained an international reputation with *Le Diable au Corps*. Subsequent films included: *Les Sept Péchés* (one episode – 1952); *Le Rouge et Noir* (1954); *Le Comte de Monte Cristo* (1961) and *Le Journal d'une Femme en Blanc* (1965). He was one of the 'old-school' directors most virulently attacked by François Truffaut and the *Nouvelle Vague*.

me. So, every fifteen minutes, after every take, Garad came over and asked me, 'Have you got my money yet?' After about an hour of this Korda lost his temper and yelled out: 'What the hell is this about change?' I told him I owed Garad twenty francs and so Korda took out twenty francs and paid for my ties. After that we became great friends!

I liked him very much. We talked a lot – I think he felt more comfortable with me because I was a fellow European and so many people at the studio were American. We discussed literature – the Russian classics and that kind of thing – and he seemed very cultivated. Something I really liked about Korda was that after lunch, at about one-thirty, he used to light a big cigar – a special cigar marked 'Alexander Korda' which he received personally from Havana, Cuba – and when the cigar was burned down to a certain length he would say, 'Well, we're done for the day!' no matter where we were in the schedule. The crew spent all afternoon watching the length of his cigar!

At the end of the picture Korda announced to me that he was leaving for England and said, 'You are too clever to be a cameraman, so why don't you come with me?' I thought it over for a while and decided that being a cameraman is a profession, while being Korda's assistant in England is not, and so I turned him down and stayed with Harry Stradling.

KM: Can you tell me a bit about how you used to light things in those days?
MK: At Paramount everything was lit in the most straightforward manner: flat light with not a shadow in sight. But then a cameraman called Gordon Pollock, who had worked with Chaplin in Hollywood, did a film at the studio and used a completely different style of lighting. He used lots of little lights – key lights – and achieved a very interesting, varied effect which really impressed me. I remember that one night I was in the projection room watching Pollock's rushes and the big head of the studio, a Mr Cain, came in with a cigar between his teeth. He said he'd never seen such bad lighting in his life and asked everyone else in the room what they thought. Of course, everyone said, 'Oh, yes, Mr Cain, it's lousy.' But I said that I liked it and everybody turned to look at me as though I were mad! They all expected him to fire me on the spot!

KM: Did this change the way that you and Harry lit things from then on?
MK: No, but then we saw a picture at one of the Saturday night screenings they had at the studio, a film from American Paramount called *City Streets* [1931], directed by Mamoulian with Gary Cooper and Sylvia Sidney, lit by an excellent cameraman called Lee Garmes. It had really interesting lighting: just direct lights, with nothing to fill it out, and lots of nice shadows. He used what they call 'key light' – one single light directed on the face, as you find on Marlene Dietrich in *Shanghai Express*. We liked it a lot, so Harry asked and received permission to try this kind of lighting on our next film. We spent a great deal of time discussing how we were going to achieve it. It was very interesting for me to be involved right from the beginning when nobody knew how to get these effects. So when I started getting jobs as a director of photography in 1933 I used this kind of lighting; it was new and people liked it. I was only

twenty-four or twenty-five, so I was a very promising young man. Actresses, in particular, liked my photography. You see, at that time actresses were not as young because most of them came from the theatre, and so there would be a forty-year-old playing an eighteen-year-old girl. This kind of lighting gave me the opportunity to make them look younger and they really appreciated it.

KM: Were you influenced by the Germans' so-called 'expressionist lighting'?

MK: Not really. I liked that kind of *Caligari*-influenced look, with long, deep shadows, but in France there weren't really opportunities to try it because we produced very few dramatic pictures at the time. It was mostly comedies and musicals.

KM: How long did you stay Stradling's assistant?

MK: Some time in 1931/32 Paramount closed the studio down and Harry decided to go back to America, but he couldn't find any work there. I was also unemployed for about six months, so what I did was find Harry a job in France: he came back and I was his assistant. Shortly afterwards, he became the most sought-after cameraman in the country.

KM: Your first credited feature film is *Incognito*, directed by Kurt Gerron.*

MK: In 1933, Paris suddenly became flooded with German-Jewish émigrés, among them lots of film people, and since I spoke a little German and was cheap, I was a natural choice! Gerron was a lovely man – big and fat and funny. He had been an important cabaret and film star in Germany – you probably remember him as the leader of the clown troupe in *The Blue Angel*. *Incognito* was a very commercial film, starring René St Cyr and Pierre Brasseur, and we shot it on the Riviera. Gerron would often fall asleep on set after a good lunch and we developed a code: I would squeeze him on the arm once if the take was good and twice if it was bad and, without opening his eyes, he would yell out: 'Let's try it again!' or, 'That's fine, next set-up, please!'

KM: Your next two films were directed by Jacques Tourneur and Kurt Bernhardt, another refugee, and then you made *Zou-Zou* with Marc Allegret, starring Josephine Baker and Jean Gabin. What was Baker like?

MK: When I signed my contract Josephine Baker had just married an Italian gentleman called Abbatino, who looked a bit like the actor Mischa Auer – a very thin, comical-looking person, with a drooping face and a pencil moustache. She was a lovely person and we always got on very well. She was very

---

* Kurt Gerron (1897–1944) was a popular musical and cabaret star in Weimar Berlin, often in partnership with the comedian Sigi Arno. He appeared in the original production of Brecht and Weil's *Threepenny Opera* (1928) and in many films including E. A. Dupont's *Varieté* (1925), Sternberg's *Der Blaue Engel* (1930) and Wilhelm Thiele's *Die Drei von der Tankstelle* (1931). He directed many short 'cabaret films' for Ufa and a number of successful German features. In exile from 1933, he directed several features in France and Holland, where he settled in 1936. He voiced the Dutch version of *Snow White and the Seven Dwarfs*. With the fall of Holland in 1940 he remained there as director of the Jewish theatre. In 1943 he was deported to Westerbork concentration camp and from there was sent to Theresienstadt, where he was forced to direct a Nazi propaganda film called *Der Führer Schenkt den Juden eine Stadt* (The Führer has Given the Jews a City). When the film was completed, Gerron and all other participants in the project were deported to Auschwitz.

Kurt Gerron et moi

Kelber on the set of *Incognito* with Kurt Gerron.

sweet and rather naive, with the mind of an eight-year-old girl and the most beautiful body I ever saw. She was not at all arrogant and never difficult to work with. However, every time she had a night of love with her new husband she would arrive on set terribly tired and I told her that she had to stop because I had no way of hiding it! After that she would come up to me on Saturday evenings, at the end of the week, and say very sweetly, 'Is it all right if I make love to my husband tonight?'

KM: And Gabin? This was one of his first screen roles.

MK: Gabin was never very easy to work with. Sometimes he'd be good-humoured, sometimes ill-humoured – you could never guess what he'd be like.

I worked with him quite a lot over the years and I'd even say that we became friends, but he was extremely capricious. I remember once in Nice I saw him come out of the Negresco saying, 'Ah, *merde*! The sun is shining!' and then the next day he came out and said, 'Ah, *merde*! It's raining!' Quite frequently he'd tell you, 'This is a profession for pricks!' And once I asked him, 'What's the matter, Jean? You're earning a fortune. Imagine if you were an electrician or an extra . . .' And he replied, 'I was happier when I was a workman at Citroën!' Another time, much later, a friend of mine asked me to show a couple of young Danish directors around the studios when a Gabin film was shooting. They asked me if they could watch him performing and I said that I'd have to ask the producer, which I did. But the producer said, 'Oh, no, I couldn't give you permission, ask the director.' So I asked the director, but he was too frightened to give permission either. Then I went to see Micheline, Gabin's dresser, an old woman who worked with him for ever. She said that she thought it would be OK, but that she'd better ask Gabin. Finally Gabin called over to me: 'This is ridiculous, Michel, can't you ask me directly? Of course your friends can watch – your friends are my friends.' So we waited at the edge of the set and Gabin kept getting his lines wrong – remember, this was towards the end of his career – and they started to put his lines on a blackboard. And suddenly he got mad and started to yell: 'How the hell do you expect me to work with a load of foreigners around!' And so we were thrown out of the studio!

But you know, he always put forward that tough-guy image, even though I think he was a bit of a coward. I remember a picture I did with him and Autant-

Lara when the two of them had a huge row. Autant-Lara – a little man with a fierce temper – slapped Gabin. I thought, oh my God, he's going to make mincemeat out of poor little Claude! But nothing happened, he didn't move.

KM: On *Zou-Zou*, Boris Kaufman has an additional photography credit. How did that come about?

MK: Both Boris and Vigo had a very difficult time after *Zéro de Conduite*. Gaumont looked on the film as a huge flop and neither of them could get any work. Both of their wives had just had babies, so it was particularly hard. Consequently, whenever I could, I helped Boris out by getting him a job as an operator or second-unit cameraman. I got him a job with Harry at Paramount for a while when I was away, then on *Zou-Zou* I needed a second cameraman and I got Boris in. After *L'Atalante*, things got better for him, although he never lived down the undeserved reputation of being 'slow and artistic', which he had got from being associated with Vigo.

KM: In 1937 you shot *Un Carnet de Bal* for Duvivier. That must have been an enormous honour for a cameraman who was still under thirty.

MK: Yes, I was terribly excited when I signed the contract. I turned down Carné's *Drôle de Drame* [*Bizarre, Bizarre*, 1937] to do it, because Duvivier had such a high reputation, and as you know the film was an enormous international success. But he turned out to be a most disagreeable man. I wanted to leave in the middle of the picture because I couldn't stand Duvivier any

Un Carnet de Bal.

more. Every night he'd come out of rushes swearing and cursing, but he never told us what he was upset about, if it was my photography or what. He never complimented anyone, he never told them they had done a good job, and on the set he made personal, really wounding remarks. Everyone was terrorized. I remember that he once told the star Marie-Bell, 'That expression is hopeless! You look like a cow who's just seen a train go by!' She burst into tears. Because of this pressure, my camera operator had a nervous breakdown in the middle of the picture and I said to myself, 'Why the hell should I put up with this?' So I went to the producer and told him I wanted to leave and, very reluctantly, he agreed, as long as I found a good replacement. I went to see Eugene Shuftan, the famous German cinematographer, who was out of work at the time, and he agreed to take over. I told him to come to the set that afternoon and I'd show him how I was lighting it and he could continue. That afternoon it was a really big ballroom scene with hundreds of extras in white dresses and dancers; I was lighting when suddenly Duvivier caught sight of Schuftan and said, 'Who the hell is this man?' They told him that it was Schuftan and Duvivier asked, 'What the hell is he doing here?' They said, 'Well, he is taking Kelber's place.' 'Why, is Kelber sick?' 'No, Kelber is not sick – he wants to leave.' Duvivier got really mad, yelling from the other side of the room, 'Kelber, come here!' Then he said to me, 'The only people who leave my pictures are the ones I fire – the others stay!' And he told Shuftan to get out. After that, however, he did become a little nicer.

After *Carnet de Bal* he offered me maybe ten different pictures over the years to do and I never wanted to work with him. Only twenty years later did I agree to do another one, *Pot-Bouille* [1957]. Before we started shooting we had lunch together and I told him what terrible memories I had of our last film and how, now that I was much older, I wouldn't put up with so much, so, I said to him, let's be friends and make this picture nicely.

KM: And had he changed?

MK: Yes, he was fine, but he was never exactly sympathetic, he never joked. If he smiled, it looked as though it would kill him. But he was a wonderful technician. For instance, on *Pot-Bouille* Gerarde Philipe, who was a great friend of mine and had the lead, told me that very few directors gave him such precise direction with so few words as Duvivier. He knew exactly what he wanted. He'd arrive on set, walk to a certain point and say, 'I want the camera here with a 35mm lens.' The only thing he did to annoy me on that second film – and I think he did it deliberately – was to tell me, after I'd lit the whole set, that he wanted it with a ceiling piece, so I'd have to redo the whole thing. He did that all the time. I think that he was a shy man and was disagreeable because of it. He was afraid of being nice to people.

KM: And after you turned down Carné's *Drôle de Drame*, didn't he ever offer you another film?

MK: He was mad at me for turning him down for his first film and told me, 'You'll never work with me again!' So even though his main writer, Jacques

Prévert, was a great friend of mine and tried to get me to work with him, he refused. Then about twenty-five years later, when he was perhaps the most famous director in France, I got a telephone call from his production manager with the message that he wanted to meet with a view to having me shoot his next film. I put on my Sunday suit, went to see him and we talked for about twenty minutes, then I went home. Then the telephone rang and it was the production manager: 'You're crazy!' he said to me. 'You had a green tie on!' And I said, 'So what?' and he told me, 'Carné hates the colour green and so you're not going to get the job!' Can you believe it?!

KM: Over the years you did a number of films with Robert Siodmak, the first being *Pieges* [*Personal Column*] in 1939. What can you tell me about him?

MK: He was an agreeable man to work with and extremely skilful. He never doubted, not for an instant. But he could have been a much better director if he had taken himself seriously. He was always joking and he had a very strong and very Jewish sense of irony about everything. He had really exciting ideas from time to time, but he didn't believe in himself enough.

KM: Both *Pieges* and another film you did in the same year, Bernard Deschamps' *Tempête sur Paris* [*Thunder over Paris*], starred Erich von Stroheim. What was your experience of him?

MK: Well, he was a terrible drunk – that's what I remember most! On both pictures he acted only in the morning, because after lunch he was so drunk that it was impossible to work with him. We once tried to bring him on in the afternoon and he tried to fight with the electricians! Impossible! He had a nice French mistress whom he used to beat terribly in his dressing room. I also remember that he had to be paid in cash every morning before he would start work – several thousand dollars a day.

KM: Did he tell the director how to do things?

MK: Yes, he always made a lot of suggestions, just to show, I suppose, that he was really a director himself too. Deschamps let him more or less direct himself, but Siodmak was not so easy. I myself once got into an argument with him during a scene in which he had to cry with [Maurice] Chevalier. At that time I'd just got some new, extremely sensitive stock and so I'd used very little light in the scene. He got angry and told me that it would be underexposed. 'With the light you've got nobody will see my tears,' he said. I guaranteed him that he'd be able to see them. Then he bet me a week's salary that we'd have to reshoot. Siodmak thought this was very amusing and encouraged him, saying that he'd be a witness to the wager. So the next day we went to the projection room and, of course, you could see everything perfectly and Siodmak said, 'OK, now pay him his week's salary.' Von Stroheim took out his cheque book and asked how much it was, but when Siodmak told him he refused to pay up. So I said, 'OK, we'll do something else. You put this money at the bar and whenever anyone from the film wants a drink you can pay for it.' He agreed, but I found out later that he left only half the amount of my salary!

KM: Was he very aloof from the crew and other actors?

MK: Well, he thought he was superior – and maybe he was!

KM: One thing I've noticed on your filmography is that you've worked on several films which are credited to one individual, but which were actually directed by somebody else. For instance, two films which were credited to Maurice Lehmann were actually shot by Autant-Lara. Another one, *Hercule* [1937] with Fernandel, was credited to Carlo Rim, but was actually directed by Alexander Esway.

MK: Yes, Carlo Rim used to appear on set occasionally, but Esway did everything, I don't know why. But I do recall a very funny coincidence from that film. Esway was a very sweet, friendly Hungarian man, and also extremely adroit as a director, but he'd received a bad wound in the war, during which he'd been a German aviator, and he had a completely false jaw bone and false teeth. Now the producer of the film had also been an aviator, on the French side, and one day these two started discussing the war and it transpired that on the day that Esway received his wound only one German plane had been hit – that piloted by Esway – and the man who had shot it down was the producer!

KM: Why was *L'Esclave Blanche* [1939] credited to Pabst's assistant, Marc Sorkin, when you say that Pabst himself directed it?

MK: Because Sorkin was the nephew of the man who financed the picture and he agreed to give the money only if Sorkin got the chance to direct. So Sorkin sat in the chair and said, 'All right, let's turn over!' and 'Cut!' and all the other work was done by Pabst. Sorkin couldn't really have directed it anyway, because he had a bad speech defect which meant he could hardly speak French, just a sort of broken Russian. Pabst agreed to do it, I'm sure, because he was very fond of money.

KM: Did you find him a good director? He has a particularly high reputation for working with actors.

MK: He was a brilliant director in every department. He gained a lot of respect on the set. When he arrived each morning suddenly everyone would go quiet, nobody spoke, and if somebody did, Pabst would just turn around and walk off again. He was one of the few directors who gave me direction about lighting – 'effect' lighting. He would tell me that I was still very young and had yet to learn how to give expression. 'Even if it's not a very nice shadow, it gives a very interesting effect which I can use for my scene': he'd say, things like that, and of course I didn't argue with him.

KM: Was he popular with the actors?

MK: No! He would direct the actors like a judge handing out a sentence. The actors weren't allowed to alter a thing. I remember one actor – a slightly crazy fellow – refused to do what Pabst wanted, so Pabst told him, 'OK, I'm just going to call the company lawyer and tell him that you are delaying the production, at a cost of so many thousand francs a minute, and he will sue you for it!' The actor got scared and did what he was told.

Pabst was a very mysterious character. I remember one day in 1939, just after I'd finished working with him on *Jeunes Filles en Détresse* [*Young Girls in Danger*], I went to the cinema in the middle of the afternoon – which is when I like it best because there are fewer people about, so you can concentrate better. Anyway, the lights went down and I felt a pair of hands grasp my shoulders from behind and it was Pabst. He told me not to turn around and said, 'Now I'm going to give you some advice. Just take your American visa, pack your stuff and leave France.' I said that I couldn't, that I had just signed on to do a picture with René Clair, and he said, 'I am just giving you advice. You do what you want. There is going to be a war.' And that was the last time I saw Pabst.

KM: Do you think he had inside information?

MK: You know, Pabst had a reputation for being a Communist, but he was extremely fond of money. When I was working with him he was an Austrian citizen, but hadn't lived there for ages, certainly not since the *Anschluss*. One day he appeared on the set terribly upset and told me that Hitler had passed a law that all Austrians now living outside Austria had to take a German passport, or they would have their property confiscated. Now, Pabst had several properties and bank accounts in Austria, and he explained to me in a terrible state of agitation that he had no choice but to take a German passport. As soon as he did so, of course, people started saying in the papers that he had become a Nazi, which was completely false. He was simply greedy and his greed led him into a terrible dilemma.

I can tell you something else about Pabst and politics. When he was making *Jeunes Filles* in Paris, he rented a very nice apartment on a six-month contract. After the film was finished the lease still had a few months to run, so he offered the flat, free of charge, to Lászlo Vajda, a young editor and the son of Lászlo Vajda, Senior, who wrote many of Pabst's finest films. Vajda was living there when the war started and I lost touch with him for a few years until we met up again in 1943 in Spain, where he had become a director. He told me then that while he had been living in Pabst's flat, quite a lot of mail arrived for the director, some of which he sent on and some of which he decided was not important and kept. Among the latter were a lot of philatelists' papers and sheets of stamps. Vajda thought this was a bit odd because he didn't think Pabst was a philatelist, but he didn't think much of it. Then one day a Hungarian friend of his was visiting, took a close look at the sheets of stamps and noticed lots of tiny pencil marks on them. He realized that it was some kind of code and after a while they worked out that it was instructions from the German Communist Party. This, at least, is what Vajda told me.

KM: At the outbreak of war, you were working with René Clair on a film called *Air Pur* [*Pure Air*]. Can you tell me about that project and your impressions of Clair in general?

MK: Clair was considered to be the greatest French director at that time. One day the phone rang and a voice said, 'This is René Clair.' I thought it was a joke and I asked him what he wanted. 'I saw the rushes of your most recent picture, *L'Esclave Blanche*, because I wanted to see the girl in it for my next film, and I really liked your photography. Would you like to work with me?' I was bowled over. I thought that this was really the high point of my career and

I don't think I have ever been so happy as I was at that time. So a few months later I started the picture, which was about young children. For about a month we shot exteriors in the South of France, then the war started and we all got mobilized. I had to drive all night to get to Paris with the roads full of cars and panicking people. After the war they tried to continue the picture, but all the boys already had moustaches!

KM: And what was your impression of Clair?

MK: To tell you the truth, I was a little bit disappointed in him. I never had the impression that he brought anything personal to his films. When I work with a really talented director, I expect him to bring something to the project that I don't expect, but with Clair I usually knew what he was going to do before he did it.

KM: In retrospect, his best films are from the late silent and the early sound periods – I'm thinking of *Un Chapeau de Paille D'Italie* [*The Italian Straw Hat*, 1927] and *Sous les Toits de Paris* [*Under the Roofs of Paris*, 1930].

MK: Yes, because then he was experimenting, he was unsure of what to do and he was trying to find a style. But later on, he seems to have stultified. I made another film with him after the war called *La Beauté du Diable* [*Beauty and the Devil*, 1950], with Gerard Philipe and Michel Simon, which was OK, but the script was very weak and he didn't seem to notice. Also, he didn't direct the actors – he left them to do what they wanted. He was so pleased to have good actors that he didn't want to upset them by giving them instructions! He struck me as rather helpless.

KM: Once you were demobilized, you were involved in two films in Switzerland.

MK: Yes. The first was called *L'Ecole des Femmes* and was to be directed by Max Ophüls, who was Jewish like myself and had taken the opportunity to get out of France. The real force behind the production was the actor/manager Louis Jouvet, who had come up with the idea of turning Molière's play into a film. All the actors came from his company, with himself and his lover Madeleine Ozeray taking the leads. However, as soon as I arrived in Geneva, where the production was based, I knew that something was wrong. There was a strange atmosphere, people were not talking to each other – that kind of thing. I met Ophüls very briefly on that first evening; he smiled a funny, nervous smile at me, but seemed quite indifferent, then Jouvet took me off to sit at a separate table for dinner. I realized that the production was completely split into two camps and Madeleine Ozeray never left her room. After dinner, Jouvet, who I knew quite well, took me walking all night through the empty streets of Geneva to explain what was going on. Ophüls, it transpired, was having an affair with Madeleine Ozeray and Jouvet was totally miserable. He told me then and there that he didn't want to make the picture but the thing dragged on for about two weeks. We did some tests and rehearsals and shot a few scenes – those without Jouvet, who refused to appear on set except for one scene that was an enormous tracking shot from the top to the bottom of a theatre. After a fortnight or so, Jouvet called a halt to the film and had to do a special tour of Switzerland with his company to pay the producer back.

When *L'Ecole des Femmes* collapsed I went back to France for a short time and then was lucky enough to get a contract shooting what was to be Jacques Feyder's last film, *Une Femme Disparait* [*Portrait of a Woman*, 1942] in Switzerland. It was a lovely shoot and we dragged it out for as long as possible because nobody wanted to go back to France. But all good things must come to an end, and I made my way to unoccupied France and rented an apartment in Juan les Pins.

KM: From 1942 you are credited on quite a lot of Spanish productions. How did you end up working there?

MK: That came about through a friend of Jacques Prévert, a film editor, who like myself was living on the Riviera. One day he bicycled over from Cannes to see me – there were no cars at that time. He said that a Spanish company had called him up to ask if he knew of any good cameramen staying in unoccupied France and he had recommended me. So I went back with him to the Hotel Majestic, where I received a call from a Spaniard who asked me if I was free and how much I charged. I told him that I was and mentioned my price in Swiss francs, since I didn't know the value of the peseta. He said, 'Fine, we'll send you a visa.' But I still had to get an exit permit from the French and this was not so easy, because they didn't generally allow demobbed officers to leave the country at that time in case they joined up with de Gaulle. However, fortunately for me, on the Ophüls film in Switzerland I had made friends with the associate producer, a man called Pierre de Herain who was Petain's stepson, and he managed to get me my papers.

KM: Spanish films at that time were quite primitive. You must have been considered quite a catch.

MK: Yes, all the more so because when I arrived in Madrid I realized that through some sort of accident they had miscalculated the exchange rate of the Swiss franc and they were paying me almost double what I had asked for. Naturally, when someone pays so much for a cameraman they think everything he does is absolutely marvellous! They even wrote about me in the newspapers: 'The Most Expensive Cameraman in Spain!' I won a Spanish film academy award for the photography of my first film and after that I had lots and lots of offers.

KM: The first film you worked on in Spain was called *Goyescas* [1942], directed by Benito Perojo. What can you tell me about it?

MK: Not much. The film itself wasn't memorable except that by Spanish standards it was very big budget and had a lot of stars in it. One thing I do remember very well, though. At that time Spain was in the German sphere of influence and so, of course, we were shooting on Agfa stock; Agfa even had a very good lab in Madrid. One day two big, blond, Aryan-looking gentlemen turned up on the set, both with Nazi party pins in their lapels. One was the head of Agfa in Spain and the other, the visiting General Director of the company from Berlin. They introduced themselves to me, shook hands and then, when the Spanish representative was talking to someone else, the General Director came up to me, put one of his hands over his lapel badge and – speaking in French – invited me to dinner that night. I said yes and he said that he'd send a car round to my hotel to pick me up. By the time the evening came I was really anxious. I imagined that maybe the Germans were going to kidnap me. When the car arrived I got in very suspiciously and spent the journey noting down the exact streets we took, in case I had to escape and find my way back to the hotel. Eventually, the car pulled up outside a nice restaurant and I went in to find the General Director there, alone, waiting for me in a private room. His name was Dr Thaitke, we started to talk and he told me that I was rather famous in Germany. I was puzzled by this comment and he explained that a few years before I had written a letter to Agfa explaining why I didn't like their stock and why I preferred to use Kodak. This was true. Then he told me that when they received my letter they had worked for six months to improve the quality of the stock – and so my name was very well known by everyone at Agfa. Then he asked me if I was satisfied with the improvements. I said that I was and that it was now an excellent stock. Somehow, during the meal it came out that I was Jewish and Dr Thaitke leaned closer to me and said, 'I'm going to speak very freely to you. In one of the occupied countries our troops found a print of *Gone with the Wind*. I saw this picture and I realized that a country which can produce a picture like this cannot lose a war. So we Germans have lost the war. I am telling you this and it is something I have not told even my wife. I just wanted to tell somebody that Germany has a madman as a leader and we are going to lose the war.' I was very touched by this – it meant a lot for someone like me to hear this from a German, particularly one so high up in an important company, and we parted as excellent friends. About ten years later I was in Berlin shooting a Robert Siodmak picture and I decided to look him up. I called up Agfa and asked to speak to him, but nobody seemed to know his name. Eventually I was put through to somebody who said, 'I'm sorry to tell you, but Dr Thaitke died during the Allied bombardment of Berlin in 1944.'

KM: After the war you worked with Cocteau on two occasions.

MK: Oh, yes, I liked him. On the first film I did with him – *Ruy Blas* – he was only meant to be the 'supervisor'. We had wonderful sets by Georges Wakhévitch* and the director was a nice man called Pierre Billon, but the personality of Cocteau was so strong that I recall Billon asking me from time to time, 'What the hell am I doing here?'

KM: Why was Cocteau only the supervisor, not the director?

MK: I don't know. All I know is that he didn't trust Billon as a director for Jean Marais, and Cocteau directed all the scenes with Marais himself.

KM: Did he direct the technicians too?

---

* Georges Wakhévitch (1907–84) was a Russian-born production designer who worked on numerous French and American productions including: Jean Renoir's *La Grande Illusion* (1937), *Bluebeard* (1951) and *King of Kings* (1961).

MK: Yes, he started to direct everybody. You know, at the beginning of every day he let Billon decide where to put the camera, which lens to use, and say, 'We'll do a tracking shot from here to here . . .' or whatever, but then Cocteau would start to change practically everything. I remember, for instance, one day we were in the projection room viewing rushes and they were quite nice, but suddenly Cocteau started to say to me: 'You see! You spoiled everything, I told you that I didn't want this and you did it!' And I didn't know what the trouble was, because he didn't tell me. I got out of the projection room and the producer came over to me and asked, 'What happened? What's the trouble?' And I said, 'I really don't know; everything looked fine to me.' Cocteau disappeared and went to the cutting room and appeared half an hour later, much happier, and told me that it was OK, he had fixed everything. Only later did I find out from the editor that Cocteau had been upset because in one particular shot Marais was shown from the wrong side! This was the kind of thing Cocteau spent his time worrying about! But he always had brilliant ideas – I liked him very much.

KM: Did Cocteau want anti-naturalistic lighting?

MK: No. Sometimes I would try to light something in a particular way, then decide that I didn't like it, and he would say, 'No, no, don't touch it, don't move the lights, because this light is exactly what I imagined.' I never argued

Les Parents Terribles: Jean Marais.

with him. I said, 'Of course, Jean, I'll leave the light.'

KM: Did he give you much specific direction?

MK: On *Les Parents Terrible* – which is a very nice picture, I think – he gave me direction. For instance, he told me, 'This room must be like an aquarium, only more greasy. They are just swimming in it. So I want you to give the impression that it is an aquarium.' On another occasion, speaking about Marais, he said, 'Don't light him, he's lit by his anger.' It was all very subjective and I would light according to what I felt was the best interpretation of his instructions – there is no light that is greasy; I decided that he meant he wanted a light without contrast, in the semi-darkness.

KM: Did you get on well?

MK: Yes, he liked me. Practically every Sunday I went to his house outside of Paris at Fountainbleau [actually Milly-la-Forêt], during the shooting of the picture and afterwards. I liked him because he was very interesting; you know, he was always inventing things. I remember that I went to Venice with him for *Ruy Blas*. Everywhere he went, there was a crowd of well-known French homosexuals tagging along with him. Whenever he went to the Café Florian, they had to join three tables together there were so many friends. And one day, I remember, when Marais had gone to the Lido with a young friend, I was walking through Venice doing a bit of exploring and I came across Marais's dog – he had a famous dog called Malouk – and I called him and he was very happy to find me. So there I was with Malouk when I met Cocteau and he asked me if I would offer him a coffee – you know, Cocteau hated to spend money! I said, 'Of course.' We went to the Florian, the two of us and the dog. Cocteau started to improvise wonderful things, witticisms and paradoxes, a bit like Oscar Wilde, and I said to myself, 'I must write this down when I get back to my hotel because it is so brilliant.' Shortly afterwards his friends started to drift in and every time somebody new arrived, Cocteau would say, 'As I said a couple of minutes ago to Kelber . . .!' And he repeated to everybody who came these exact same witticisms! And I thought they had been just for me! He was somehow frightened that something he said – something he invented – was going to be lost!

KM: Did Cocteau treat the cinema as an art form?

MK: Absolutely. He was a very interesting man – one of the most interesting men I ever knew – but the only thing which I could reproach him for was that, because he doubted this, he would try a little too hard. He didn't really need to go over the top, he was such a unique person, but sometimes he would overdo it . . . This is just my opinion, of course.

KM: Was he a pleasant man to work with?

MK: Always. Very pleasant. Cocteau always got what he wanted from people. He played the helpless man – saying something was too difficult for him, or that he didn't know how to do it – so that everyone would fall over themselves to help him. This was how he got what he wanted.

KM: Did he visualize things very clearly? Did he know what visual quality he wanted?

MK: Yes. In the beginning I wasn't very sure that I understood him, but then I

French Can-Can.

got used to him and would know what he meant. I was sorry that I couldn't go on working with him afterwards, but I had other contracts – one from René Clair. I think we had a very good rapport.

KM: In 1954 you finally worked with the man now considered by many to have been the finest French director, Jean Renoir, on *French Can-Can*. Had you ever had any dealings with him before that time?

MK: No. We had mutual friends, particularly the Préverts, but we never met until *French Can-Can*, and I think it was the producer, Deutschmeister, who recommended me for that.

KM: Do you agree with the generally high regard people have for his work?

MK: Yes, but he wasn't as talented as his father! I don't think all his films were that good. His best films were undoubtedly *La Regle de Jeu* and *La Grande Illusion*, but his early films – *Nana*, *La Chienne*, etc. – I don't like them; the lighting and the sets are terrible. I think they are the films of an amateur, although I know you're not supposed to say so.

KM: But what about *Une Partie de Campagne*?

MK: That is a masterpiece – but it was all shot in exteriors.

KM: And *Le Crime de Monsieur Lange*?

MK: Oh, wonderful! I loved it! You know, when I met Renoir, within the first ten minutes I felt he was a wonderful man. I really enjoyed working with him – I think everybody did, it was more like play than work – and when we finished he told me that he was sorry, but he had to use his nephew Claude on his next film. I met him only once again, when he was already quite old, in a studio restaurant, and he was so glad to see me that he started to cry. I was very moved, because there were big tears on his cheeks.

KM: Was this one of your first Technicolor films?

MK: No, I'd done two previously. My first was *Le Grand Jeu* [1953] by Robert Siodmak, with Gina Lollobrigida. Before we started shooting I spent a fortnight in London with Technicolor learning about the process. They took me round different sets at Pinewood and Shepperton so I could watch various cameramen and see how they used it: Otto Heller, Chris Challis, Jack Cardiff – who was perhaps the one who had the most sensitive and interesting approach to colour, although I learned from them all.

KM: The British had a very high reputation for Technicolor at the time.

MK: Yes, but they also had very good facilities. We were never given as many lights or as much time. In England they took their time, while in France they were always telling you to hurry up. The only Technicolor picture where I had all the facilities I wanted was *The Hunchback of Notre-Dame*, with Anthony Quinn and Lollobrigida.

KM: Did you find Technicolor cameras difficult to use?

MK: Not really, except for the enormous quantity of light needed. You know, the whole process was shrouded in secrecy. I had to have English assistants especially supplied by Technicolor, and when they were changing the magazine, or doing something inside the camera, I wasn't supposed to look – I had to turn my back to them.

KM: Did Renoir like shooting in colour?

MK: Yes. We did a lot of tests before starting. He was very interested in seeing the effect that certain colours of dresses, for instance, would have against certain colours of wall and furniture. Douy [the designer] and I spent a lot of time experimenting with him and it was very interesting.

KM: Did you observe how Renoir directed actors?

MK: He was wonderful with actors – even with Gabin, who was usually so difficult. He was very polite to them and to the whole crew. He didn't differentiate between people. He would use only the most polite expressions, as though he were at the court of Louis XIV. Even when an actor did something which was totally wrong, he would say, 'It's wonderful, really wonderful . . . Now, would you mind if we just tried doing it a little bit like this . . .?' I remember the only time he scolded me. Renoir had told an actor to do whatever he liked in a particular scene. When the actor had finished he asked me what I thought. I said it was a little vulgar and he got angry. He told me, 'But don't you understand that vulgarity is something that you need in your cooking – it adds taste!'

KM: What was your reaction to the *Nouvelle Vague*?

MK: I hated them. It was ridiculous. They wanted to create a revolution, invent a new kind of cinema and get rid of all the old 'classical' directors. But all they invented were things which we had known for years. Look at the 'mature' later films by Truffaut. When he finally made his most professional and 'complete' picture, *Le Dernier Métro* [1980], it was like a film by Henri Decoin!* After many years of despising and attacking classical cinema, he made something exactly like the worst of old French cinema.

KM: Did you work on any *Nouvelle Vague* films?

MK: Yes, I did a couple of ridiculous Eddie Constantine† pictures [*Incognito*, 1958, and *L'Empire de la Nuit*, 1962]. He liked my work a lot and put me under a personal contract, offering a lot of money. I regretted it ever afterwards because I missed some good pictures. Not that I disliked Eddie – he was a nice, extremely generous man – but as a film star he was a ridiculous figure.

KM: Did you object to the style of the *Nouvelle Vague*: the hand-held cameras, the real locations and naturalistic lighting?

MK: Of course not – if there is a reason for it. But too often there was no reason at all. Vigo had done the same things thirty years before in a context which made sense.

The *Nouvelle Vague* cameramen didn't know how to do anything other than light real locations. I had to teach several of them how to light in a studio. Once they understood, they were amazed by the possibility of having complete control by working in a studio – you can do whatever you want with the light – whereas on location, you are always restricted by what's available. And because the *Nouvelle Vague* had such a prejudice for real locations, we have no real studios left here in France: Boulogne, Joinville, Billancourt, they've all closed down. Now if you want to make a film in France requiring special craftsmen, plasterers or set builders, you have to get them in from Italy or Spain. It's a terrible shame.

KM: What do you think makes a good director of photography?

MK: I don't know. What makes a good painter? To start with, on a practical level, you have to be a diplomat and you have to know the capabilities of your crew, so if the director asks you, 'How long will it take you to light this set?' you can give him an exact answer. On an artistic level, being a director of photography is to build a kind of picture with light, to give tonal values to a set which has none. The cinema screen has two dimensions and it was my job to add a third dimension with shade, depth and light. Of course, I have worked with the best set designers, people like Andrejew, Wakhévitch, Trauner and Meerson, which is important for a cameraman – you can't do anything unless you've got a good set. For me, a set is like a black hole and if you switch on just one light you get a certain effect, a certain character comes out, and every light after that discovers something else. I spent my entire life doing this and I enjoyed it.

* Henri Decoin (1896–1969) was a competent and prolific director who churned out impersonal, unoriginal, but highly successful films from the early 1930s to the mid-1960s. He represented everything the New Wave affected to loathe about 'classical' French cinema.
† Eddie Constantine (1917–93) was an American singer who came to Paris in the late 1940s and befriended Edith Piaf, becoming a successful recording artist and then an actor. Throughout the 1950s and 1960s he was an enormous film star in France, usually playing the role of Lemmy Caution, a tough-talking, whiskey-guzzling, American private eye.

Vittorio Storaro with Bernardo Bertolucci (behind camera).

17 A Journey into Light

Vittorio Storaro in conversation with Ric Gentry

Perhaps Vittorio Storaro's stature is best summarized by his peers, fellow Academy Award-winning cinematographers. The late John Alcott once remarked that Storaro's *Reds* (1981) was 'the most beautifully textured film ever made'. Haskell Wexler described his work on *Agatha* (1978) as 'the pinnacle of what can be accomplished in our profession with light'. Owen Reizman called Storaro 'the standard of excellence'. And Robert Richardson: 'Storaro, well, he's the greatest.'

As he discusses here, Storaro prefers the term 'photography' for what he does which, as he points out, means 'to write with light'. Lush, lyric, sensuous, exquisitely illuminated, each of his films is the product of deep aesthetic premeditation and a mastery of film technology.

The youngest assistant, then the youngest camera operator in the history of the Italian film industry, a fully ranked cinematographer by the time he was twenty-six, Storaro's career took a dramatic turn when he met another burgeoning prodigy, Bernardo Bertolucci. Their subsequent films together include *The Spider's Stratagem* (1969), *The Conformist* (1970), *Last Tango in Paris* (1972), *1900* (1975), *La Luna* (1979), *The Last Emperor* (1987), *The Sheltering Sky* (1990) and *Little Buddha* (1994). 'Not even my marriage was as close as my relationship with Vittorio,' Bertolucci once said.

Storaro divides his career into three stages, each of the first two demarcated by exactly ten years: concern with the properties of light itself, then with the properties of colour, finally and currently with the four elements 'that caused life to begin' as Storaro puts it: earth, air, water and fire.

Equally important, artistic progress is synonymous with self-realization for Storaro. As sensitive, generous and altruistic ('the most kind-hearted person I ever met', Bertolucci says) as he is introspective and passionate about his work, Storaro discusses his background, the methods and aspirations for his major films and what culminated in something of a personal epiphany through photography.

A three-time Academy Award winner, for *Apocalypse Now* (1978), *Reds* and *The Last Emperor*, Storaro's work is further distinguished in *One From the Heart* (1982), *Wagner* (1982), *Ladyhawke* (1985), *Tucker: The Man and his Dream* (1988), *Dick Tracy* (1990, AA nomination), and the recent fifteen-part documentary of ancient Rome entitled *Roma: Imago Urbis* (1995), which took six years to complete.

Our conversation was in English.

Ric Gentry: I understand that it was your father who originally inspired you to consider a career as a cinematographer.

Vittorio Storaro: My father was a projectionist with a major Italian company [Lux Films in Rome]. He encouraged me into a school that taught photography. It was something my father always wanted to do, so he influenced one of his sons into photography as a continuation of his own ambitions. I was about fourteen years old when I began the school, so I really didn't have a good idea of what this was about. Much later, however, I discovered that photography allowed me to express myself.

Photography originally meant 'writing with light' and it is the term I prefer for what I do. It's writing with light in the sense that I am trying to express something within me: my sensibility, my cultural heritage, my formation of being. All along I've been trying to express what I really am through light. When I work on a film, I am trying to have a parallel story to the actual story so that through the light and colour you can feel and understand, consciously or unconsciously, much more clearly what the story is about.

Very early on I thought that light and only light was the primary thing. I was really concerned that the [technical] elements – the camera, the different lenses, the different film stocks, different developing processes, different printing techniques and even different projectors in different screening environments – were obstacles to expressing myself clearly, that these things were mediums that interfered with what I was trying to say in a story to the viewers.

But then (in the early 1960s) I had a very interesting experience working in the theatre. I was invited to do the lighting by director Luca Ronconi for *Kathchen von Heilbronn* by Kleist and later *Oreste* by Euripides. I stopped working in the cinema and worked in the theatre for one season. In the theatre, you don't have these elements that mediate the light between yourself and the audience. It was an opportunity to show an audience exactly what I was doing with light. That was one of my primary considerations in working in the theatre, that and the fact that the story of light had not changed in the theatre for a very long time.

But what I discovered was that my total expression wasn't merely through the light. The light was the primary thing. The light was the start. But the mediations, any single technical element that would affect the final positive image, that's what my expression was about. When I realized that, I really understood photography.

It was a very important discovery for me, because until then I was very concerned with light in its purity. Until then I almost wanted to do away with the mediations that transformed the light because I was so preoccupied with the nature of light, the reality of light, the wonder of light.

RG: You mentioned the 'parallel story' that you're trying to create in terms of imagery, which I presume complements the director's vision.

VS: Yes. I believe that making a film can be compared to conducting an opera. Whether the director is the author [of the screenplay] or not, he is still similar to the conductor. The orientation, the language, the style that we are going to seek for the story originates with him. As the photographer, I listen to what his feelings are, how he thinks about the material that is before us, what his concepts are. Then I read the script with all of this in mind, trying to visualize his concepts in terms of a style. Essentially I am trying to continue our dialogue. Then I suggest to him what can be done to augment his concepts in the photographic area, how the story can be represented in an emotional, symbolic, psychological and physical way. If we reach an agreement, if we really know in which direction we are going, I go back to the script and, scene by scene, apply to it, in a specific way, the general concept that we have established, the principle that guides me in lighting any single shot.

Of course, step by step, day by day, I can make changes, always trying to come closer to what the visual concept is. This visual concept will take you through the picture as it is made, as it evolves. Because you can see something along the way that is more attractive, more beautiful, but that is not right for the picture you've set out to make. You should always be very strong in resisting these distractions. You must select only the right kind of light, the right kind of tonality, the right kind of feeling, the right kind of colour for the story. This is my approach, and the work I do with the script has helped me a lot.

Also, from the moment I begin a picture, I also try to find stimulations, corroborations through external sources – such as images, museums, films, music, people, locations, costumes – that add to my feelings about the material. I am always trying to come closer to my original impressions of what is photographically needed.

RG: Let's discuss your first film as director of photography of *Giovenizza, Giovenizza* in 1968, directed by Franceso Rossi.

VS: That was an incredible time for me. It was like my first love. It was my first opportunity to really express myself in a complete way. I had done some short films before that, but a feature allows you to realize the fullness of what is inside of you.

Each picture I've done since then is an outgrowth of what was born on my first picture. I basically developed everything from that first expression. I think what is in my first film is like a fingerprint. After that, I tried to take every principle in that film and develop it. I tried to make it clearer, more evident, more refined.

Not all of it was always conscious in the beginning. Sometimes what I did was very intuitive. Sometimes I only understood it much later, often after more study and more research and after looking back at my work. I was actually

257

directing myself towards a goal of which I was only partially aware. But there were certain ideas and concepts I was very aware of even from the beginning.

RG: Let's discuss some of those concepts.

VS: It is basically the conflict between opposites. Day opposed to night, light opposed to shadow, natural opposed to artificial, male opposed to female, energy opposed to matter. These are things you can always recognize in my work: the dialectic between opposites, always two things in collision.

RG: This seems quite evident in *Giovinezza, Giovinezza*. While it's a story that recalls the Neo-Realist preoccupation of the Italian working class under Fascism, the high contrast of the black and white imagery diverges from the more even tones, the dependence on available light of the traditional Neo-Realist documentary style.

VS: Yes, it was a different look. I was trying to separate light from penumbra, with variform light and punctiform light, with sources of radiance both natural and artificial. I was also trying create a dialogue and conflict between the passage of the sun and moon to express a sense of continuous transition which would produce a ledger of feeling that corresponded with the changing light. So it was there in the beginning. Two things in contrast. Two different poles in conflict.

But you will also see in *Spider's Stratagem*, *The Conformist*, and *Last Tango in Paris*, that the shape of the lights I used was often round, a globe. It is the image of two halves put together. The circle has always been my symbol. Again, it was not always conscious.

RG: So in the beginning there was an effort to articulate polarities, yet there was also the suggestion of an ideal, a latent sense of balance and harmony.

VS: As I was saying, I really think my work is not only a professional story. It is my own story. There were always two things in collision, but when they are brought together there will be a balance, which is the level all things seek. It is the level I must seek. I am trying to reach an equilibrium with my life. The opposites should come together.

But everything evolved, especially in the transition from black and white to colour. There was the exploration of light, from my first movie until *Apocalypse Now*. From then until *The Last Emperor*, the exploration was into colour, 'the children of light', as Leonardo put it. After *Last Emperor* came the exploration of the elements – earth, air, water and fire – that caused life to begin. Each progression included what was discovered before, but I would become primarily concerned with the tenets of the next subject of exploration.

RG: Let's discuss your films with Bernardo Bertolucci and how you developed the look of those films, especially in terms of light, colour and theme.

VS: *Spider's Stratagem* was our first film together. When we were trying to get an idea about the style of the picture, he talked to me about the paintings of René Magritte. In a Magritte painting there is an open perspective. That is, the picture, the depth, does not end at a specific place. It is always through something, through a window, through a wall, through a tree, through a body, through a medium or a barrier.

On top of that, in speaking with Bernardo, my idea was to bring the naive,

The Spider's Stratagem.

the primitive painting into the style of the movie. The story was about a young man living in a town who was going to visit a part of the country where his father once lived for the first time. The idea was to show this little isolated place in the country as an enormous stage. The kind of colour we decided to use was very strong, very pure. But in the city where he came from, whether it was Rome or Milan or another, there are things which interfere with the true colour of things, like the red of the sunset, or the green of the grass. So it was an incredible and moving experience for him to see the pure colours of nature in the clear air. It was also impressive to hear without the noise of cars, televisions, humming refrigerators, machines, everything that is in the city. When you remove this camouflage of noise, you suddenly hear the leaves move, the wind blow, subtle things with new clarity that open up a new world to the senses. This kind of experience had to do with the whole style of the film.

So in other words, the city was always very monochromatic, but leaving the city for the country was a discovery, a kind of new emotion about to be experienced. This is what I proposed to Bernardo, and he went along with it.

During *The Conformist*, he did research by looking at films of that era in Italy (the late 1930s and early 1940s), and so eventually he was to construe a style for the film that we saw historically, and that we saw through the history of the Italian film industry. That's where we started, but I was also developing the concept that the Fascist period in Italy was very closed, very claustrophobic, without any communication between shadow and light. The line in pictorialization was very hard, but broken.

It was also a time when things were not completely real. It was the time of Mussolini, a dictatorship. The promises in that historical period were very great but their impact on reality was very small. One of the things we did was to shoot interiors on location, but outside the windows there would always be

The Conformist:
Historical style.

something artificial, never the reality of the setting itself. It would be a painted background, something unreal. We wanted to show the conflict between the reality that was stated and the reality that existed.

RG: The train sequence was a good example of that.

VS: Yes, we did the train sequence with rear screen projection. Once more, I applied the idea that the light was not reaching the shadows. They were not communicating and they were very separate. *The Conformist* is almost a black and white picture in the beginning. I was trying to get a very high contrast between light and shadow in the first part of the picture. But then, step by step, when the characters move out of Italy on the train to France, the style changes. I wanted to express a sense of freedom by letting the light go into the shadows, very gradually, and to have colours that were not in the film before. In Paris, you see the world very differently. The colours come up more and more. The idea of being caged, the claustrophobia of the light, is relaxed.

For *Spider's Stratagem*, the blue colour of the little town was suggested by the script itself. The eulogizing of the protagonist's father was based on something that had never really occurred. The murder of his father was accepted as part of their local history, but it had never happened the way they believed it did. So the idea was to show the little town as a stage, as the setting for a fiction. The way we shot the night was very close to a Magritte painting, in the sense that there was always light in the sky.

I took this idea of night once again and used it in *The Conformist*. I was using blue as the colour of the intellectual, as a display of intellectual freedom,

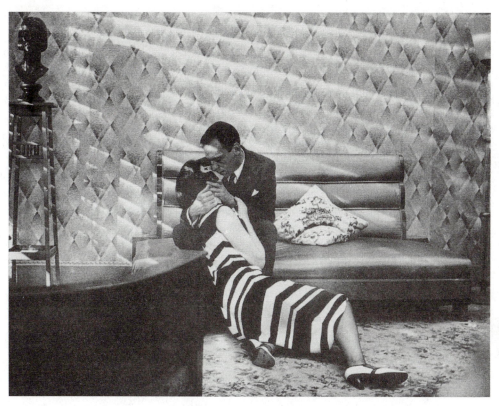

The Conformist: High contrast between shadow and light.

The Conformist: Light enters the shadows.

as the colour that returned to us in Paris or after the fall of Fascism. Also, whenever the character (Clerici, the protagonist) is going to make an admission about the killing of the young teacher when he was a boy, the light changes. It becomes more like the claustrophobic light in the beginning.

When we did *Last Tango in Paris*, one of the first impressions I had was how interesting the town was lit in the winter time. The sun in the sky was very low. So each shop, each apartment, everything was lit from within by artificial energy. The conflict between the natural energy and the artificial energy was very distinct, very significant, very dramatic. In that situation, the high wavelength of the artificial energy was approaching the yellow-orange and red of the colour spectrum. It told me what grade of Kelvin to use and which colours would approximate this tension between energies. Orange became the prominent colour, the colour of passion. The apartment where the two characters meet was to be orange. We incorporated the winter sun which, again, was very low, into our photography in the daytime. The sunlight gave us warm tones, and the colour of the artificial light beside the daylight hinted at the colour orange.

I was always trying to show these colours as part of the story, as a kind of vibration, a kind of conflict between male and female, between natural and artificial energy, between night and day, between positive and negative, between light and shadow. It was as if two different worlds were fighting to exist in the same place together.

Also about *Last Tango*: Bernardo and I discovered that there was an exhibition of the works of Francis Bacon in Paris while we were there. We went to see it. By this time we had already talked about the concept of the picture, the idea of pictorialization and the style. And what we saw when we arrived at the exhibition amazed us, because there were so many ideas in Bacon's paintings that were similar to what I had already discussed with Bernardo. From then on, we kept Bacon in our minds. What Bacon had to add to our point of view was that you often seemed to view (his subjects) through a sort of translucent material, which would split the image and blur the form. Often he used a kind of glass to do this, the glass of a kind of shower door or dull eyeglasses, anything that was breaking up the clarity of the line in the image.

RG: What about *1900*?

VS: *1900* was like the realization of everything Bernardo and I had done together until then, a culmination of the three films we'd made. But on top of what went before, we added one specific concept: the four seasons. The four seasons reflect the development of the human being, from a child, to the adolescent, to a man, to old age. With that in mind, Bertolucci plotted the history of this century for Italy. For childhood was summer; adolescence was autumn, when the rise of Fascism was approaching. Winter was the Fascist reign, the adult, the man. And spring was the old man when, after Fascism, the world as we knew it was ruined. We were trying to demarcate these four aspects of the human destiny according to this century's Italian history with the story we had. At the same time, Bernardo and I were revisiting our own past, together, our work up to this moment.

Last Tango in Paris: Marlon Brando and Maria Schneider.

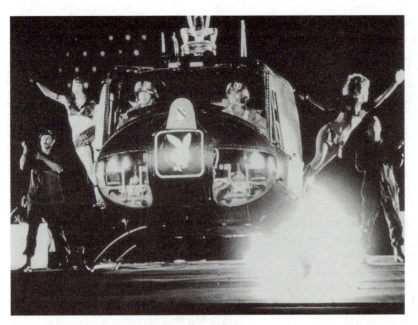

Apocalypse Now: The showgirls.

Apocalypse Now: Brando with Coppola.

RG: Let's discuss your visual strategy for *Apocalypse Now*. As I recall, natural and artificial were tensions you created in that film as well.

VS: Yes, that's right. The original idea was to depict the impact of one culture which had been superimposed over another culture. Here again, I was trying to show the conflict between natural energy and artificial energy. For example, the dark, shadowy jungle where natural energy reigns, in contrast to the American military base where big powerful generators and huge, probing lights provided the energy.

Another example is the USO scene with the showgirls on stage. We framed them in big spotlights in a way that conflicted with what the eye expected to see against the background of the jungle. It wasn't glaring. It was just a suggestion, something that slightly disturbed your perception. Often, we tried to use colour and light to create the mood of conflict in subtle ways. The way that a red fire in a camp contrasted to the blue or black gun in the foreground, or the way the colour of a weapon stood out against the sunset, or how an American soldier with a blackened face was seen against the green jungle or the blue sky. All of that helped to create the mood and tell the story. Even the surfing sequence indicated a collision of energies, that something was askew, out of context, unnatural to that environment.

The Americans, as depicted in the film, were out of place; where people live and think in a different way, a more primitive way. They were bringing their culture with them, which was also their mentality, so they didn't understand the people they were at war with. If they understood this culture, they would have thought differently about the war fought in this land. This was the tragedy of the story, really.

The Marlon Brando character represents the dark side of civilization, the subconscious, or the truth that comes out of darkness. He couldn't be portrayed in an ordinary way. He had to appear as something of an idol. You can reveal patterns and moods against black that aren't possible in other ways. When I pictured these scenes before we shot them, I always saw Brando in the shadows or partially lit. Coppola gave me the opportunity to express this idea. We also tried to use the changing light and the seasons to our advantage to establish a continuum of time. But it was very difficult work. Very, very difficult.

Apocalypse Now was the sum of my work up to that time. It was everything I did in the moment of my past, and everything I could do in the moment of my present. It was through Conrad, in part, and the title of his novella *Heart of Darkness* on which Coppola's film is based, that I began to re-evaluate everything that went before. The concept of 'darkness' itself was revealing. It is where light ends. But I also realized that darkness is not the absence of light but the antithesis of light. In other words, they are aspects of each other. Light and dark are not only metaphors but the means by which we perceive and understand.

But after [*Apocalypse Now*], I was so exhausted, so terribly exhausted. The world was so empty because I'd given everything I could up to that time. It was very difficult to begin again. There was nothing to give me an idea, or inspire me, or replenish me. I refused several pictures because I felt that I had nothing to offer them. My battery needed to be recharged again.

So as I did once before, when I was very young and the Italian film industry came to a halt – I retreated into my books and all the knowledge I had gained before when I was in school. I became a student all over again. I went through all the books I have at home, and books in the libraries, and in particular I began to research the meaning of colour and the philosophy of colour. And as I went along, I began to evaluate my films and, step by step, I became more conscious of why one story was this colour or that colour; why I did *The Conformist* in blue, why I did *Last Tango* in orange, why *1900* is the way that it is. And progressively, everything became clear to me. It was a kind of visitation into myself – who I was, who I am, who I will be.

It was after this that I began the second journey. *La Luna* was the first film I did with a more conscious idea of the meaning, the symbolism of colour. *La Luna* was very clearly a movie designed around psychoanalysis. And in psychoanalysis, luna, the moon, is the symbol of the mother. I tried to find colours for the mother that would identify her with that. Also, I tried to give the characters depth, volume, by encircling them in light. I tried to give them all a dense, strong physical presence.

RG: As with sculpture, perhaps?

VS: In a sense, yes, but not so that they were marmoreal. Only that they were massive in this presence, in their occupation of space, almost as if there was an attraction or resistance as in planetary bodies that are very strong, very

La Luna.

One from the Heart: 'The environment works to ease restraint.'

defined, very separate yet somewhat interdependent, affecting each other, almost irresistibly, as with gravitation.

But primarily I wanted to work with the symbolism of colour to arrange the emotions in colours. Everything represents something specific in an emotional sense, according to colour in psychoanalysis. When you dream, something is dramatized by the colours, something perhaps additional or separate or complementary to what is happening in the dream. In *La Luna*, I used this idea of what is symbolized by colours to correspond with the emotions of the characters.

In *One From the Heart* I went to the physiology of colour, in the sense that I wanted to show the kind of reaction the body itself has in the presence of one colour instead of another. Part of human development, through the centuries, has been the way we respond physically to colour. It is not something new. Scientists have known this for a very long time. When the body is exposed to light, you are likely to be active, and you want to be active. When the body is exposed to darkness, the body tends to want to relax or rest. Working conditions are often improved when the colour of the walls and the environment are conducive to work. People could not work very well if the walls were black, especially if it is daylight outside. The contrast is too great. It is also hard to work if the walls are red, because red excites and distracts from the work. Scientists have determined that a red environment can make your heart beat faster and your pulse go up.

When Francis Coppola and I went to Las Vegas to prepare *One From the Heart*, I was amazed at the incredible amount of light that pulses in the casinos and the hotels. It is all artificial light. You cannot see outside. The windows are tinted blue to keep the sun out. You are not sure whether it is early or late. The casinos are always open, and all the light inside stimulates you, regenerates you, surrounds you with energy. The purpose is to make you want to stay and wager. The principle of light and the principle of colour are used in the casinos to have a specific unconscious stimulation on the body and the people there.

For characters in a story which takes place in Las Vegas, I wanted to use this physiology of colour to create an atmosphere. *One From the Heart* was about the feelings of people in such a place, where the environment works to ease restraint.

RG: Let's talk about *Reds*. The title of the movie is a colour. It's also a colour often associated with a certain political disposition.

VS: At first, the film was entitled *The John Reed and Louise Bryant Story*. It was not called *Reds*. That came later. So my approach was not through the title but through the story. It was the story of a relationship that was very modern, yet relationships are always the same between man and woman, husband and wife. That is to say, timeless. As I was telling you before, there is always the same kind of polarity, male and female. It is as if there are two halves or two souls in the human being.

RG: In a way, you've been describing the principle of Tao, the yin and yang, the struggle between two primary forces, which give each other definition as they are drawn together and try to assimilate.

VS: Yes, that's right. Only when opposites complete each other is there a balance, which is the level all things seek. It is a very beautiful moment, but it is very hard to attain.

With *Reds*, I started out from a monochromatic tonality of colour, from brown. Brown is the colour of the earth, the colour of the roots. Brown is the one major colour that does not exist in the rainbow. A pure brown light is something outside the realm of nature as we know it. It is an earth colour. That's why the story starts from the floor of the dwelling, from what is beneath, from the earth.

My interpretation of the story was in the configuration of a tree, coming out of the earth from the roots. And the roots for me were 'the witnesses' [documentary interviews with John Reed's contemporaries], the fifty-five people telling the story to us, so that even if they were very old, the story is very much alive.

Reds: The witnesses.

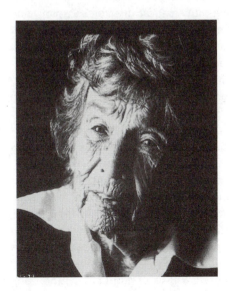

The roots generated the trunk of the tree, the body, which was the politics and the imperative to write for John Reed. I saw a relationship between his need to complete himself with either a woman or with politics, which are reflections of each other, coming as they were from the same impulse. The balance of the world and the balance of himself were the same. Ultimately, he is trying to reach the light, which is the harmony between emotion and reason, light and dark, roots and heights, earth and sky, heart and mind, male and female.

So the roots were coming up through him. The old people, too, wanted this balance. He was like them. He represented their impulse too, which made them seekers. In John Reed's relationship with Louise Bryant, I started out with something totally monochromatic, coming through a brown tonality, but which progressively opened up into all the colours of the spectrum, all the emotions between a man and a woman.

I also noted how the camera movements might progress through the story. With 'the witnesses' the camera is fixed, like a photograph. Only the characters move within the frame. Later, the camera moves but in linear motions, straight forward or in parallel, describing the scene or leading us to the actors. The light is very sharp, with dark shadows, very distinct from each other. Eventually the camera movements become more curvilinear, more encircling. Everything at that point is in movement, just as there is more and more light and colour. The light which is soft and direct envelops the characters, providing them with consistency and depth. There is no more separation between light and shadow. The colours come out clear and vivid in all their distinct wavelengths.

RG: Was there a cultural difference in working with American directors? Each of your next three films after that with Bertolucci involved foreign lands and cultures that were very old: *The Sheltering Sky* (Morocco), *The Last Emperor* (China) and *Little Buddha* (India). There was a kind of movement away from your origins in the strictly Italian cinema.

VS: Yes, there was a difference. A cycle that began by exporting the indigenous world that I knew and had developed with Bernardo continued with my experiences with Francis Coppola and Warren Beatty, so that I ended up bringing something new again when I went back to Italy. Which prompts a phrase I often repeat to myself and to others: that I don't believe that any person or culture or civilization can develop in a balanced way alone. We grow together through exchange, and by learning from and teaching one another.

When I returned to work with Bertolucci on *The Last Emperor*, everything I'd been developing visually up to that time seemed to reach its rightful conclusion. The principal idea was that a man takes a journey through memory, re-examining every moment of his life, which I tried to visualize in terms of the colour spectrum. I thought that each part of Pu Yi's story should be symbolized by one type of colour. For example, his years in the palace [of the Forbidden City in Beijing] are in 'forbidden' colours, the warmest colours, because it was a kind of protective womb for him as well as a kind of prison. There was the red of his imperial birth, moving to the orange glow of family warmth in his youth, then the splendid yellow of his imperial robes for the coronation when he became conscious of himself as an individual. The arrival of his English tutor enabled him to reach the years of learning in green as he broadened his knowledge and awareness. Then, the discovery of a part of life that had been forbidden to him before could not help but be represented by entering the blue of free-thinking and the freedom of the Western world. The newly acquired sense of omnipotence and materialism that followed was represented by indigo, as he sought to become emperor a second time. Later, as an ordinary Chinese citizen, he reviews his life in violet.

Beyond the colour scheme was a lighting concept for *The Last Emperor*. In the Forbidden City, he is never exposed to direct sunlight. He is always in penumbra, as he is still shielded from the outside world at this point in his life. Later, the more he learns from his English tutor, the more the rays of light from the outside begin to reach him. Gradually, a fight develops between light and shade, just as a person has a conflict between their conscious and their unconscious. In the Manchukuo part of the story, when he's established as a puppet of the Japanese and dreams of rebuilding his empire, the shadows almost overwhelm the picture. It almost returns to how it was when he was very young. Then, when he's in prison, Pu Yi thinks back over his life. The more he understands, the more light and shadow come into harmony.

With *The Last Emperor*, as I had immersed myself in all the colours of the spectrum, it was as if I'd passed through a second circle of life on my journey. It was soon after that I began to explore the third circle of the elements.

After *The Last Emperor* I knew that I had to take another step. I had to take another step in trying to find a balance between all these different things. Mainly, in the beginning I was trying to divide, to separate light from shadow, then red from blue, one colour from another. Now it was time to see if I could put them together, to find more harmony.

It was then that the idea came to me to go back to ancient Greek philosophy, the pre-Socratics, who determined that life consists of four basic elements: water, earth, fire and air. I wanted to understand how I could begin to visualize life itself through these four elements. That was my main concern.

When I began the documentary *Roma: Imago Urbis* with Luigi Bazzoni, I began to think that maybe with these fifteen programmes of one hour each, I might be able to do a kind of résumé of my professional life. In other words, maybe I could divide the series into three parts. One would mainly be the journey without light. One would be the journey *within* light, into colour. And the third would be to try to find a balance between these two, but mainly the idea of balance between the four elements.

Aside from the opportunity to work with my good friend Luigi – and to create a unique kind of documentary that would portray ancient Rome without any reference to contemporary times – this was another reason to work on *Roma: Imago Urbis* and to spend six years on the project.

RG: Through the course of *Roma: Imago Urbis* you made *Little Buddha*.

The Last Emperor: The four stages of Pu Yi's life: In the palace . . .

. . . the arrival of the tutor (Peter O'Toole).

... outside the Forbidden City (John Lone).

... and an ordinary citizen.

VS: That's right. But you know, *Little Buddha* is not just a movie for me. It is trying to come to terms with the meaning of your life, trying to come to terms with all the fundamental questions that confront the human being. That's why I believe I started thinking about *Little Buddha* from the beginning. Since the day I was born, everything in my life was unconsciously moving me towards it.

RG: In a sense, you also started progressing towards a life as a director of photography from the beginning, since it was something your father instilled in you and, considering the nature of his work as a projectionist, you were actually raised in the presence of the moving image.

VS: Well, yes, that's true, too. Everything is very well connected. Everything. For example, well before *Roma: Imago Urbis* or *Little Buddha*, Luigi Bazzoni gave me a book entitled *Adventure of Consciousness* by (Sri) Aurobindo, who was a great yogi living at the turn of the century. Aurobindo was unusual because he was a very active yogi, a revolutionary yogi, fighting against the English to liberate India. He was very political, but at the same time a very deep philosopher.

One of the things that really touched me about his book was the basic idea that you can research, that you can discover your own subconscious, and that the deeper you go into the subconscious the more you can understand the outer levels of your consciousness, which is the over-conscious. Do you understand what I mean?

There is a line where you are right now, your conscious. The deeper you delve down into your subconscious, the more proportionally you can understand when you return back up to your over-conscious, which is above the level of the conscious. Many philosophers have studied the relationship between the subconscious and the conscious. Freud was one of the most important; he used this theory to help people, because human beings can live better when they're in balance between these two levels of consciousness. What is inside yourself is what you use outside yourself.

So Aurobindo said the deeper you go, the more you will understand and become aware of. Yogis use the word 'meditation'. In psychoanalysis, you use the word 'analysis'. The two are not unrelated.

And one thing that really touched me while I was reading Aurobindo's book was the fact that any human being, in the moment that they have an idea, in the moment that they have an inspiration, that is the moment when they go above the line of the conscious to look into the over-conscious.

And I think that is such a wonderful principle, the fact that we are moving along the level of the conscious, but in that moment – when you are writing and you find the words to express an idea that jumps forth, or when I am working in photography, and I have an idea of how to make that light – that moment is our chance to go into the over-conscious, and come back afterwards into the normal level of consciousness. Don't you think that is beautiful? It was an idea that really touched me a lot, the fact that at any moment you have an idea is the chance that you can go above the consciousness. It's fantastic.

So, as I often do with things I read, I gave this book to Bernardo. A few years later, after *The Last Emperor*, Bernardo said to me one day, 'You know, Vittorio, what I did yesterday? I was in my sitting room, wandering around, thinking, when suddenly my eye caught one book on the shelf. I went over and I picked up this book. I opened it and read what you inscribed to me, that I may not be able to read the book at the time that you gave it to me, but there was going to be a day when I would. I sat down and I read the book.'

It became a turning point. Bernardo had begun his own research when he started putting together *The Last Emperor*, and step by step, through other books and other friends and through his own thoughts, he was coming into oriental philosophy, but now there was something else. And from my side, I began to read more and become more acquainted with oriental philosophy because I had become very interested in it.

So there was this connection between myself and Bernardo through this book, *Adventure of Consciousness*. Finally – it was I think 1989 – I was doing *Dick Tracy* when we spoke on the telephone – Bernardo was in London, I was in Los Angeles – and he said, 'What do you think about doing a movie about Buddha?'

RG: Were you surprised?

VS: Not at all. In fact, it was an idea that practically came as we were speaking on the telephone. And at that moment we began to discuss the story for the first time, because until then, though there were all these other things in the atmosphere, we weren't yet conscious of the fact that we were going to do a movie about Buddha, which is an extraordinary, very captivating idea. Everything was leading us towards this, though we weren't aware of it until this telephone conversation.

RG: So in a sense, Bernardo and yourself were exercising Aurobindo's principle, only in unison, together.

VS: That's right. The principle he was describing enabled us in a way to come forward with something new. It had been coming for some time and so there was no surprise when it happened, only a kind of gratification, only a kind of momentum and joy in this realization.

And after that, I began to consider ways to visualize it, what I would need for the photography while Bernardo began to further consider the story itself. And we started to pick up all kinds of books after that, histories of Buddha and Buddhist philosophy and Buddhist practice and Buddhist culture.

And you know, the moment I began to think about visualizing the film was a major step. I mean, how can you visualize Buddha's 'enlightenment'? As soon as I began to think about that, I knew this would implicitly have a very significant meaning for me.

Then later on, Bernardo came to my house one day. We sat down and he said, 'Vittorio, I've decided not to do a movie just about Buddha. I think I'd like to do a movie about a lama in search of the reincarnation of his own master and who finds three children (each of whom he believes may be the master reincarnated). And when the lama finds the children, he begins to tell the story of Buddha.'

And I remember he said, 'Vittorio, what do you think? I strongly feel that this is the way to do it, using this relationship between modern time and ancient time rather than just doing the story of Buddha itself.'

And I said, 'Well, if you have this idea it's no doubt because you feel more comfortable [with it].' And also, it was very important for Bernardo to make this a story that would be open to children.

But from the moment he gave me this basic structure, I saw that we had three different countries, one for each of the children. Three children and one master. And the basic idea of Siddhartha [the original name of the Buddha, which means 'the awakened one'], is that he finds his balance, his equilibrium, his realization, his enlightenment. And I thought, 'My God, this is exactly what I was looking for with this further step into myself, this research into how to visualize and achieve balance through the four elements.'

Then I said to myself, 'Let's think for a moment if the lama Norbu can be represented by the element of earth. Earth is an element of nourishment, and to nourish is also to impart knowledge. The lama is the teacher of these children, like the father and the mother at the same time, because in the ancient philosophy, earth is a feminine element because it gives nourishment to all life.

So I decided to represent the lama by the element of earth with the colour of black, which is the symbol of matter. Matter is the loam, the vital soil. Matter is the material.

RG: I believe the word 'mother' is derived from the Latin for matter, or material, which is 'mater'.

VS: Exactly. That's right. So lama Norbu would be portrayed as the element of earth through the colour black, and sometimes also the colour orange, which is the warmth of the mother in the mother's embrace of the child.

So the lama is nourishing the children, through knowledge, through the story of Buddha. And from this idea, for example, I suggested to Bernardo that we shoot the first scene of *Little Buddha* – when we see lama Norbu speaking to the classroom in the Bhutan monastery and telling the children the humorous story of the goat as a parable about reincarnation – at night instead of day as it was originally written so that we could start with black and orange to give it this feeling in relation to him.

Then with each of the three children, I ascribed an element – water, fire and air – and the corresponding colour. Jesse in Seattle was the element of water and the colour green. Raju, the other little boy of Kathmandu, was the element of fire and the colour red. Gita, the girl of Nepal, was the element of air and the colour blue. This was not arbitrary. These elements were in the nature of their characters and their geographies.

So this was my basic approach to the visualization, and throughout *Little Buddha* you will see the elements in these and other ways – sometimes more independently, sometimes simultaneously, sometimes symbolically, but always striving for harmony – leading to a fifth manifestation which is energy, the energy of pure white light, which is the enlightenment.

RG: In terms of using the elements and the colours, did you achieve this through filtration over the camera lens, through the colour of the lighting, in the printing process of the film in the lab, or perhaps also in working with the set or costume designer, or a combination of these?

VS: Each of those. In other words, in order to apply what I have described to you on screen, that combination of light and colour, I used everything in my knowledge of photography to achieve that goal. So naturally I used one specific film stock, one specific set of lenses, one specific kind of filtration, one way of printing to achieve the colours for Seattle and the element of water. I did something nearly the opposite in Kathmandu to achieve the element of fire, another film stock, different filtration, different light, different lenses, different printing. There was something different for the sequences of lama Norbu in Bhutan and something different for the girl in Nepal. And when I did the sequence of Siddhartha for the enlightenment, I used *all four*. It's like you're using different punctuation and different adjectives to create a style out of language to describe one part of the story you're writing in relation to another part.

And then, of course, the transition of one section to another, the fusion or the pulling away or the prominence of each element in the story as it happened, told me how to prepare, what I would need technically to bring all of this forth. To put it simply, any ideation in the film which concerns photography is always very, very important to me.

When I went to Kathmandu to scout locations for the first time, Bernardo was still in Los Angeles casting. I had to wait for him for two weeks. In that time I entered into the script, scene by scene, the entire visual structure for the photography. When Bernardo came, we went back to each location once again, and in doing that I was able to refine the structure even more. Then, when I went back to Rome, before shooting the picture, I did more work. I wrote down the philosophy of the film through an ideation of photography and wrote down beside each scene which lens, which filter, which colour, which formation of lighting I would use to achieve the kind of feeling that was appropriate.

What is the story of Siddhartha? It's about a young man who lives in this perfect world of his father's palace who must be reborn once again, but now as a man. It is only through experience and a balance between extremes that he finally comes to the tree prepared for the fulfilment he's been seeking; he can now meditate and in a conscious way find enlightenment.

Throughout Siddhartha's journey to the Boddhi tree I was trying to give a cyclical feeling, to give a sense of his birth and rebirth. In each scene there was a light from a certain time of the day to move the cycle forward – day, sunset, dusk, night, dawn, day again – but at a different moment than before. And in having this different aspect of light for each scene to give this cyclical feeling, there was the earth in relation to the sun, to the other planets, to the larger sphere beyond, to a motion within all space and time.

RG: And what about the enlightenment scene itself?

VS: This cyclical sense culminated with that scene. If you notice, when lama Norbu is beginning to tell the story to the children of Siddhartha seeking his own enlightenment under the tree it is daytime. When the children enter the scene to observe Siddhartha under the tree and he is distracted by the daughters of Mara (lord of darkness), everything gradually progresses into sunset. When the wind begins to blow to signal the approach of Mara, night is arriving. As the children go around to the other side of the tree, they find that night completely covers the ocean. Over the ocean is the gathering battalion of soldiers whose arrows become blossoms that shower down on Siddhartha, and after that the moon begins to rise at the same time as the dawn is impending. When Siddhartha confronts the embodiment of his ego, the root cause of duality, it's dawn and at that moment the sun and the moon are in balance. Each is a symbol representing the conscious and the unconscious. Sun, day: the conscious. Moon, night: the unconscious. So I put them in balance, gave them equilibrium. Soon Siddhartha is winning the struggle with the ego, so that now the conscious dominates and becomes the over-conscious. And the story continues, with daytime returning once again and so on.

So in one sequence I did the entire cycle of the four elements and the entire journey of the sun and the moon. When the children are approaching Siddhartha, you have the feeling of the earth, and where he is sitting firmly on the ground. When the wind arrives with the daughters of Mara and disperses their bodies into ash, there is the element of air. When the children cross over to the other side of the tree, there is the ocean, the symbol for water. When the soldiers attack, their burning arrows are the symbol of fire. And when the struggle ends and everything is calm and the petals are falling, all the light returns to white as the symbol for energy, the over-conscious. So there is in that sequence the four

Little Buddha: The enlightenment scene (Keanu Reeves).

Little Buddha: The enlightenment scene — the wind begins to blow.

elements, the four different aspects of the day, the four colours.

RG: You've been speaking of the implicit polarities in your work, the dialectic between opposites, day opposed to night, natural as opposed to artificial, male opposed to female, intellectual as opposed to sensual, energy and matter, moon and sun. It seems that everything, the ideal first expressed through the round, global lights in the earlier films, culminated for you in the enlightenment sequence, in a circle of pure white light. It must have been a very moving experience for you.

VS: Well, yes. It was very moving. The visualization is a kind of synthesis of all those opposing energies in my work until this time. But at first I didn't know how to visualize the enlightenment. It came step by step, with the cycles of light, the elements, the colours. But the actual moment of his realization was suggested by the word itself: 'enlightenment', to be filled with light. It is not only a metaphor. It is the moment when there is a union with all things, all opposites. A pure white is the synthesis of the spectrum. Don't forget that all relation to the outside world originates from the senses. We might call this moment of enlightenment by another name, something abstract, but it begins with a feeling that is familiar to the senses. It comes when everything is in balance: all feeling, all thought, all time.

RG: You once mentioned that light itself has a mystical quality.

VS: Light is energy, and I not only think that we derive from this energy, but we originate from this energy. It is also our reality. Energy is everything. I mean, the essence of light has this spiritual quality whether we know it or not. Even if we don't understand, even if we don't believe, even if we refuse, even if we don't know, it has to be.

As I told you, *Little Buddha* is not just a movie for me. It is really a part of my own life. Without *Little Buddha* it was like a journey that was stopped. Then for a moment I had the fear that *Little Buddha* was almost the end of the journey, the end of what I had been seeking. It was something that you could not go beyond.

But at the end of the movie after lama Norbu dies and the children are receiving his ashes, there is once again the symbol of the four elements. They go into the ashram, before the huge figure of the Buddha, and the light is completely red. The red light was to invoke the sense of fire incinerating the body to create the ashes. So the symbol of fire. Then, later, the young girl is disposing of the ashes from the tree to the earth, the second element. The American boy is disposing the ashes from the boat into the water, the third element. And the boy from Kathmandu is sending the ashes up with a balloon into the air, the fourth element. It's like taking the human body and dividing it once again into the four elements. It's a kind of step forward again.

In other words, this was something I understood because I had already come to this realization about the elements and this in *Little Buddha* further confirmed it, that as we are each composed of matter, we are also composed of energy. I don't really believe in this form of reincarnation, something very direct, where when someone dies they can be born exactly the same but with a different body in a different part of the world, as the movie depicts. But it is clear to me that the human body will separate into the four elements and unite with other energy and other elements and restructure again as something else, perhaps as a human being again one day. So matter is something impermanent that belongs to you, to me, to every one of us. But the energy is universal. The energy is indestructible. The energy is irreducible.

My fear about completing *Little Buddha* was that maybe there would be no other chapter as strong or as important. But when it was finished I said to myself, 'No, this is not the end at all. This is the beginning of something else. I have opened another door. I will undertake another journey.' I don't know if I will be able to complete it. I don't know where it will take me or how it will end. I don't know what I'm going to do tomorrow. But that's the beauty of discovery.

18 Images and Accidents

A Diary of *Kids* by Eric Alan Edwards

Introduction

I was in San Francisco filming a music video for Chris Isaak directed by Larry Clark. In fact, it was the first time I worked with Larry and the first time he had ever made a movie, albeit a small one. As part of his concept, Larry wanted to use real strippers, and we did our research by watching lap dancers at the O'Farrell Theater one Friday night. We hired a hotel room, and amazingly all the girls we'd asked to audition showed up to do their strip act while a pitifully low-quality, low-volume CD-playing boombox whined out in a tinny fashion. It was very on the up and up; just me, Larry, Harmony Korine, Bob Jason the producer and a quite clerical-like woman – some sort of legally required participant – who sat looking down, motionless. What interested me was that, almost without exception, each woman told us how nervous the event made them. They were out of their domain and therefore away from the kind of control they're used to having on stage and lap.

During a break in our filming in a tall Victorian house where the three we'd chosen were in bed together, Chris was in the hallway listening to one of the girls telling him about painting, about the other pursuits that interested her. It seems a little hard-assed now, but he told her, 'Look, *you're* carny trash, *I'm* carny trash . . . we all got into this biz for one thing . . .'

But it rang true. I *was* carny trash. Isaak may as well have been speaking for the entire crew. Well paid by some standards, certainly far better paid than the girls were that day; I had 'joined the circus'. I had joined it years ago.

I bypassed a liberal arts education for art school (Rhode Island School of Design). In the first year my floor counsellor said to all of us that only a total fuck-up could get expelled from this school. He was right, although attrition in the freshman class was quite high. More than likely, many others chose art school because it sounded much easier than real learning.

Gus Van Sant and I graduated from RISD together in 1975 and went into the real world where no one would ever ask to see our degrees. I never doubted our academic or formal interest in the medium and neither his nor my own abilities as film-makers. I never doubted our talent. It wasn't until he made *Mala Noche* that I knew how good a storyteller Gus was. The thing that I did doubt for the longest time after leaving school was whether either of us would ever get the chance to make a 35mm film. Finally it happened. We did *My Own Private Idaho* (1991) and then, *Even Cowgirls Get the Blues* (1993).

I was in Toronto with Gus finishing the filming of *To Die For* when Larry Clark gave me a plane ticket to New York to talk to him about his first feature film, which Gus was executive producing. The script I read was a very ambitious piece, written in one powerful, seamless stroke by a very young Harmony Korine, a kid he'd met in Washington Square Park two or three years earlier. It was so unflinching and direct and without the requisite devices that usually clean, reduce or homogenize films for the big market. It was a film that could never be reasonably made by those who control the kind of money it takes to make movies. Producer Cary Woods made it happen.

Because he'd worked with me before, Larry asked me to shoot the film for him.

When I wrote in this journal, usually I would be sitting down tired, with little time or resource. So, it is a fragmentary and incomplete record of my experiences. As if wearing blinders, I wrote what was immediately troubling me in my intense narrow world, keen on those things that I needed to get through in the film. In retrospect, I find what I've written is myopic and self-focused. I always wonder: what is going through everyone else's head?

Wednesday 22 June 1994

I'm leaving Canada after fifteen weeks of shooting *2Die4* for Gus Van Sant. Three weeks ago, Larry Clark called me in Toronto to tell me he wanted me to shoot his first feature, *Kids*. I will have only two weeks before starting *Kids* in NYC. I need more time off!

Thursday 23 June

Portland, Oregon. It looks like my choice of gaffers, Christopher Porter, won't be able to do *Kids*. The money isn't good. I asked him to get in touch directly with the production office. I talked with *Kids* producer Lauren Zalaznick at the office on Tuesday. She urged me to get key grip Eric Schmidt signed up. I'd OKed Jonathan Mintz already. They're paying them so little that they want to get 'em before someone else (which means *anyone* else) offers them more.

Tuesday 28 June

My first assistant cameraman, Richard Rutkowski, suggests we use the bloop-slate like in the old days of documentary: the soundman holds in his hand a light which, when he pushes a button, simultaneously blinks a light and puts a beep on the tape running through his Nagra. The producers, however, may insist on the usual time-code slate. In putting together the camera truck he has recommended a converted Snap-On Tools truck from Brian Heller in Providence, RI. It's a step van and we can put all the camera gear in it; also, there is a platform with rails on top that, maybe, we can shoot from. A great NYC spirit, Richard comes Harvard-educated and, like many on the East Coast, started with the smallest of productions, earning him an aptitude for doing things innovatively. He agrees to do it for the money offered. This I like.

Thursday 30 June

Portland. A talk with Lauren Zalaznick in which she says she doesn't like the fact that Christopher Porter hasn't called her back. Christopher told me he wanted $1,400/wk and my thinking was: how far off can that be? Just pay it, don't tell anyone else, whatever. Fuck, take it outta my salary! She doesn't like the fact that he's having me negotiate his wage through the director. 'Why can't Christopher talk through the unit production manager, Pam?' She'd hate to see me have to lose another zoom lens off the camera list. I tell her that we already have. She agrees to talk with him. The producer is hired to draw up a budget and decide how much will be allocated to each department. What is odd is that Larry hired the producers, yet he lets them have complete say in these matters.

I can't go to Larry and get anything done regarding money.

I've been trying to get Christopher on the film because he's the fastest gaffer I know. He can orchestrate the electricians under him in a rapid, motivated way. This is all I care about. This is what I'm going to need if I am going to do a $2 million film in twenty-four days.

All I've gotten from Lauren Zalaznick, Christine Vachon and Pam at the office is that the wage for every department head will be $1,000/week – something about 'most favoured nation status'.

Christopher has talked to Lauren and Christine, as well. He reports back to me that the last time someone talked to him about 'parity', it simply meant that they were trying to screw him outta a reasonable wage.

They want to pay: me, the production designer, the soundperson, wardrobe, make-up, the writer, the director, everybody, $1,000/week; to bunch us all together in one big, happy, evenly paid family.

One reason I'm doing this for the money I'm being offered is that I like the project. I liked Harmony Korine's script and the hit I got off Larry when they flew me down to interview me. Also, I am getting to work with a small crew and put the means of production into my own hands. I don't wish to repeat what I was so eager to get away from back in Toronto. The presence of the camera operator always seems to cement a separation between me and the director. If the director wants the framing changed, he goes through the camera operator. I lose a say in something that is fundamental to what I do. It is disruptive to the work, counter-productive.

Now, my heart is in it. I just want the man who'll make me go as light-speed fast as I can – Chris Porter – and I've tried to side-step the usual powers in this case.

Larry Clark gets back on the phone. 'Have you seen Cassavetes' *Mikey and Nicky?*' (He has a copy from Martin Scorsese. Martin and his company are possibly in as executive producers on *Kids.*) He stresses the harsh light, the out-of-focus moments. I say we should prepare first assistant director Van not to hire too many crew people. Everyone in this industry is convinced you need so many people to make a film.

Larry sounds like he's totally in the midst of what directing is: ten major crises before lunch.

Saturday 2 July

Portland. In my basement, I gather what I need from the overflow from three films. Boxes of various-sized incandescent bulbs, uncountable rolls of gel, aluminium honeycomb grids that electricians have framed with mahogany, lights I've bought that are difficult to rent. A testament to my annual output.

Thursday 7 July

I arrive in NYC at 6 p.m. At Larry's loft he mentions foreground in the frame. He likes that about *Mikey and Nicky*. When I look at the film, I note the amazing lack of light in the night-time exteriors. Zero-budget kind of film-making. By this time I have watched *Shadows* with Gus in Toronto. Larry and I run through the pieces that he keys in on. It's clear that in the late '50s, early '60s, on their budget, they didn't have fluid heads on their tripods. Nor through-the-lens reflex viewing. There is an Etch-a-Sketch quality to the pans and tilts, and the framing/compositions, and when the camera comes to rest in a shot, it often leaves great headroom – though this could be the TV transfer. They may be showing the entire frame, something unintended by the film-makers. Larry loves this about it. He wants me to frame similarly in close-up. This might be difficult for me. It just looks too odd, unsettling. He likes the hard light of the interior shots.

This aesthetic we're locking on to is the result of the technology they had at that time, as well as the budget. Arri 2cs were often blimped in a metal housing, with only non-zooming, prime lenses used; handheld meant looping the dialogue. I love heading back to this kind of film-making, a method that now seems like a distant artefact, a thing to be found under glass in a museum.

We also look at *Killing of a Chinese Bookie* a thousand times. Each day we get our 'Bookie' hit'. Larry likes the out-of-focus moments where the focus puller made mistakes. The harsh lighting. In retrospect it should seem so alarming, but I am blown away at how sloppy things get in this film. Larry loves the ballistic heat of a face getting too close to a film light. People go into shadows and stay there. Cassavetes was in it for the actors.

I believe it's 'the accident' we're after. To polish a thing is to put it too deliberately in the realm of the professionally serious. Gus always had a desire for the occasional flare in the lens. We constantly had to fight the crew for this. And I think Larry is right. He's right to head for this 'zone', this place where accident gives us the evidence of life/film-making on the edge. The big question, and it's one I often find myself up against, is: how do I make accidents? Sometimes I'll surprise the focus puller with a framing change; often at the start of lighting a set, I'll turn on the nearest light that just 'fell off the truck'. Or, after setting up lights, I'll start to turn the damn things off, playing: 'How low can we go?'

My apartment, subrented for me by the production, is on 7th Street, between 13th and 14th. A comfortable, lived-in twelfth-floor space overlooking the four-storeyed West Village.

Friday 8 July

NYC. First purchase, a backpack. I rent the totally illegal *Cocksucker Blues* from Kim's Video on St Marks Place.

The production office is a sizeable loft on Broadway near Houston, the third floor of a building with tall storeys and large windows, bare-wood floors and brick walls. The elevator is the world's tiniest (we always choose the long stairs), as well as slowest. I have to find a desk with a phone on it. Larry is in the middle of rehearsals, so I grab his until he comes in.

Production designer Kevin Thompson has asked what I want for window

Kids: Justin Pierce and Harmony Korine.

treatments and practical lighting. 'Lots of them!' Kevin is amazing. He's sensitive to light. Where has this man been all my life!?

My first assistant cameraman Richard Rutkowski is in place. So are key grip Todd Klein and best boy Joe Zizzo. Unit production manager Pam Koffler and co-producer Christine Vachon want my camera, grip and electric lists as soon as possible. It's only ten days till we shoot (!), but I can't narrow them down until I've had more conversations with Larry and see the locations with him. These lists are always a panic because we need to tech-scout the locations with the department heads to narrow down how we're going to make the film.

Chris Porter calls from Toronto and says his wife hasn't had her baby yet. I seriously worry about his involvement. I've rented Bill Plympton's loft, in addition to the apartment provided by the production. At the production office, Lauren had a confab with Chris and she says that he's on and for the going rate. I tell her, 'I don't know what you said to him, but it must have been good.'

Larry is still casting minor roles. He has a casting director, but finding the authentic street kids often requires going out with Harmony on the weekends – and now, with production looming near, on weekdays – to find them in Washington Park or Astor Place; anywhere they can be found.

Me, Larry, first assistant director Van Hayden, and often Harmony and production designer Kevin Thompson, go off to look at the locations that they've either found (ahead of my arrival) or need to find. Today, location scouting started with Harmony's grandmother's house, where he grew up. I make notes about the lights we need. Company move and the van won't start. A neighbour jump-starts us; we get through the tunnel, but ten blocks short of St Marks the van dies again. Five of us jam into a reluctant taxi. Egg creams at 2nd and St

Marks Place. Benetton/AIDS poster of Reagan with Kaposi's sarcoma all over his face, harsh. Larry wants it in the film.

10 p.m. At the Tunnel nightclub, now replacing Rave NASA in the script, Larry confides to me that Harmony knows the club scene better. When we arrived, the place was literally dead. By 11.30, the floor is filling and the two DJs have the fog machines going good. The skateboarders oscillate in the fenced-in cage, showing their chops.

Saturday 9 July

A.m. At Larry's loft, he is concerned about his tennis shoes. He laces up unworn, vintage ten-year-old shoes, bought by a warehouse-hunting, career shoe searcher. 'I spend a lot of time checking out other guys' shoes on the sub-way, when ya look down avoiding eyes. I need longer laces like yours,' he says, pointing to my soiled New Balances. 'These look like women's shoes, all neat.' He's been rehearsing with Mia Kirshner (the lead in *Exotica* and *Love and Human Remains*) and is amazed to be working with a pro. 'She cries, laughs, does all that.' He has to remind himself that he's working.

I'm totally uncertain what I'm into with Larry. There's a lot of stoppin' and starin', thinking carefully about things. I just have to let him have his space. It will test my resources. I really now have to think about the oddness of being a fluent cameraman collaborating with someone who's known as a great photographer. How do I make my magic work for someone whose magic works for them in the two-dimensional world?

Sunday 10 July

Go to watch rehearsals at Larry's small loft. Mia Kirshner, who has been flown in from Toronto, has been whipping up the group of five girls talking intimately about sex in Ruby's room. We watch once. I tape with the 8mm camcorder for a solid forty-five minutes. They totally get into it. The girls are like talk machines. They exchange lines with each other and toss them around like they were flowing naturally. It blows me away how easily they slide into the rhythm of speech. Harmony Korine's lines are pure, extracted by syringe from real life. Even though (I hear later) some of the girls are virgins, they know exactly how to fake graphic details of their first sexual encounters, preferences and orgasms.

An endless source of entertainment is the garbage chute just outside my door. I relish with pleasure the sounds of items (bottles) gaining velocity in the narrow metal shaft and then impacting bottomwise. Very satisfying. Job well done!

Tuesday 12 July

In the production office. Right now, Larry Clark brings me into it. A real 'carnale'. He gives his large handshake and, in a kind of guileless way, says, 'Mia's out of the picture, I fired her. I've been on the phone to Cary Woods and her agent all night.' He will try Chloe Sevigny, one of the original skater people, in her place. It's a pivotal role.

He wants my opinion on the actors. I had said how 'white' Mia was. Just an observation. Uptight, in contrast to the black girls. But I hadn't said it negatively.

Five days till we shoot and we still need to cast Ruby, the other leading girl role. While we were looking for an apartment house in Alphabet City, a crew was filming a TV commercial for *Vibes* magazine. Walking through the forest of chrome, silver and black shit that landscapes a shooting location, we heard a voice coming from a balcony above a bombed-out stoop. Larry said, 'She looks like the perfect Ruby!' He and Harmony went up to ask her to audition tomorrow. Her name is Rosario Dawson.

We do the location survey in a rented van. Larry rides shotgun. First AD Van Hayden has the daily schedule of where we want to be by when. We have to see what electrical needs are: dolly or crane or ??? How noisy is the location for sound recording?

Back in the van, best boy Joe (standing in for Christopher), key grip Todd and I go over the grip and electric lists. The size of the film is shaping up now with these location surveys, but I know how small we want to keep the crew and the equipment we use. Joe pushes for all the usual gear. I bring him down as low as I diplomatically can. I don't want to be an unreasonable, unlistening jefe just yet.

We talk to unit production manager Pam Koffler with the lists. We go over each detail.

We pare off a few items, but Joe holds his ground. I let him have it, feeling a little foolish, but justify it to myself by thinking I can come in later and heroically knock off other things.

Larry Clark wonders who may get it on with Ruby. She's stunning. We're already anticipating the male cast's interest in her. There is this immediate, close proximity of a bunch of young actors to each other like a clan, an extended family.

At Jerry's on Prince Street, the Stones' 'Parachute Woman' plays. I'm feeling a lot less alien now with the scout team together. Still no Christopher Porter. He's been waiting in Toronto with his wife Megan, who is overdue to give birth. Doubts about the Body Cam from Abel Cinetech. We watched a tape they'd sent us. Looks swayingly like a poor man's Steadicam.

Larry invites me to watch rehearsals again at his loft. He's easing into this. I find him standing, staring into his hand which is drawn up to his nose, in sultry, East Coast humid sweat. Shining, like he's just gunned someone down. Imagine, you've never had to think about a close-up, a cutaway before, never had to overlap real-time coverage of something graphic and flowing – and now you're directing a feature.

Wednesday 13 July

I don't want the mechanics of movie-making to interfere with Larry's work with the actors. I want everything to come from what he wants to do with them. Obviously, I don't need to show him what a movie camera is, but how many angles we do, how many takes, how we block the action, what length lenses, do we handhold? tripod? or have the camera tracking along?? I want to reduce the focus of everyone's attention on the camera, the time it takes to light, and give him every inch he needs to get what he wants out of the actors. It's their first time at this. I'm sure their act will be perishable.

I can tell already he has good enough sense to mix and stir it up regarding lenses and camera mounts.

Towards the end of today's location scout, at the Korean deli, Larry wanted to run the scene through, even though we had no actors to rehearse with. It was a tiny place, filled aisles, and there was me, Larry, Van, the gaffer, the script person and Pam. I said we should just go through it, with two of us moving through the place saying the dialogue. I cleared everyone out, asked them all to leave except the two doing the lines: an experiment for Larry. I angered Van, but I got him out too. Just Larry and me, with Pam and Harmony to run the scene. Running the action and finding the angles from their movements. It was a contained situation. There are only so many practical solutions. We blocked it several ways, me playing with it, offering camera angles that popped into mind.

I want to have a procedure with Larry. I keep saying to him, 'Just run the thing. See where your folks naturally go.' This can be done only when the room is clear. Often, with Gus, he will ask even me to leave. Every-fucking-body out. Liberating, for a director who's spent the last five days with an info-seeking crowd of technicians mimicking his every footstep.

(Back at the office, Larry said, 'That was a goof. I didn't know I could do that.')

Leo Fitzpatrick (Telly) and Sarah Henderson (Girl #1) rehearse the first scene. I know what to expect, I've read the script. I know that they're young. But I think of Sunny Jim, skinny, middle-American wholesomeness. Leo and Sarah are kissing for the longest moment. Larry wants them to go at it slowly. Actually, it's the magic that makes it work. He draws it out so that it's uncomfortable. A pregnant pause that forces one to confront their youth and the real-time in-your-faceness of their sexuality.

We have a big production meeting, everybody in a large circle on folding metal chairs, with notebooks open. Kevin has his set/location sketches together, showing placement of furniture. Larry spent nearly the entire time intently looking straight down at his shooting schedule. It took his entire attention. We introduce everyone and go through the script page by page, the department heads hashing out what gear, people, costumes, props, special effects we need on what days. We've seen all the locations.

Larry pours a continuous stream of eye-drop solution into his eyes.

At Kim's Video, I finally find Richard Lester's *The Knack (and How to Get It)*. If I could only find *Lovers* with George Segal, my revisiting of my early film-going influences would be nearly complete.

Saturday 16 July

11 a.m. at Time Café. Meet Larry and producer Cary Woods. Larry talks about the opening virgin scene. It's to look like his photos. Cary holds a good poker face. Larry and I leave Cary on Lafayette. Walk down to Kim's and get laserdiscs of *Breathless*, *Taxi Driver* and *Night on Earth*. With *Taxi Driver* we figure out the car angles. Pans and stuff. How complex do we want to do our travelling car shots? It always takes huge amounts of time to do *any* car rig. We need atmospheric shots of the city; evening shots to establish time transition after Jennie's drop-off in Washington Park.

Christopher arrives from Toronto. Megan had the baby. His foot is hurting enough to make him limp – a slip while running.

Sunday 17 July

7 p.m. Taxi from Larry's. It's the eleventh hour. He's stoked. I'm already stoked. Butterflies briefly in my stomach. Harold missed one rehearsal, Justin Pierce (Casper) has also missed one. One fear of mine is that there will be a day when an actor doesn't show up for shooting. Do they know that $16,000 a day is being spent and forgetting a call time or a day means something?

Larry gets more and more certain about the image. He talks of the 50mm and the 35mm on his Leica. *Tulsa* was almost all 50mm and *Teenage Lust* was 35mm trying to look like the 50. I wonder about the arbitrary lens ruling. Wim Wenders' *Tokyo Ga*. Ozu and his 40mm lens at sitting height, etc.?

As we watch *Breathless*, I stress the non-stop aspect of the film owing mostly to the action and the busyness of the characters. We watched *Night on Earth* yesterday and Larry felt the interiors of the cabs were way overlit.

Chris and I take a cab to the Carmine Street Pool location, our one big night exterior. His foot is plainly hurting. Italy plays Brazil's soccer team and the Mambo bar near the pool has a block-long line around it. This part of town near the Holland Tunnel seems to be going nuts about it.

Van Hayden comes over to Larry's loft to suggest logistics. It's really to give him a sense of security. The producers, Chris and Lauren, are nervous about this too. They want a shot list. This won't happen. Larry waits to find angles and coverage until we're on the set – which will unsettle them throughout the schedule. I think I have Larry's undivided attention. I feel secure about this act right now.

Dinner. Larry is definite about press. Nobody! The press would be harmful to the process. He's right, the kids would flip. He tells me that this, the making of a film, is an extension of his photography, his work. It was the 'next thing', the logical extension of his art. He feels securely in the right place. Fuck, it's a big move for him. I say, 'Get some sleep and don't worry about tomorrow.' 'I'm not worried,' he says. And he isn't.

As Christopher and I go into a bar on Varick, he talks about working on *Hail, Hail, Rock and Roll*. He tells me about the lighting on that one, about Keith Richards and his cases of guitars and roadies to keep them in tune, and about

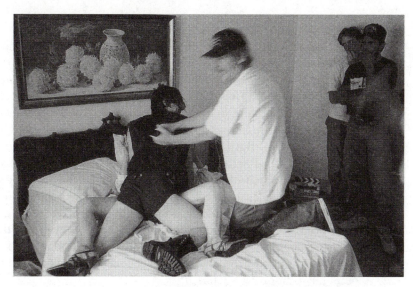

Kids: **The fucking-like-rabbits scene.**

Chuck Berry getting off the plane, grabbing his one guitar off the moving baggage-claim belt. I feel tired. I feel like I could sleep. Not too distracted with thoughts about tomorrow. Chris has missed the technical scout, his best boy filling in for him. We both know this will be an adventure. Uncertain, but . . . ? 'As long,' he says, 'as we can keep smiling.' He knows the turf.

Monday 18 July
two shot: Telly/Girl #1
singles
overhead
exit room
spit close-up
down stairs
out door

First day shooting. 84th and York. We finish shooting at a three-storey brownstone (next to Walter Cronkite's, somebody says). Leo and Sarah had the hardest time doing the fucking-like-rabbits scene. We worked them to the bone. It was me, Larry, script person Chiemi Karasawa, Jan the sound mixer and first assistant camera Richard in the room. Amazing that Leo and Sarah trouped on through it, feeling uncomfortable at first with this crowd, but maintaining. I suggest we cross the eyeline for the close-ups. Keep us on edge.

On the sidewalk at wrap, everyone stuffing pizza. I talk with Lauren. She and Pam think the day's gone well. Lauren wants to know what took so long after the first team was brought in for the overhead shot. I say 'the agonizing over the POV'; we couldn't find a way to stage it with Leo's head outta the way. It was really the arrival of the owner back home that forced the last shot or two. I felt that we spent way too much time on the getting-down-the-stairs shots.

Christopher blew up. His foot was killing him. Larry wanted the entryway dark, insisted on it. I felt, guiltily, we were up to our same old dirty goddamn lighting tricks, hauling so much shit outta the truck. Now, I just chalk it up to nervousness on the first day and wanting the day's footage to be impressive in dailies tomorrow. But I really don't want this to be a pattern. I feel Larry's mindset intensely. I'm totally with it and agree. The hard part, I anticipate, will be to convince Chris and the crew that it really is OK to use something only as blindingly simple as a photoflood in a naked socket, when all the marvels of contemporary high-tech film-making are at the fingertips of qualified technicians waiting truckside. Pam says she's got a daily journal on the production, noting its accidents. Chris's foot, for one. I tell Lauren that a weight seems lifted after watching the rehearsals of the scene we will film tomorrow. We're outta the location by 8 p.m.

There are times when you look at the sweating walls, the tired hot lamps, and you know how many shots you need to satisfy the designs of the director. I just grit my teeth and push on. Shortly, there is the cutting of things that originally seemed so precious and necessary.

Tuesday 19 July
low-angle, exterior, Telly greets Casper
tracking medium shot
tracking close-up
Six-dollar cab to the set.

We've got the camera on the vibration isolator (a simple analogue gig) on the peewee which, in turn, is on the bed of the pick-up truck. With it I can get very close, always using the 25–250mm zoom, and intimately track along with them. I keep my eye on the focus through the viewfinder. I don't miss Panavision, except for the large barrel markings on the lenses. Richard handles the focus with the Zeiss lenses perfectly.

The atmosphere at dailies was of nervous humour. We were quiet, but couldn't stop laughing at Sarah's inability to scream while having sex. Larry is brutally direct as a director. Commands her to do so.

Afterwards, Lauren makes a big deal of asking if we got a CU of Leo in his walk from the stoop.

I'm so fucking exhausted, I feel like Malcolm McDowell in *Clockwork Orange*. I could drop my head into my pasta. First dailies. Larry's happy.

Wednesday 20 July
walking: sidewalk

Shooting Telly and Casper walking. I keep wondering when we'll run out of visual tricks. We have an intimidating seven, eight pages of dialogue to slog through and I try to think of a way to do it in the least number of set-ups. The scaffolding with the 600mm lens. It worked nicely and allowed the boys to do their action without onlookers.

Handholding on the sidewalk, tracking ahead of Leo and Justin, I scraped the shit out of my arm on a tree, stumbling with the Movie Camera on my shoulder.

During a lull, I get anxious for the whole show to move along quickly. I talk to First AD Van. He has a difficult job, harder even than that of my camera assistants. It's a big juggling act. He needs to be on top of all the things happening on the set: what wardrobe, make-up, hair, grip and electrics are doing; what the next scene is, and telling all concerned on set where we now stand. He needs to be checking with everybody, asking them 'How long?' all the time. Occasionally, the crew may wonder what we're waiting on. It's a job I don't think I could ever do.

I tell him, 'Van, we've gotta move things along here.'

He says, 'I just don't want to be on your case.'

'Stay right on my ass!' I say.

'This is war,' he says. We talked later, seems we're both capable of being bitchy. It's a good-intentioned crew.

At dailies, the tracks sound like shit. Too much ambient sound. I ask Jan if she's separating tracks.

Thursday 21 July
Korean deli
subway entrance

Larry was sensitive to Leo's mood. His girlfriend was there on Lexington Ave. Justin was goofing and getting on Leo's nerves.

The aesthetic this far is natural and rough. It's a legitimate synthesis already. I keep choosing the long lenses, cropping out expensive-to-shoot-in New York City. Larry always says, 'Yes, closer, that's it.'

Christopher has gotten hold of a loft on Broome Street. Nice for him, but I'm holding two places for me now: Plympton's loft, which I've paid for, and the homey apartment with no air-conditioning on 14th Street. Depending on the heat, I will go between the two. The bed at either isn't my favourite. I'm really not keen on figuring out my keys at 9.30 p.m. after shooting. My neighbour's long-nosed grey and white cat slinkily poses before my chair. A new stroke-friend, a real porcelain figurine. On Plympton's east wall are several hundred 5 x 7 pieces of hand-pencilled, coloured drawings from every scene of his next project, a feature-length animated film. Very funny, all of these: a decorated military sort with a telescoping gun for genitals, a smile with a top hat and legs, shoe trees doing curious things.

Kids: Larry Clark and Eric Alan Edwards.

Friday 22 July

Jennie phones home
Telly picks up Darcy

All day, script/continuity person Chiemi hounds me to tell her the coverage. Every time, I tell her the two reverse shots of the phone booth. Then, a possible third of the man-walking-up business. Over and over she asks. The producers are trying through both Chiemi and Van to pressure us into getting more coverage.

More close, telephoto shots. I have this aversion to another New York postcard. Streetwise, I believe, the feeling is that we all know this town well enough, and selling it would just mean a brand of self-consciousness. Any conventional producer would be sending us memos by now.

Larry didn't get together the group out at the car in front of Darcy's till 4.30. We are shooting a street in Alphabet City. He looks suspiciously at the light we set up in Darcy's window. The reflection off the ceiling fan is too bright. I have the boys soften it down a bit.

Chris says to me, 'It's your work, man. At least get the space to light it the way you want.' He doesn't know that I embrace Larry's simplicity on this film. On the other hand, I don't want to lose Christopher's interest.

All day the cam on my shoulder. Thousand-foot magazine and the zoom. I was nuts. The physical effort required to do this film! I've never had a camera on my shoulder this much before, and I'm loving every moment of it!

Chris's wife Megan and seven-day-old, as-yet-unnamed son 'Boy' drop by at wrap time. Handshakes to all. First week down. Everyone shakes hands.

Saturday 23 July

At the Angelika I watch *Spanking the Monkey*. A good young first film. A reference to *Five Easy Pieces* (one of my favourites) at the end. Matinées are all I really wish to get into. Their policy of making you stand in line and wait, while listening to loud classical music and the angering, interrupting PA system calling for boarding is too much. The theatre's sound system is dangerously over-pumped and it was fucking freezing. Absurd air-conditioning, I wanted my coat. A truly righteous film-going experience, this Angelika!

Sunday 24 July

I feel rested, finally! I will have dinner with Larry later after seeing Kieślowski's *White*. He's at the office where the edit table is installed with editor Chris Telefsen; he's selecting takes.

I wonder if I need to clarify things about our working together? There has been no idle time to reflect. No time to figure out whether the things we're doing make sense or not. On Friday, I wondered if I was in his face too much. We have to get so much done at the outset, and it's all so new to him getting all this down.

I watched *The Red Shoes* last night on Channel 13. A real artefact. A vintage piece of special-effects work. Technology really shows its date in that one. But beautiful Toulouse-Lautrec dance-hall footlighting. Lots of white things, puffed out dresses and light splashing through from behind like we've never seen in cinema before.

Jerry's on Prince Street for dinner with Justin and Larry. He's happy with the footage. We feel we have plenty of coverage, even this early in the process. Justin has a nick over one eye from his adventure with an Alphabet City girl. We talk sound problems. I explain the various mike patterns; most importantly, the ability the soundperson has with the stereo Nagra to isolate each radio mike, which the actors are wearing, on to separate tracks, giving the best quality. Justin is smart, follows us close.

Monday 25 July

Casper hides beer
walk thru house

More noisy, bad sound at dailies. Lauren asks me about it. I say that I think it's problematical, yet I can't be the final word. Can we get editor Chris Telefsen to take the tracks that we have to a sound house and have someone evaluate them for their usability? It seems Jan has been mixing the lapel/radio microphones in with the hand-boomed overhead shotgun mike which picks up almost entirely street noise. It's a good thing to have this second mike recording, but it must be discreetly separated on to the stereo Nagra's other track. I think she's unwisely doing a mix on location. I say so to Lauren. I know what it's like to work on films with terrible sound. I've done it too many times.

Tuesday 26 July
Telly's mom's bedroom
Telly's room; he pumps up

In Telly's room the action starts seeming repetitive, from my POV. Another room with our two guys in it. I ask Larry to take a chance. We'll shoot the sequence with Casper and Telly doing their 'mad diesel!' weightlifting/buffing up in all their positions, knowing that the scene runs long and the fat will have to be pulled out. Take 2: same thing with a longer, closer lens. We force the editor (fortunately, Chris Telefsen did *Barcelona*) to jump-cut it, using the salient pieces. No convention precedent thus far, but it's that kinda film! Larry digs it.

I like the crew this far. Everyone seems to be keen on making an interesting film. I often hear people talking about foreign film-makers, favourites, etc. This is almost never the case on the West Coast. It's refreshing, and I feel like we're getting back to what I facetiously call 'College Film-making'. We actually can throw the camera in the van, go off and grab something. I don't have to talk the guys outta taking the generator with us, 'Just in case.'

12.30 a.m. Ileana Douglas, from *2Die4*, is celebrating her birthday with her friend Scorsese and has invited me to his place. When I get there, I can't seem to hear a word Ileana is saying. The usual fish-inna-tree blues for a moment. Griffin Dunne shakes my hand, I tell him about Sundance. I talk with Margaret Bode, Scorsese's assistant, about *Kids*. 'A "B" movie,' she asserts, in a good way. 'Like a Sam Fuller film?' I say, yeah. I speak of avoiding postcard clichéness of New York. The use of our telephoto lenses. The centre of the story.

I sit with Marty and Ileana. He has a new Polaroid, the likes of which I have never seen. It takes little baseball-card-sized photos, with big paper margins for writing in. His mother, incredibly warm and very short, serves up two kinds of cake with mascarpone. Marty has nervously busy hands, often turning down the stereo with his handset button pad. Everyone around him is gentle.

I reintroduce myself to Alison Maclean. She tells me about her new film, a remake of *Bedlam*, a tale set in a lunatic asylum, filmed in 1946. I talk about *Man Facing South-East*, the sound work and avoiding clichés. We sit as Martin tells me about *Casino*. The end of an era. Organized crime. Greed. The last Western town.

Ileana wants to interview me on camera for her Bravo Channel show. Independent film-makers. She'll get Marty to do it too.

'They make the same choices for the same reason,' I tell myself on the wet pavement on 62nd Street, thinking about being out-leagued. Hey, right place, just a little early is all. Don't sweat it if no one else does.

Thursday 28 July
Jennie and all the girls confess about sex

I have Christopher operate B camera with a 100mm lens while I shoot with A camera. He has the ageing Arri BL3. Larry has to decide what to do. We set a dance floor down. The shoot is taking on a leisurely pace. Makes me nervous. I'm a racehorse; the clock usually waits on me and my lighting. I'm always maintaining a high, even strain.

We looked at dailies at 1 p.m. rushing up to Technicolor with caterers' boxes on our laps. I nearly fell off to sleep. A body desperate.

P.m. I grab the nearest cab. The bistros, Italian restaurants with excessively rococo names, are almost bursting on to the sidewalks with white shirts, black slacks, professional types. The taste of newly ripped tree bark and freshly exposed dirt as light rain drops.

Chris and I find a crowded, expensive Thai joint/bar, dark, animated, and candlelit on Spring Street. At the back we watch the cooks just across the counter, marvelling at the sliced-up fish, the sauces made by sur-chefs, shrimp piled high in stainless-steel sinks, under stainless-steel hoods. He was saying how he'd like to have his own restaurant. A dream. The poetry of so many meals made in a kitchen not much larger than one's home. He says, 'Look who's doing the real work! And guess who gets the credit?'

Here's the thing about the gaffer. On every film I have ever shot, the weakest link is the speed with which the gaffer and his guys do all the things I want them to do. As he, the key grip and I go around the set at the day's beginning, there are fifty things to be set up. I always want a thinking gaffer. One who's seen as many (and usually more) ways to light than I have. The gaffer often has a newer/different/unexplored/more efficient solution to setting up what I'm after. (In Chris's case, he's introduced me to the use of fluorescent fixtures more than I'm used to and he's completely open-minded about the oddest piece of gear I push in his direction.) The gaffer has to get his crew of electricians going on five things at once. He's the ringmaster of that crew. Lighting is what always takes the most time on a set and we need to get it done in the least amount of time. Every first AD waits for the moment that we can shoot.

Friday 29 July
Paul's, boys buzz up
Jennie looks for Telly
boys' pass shirts

Short day. Outside Paul's apartment. Then a tracking shot to show the 'Presidential AIDS' poster, the 'Blow Me' and 'Fuck Me' T-shirts offered streetside on St Marks – a shot that defied setting up and I fear might be too conventionally set up. After dailies, I wonder if my work is too conventional. Shit, I'm trying things as experiments. The through-the-banana shot that Christopher operated in the girls' room was filled with energy and I regretted not doing much more that way. I was intimidated by the set-up. Afraid to impose my blocking so early. Letting Larry do it and adjusting my position.

I'm trying so hard to read Larry. He is the creator of two books, published in the '70s, when I was in art school, and doing a similar kind of work with the same camera, the Leica, favourite of all hip art photographers the world over. The Leica was the first 35mm stills camera. Germany pioneered the field and it was always known for the high quality of its Leitz lenses. I know the aesthetic found in his frames in *Tulsa* and in *Teenage Lust*, but have a big question mark when it comes to the moving image. We won't have the abstract power of that frozen, black and white moment. The abstract of a singular enclosed frame.

I decide that I can be only honest, graceful, with the camera on my shoulder. To put the subject through the rigours of fat, large crew/gear cinema-making would be conceit.

But has the edginess fallen by the wayside? At the girls' room, my coverage was set up to encompass the different actors in a single take, and to put me right into the mix. But we unconsciously abandoned Larry's original through-the-foreground concept. A mistake? I vow to try to do the boys differently.

Kids: Larry Clark in the boys' room.

We scout the boys'-room location. Kevin's work is perfect, porn magazines all around the floors. The crew guys keep flipping through them. We've finished Ruby's in two days. The footage we saw this afternoon of the improv had us all laughing.

Today, the traffic leaving Manhattan by tunnel created unfathomable gridlock. We all bailed off the van at about 38th Street. Everyone drives like a sociopathic fuckhead here.

Saturday 30 July

Christopher says that Larry told him what he wanted to hear: that the girls looked beautiful, and very naturalistic, in Ruby's room.

Sunday 31 July

Dinner with Larry at El Quijote next to the Chelsea. I tell him my likes on this project. We're telling this story in a down way. A no-bullshit, straightaway shot at the subject. That the truth is that we all experience sex this young before we really experience people. Larry and I share an irreverent spirit, a rebellious, botched childhood thing that prevents us from buying the clownship of adulthood. His soul and heart are large.

Monday 1 August

boys score pot in Washington Square

I agonize: how should we treat Washington Park, notorious landmark of NYC? It's a postcard waiting to happen. So, of course only one solution. No wide shots! Totally nuts. We wait an hour and a half for an extra radio mike (I wanted to murder Jan on Friday for waiting to wire the talent till after we'd set up the dolly shot) and for a goddamn 18-inch riser to arrive.

Now we've broken again at 4 p.m. because we had so little scheduled for this day. Frustrating.

Tuesday 2 August

boys roll blunt
Telly lies to Misha, notices fight in park

8.45 p.m. We shoot in Washington Park with a hundred extras. The biggest crowd we've had to deal with. We have extras, who are really more than extras, here for three days. It's a struggle for everyone. We're not used to managing a large group. They will have to do the fight scene. It's a sunny day and the kids are incredibly mellow, wanting just to do the usual: hang out, talk and get messed up.

Christopher advises a meeting. 'Nobody listens,' I say. It's hot. After each completed scene we need to have 'New deal!' called and then a blocking rehearsal, clearing whatever shit needs to go outta the way. What colours this situation is that, unlike a big-money show, where every shot is blueprinted, we have to discover things as we go. And once we've made a decision, call it out. I mentioned that the grip, Todd, wasn't near us today when Larry was deciding that we needed a dolly shot.

I sometimes look at Larry getting into the van, or calling out that reaction shot he's gotten into his head of Misha and Telly looking back at the gay-bashing group, totally into the complete complexity of this brand-new adventure.

He's totally, 100 per cent on top of the fucker. I'm in awe. A director that's been waiting to happen.

He gave me the tape of the real fight event that we are filming. The scene in the script that I had thought was the most implausible is factual.

But what a fucking day! Yesterday's footage (all twelve minutes of it) left me hopeful and even proud. We got the dope drop – the Rastafarian was total real-time mode – and we got the foot uncovering the cake. I feel like we are all well-intentioned folks, but young at group dealings. I looked around me in the heat of my anguish about the slowness of it all and could find no authority about me. Larry and Van? The fish was stinking from the head and we were that head.

Pam says this is the halfway point. We've put some serious shit miles behind us. Still, for me, ain't this a long way from driving an oil-delivery truck in Tillamook?

Wednesday 3 August
hoodlum, fight
Jennie looks for Telly

The light at the end of the day was fucking us. I was a hustle of activity. I hate this shit. Because we were inefficient earlier, we get fading light where we don't want it: the fight scene. When I read the script I felt violated. It's brutal and surprising, and hardly makes one empathetic with our heroes. Shooting it was just as brutal. I give the B camera to Christopher for the low POV shots of the black guy getting beat up. One of the kids gets too carried away and Chris reams him.

Kids: **Hanging on the rig; Eric Alan Edwards and Christopher Porter.**

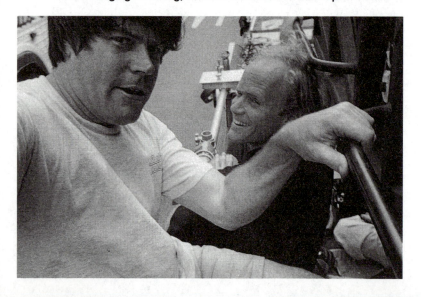

Thursday 4 August

int taxi, Jennie

We are filming the aged cab driver. We start at 110th Street at the top of Central Park. The shotmaker truck pulls the cab, rigged with sound, light cables and the half-dozen of us clinging to the hardware like a South American mountain road bus ride.

I looked over my shoulder at the hulking, lurking crane inches from my head. I looked at the bearings that hold its pivot, the bucket made of steel holding the weights, a gargantuan piece of gear, a Damoclean sword ready to fall.

The cab zips away from 25th and 6th. I feel there is so much peril around me in this town. I could get dragged down blocks by my collar before anyone'd take notice. I'd be dead.

Friday 5 August

young Casper comes home
rape scene

Rained all day as soon as we finished the exterior. Interior with Casper-as-a-youth fantasy scene. It's a flashback where a young Casper comes home early from school one day to hear the screaming of his mother. Thinking that she is in peril, he grabs a large knife from the downstairs kitchen.

We had a young boy (ten, maybe) who was cool enough. I can't imagine doing this when I was his age but . . .? He has to open the door slowly, knife in hand, and dash across the room to the bed. His mother, played by a bare-breasted woman, is having mad sex with a man dressed in high-bondage leatherworks, and the kid stabs him. The boy was totally focused (to the point of it being tiresome) on this task. The hardest thing Larry had to deal with was getting the kid to make it look real by actually putting his weight into it. The knife was an FX rig that collapses. The kid was pulling his punches. After many rehearsals we let the kid's real father in to see what was going on. The deal was he'd have approval. He looks in at what must be the craziest shit ever. Looks at all the assembled crew and says sheepishly, 'Sure . . . ah, OK.'

The van ride back to Manhattan was filled with laughter.

Saturday 6 August

Larry is directing the real way. He doesn't look through the lens. He lets me call it. Then he views the first run-through with the 3-inch monitor to see the camera coverage. After that he leaves it alone to direct the actors. When we shoot, his eyes are on them, not on a monitor.

Sunday 7 August

At the Guggenheim I fall in love with close viewing of Van Gogh's work. Chris

Porter and I head uptown. See *The Mask*. Laugh insanely at some really corn-ball stuff.

Lauren and Larry *finally* fired the soundperson. She'd called me to ask about the sound inside the taxi. Larry wants to reshoot that sequence completely.

I watch *The 400 Blows*. Would it be outta line to call *Kids* a contemporary *400 Blows*? Maybe so. In the film's beginning is a title sequence, handheld shots from a car going through the streets of Paris, looking up at the Eiffel Tower. I could shoot through Manhattan looking up.

Arrival of our new soundperson, Charles. When he needs to get room tone, one of the actors, Hamilton, can't shut up, blowing his nose and not comprehending what the fuck room tone is. Charles says to get him out. I get him outta there.

Later. When I started *2Die4*, I dropped my Los Angeles apartment. A good view, light and a short elevator ride. I hated to get rid of it. But it was a waste. I was doing only three music videos/meetings a year. The further away I get, the more amazing places I go. The worlds that open, and especially the people, all reinforce my ties to Portland, a strange corner of this world.

Monday 8 August
Telly, Darcy sleep
Casper peeks in
Jennie peeks in
Telly seduces Darcy

Chris lights the bed where Telly and Darcy are asleep on the final morning of the picture. He put the Kinoflos in the ceiling, but the effect was harsh. Nothing seemed to soften it. I just got up there and wrestled with it. In the end, the adjustment was minor. But everyone was frayed. The fucked-up guy in the neighbouring condo had kicked us off the roof, putting a serious crimp in our lighting style. I talk with him at lunch. He'd lost his funk by then. Both of us frustrated.

I curse myself for not having the gift of humour, the gift of the gab. That would surely slide me through the moments when I want something different from Larry's inspirations and I can't provide that.

Thursday 11 August
everyone's makin' out
Jennie looks for Telly
Jennie cries on couch
everyone asleep (dawn)

6.15 a.m. My Birthday. I told Pam on the sidewalk that a ten-hour turnaround was a joke. Sure, it's in our contracts, but that doesn't mean that they should do it to us.

Christopher Porter cracked a bottle open from the camera truck. I got my flowers, a huge and wonderful bouquet from Kristi, and presents from the crew, a Sin-e T-shirt and bottle of Mezcal, no doubt from Chris, at dinnertime. No sense of time, but for the blueing sky getting ready to turn to the hurting white light of fully fledged morning.

Thursday – Friday 12 August (actually)

everybody sleeps
Casper, 'What happened?'
Jennie stumbles in
Jennie rides elevator

4.30 a.m. Speaking of New York's finest: six squad cars show up on the street below for our last take. Upstairs on the fire escape, a bunch of us look down. A car full of kids were smoking a blunt and making noise. Someone called the cops and told them there was a gun involved, the common reference when you want them to show up. One of us, Larry or whoever, tells the cops that they're actors in a film.

Larry is direct: 'Ask her for a blowjob,' he requests midway through a take of Billy and Gredda. I think his connection – though unsophisticated or cool or distant or intellectual – to the actor kids is direct and understood. There's no bullshit. No guilt. He speaks like someone who's had kids, dealt with the life shit, like Chloe and her period. He says that tonight, because it's her period, she's uncomfortable. She troops through the scenes.

A new wrinkle in the show: we lined up four boys and filmed them improvising. They went off slowly at first and then picked up momentum. We rolled fourteen minutes in all. I liked what I was seeing: the sensuality, the youth expressed in the elements that Larry mentioned, hairless armpits, pimples.

Kids: Improv with the boys.

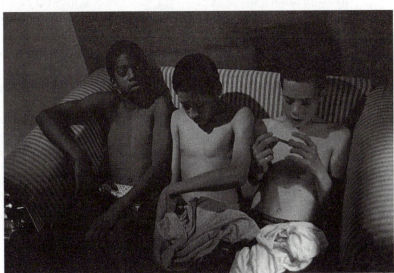

How this lyrical, round moment can be pounded into our square, established format is totally beyond me. I long to do that film in which it fits. Harmony thinks it's gold. It's priceless shit that can't be written.

When Chris points out the scraping light from the street below that slices through the window, I tell him he's a backlight junkie. He spends the next fifteen minutes finding the moment to tell me I'm wrong about that. What the fuck can I say? It's how I feel, it's how I read the situation. This is the end of the most difficult three days of the show.

The fall of evening night chased through our set-up with Justin. We are shooting dusk for dawn. By the last take, when it was getting interesting, there was darkness.

Goddamn, the camera crew's together, though! Always get my meters on cue.

Dailies were lighter than imagined. Casper's rape of Jenny worked well. Larry commended Chris on his shot of Xavier. Naugahyde couch. There is the overbearing squeak and crunch of false leather. All I can think about is a Benny Hill skit seen years ago.

Tuesday 16 August

Four more days! Yes!

Watching dailies with Chris and all. We talk of lighting. A backlight at Paul's made sense where normally it wouldn't have because of my 'artifice clause'. I really think it's a kind of philosophy of honest image-making. We've stayed small. The look is a combination of restrained pro work and honest handheld-accident-welcomed image-making. Accident-adapting, discovered compositions. Maybe that's the argument. Discovery and the uncontrollable versus the planned and controlled.

We spend two and half hours on the goddamn car mount again. All Chris and I can do is shake our heads. A pox on us. Then after one run down 5th and back through the park, the police come and talk to Pam. Production decided to go ahead without a permit for today. Short notice because this is a reshoot. We haven't been given a SOD cop and they won't let us tow the car. So, more dangerously, we get non-actor Joe to drive without his glasses, with the cab stuffed full of us all. No one wants to come back a third time with the expense of a tow rig. And now it's been made useless.

Even in my semi-resigned state I manage to piss Van off completely by pointing out that he doesn't know what is going down as Larry and I discuss the next shot. Everyone asks me for info, not him. In his anger, he decides to ride camera's ass: 'Are you ready yet?! Two minutes? OK! Cameras not ready! Two more minutes.' Little does he know that this is doing his job perfectly: to know where camera is and how long till it rolls, and telling everyone else. One thing about Van: he has the right attitude – unneurotic and (usually) never angry or offensive, unlike so many ADs.

Wednesday 17 August

tunnel
Fidget comforts Jennie
Jennie in rave

There're a lot of shady kinds of dealings afoot early today in the extensive bathrooms at the Tunnel. It's wild, folks with two-foot-high lace-up platform boots.

We have three hours to set up the lights at the Tunnel. Jay McInerney is here to write a story on Chloe and her choices of clothing. She is New York's 'It Girl'.

Lighting this is a bitch. When we finally get going, I operate all the entering-the-club stuff, and have Chris operate the mad-public-kissing stuff and Fidget giving drugs. It's our slowest going yet.

We shoot Chloe on the dance floor, stoned. The last shot is outside the Tunnel as Chloe enters it. It starts raining and we just get it. At this point Justin comes breaking out the side door, held in a head lock by the bouncer. Apparently he had slugged a cop who was questioning him downstairs, where they'd taken him after finding him stealing bottles from behind the bar. Larry grabs Justin and we get him into the camera van. Justin's insane with rage. The cops appear at the Tunnel door looking for their escapee. Larry has Van get a car and meet us on the other side of the truck. Fortunately, there's a back door on the camera truck and we can slide out of that to the waiting car.

Thursday 18 August

Day off!!!!

Chris and I hit Jaap Rietman Books. Great shit. A thickly bespectacled, frothy, wise-looking bearded dude talks Larry Clark books with us. 'This guy must have a fabulous collection of first editions,' says Chris as we walk away. Headed for the door. (I pick up the vanilla-coffee-bean-wafting burlap bag full of cheap used-up horn mutes, purchased minutes before off the pick-up-truck hood of a Spring Street vendor.) The proprietor has *Teenage Lust* in stock for $180 apiece, *Tulsa* is $400.

Next, a swaggering cab hail to: 'Wall Street! Got to go buy some stocks and bonds!' Chris says aloud as we roam off. We get out a block short and admire the vertical money architecture on the narrow antique street.

At Wall Street Camera, Chris and I dwell on the possibility of buying Leica M-6s. Chris is way excited. He mocks shaking. 'Why am I doing this? My heart is pounding!' We put out our plastic and go for it. I have reservations thinking about the possibility of saving a few hundred by looking further for a used M-6.

A man, shorter than the two of us, walks through the door saying, 'You're ugly!' to the white, neck-tied dog on the floor. 'Who me?' Chris responded. 'No, I don't know you. I don't like you, but since I don't know you, that doesn't matter.' He's Andy, one of the owners. He holds aloft a 1968-built Nikon 35–250mm zoom lens in pristine condition, clearly impressed with it. He wants to show us things, invites our asses upstairs.

Three flights up, it's the mail-order wing of Wall Street Camera. The shop is abuzz with several customers, including a dude who wanted to bend my ear. An older man, really older and frail, is standing fixturelike, staring at the proceedings (day in, day out, I suppose); silent, but mobilitating, hovering about. Andy has taken us under his cranky wing. Chris told them he was from Nova Scotia and I mentioned my large-format cameras. Andy got off on a serious show and tell. 'Hey Chris!' he keeps saying or, to me, 'You! Mr large format, over here!' (To Chris) 'Hey, Blondie.'

He went through cabinets of Leicas, shelves of Nizos, cardboard box after box, explaining the disarray to recent purchases. Neither of us had ever seen such a used collection. Floor to ceiling! 'Don't get so excited,' he scolds. A Jolly Green Giant Military, Leica-style, American-made 70mm reconnaissance camera. In a back room piled high with every camera manual: shelves of every demo model, clear plastic see-through, that has entered the shop. 'Come back any time you like. But, don't *ever* bring anyone in here who isn't totally crazy about cameras! I don't want that!' On our way uptown, 'Yeah, but won't you remember this every time you pick up your Leica and take pictures!?' says Chris.

Friday 19 August

Day off!!!

I keep thinking about apes in the jungle. We exist in such a neurotic situation in society. But aren't the only things real to us our friends? Does anyone really have more than just a few intimate or important friends? I wake up this a.m. and worry about being forty-one. One thing the kids are awake to is their connection. They hug each other when they meet. It surprised me when I first saw it.

When I talk to Larry on the phone, he gives me a dutiful rundown of what's-happenin'-now. And his stutter is alive and well.

Justin broke his hand on the door of the truck, would like us to think it was on the bouncer's face. Yeah! So, Lauren was in a panic because he didn't show up at the hospital today. But he did. We're so close I can taste it. Watch *Hannah and her Sisters*.

I'm a short-timer once again.

Saturday 20 August

A.m. We ate those foil-wrapped buns with two fried eggs and mayo that gourmet delis (a serious oxymoron) pawn off to New Yorkers believing them to be breakfast. We are shooting the morning shots to go at the end of the film – camera mounted on a tripod in the back of a pick-up truck. My thought was that the truck should just keep moving. Nothing static, stolen from *400 Blows*.

NYC looks incredibly different at 6 a.m., at least from the point of view of having had sleep. It's funny in film. You get up after a night of relative debauchery and rise to the task. Nothing, I mean nothing (still, at this time in my life) equals the adrenaline of film rolling through the camera. Hundreds of dollars per minute. As Richard Rutkowski says, 'I've ended an evening at this hour many a time.'

We filmed the homeless, the Tai Chi-ing, the buildings and trucks, the heroin addict nodding, a man hosing down the sidewalk (a cliché I'd promised myself not to do).

At Kim's Video I get *Drugstore Cowboy*, *Jacques Brel* and Maysles's *Beatles*.

Watch *Drugstore Cowboy*. I'm touched by the amazing performance of Matt Dillon. Clearly the best role he's ever had. It is Gus's best work. The home movies were perfect, bold. Also, the close-ups. The material is far better written than I ever realized. Always a tear in my eye when Kelly/Diane returns to the dump apartment. Powerful ending, a close-up on Matt's head à la home movie. I really wish I had shot that film. The camera angles and moves, clearly Gus's, are very new and uninhibited, untrained. The shot of the bus rounding the country corner. The shot through the final apartment window as Bob first enters it. Amazingly straightforward. Those are the angles Gus finds. You can't make that shit up!

Watch *Jacques Brel*. Sad, in the end, never finding what he was looking for.

At the International Photo Museum I watch the Henri Cartier-Bresson video programme. I feel I am beginning finally to be able to have time to view and like photography more for what it is than just content. Isn't that the more important thing? I've always had time for movies, television. Maybe some day for literature.

Larry comes over. Talk of the Carmine Street Pool sequence, of doing it in one day. Dinner at Jerry's. Larry won't sign my copy of his third book, *The Perfect Childhood*. Unhappy with the foreign publisher.

Larry's story about *Drugstore Cowboy*. That he didn't think it went far enough, but that it was his turf. Gus helped him to get into making this film. It was a push for him to make a film himself.

Sunday 21 August

pool
pick-up taxi

Night. Rain, fucking rain takes five or six hours from us. They want us to do the park reshoots tomorrow.

The bastard about keeping me here for two or three more days is that with the rented loft, food, cabs, my expenses back in Portland, I'm spending money to be on this shoot. I'm loving the work we do, but it is no favour to me to watch us get rained-out or to have Justin get arrested.

We're all standing in drizzle opening round foil-plastic containers with burgers, grilled tuna melts. They roll down the last gates as we huddle in the van. New York camera crew discusses fifteen-minute second meals. Time and a half.

Monday 22 August

Telly lies to Misha
Jennie exits taxi
kids hop fence

I sit in the 14th Street apartment hiding out from the rain and the company move to the Carmine Street Pool from the rained-out park. Larry's blow-up in the office. He didn't want to keep the crew waiting in the rain when we knew it would just keep raining. Producer Lauren Zalaznick's position is that we are paid for.

While waiting out the storm, Christopher and I go to Larry's loft. He feeds us his grandpa's chilli: kidney beans, canned stewed tomatoes and light meat sauce. Christopher and I remark it's the first home-cooking we've had in Manhattan – truly surreal in its own way, and wonderful.

We wait out the storm in a lesbian bar. Larry wears a hat and a flannel shirt. I can see the Indian he says is in his blood when I look close in certain light – awash in another era. An era that slightly scares me, the ghost of a grandfather, wearing wool wet from the rain.

Seventh Avenue arrows off past solid blocks of black with darkened windows to the right of that crackerjackass box of lit World Trade Towers. 3.17 on the red LED clock radio. The sparkle of high-rise spectacle is upon me. I'm off to sleep. What a glow.

Van calls after dailies, we will try the park. Justin's 'availability' is in question. He's in jail. He went to his girlfriend's early this morning. Some row, no doubt. Gone apeshit at the cops, so they took him to jail. All I can think is: what an arrogant, fucked-up asshole. I resolve not to change my Thursday a.m. plane ticket, even though now, with last night's weather-cancel halfway through the night, it means going from the pool at 6 a.m. straight to the airport without sleep.

Tuesday 23 August

subway car

At LaGuardia sushi place, Larry explained Justin's getting arrested. 'It's not this psycho bullshit.' He doesn't want to hear anything about extended family, father-figure, or end of project. He says, 'Justin is just doing the fucked-up, drunk kid thing.'

7.15 p.m. At Washington Square, the sky and light was clear blue. Felt like autumn. Everyone is saying we will decide by 6 p.m. In court, Justin has an ex-

Kids: Justin Pierce – 'He's just doing the fucked-up, drunk kid thing.'

detective with him, there are thirty cases, ten per hour. Larry has $2,500 in his pocket, anticipating his bail. Midnight, he'll go down to the station.

St Luke's. Justin said he'd commit suicide. The cops took him to the mental ward of the hospital. Larry talked to the shrink. She mentioned something about keeping him from the system, from being booked.

I go to the Mayflower bar with Chris, where we will meet Robby Müller. He's here to shoot some International Paper commercials, before he starts *Dead Man* with Jarmusch. I ask him about *Kings of the Road*. 'From my gut,' he says. I talk about how I felt the compositions were like Walker Evans's WPA photos. He has no idea what I'm talking about.

During Chloe's taxi scene, Larry asked about my staying until Thursday. 'Yeah, I'm pissed, I don't want to stay.' He hears me. His mind works. Cogs and gears. We're all bummed.

Wednesday 24 August/Thursday 25 August

kids hop fence
swimming pool

Handshakes all around seem appropriate enough. Manhattan, emanating end-lessness above the corridors of faceless buildings. Black, blue, glum edifices facing off into infinity. The orange sunrise. I'm at peace, no fear. Everyone is starting to load into the city. I'm on the other end of the deal. It's 6.30 a.m. and headed for sleep. I'm in a mild hallucinatory state. I don't fear the last subway day. All is under control. I will miss Chris Porter, but two overtime days were insufferable, and one is possible.

Larry is already on to the subway as we knock this off.

Above and below:
Kids: Larry Clark and the legless beggar.

1.50 p.m., or is it a.m.? I look at Larry's copy of Walker Evans's *Hungry Eye*. The amazing photo of the accordion man in subway, tin cup and eyes squinted. This is what he's after in the subway.

4 p.m. Dailies are like battle. Why can't I just turn off one more lamp before I shoot. I mean, turn it off! That's all that stands between me and great images. I kick myself for not having been bold enough. In the pool's case, Larry wanted 360-degree lighting. It makes one take the safer route. Using more light. But, I go through self-recrimination, hatred. The work is wrong. Then, slowly, I will

start (if it's not too bad) to respond to what is up there. I will take it in, appreciate it as artefact, our own novel contrivance.

SUBWAY!!

We shoot for six hours on a specially hired train that doesn't stop. The legless, carted beggar is great. Heartbreaking. Rocking and rolling, it seems I never took my eye from the viewfinder. It takes mere minutes to exit the train at 77th Street station. We do the accordion man and the boys hopping the turnstile. The authorities don't know this.

Out on the street now, early a.m. I take a flash photo of Justin naked, skateboarding the avenue. Two cops in a cruiser see this and nearly stop.

It's the real 'wrap'. We're out on the street with no open bars in sight. Larry, Van and me talk about anger. Talk about the soundman. Me: 'Arguments are like airplane landings – if you can walk away from them, they qualify as good.'

Edward, Justin and Harmony and I are in the back of the seatless red production van, throwing beer in this nice enjoyment. Emptying bottles in the direction of driver Graham. Larry rides shotgun. I take flash photos.

In the street outside Larry's loft, Harmony and Justin christen each other with 40s. When Harmony throws Justin's unfinished Old Gold Milwaukee crashing to the pavement, he attacks him, catlike. I try to take records of it, missing many moments.

Friday 26 August

6 a.m., Newark. There's something about a cardboard, life-sized Ronald McDonald greeting me at my United gate that makes me uneasy. I'm here at the airport, one and a half hours early.

These kids don't know the world. They don't know how big it is. Richard Rutkowski's bummed that I won't stay for the wrap party. Without sleep and smelling like a brewery, I get on the plane, back to Oregon.

The Centenary

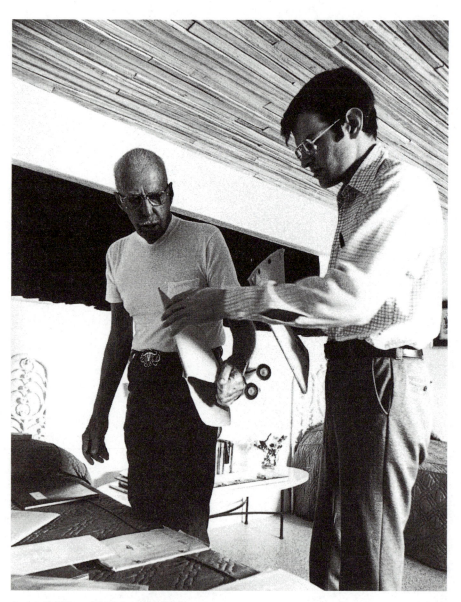
James V. D'Arc with Howard Hawks.

19 Howard Hawks and the Great Paper Chase: Memoir of a Desert Encounter

James V. D'Arc

When the seventeen-foot long truck pulled up to a modest frame rambler on Stevens Street in Palm Springs, California, I double-checked the address from my correspondence file. Could this home, which appeared no different from the other homes in the housing tract, really be the residence of Howard W. Hawks? In the driveway a teenage boy was working on a motorcycle, his head bent close to the piston. My supervisor at the time, archives curator Dennis Rowley, and I looked at each other, silently asking the same question. 'Is this the Hawks residence?' I hesitantly – almost disbelievingly – enquired of the young man. He raised his head and smiled. 'Yes, it is. My father's inside. Go on in.'

This acquisition trip, taken in early April 1977, had already been a momentous one. The truck we had been driving for more than two hours from Los Angeles eastward into the barren, hot desert of inland California was now completely full with the first instalment of Cecil B. DeMille's papers, memorabilia and production artwork to be housed in the library at Brigham Young University. I was in my second year in the Archives and Manuscripts Department, and trips of this nature to pick up archival materials were – and often continue to be – an exhilarating part of the job. However, in the case of DeMille, this trip was as exhausting as it was exciting. We had just spent the better part of a week, sometimes ten hours a day, combing through the basement, garage and selected rooms of the DeMille mansion in the Los Feliz area of Los Angeles, packing up papers, unloading filing cabinets, and carefully removing much of the 8,000 pieces of production artwork created for most of DeMille's seventy motion pictures. We would return three more times in the same large truck before the entire DeMille archive was safely transferred to BYU. But on this picture-perfect, if warm, day in southern California, we were now at the home of a film director of a very different stripe from DeMille. Ironically enough, at one time Hawks and DeMille were employed at the same studio, Famous Players-Lasky – DeMille as Director General and Hawks in the prop department and then as an assistant director. During the early 1920s, Hawks was employed in the story department where he was commissioned to acquire literary properties for that ambitious studio's expanding need for film subjects.

Our knock brought the eighty-one-year-old director to the door dressed in a crew neck white T-shirt, denim trousers and a striking belt buckle sporting the intricately carved head of a water buffalo. To a budding archivist and long-time film buff in his mid-twenties, this was a day both dreamt of and at the same time approached with some reluctance. Would I be disappointed in my encounter with one of the top-ranked directors of all time? Had the aura of the movies themselves set me up for a let-down when meeting one of the greatest of creators of these 'ribbons of dreams'? Growing up in Glendale, California, in a quiet bedroom community five miles from Los Angeles, I had been steeped in movies. The hundreds of old films shown regularly on Los Angeles television, combined with the increasing number of revival screenings at UCLA and at smaller commercial theatres in the Los Angeles area, gratified an insatiable interest in films during my teenage years. By the mid-1970s, many film-makers of the classic era were still around, but generally were not working. Although Hawks directed his final film *Rio Lobo* in 1970, he, along with the other living past masters, was a tangible connection to our motion picture heritage. In addition to Hawks, directors Henry Hathaway, Allan Dwan, Orson Welles, King Vidor, William Wyler and even Raoul Walsh were still alive. Paramount mogul Adolph Zukor died the year before at the age of 103, but Darryl Zanuck remained a living link with the golden age of the movies.

The Howard Hawks who greeted us and graciously welcomed us into the living-room of his Palm Springs home was alive, lucid and generally self-effacing as we went through the details of the transfer of the Howard Hawks collection to BYU. Our first question, after some weeks of conversing over the phone, was how much material had survived? By way of comparison, DeMille kept everything from scripts and photographs all the way down to desk calendars and cardboard backing for the onionskin radio scripts he used on his popular *Lux Radio Theatre* programme during the 1930s and '40s. The evidence of over 1,200 boxes of papers was clear; DeMille was a supreme egoist. His collection, in addition to his films, is his monument. Hawks, on the other hand, confessed that some files had been destroyed in a garage fire some years ago; at other times secretaries simply threw material out. 'When a film was finished, I didn't think about it any more,' said Hawks. 'I was on to the next project.'

Hawks displayed none of the machismo thought to be standard equipment for a man whose brisk marital tour through three wives and who knows how many starlets were matched only by his reputation as an avid hunter, fisherman, aeroplane pilot, tennis player, race car and motorcycle driver. He encouraged us to talk and answered every question after thoughtful deliberation, whether it concerned his career or with the details of the donation of his papers to the university. Hawks was not given to idle chatter or small talk. This no-nonsense demeanour was disrupted briefly when questioned about film critics and their opinions of his films. He became animated in his response (a few chuckles), but not loud, as he disparaged most film critics as a sorry lot who found more symbolism and meaning in his films than was ever there. He recounted the familiar story of making *Rio Bravo* in reaction to what Hawks considered the anti-heroic marshal played by Gary Cooper in *High Noon*.

Acquiring the Howard Hawks papers meant gathering up the files, scripts and photographs on a room-by-room tour of the house led by Hawks himself. In anticipation of our visit, he had laid out some scripts and correspondence files on a bed in a small guest bedroom. Five unproduced scripts by William Faulkner (one of them entitled *Ghost Story*) were in plain view as I leaned over to look at these treasures more closely. Hawks told us that from time to time Faulkner needed money. Throwing him a project that Hawks knew full well would not see a turn of the camera kept the southern novelist available for script doctoring, rewrites or simply within the vicinity of the director, who admired writers and writing as much as any other facet of the film-making process. Titles to other scripts caught my eye. Neither *Gunga Din*, *Morocco* nor *Shanghai Express* were Hawks titles, but he explained that he was asked to help write these screenplays – and many others over the years – without credit. Various script drafts of *Red River* lay on the simple bedspread along with censorship and publicity files.

I asked if he had kept any photographs over the years. 'Yes, I think so,' was his response. He guided us through a sliding glass door and on to the patio adjacent to the back yard. I was getting nervous. Was Howard Hawks leaving files outside in the oppressive summer heat and in the cold winter winds of Palm Springs? Nightmarish visions of mould or paper shredded by vermin came to mind. Silently gasping as the ramifications of such unarchival practice sank in, I noticed that Hawks was pointing to a filing cabinet standing alone on a barely surviving patch of grass. 'Take anything you want out of there,' were his parting words before retreating to the inside of the house with my colleague.

These moments of discovery are perhaps the most exhilarating to an archivist. What will remain after all of these years of what in most cases has not been seen by anyone else? Opening the first of four old steel file drawers, I noted a batch of eleven by fourteen-inch photographs of a very slim, chicly dressed – for the 1940s – woman with long, flowing hair. Some of the shots were artistically lit with expressionist shadows accentuating the lines of the outfits worn by their subject. This looked like fashion photography rather than movie stills. Then the distinctive features of a very young Lauren Bacall became evident; these were test shots of one of Hawks's major discoveries. A search through the other drawers revealed action shots – nearly 100 of them – of a rhinoceros hunt in Africa. Hawks told us that during the production of *Hatari!*, he had personally opened up a contest to local photographers. They were to be allowed to accompany the production troupe during the filming and the person who submitted the best set of photographs at the end of the production period would win, which meant that Hawks would purchase the winning photographs from the winner. Other photographs, some included in this photo essay, documented an active career in the motion picture business both on and off the lot: small snapshots with second wife Nancy Gross taken in the new playground of the stars in Sun Valley, Idaho, in 1941 (where he met Gary Cooper and novelist Ernest Hemingway in a failed effort to convince Paramount to allow him to direct *For Whom the Bell Tolls*), and colour transparencies taken on location while filming *Sergeant York*.

Our visit was brief – no more than three hours – as we gathered together what amounted to about five large boxes of papers, photographs and other memorabilia. We managed to find space among the DeMille papers, which alone threatened to burst the sides of our large panel truck. Ahead of us were twelve to fifteen hours of driving before we reached home base in Utah. Before our departure, we discussed our plans for the arrangement and description of the collection, as well as our desire for a return visit after we had had an opportunity to thoroughly review the collection's contents. At that time we asked Hawks if we might begin a lengthy oral history to fill in the gaps left by the fragmentary documentation of the papers. 'I don't mind,' said Hawks. 'You can ask me anything you want.' He was genuinely appreciative of our visit and wished us well on our journey. His son, Gregg, still in the driveway and happily working on the motorcycle under the warming California sun, shook our hands and said goodbye.

In 1977, amid what some critics were calling a 'new Hollywood' influence in motion pictures, my supervisor and I noted the recent films of directors Hal Ashby, Arthur Penn, Mike Nichols, Francis Ford Coppola, Sam Peckinpah, among others. The cinematic mood of the day, as we observed in the long drive back to Utah, was certainly innovative and often filled with surprises, but the messages of many of the decade's films were also violent and unrelentingly pessimistic. Deeply personal, even quixotic, films by American directors were no longer considered subversive of the Hollywood system. These *were*, in fact, steadily replacing the rapidly crumbling studio system within which Hawks, one of its greatest *auteurs*, functioned so well. The memory of Hawks's quiet authority, evident during our conversation with him, and our discussion of his body of work, reinforced the need to preserve and make available what little paper trail was left of his contribution to a rapidly changing film culture. We felt like crusaders on a paper chase attempting somehow to capture the receding past and, in this archival venue, to preserve the remaining effects of one man's cinema that was, as Andrew Sarris concluded at the time in *The American Cinema*, 'good, clean, direct, functional cinema, perhaps the most distinctively American cinema of all'.

In the months subsequent to our brief visit with Hawks, I went through every item in the collection, pausing to stare longer than the few words on one piece of correspondence justified. In this letter, written to Hawks in 1946 on 20th Century Fox letterhead, is typed: 'I wish you all the luck in the world on the picture . . . and take care of my boy Duke and get a great picture.' This closing line was followed by the bold signature of 'Jack' [John Ford]. John Wayne's acting matured considerably under Hawks's direction in the role of the ageing and angry Tom Dunson in *Red River*, filmed later that year. We exchanged letters with Hawks about providing photocopies of designated items in the collection. Frequent mention was made of a return visit to conduct the taped interviews.

In December, news came that Hawks had suffered a fall in his home resulting in a head wound, possibly concussion. One day after his accident, when Hawks was still on the floor, a neighbour discovered him and called an ambulance. Following a stay in the hospital, Hawks returned home and there, on 26 December, passed away. I remember the shock on hearing the news of his death. The harsh reality of future appointments never to be kept and of interview plans now unrealized brought with it the sober recognition that this, too, is part of the paper chase. Sometimes we just cannot run fast enough to catch up with the past. The photographs documenting our visit with Hawks taken by a professional photographer, who was the faculty adviser to the university's student newspaper and who crowded with us in the truck's small cab, retain to this day a graphic reminder of that visit nearly twenty years ago. Those photographs may quite possibly be the last ones taken of Hawks before his death less than nine months later.

'The Hawks career reveals an almost total lack of public recognition,' wrote Gerald Mast in 1982, 'not only of what he did but even of who he was . . . Only after he had finished making films did the general public come to discover who he had been – a belated discovery that perhaps led some critics to overvalue the importance of Hawks's last five films.' 'Who the Hell is Howard Hawks?' was the title Robin Wood chose for his article in 1969 for *Focus!* Answering that question today is probably as difficult as it was for Matthew Garth (Montgomery Clift) to figure out the seemingly inscrutable Tom Dunson in *Red River*. But, as Tess Millay (Joanne Dru) and Matt found out, the end result was worth the quest.

Left: This early 1930s portrait presented Hawks as a dapper man-about-town. Indeed, Hawks was fastidious in his expenditure on clothes, automobiles, firearms and on virtually everything in his life. His image as an excellent horseman, tennis player and general Hemingwayesque outdoorsman was legendary in Hollywood. However, this portrait, in half-lit three-quarter profile, may also be viewed as something of a metaphor for the kind of two-sided man Hawks's second wife, Nancy Gross, claimed him to be in her book, *Slim*: 'Howard built such a fantasy life about himself that he came to believe it was true. He never thought I would square the fact with the fiction, but I did, simply by hearing him repeat the same stories to fresh audiences. Each time, the material was different – he would completely rewrite the script.'

Left: *Sergeant York* (1941) was an important commercial success for Hawks. Here he is seen with cameraman Sol Polito (centre) and Assistant Director Jack Sullivan (right). 'We just kept about three days ahead of Johnny Huston writing,' remembered Hawks. Hawks's conditions on making the film were that Jack Warner not be allowed on the set and that Gary Cooper be hired in the lead role.

Below: A jovial scene with influential columnist Hedda Hopper wearing her signature outlandish hat at a party some time during the 1940s. On critics and comedy Hawks once remarked, 'I don't know why a thing is funny. It just happens to be funny, but the poor damn critic has to write about it. But, actually, very few critics, in my opinion, know what the hell it's all about. Some of them I think are very, very smart, but I don't pay any attention to most of them.' (Joseph McBride, *Hawks on Hawks*, Faber and Faber, London, 1996).

Opposite: Hawks's wedding to Athole Shearer (sister of Norma Shearer) in 1928 is documented in this photograph, which also shows other Hollywood luminaries of the day. From left to right: Virginia Valli, William Hawks (brother), Norma Shearer, Mary Astor, Kenneth Hawks (brother). This marriage produced two children, David and Barbara. Following the divorce from Shearer in 1940, Hawks married Nancy 'Slim' Gross, with whom he had a second daughter Kitty. From 1953 to 1959, Hawks was married to Dee Bradford and they had one son, Gregg.

Left: Hawks with Joanne Dru (playing the role of Tess Millay) on location near Elgin, Arizona, for *Red River* in 1946. Dru was selected close to production time when Hawks's first choice, Margaret Sheridan, reported that she was five months' pregnant. This new 'Hawksian woman' proved more than able to stand up to the two men in her life, played by John Wayne and Montgomery Clift. 'She is the link between the two men,' wrote Gerald Mast.

Below: Hawks going over a scene on the Arizona location of *Red River* with John Ireland and Montgomery Clift. *Red River*, filmed in 1946, was plagued by cost overruns and tampering by Howard Hughes, and was not released until 1948. It remains one of Hawks's most popularly recognized films along with *Sergeant York,* as well as one of his most narratively interesting ones.

Above: Hawks among the monuments in the *Land of the Pharoahs*. Hawks's first film in CinemaScope was a stunning visual experience, but it was hampered by stilted language, invented out of frustration by co-screenwriter and novelist William Faulkner. During an era where Cecil B. DeMille reigned supreme in spectacle, Hawks produced a handsomely mounted epic production that caused some concern to his one-time fellow Paramount colleague.

Right: Gregg Hawks watches as his father Howard Hawks lines up a shot for *Hatari!*, as cinematographer Russell Harlan stands by. Harlan photographed four films for Hawks, including *Red River* and *Hatari!*

Hawks was often the subject of retrospectives, interviews and seminars shortly before his death in 1977.

On Hawks and movie-making, his second wife, Nancy 'Slim' Hawks, remembered: 'Howard wasn't complicated about what he did. If anything, he was slightly frightened of movie-making and, I suspect, surprised that he was able to do it at all. He used to tell me that on the first day of shooting a new picture he would stop the car, get out, and throw up a couple of times on his way to the studio. That process would go on for about a week until he got into the rhythm of the work and the movie started rolling along. He once said, "You know, when you walk on to a set and there are three hundred extras and a crew of fifty people, and you're the one with the microphone in your hand and you haven't got a thought in your head – it's a terrifying experience."'

From: *Slim* by Slim Keith with Annette Tapert,
(New York: Simon and Schuster, 1990, p. 87)

20 Working with Writers

Howard Hawks interviewed by Joseph McBride

Joseph McBride: Most of your movies, even the oldest ones, look very fresh and modern today. Why do you think that is?

Howard Hawks: Most of them were well written. That's why they last. I've always been blessed with great writers. As a matter of fact, I'm such a coward that unless I get a great writer, I don't want to make a picture. But Hemingway, Faulkner, Hecht and MacArthur, Jules Furthman, all those people were damned good. The only time I tried to take somebody that I didn't know was good, why, I had to do it over again. So I've been very lucky getting good writers, and I think that they make an awful lot of difference in the picture.

JMB: How much writing do you do on your own pictures?

HH: Well, I think that if you see the pictures that I make, you'll find a certain similarity in the dialogue and the fact that it's short and quick and rather hard. I practically always work in a room with the writers.

JMB: Why do you so rarely take a writing credit on screen?

HH: Because if I did, I couldn't get such good writers to work with me.

JMB: Could you explain how the day-to-day writing goes on a script? Were you all together in a room battling it out on a typewriter?

HH: I can't play the typewriter. I couldn't write anything *per se*. I mean, I couldn't write a book or do anything like that. When Hecht and MacArthur and I used to work on a script, we'd get started around 7.30 in the morning, and we'd work for two hours, and then we'd play backgammon for an hour. Then we'd start again, and one of us would be one character, and one would be another character. We'd read our lines of dialogue, and the whole idea was to try to stump the other people, to see if they could think of something crazier than you could. That is the kind of dialogue we used, and the kind that was fun. We could usually remember what we said, and put it right down and went on working. And sometimes you're so far in a picture, and you get an idea that you're going to change a character, so you just go back and change the lines that you've written for that character, and start all over again. Hecht and MacArthur were just marvellous. The first picture we worked on they said, 'Oh, we're all through now.' I said,

'No, tomorrow we start on something new.' The fellows said, 'What?' I said, 'Different ways of seeing things.' And they had more fun, we had more fun, for about three days, saying things in different ways. I'd say, 'How do you say this – you've got a line, "Oh, you're just in love."' One of them came up with, 'Oh, you've just broke out in monkey bites.' The audience knows vaguely what you're saying, they like the method of saying it. We go through the entire script in sequence; one of us suggests something, and what you suggest somebody else twists round. I learned it from Hemingway. Noël Coward came to see me once when I was over at Columbia, introduced himself, and said, 'Well, what do you call the kind of dialogue that you use?' And I said, 'Well, Hemingway calls it oblique dialogue. I call it three-cushion. Because you hit it over here and over here and go over here to get the meaning. You don't state it right out.' We discussed it for quite a while. Another time Capra and I spent a couple of hours talking about it, and he went off and made I think the finest example of that kind of dialogue. Jean Arthur was in love with Jimmy Stewart [in *Mr Smith Goes to Washington*], and she was trying to persuade Thomas Mitchell to marry her because she was in love with Stewart. That was oblique if there ever was one. We talked it over until he got the line, then he went and did it better than I did. I believe that this particular method makes the audience do the work rather than coming out and making a kind of stupid scene out of it.

JMB: Plots tend to be more important than characters. Quite often the characters behave according to the dictates of the plot. But you usually did it the other way around.

HH: There's a very simple theory behind that. There are about thirty plots in all of drama. They've all been done by very good people. If you can think of a new way to tell that plot, you're pretty good. But if you can do the characters, you can forget about the plot. You just have the characters moving around. Let them tell the story for you, and don't worry about the plot. I don't. Movements come from characterization. A lot of things in *Rio Bravo* happened because Wayne was watching an old friend get rehabilitated. And then just when Dean Martin started to come out of all this trouble and get better, he got caught while he was taking a bath. Because somebody said 'You stink' to him. I like that kind of storytelling. And if you'll notice, almost all the men in my pictures have gone through some troubles. Then they have to be straightened out. That makes interesting writing.

JMB: Hemingway said that the best storytelling is like an iceberg – only one-eighth of it is above the water, the rest is below.

HH: Yeah. If a girl is gonna say how broke she was, you've got to find an awful good metaphor to use, you know. Something happened, that's how broke she was. You make a picture, you draw a picture of it. See, if you're gonna do something, do it with characters. Do 'em a little differently. Every scene's been done. Now, your job is to do 'em a little differently. To get mad a little differently. To steal a little differently.

JMB: Are there scenes in your films you look back at and think, 'Oh, that's flat, I should have done it differently?

HH: Sure. That's why I steal it and do it again.

JMB: Are there books you've wanted to make into movies, but haven't been able to buy?

HH: Oh, Lord, I've tried to buy lots of stories that I haven't gotten. I wanted to do the Bond series. It was done by my former assistant director Cubby Broccoli.

JMB: What was it about the Bond books that appealed to you?

HH: The great imagination that the writer [Ian Fleming] had. As far as stories go, if I like a story, I make it. Not always – I buy three stories and throw one away, or maybe two out of the three, after I work on them. I don't have to throw 'em away, I can usually sell 'em to some poor guy who doesn't know enough. But if you get a good story, it's easy to make, and if you get a bad story, you have an awful time.

JMB: I wonder why you never made a film of the Maxwell Anderson–Laurence Stallings play *What Price Glory?* It's almost like one of your stories.

HH: Too much like 'em! There's no doubt that I've been influenced by *What Price Glory?* It was a really good play, and it was beautifully done as a picture by Raoul Walsh.

JMB: How do you come up with the names of the characters?

HH: By just thinking of people. Wayne said to me [on *Rio Bravo*], 'Hey, that's a good name you've got for me – Chance.' And I said, 'Well, she was a damn good-looking girl.' In *His Girl Friday*, we had a fellow called Stairway Sam. He was always watching girls' legs go up and down a flight of stairs. That came after we finished the script. Another thing was when Cary Grant said to this gorilla, 'There's a guy down in the car waiting,' and he said, 'What does he look like?' Well, they had a description of him. I said, 'That's kind of dull.' Ben Hecht said, 'I know what he could say – "He looks like the actor Ralph Bellamy [who was playing the part]."' Now a line like *that* you could remember. That got a big laugh.

JMB: You're fond of giving your characters nicknames. Does Bogart call Bacall 'Slim' in *To Have and Have Not*, even though the character's name is Marie, because you called your wife [Nancy Gross, Hawks's second wife] 'Slim'?

HH: Yes.

JMB: And why does Bacall call Bogart 'Steve', even though his character's name is Harry?

HH: Because my wife called me Steve.

JMB: Didn't you say one day that Victor Fleming and you used to call each other 'Dan'? Why was that?

HH: Well, I think we just started. He'd say, 'Dan, what are you gonna do?' And I'd say, 'Dan, I don't know.' And we'd go out and get into some kind of trouble.

JMB: You like to rewrite dialogue on the set, don't you?

HH: Because if you don't write big, nobody can read my writing. No, but actually, if I got an actor who was particularly good and had a certain quirk or something he did that I liked, I'd rewrite the part for him. It makes it a lot easier. You're not really rewriting it, you're just saying it in different words, with a different attitude. When we started *Tiger Shark*, Eddie Robinson's character was written as a very dour, sour man. At the end of the first day I said to Eddie, 'This is going to be the dullest picture that's ever been made.' And he said 'What can we do?' I said, 'Well, if you're willing to try it with me, why, let's make him a happy-go-lucky, talkative . . . you're going to have to keep talking all through the picture.' He said, 'Fine, let's do it.' So every day I gave him a sheet of yellow paper and said, 'Here's your lines.' He's a fine actor, and I thought he did a great job. But I hate to think of what the picture would have been if we'd done the dour, sour man instead of this rather gay, futile man, because the whole tenor of the picture changed. They talk about 'improvisation'. That's one of the silliest words that's used in the motion picture industry. What the hell do they think a director *does*? How do you expect that we can go out with a story that's written up in a room, go out to the location, and do it verbatim? I have never found a writer who could imagine a thing so that you can do it like that. And somebody started saying it's 'improvising'. Well, I wish you could see some pictures that are *not* improvised – where they send them out and say, 'We don't want you to change a word or a scene or anything.' We have a scene that we're going to do: I'm interested first in the action and next in the words they speak. If I can't make the action good, I don't use the words. If I want something to happen in a hurry, I can't have a man stop and read a line coming in. I let him run on through yelling something. I must change to fit the action because, after all, it's a motion picture. Some of the stuff that's handed to you on paper is perfectly good to read, but it isn't any good on the set. [Hawks on another occasion put this point even more forcefully, telling me, 'If it reads good, it won't play good.']

JMB: Leo McCarey, whom you regarded highly, was one of the loosest of all Hollywood directors. He would literally make up whole scenes on the set. How do you feel he managed to do that?

HH: You say 'one of the loosest' – I think *all* the good ones are loose. None of them made a scene until they thought it was any good. I watched Leo McCarey sit on a set all morning and never do a scene. Then he'd do four hours' work in the afternoon. Directors are storytellers. If we can't change something, we're no good. Because you're not trying to photograph a budget or a cost sheet. You're trying to make a scene that's going to be good, the best you know how. If you don't, it's you own damn fault.

21 Dziga Vertov

Introduction: Kevin Macdonald

Dziga Vertov was born with the name Denis Kaufman in Bialystok (now in Poland, then in Russia) in January 1896, the eldest of three brothers who all left their mark on world cinema. The middle brother, Mikhail (1897–1981), became a renowned Soviet documentary director in his own right and was cameraman on most of Vertov's films, including the celebrated *Man with a Movie Camera*. The youngest of the three, Boris (1906–80), was separated from his siblings during the Revolution and educated in Paris. There he photographed all of Jean Vigo's films before emigrating to America, where he became the cinematographer of choice for both Elia Kazan, winning an Oscar for his work on *On the Waterfront*, and Sidney Lumet (Kazan introduced them). For Lumet, Kaufman photographed *Twelve Angry Men, Long Day's Journey into Night* and *The Pawnbroker*.

Of the brothers, however, it is Vertov,* still little known or appreciated outside of Russia, who has had the most notable and lasting influence on cinema history. He could be labelled the first documentary film-maker, utilizing as he did footage of real events to create narratives and communicate complex messages. However, the word 'documentary' does not adequately describe the complex experimental nature of his work. Emerging from the Constructivist/Futurist mêlée around Mayakovsky – who wanted to create a new kind of imaginative art based on 'facts' – Vertov began editing revolutionary newsreels during and after the civil war, including *Kino-Pravda* (*Film Truth*), a film equivalent to the Communist Party newspaper, *Pravda*. Throughout his career, thereafter, he never strayed from an absolute belief in the revelatory capacity of unscripted documentary footage. What did develop were his ideas on montage and filming technique which were most fully expressed in a series of 'documentaries' in the late 1920s and early 1930s: *The Eleventh Hour* (1928), *The Man with a Movie Camera* (1929), *Enthusiasm* (1931), and *Three Songs of Lenin* (1934). For all their experimental form, Vertov insisted that his films

---

* Denis Kaufman adopted the pseudonym Dziga Vertov shortly after the Revolution. It has Constructivist associations and the two words translate roughly as 'spinning at great speed', with the connotation of enormous energy.

Denis Kaufman (Dziga Vertov).

Mikhail Kaufman: the man behind the movie camera.

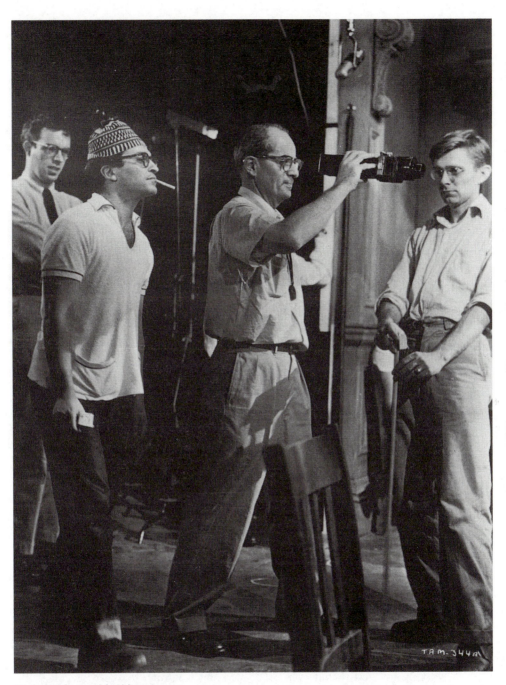

Boris Kaufman with Sidney Lumet.

had a clear purpose. 'The important thing,' he said, 'is not [to] separate form from content. The secret lies in the unity of form and content.'

Vertov theorized relentlessly, and wrote numerous pamphlets and declarations expounding his ideas. For all the complexity of their appearance (not helped by the peculiar layouts and typefaces he characteristically adopted), Vertov's basic ideas are relatively straightforward. He and his associates (whom he dubbed 'the *kinoks*') believed that fiction cinema was an irrevocably bourgeois art form and should be abandoned in Revolutionary Russia. In its place they posited a cinema of facts, made up of documentary footage of real people in real situations, if possible filmed unawares. Central to his theories is a kind of idolization of the camera. Vertov believed that the camera (which in combination with the editing process, he called the 'kino-eye') was in many respects superior to the human eye, able as it was to see at long distances, to film in slow or fast motion, etc., etc. Moreover, in the editing process, scenes from different times and places could be cut together, the same scene viewed from several different angles, impressions of speed and energy given by fast cutting . . . all of which liberated the kino-eye from the confines of time, space and normal causation. A kino-eye film was able, Vertov believed, to reveal a deeper level of truth in the world than was normally perceived by the 'imperfect human eye'.

Watching Vertov's films today, what is most impressive is their no-holds-barred willingness to explore every technical capability the cinema has at its disposal. Vertov and his *kinoks* did everything and anything: used freeze-frames, multiple frames, animation, telescopic and microscopic lenses, multiple exposures, 'subliminal' cuts of one or two frames, slow motion, fast motion, cameras in planes, cameras hand-held and cameras in cars.

Vertov was also extremely prescient in his ideas on sound film – expounded several years before the process became technically feasible. He believed in using a combination of 'direct sound', music and effects. He did *not* think sound should be used naturalistically, but wanted it to create a tension with the image, by turns counterpointing and underscoring it. His own first sound film, *Enthusiasm* (including probably the first use of 'direct sound' in a documentary), was a masterpiece that Chris Marker has called 'the greatest documentary ever made'. Charlie Chaplin, who was searching for a similarly anti-naturalistic way of using sound, wrote: 'I regard the film *Enthusiasm* as one of the most moving symphonies I have ever heard. Dziga Vertov is a musician. Professors should learn from him instead of arguing with him.'

Not surprisingly, Vertov's radical ideas about the superiority of factual film were unpopular with the Soviet Union's fiction directors, particularly Sergei Eisenstein, who publicly lambasted them (although he had started his film career working for Vertov and even asked Mikhail Kaufman to shoot several of his films). Perhaps it was inevitable that as the renown of the fiction directors increased through the 1930s, Vertov's influence would wane. Even more problematic was the increasingly hostile interference of Stalin's bureaucratic regime, which insisted that all films should have a detailed script for perusal prior to shooting. Vertov, whose films rested on the very idea of spontaneity and the rejection of shooting scripts, was crippled. He refused to compromise and fell under ideological suspicion. His position was not helped by an insistence that it was the documentary film-maker's duty to show 'life as it is' – not to show the ideal the *apparatchiks* wanted to see. He got into particular trouble for filming the great Soviet famines of the early 1920s and '30s. In this, as in so much, Vertov was ahead of his time; we usually think of the notion of a documentary film-maker as someone who exposes injustice and suffering as originating in the 1960s.

Vertov was largely forgotten in the West and reviled in Russia by the time of his death in 1954. That his reputation has been rehabilitated is, as is usually the case in these things, largely owing to interest in France. In the late 1960s Jean-Luc Godard, who shared Vertov's relentless need to rationalize and theorize the cinema, named his Marxist film co-operative 'The Dziga Vertov Group'. More significantly, a decade earlier, Jean Rouch saw and admired Vertov's films, and in homage named his new documentary style 'Cinéma Vérité' (French for *Kino-Pravda, Film Truth*). Almost simultaneously, in America, Richard Leacock and the other originators of Direct Cinema were also adopting Vertov's ideas – perhaps without knowing it – particularly his notion of 'catching life unawares', either by using hidden cameras or, more frequently, by filming people who were so absorbed in what they were doing that they forgot the camera was there. Like Vertov, this new generation of film-makers hated the static camera and thought the cameraman should move through life like a 'canoe lost in a stormy sea'. Moreover, like him they felt that a documentary film-maker's job was to record *slices of reality*, and use them as building blocks in an imaginative process to create works of art, without sacrificing the essential truthfulness of their material. 'The goal,' as Vertov put it, 'is to make things on the screen look like "life facts", and at the same time to mean more than that.'

This conception of documentary-making is now all pervasive. The ghosts of Dziga Vertov and his gang of *kinoks* enter your living room almost every time you turn on the TV to watch a documentary film.

From *The Council of Three* (1923)

1. Upon observing the films that have arrived from America and the West and taking into account available information on work and artistic experimentation at home and abroad, I arrive at the following conclusion:

The death sentence passed in 1919 by the *kinoks* on all films, with no exceptions, holds for the present as well. The most scrupulous examination does not reveal a single film, a single artistic experiment, properly directed to the emancipation of the camera, which is reduced to a state of pitiable slavery, of subordination to the imperfections and the short-sightedness of the human eye.

We do not object to cinema's undermining of literature and the theatre; we wholly approve of the use of cinema in every branch of knowledge, but we define these functions as accessory, as secondary offshoots of cinema.

The main and essential thing is:

The sensory exploration of the world through film.

We therefore take as the point of departure the use of the camera as a kino-eye, more perfect than the human eye, for the exploration of the chaos of visual phenomena that fills space.

The kino-eye lives and moves in time and space; it gathers and records impressions in a manner wholly different from that of the human eye.

We cannot improve the making of our eyes, but we can endlessly perfect the camera.

Until now, we have violated the movie camera and forced it to copy the work of our eye. And the better the copy, the better the shooting was thought to be. Starting today, we are liberating the camera and making it work in the opposite direction – away from copying.

2. I make the viewer see in the manner best suited to my presentation of this or that visual phenomenon. The eye submits to the will of the camera and is directed by it to those successive points of the action that, most succinctly and vividly, bring the film phrase to the height or depth of resolution.

Example: shooting a boxing match, not from the point of view of a spectator present, but shooting the successive movements (the blows) of the contenders.

Example: the filming of a group of dancers, not from the point of view of a spectator sitting in the auditorium with a ballet on the stage before him.

After all, the spectator at a ballet follows, in confusion, now the combined group of dancers, now random individual figures, now someone's legs – a series of scattered perceptions, different for each spectator.

One can't present this to the film viewer. A system of successive movements requires the filming of dancers or boxers in the order of their actions, one after another. The camera 'carries' the film viewer's eyes from arms to legs, from legs to eyes and so on, in the most advantageous sequence, and organizes the details into an orderly montage study.

3. I am kino-eye.

From one person I take the hands, the strongest and most dextrous; from another I take the legs, the swiftest and most shapely; from a third, the most beautiful and expressive head – and through montage I create a new, perfect man.

I am kino-eye, I am a mechanical eye. I, a machine, show you the world as only I can see it.

Now and for ever, I free myself from human immobility, I am in constant motion, I draw near, then away from objects, I crawl under, I climb on to them. I move apace with the muzzle of a galloping horse, I plunge full speed into a crowd, I outstrip running soldiers, I fall on my back, I ascend with an aeroplane, I plunge and soar together with plunging and soaring bodies.

Free of the limits of time and space, I put together any given points in the universe, no matter where I've recorded them.

My path leads to the creation of a fresh perception of the world. I decipher in a new way a world unknown to you.

Excerpted from *Kino-Eye: The Writings of Dziga Vertov*, edited by Annette Michelson; University of California Press, 1984

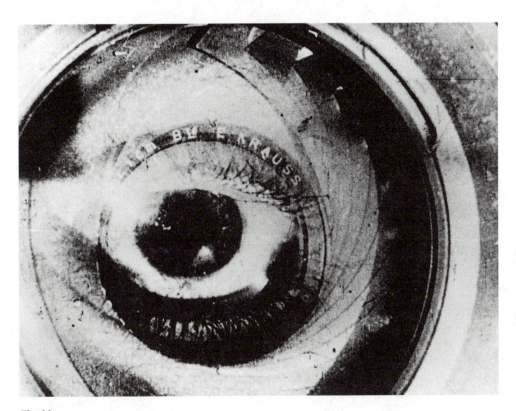

The kino-eye.

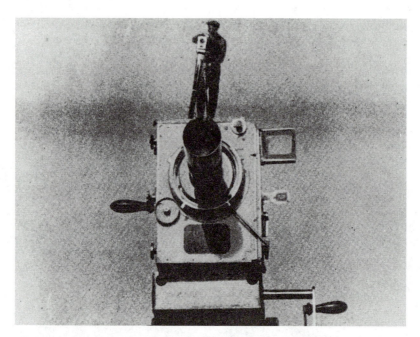

Above and below: Man with a Movie Camera.

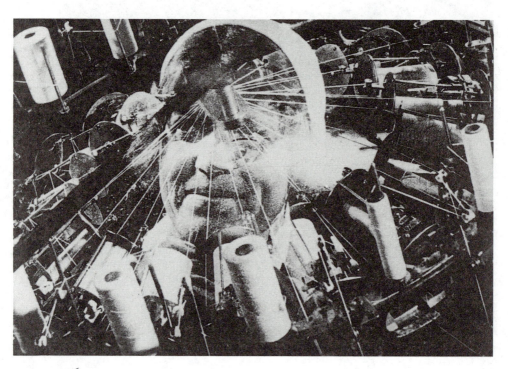

In Memoriam

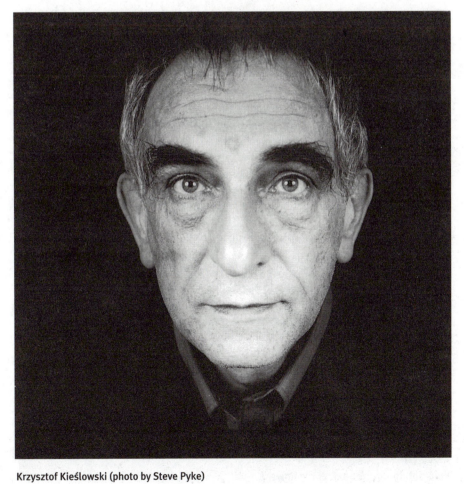

Krzysztof Kieślowski (photo by Steve Pyke)

22 In Memoriam

Film-making doesn't mean audiences, festivals, reviews, interviews. It means getting up every day at six o'clock in the morning. It means the cold, the rain, the mud and having to carry heavy lights. It's a nerve-wracking business and, at a certain point, everything else has to come second, including your family, emotions, and private life. Of course, engine drivers, businessmen or bankers would say the same thing about their jobs. No doubt they'd be right, but I do my job and I'm writing about mine. Perhaps I shouldn't be doing this job any more. I'm coming to the end of something essential to a film-maker – namely, patience. I've got no patience for actors, lighting cameramen, the weather, for waiting around, for the fact that nothing turns out how I'd like it to. At the same time, I mustn't let this show. It takes a lot out of me, hiding my lack of patience from the crew. I think that the more sensitive ones know I'm not happy with this aspect of my personality.

Film-making is the same all over the world: I'm given a corner of a small studio stage; there's a stray sofa there, a table, a chair. In this make-believe interior, my stern instructions sound grotesque: Silence! Camera! Action! Once again I'm tortured by the thought that I'm doing an insignificant job. A few years ago, the French newspaper *Libération* asked various directors why they made films. I answered at the time: 'Because I don't know how to do anything else.' It was the shortest reply and maybe that's why it got noticed. Or maybe because all of us film-makers with the faces we pull, with the money we spend on films and the amounts we earn, with our pretensions to high society, so often have the feeling of how absurd our work is. I can understand Fellini and most of the others who build streets, houses and even artificial seas in the studio: in this way not so many people get to see the shameful and insignificant job of directing.

As so often happens when filming, something occurs which – for a while at least – causes this feeling of idiocy to disappear. This time it's four young French actresses. In a chance place, in inappropriate clothes, pretending that they've got props and partners, they act so beautifully that everything becomes real. They speak some fragments of dialogue, they smile, they worry, and at that moment I can understand what it's all for.

Krzysztof Kieślowski
Epigraph for *Kieślowski on Kieślowski*

Filmography

Mike Figgis is the director of, among others, *Internal Affairs, Liebestraum* and *Leaving Las Vegas*.

John Boorman is the director of, among others, *Point Blank, Excalibur* and *Beyond Rangoon*.

Lawrence Bender is the producer of, among others, *Reservoir Dogs, Fresh* and *Pulp Fiction*.

Tom DiCillo is the writer/director of, among others, *Johnny Suede, Living in Oblivion* and *Box of Moonlight*.

Eleanor Coppola is the author of *Notes: The Making of Apocalypse Now*.

Robert Towne is the writer of *Chinatown*, and the writer/director of *Personal Best* and *Tequila Sunrise*.

Joel and Ethan Coen are the writer/directors of, among others, *Blood Simple, Barton Fink* and *Fargo*.

Suso Cecchi d'Amico is the writer of, among others, *Senso, Rocco and his Brothers* and *The Leopard*.

Walter Murch was responsible for the sound design on, among others, *The Rain People, The Conversation* and *Apocalypse Now*.

Terence Davies is the writer/director of, among others, *Distant Voices, Still Lives, The Long Day Closes* and *The Neon Bible*.

Steve Martin has acted in, among other films, *All of Me, Roxanne* and *Grand Canyon*.

Gillies MacKinnon is the director of, among others, *The Grass Arena, A Simple Twist of Fate* and *Small Faces*.

Stanley Donen is the director of, among others, *Singin' in the Rain, Funny Face* and *Two for the Road*.

Kevin Macdonald is the author of *Emeric Pressburger: The Life and Death of a Screenwriter* and the co-editor of *Imagining Reality: The Faber Book of Documentary*.

Shohei Imamura is the director of, among others, *The Insect Woman, The Ballad of Narayama* and *Black Rain*.

Toichei Nakata is the director of *Osaka Story*, a documentary about his family.

Karl Brown was the assistant to cameraman Billy Bitzer on D. W. Griffith's *The Birth of a Nation* and *Intolerance*. He was the cameraman on *The Covered Wagon*.

Freddie Young was the cinematographer of, among others, *Goodbye Mr Chips, Lawrence of Arabia* and *Doctor Zhivago*.

Frank Mannion is a lawyer with Scala Productions.

Michel Kelber was the cinematographer of, among others, *Un Carnet de Bal, Les Parents Terribles* and *French Can-Can*.

Vittorio Storaro was the cinematographer of, among others, *The Conformist, Apocalypse Now* and *The Last Emperor*.

Ric Gentry is a journalist working in Los Angeles.

Eric Alan Edwards was the cinematographer of, among others, *My Own Private Idaho, To Die For* and *Kids*.

Howard Hawks was the director of, among others, *Only Angels Have Wings, His Girl Friday* and *Rio Bravo*.

James V. D'Arc is the curator of the cinema archives of the Harold B. Lee Library of Brigham Young University, Utah, which houses the papers of film-makers such as Howard Hawks and Cecil B. de Mille.

Dziga Vertov was the director of, among others, *Kino-Pravda, The Man with the Movie Camera* and *Enthusiasm*.

Krzysztof Kieślowski was the director of, among others, *Blind Chance, The Decalogue* and the *Three Colours* trilogy.

Acknowledgements

Thanks are due to Lawrence Atkinson, Mark Cousins and the rest of the staff of the Drambuie Edinburgh Film Festival; to Tony Rayns for his invaluable assistance with the Imamura interview; to Ian Bahrami, Victoria Buxton, Dave Fairey, Claire Mellor and Justine Willett at Faber and Faber. As usual, the editors are indebted to the staff at the BFI's Stills Library, for their efficiency, good humour and willingness to come to the rescue at a moment's notice.

Photographs courtesy of BFI Stills, Posters and Designs. Copyright for the photographs is held by the following: MGM (*Anchors Aweigh, Singin' in the Rain, It's Always Fair Weather, Seven Brides for Seven Brothers, Doctor Zhivago* and *Ryan's Daughter*); Paramount Pictures (*The Godfather, Part III, Chinatown, The Covered Wagon, Reds* and *The Little Prince*); Warner Brothers (*Personal Best, The Maltese Falcon, The Hudsucker Proxy, THX 1138* and *Young at Heart*); Columbia Pictures (*Mr Deeds Goes to Town, Lawrence of Arabia, Dracula* and *The Deadly Affair*); TCF (*The Leopard, The Robe, La Luna* and *Bedazzled*); Zoetrope Productions (*THX 1138, Apocalypse Now* and *One From the Heart*); Jeremy Thomas Productions (*The Last Emperor* and *Little Buddah*); Titanus (*Rocco and His Brothers*); ICI (*Ossessione*); Artificial Eye (*The Neon Bible*); Imamura Productions (*The Insect Woman, Profound Desire of the Gods* and *Black Rain*); RAI Television (*The Spider's Stratagem*); UA (*Last Tango in Paris*); Sirrius (*Les Parents Terribles*). Copyright for the *Kids* production photographs is held by Eric Alan Edwards; copyright for the Howard Hawks photos is held by the Harold B. Lee Library at Brigham Young University, Provo, Utah; photo of Mike Figgis by Suzanne Hannover; photos of John Boorman and Krzysztof Kieślowski by Steve Pyke; photos of Tom DiCillo and *A Box of Moonlight* by Bill Bettencourt; photo of Eleanor Coppola by Sofia Coppola.

Projections 1

The first issue contains:

Bright Dreams, Hard Knocks
A journal for 1991 by John Boorman.

Film Fiction
An essay by Sam Fuller.

The Early Life of a Screenwriter
From the Berlin diaries of Emeric Pressburger.

Demme on Demme
A comprehensive survey of the career of 1991's Oscar-winning director.

Matters of Photogenics
An essay on photographing the human face by Oscar-winning cameraman Nestor Almendros.

My Director and I
A conversation between River Phoenix and Gus Van Sant during the shooting of River Phoenix's most memorable film, *My Own Private Idaho*.

Surviving Desire
A screenplay by Hal Hartley.

Making Some Light
Michael Mann discusses the making of *The Last of the Mohicans*.

Projections 2

The second issue contains:

Shadow and Substance
George Miller charts the journey he has made form the *Mad Max* trilogy to *Lorenzo's Oil*.

Movie Lessons
Jaco van Dormael discusses the creative process that led to *Toto the Hero*.

Searching for the Serpent
New Zealand director Alison Maclean discusses her work.

Freewheelin'
A free-ranging phonecall between Derek Jarman and Gus Van Sant.

Acting on Impulse
Willem Dafoe describes his approach to acting.

The Early Life of a Screenwriter
Veteran writer/director Sydney Gilliat relives the early days of British cinema.

Altman on Altman
From *M*A*S*H* to *Short Cuts*, Robert Altman discusses his career.

Bob Roberts
Tim Robbins's stunning, incisive political satire.

I Wake Up, Dreaming: A Journal for 1992
Bertrand Tavernier's diary records the evolution of his controversial film
L627 against the shifting European cultural landscape.

There are also contributions from;
Denys Arcand, David Byrne, Monte Hellman, Richard Lowenstein, Jocelyn
Moorhouse, Arthur Penn, Nicolas Roeg, Philippe Rousselet, Paul Schrader,
Ron Shelton, Roger Spottiswoode, István Szabó, Michael Verhoeven, Vincent
Ward and Fred Zinnemann.

Projections 3

The third issue contains:

Journals 1989–1993
Francis Ford Coppola
An intensely personal and highly revealing documentation of the creative
processes of one of America's greatest directors.

The Narrow Path
Chinese director, Chen Kaige, discusses his life and work, culminating in
his Palm d'Or-winning success, *Farewell, My Concubine.*

Acting Is Doing
Veteran director Sydney Pollack discusses his approach to working
with actors.

Art Direction: Wajda to Spielberg
The Oscar-winning art director of *Schindler's List* describes his approach
to his craft.

Making Music for *Short Cuts*
Hal Willner discusses how he created the rich musical texture for
Robert Altman's film.

Pixelvision
Michael Almereyda reveals the mysteries and beauties of this video medium.

Kasdan on Kasdan
From *Body Heat* to *Wyatt Earp*, Lawrence Kasdan discusses his career.

Screenwriting
Michael Tolkin, the author of *The Player*, discusses the struggles of the screenwriter in a town where writers are treated with ambivalence, if not disdain.

Producing
Art Linson discusses his tussles with David Mamet on *The Untouchables.*

Answers First, Questions Later
Quentin Tarantino traces the journey that led to *Pulp Fiction.*

On Tour with Orlando
Sally Potter's diary of her promotional tour for *Orlando*.

The Hollywood Way
An excerpt from Gus Van Sant's 'biographical novel, with a few movie hints'.

'I Wake Up, Screaming'
Richard Stanley's diary of the trials and tribulations of shooting *Dust Devil* in Namibia.

Flirt
The script of Hal Hartley's latest exploration of love and manners.

Cry from Croatia
Croatian film-maker, Zrinko Ogresta's lament for the destruction being wrought on his country.

And the Dreams of:
Denys Arcand, Monte Hellman, Richard Lowenstein, Sally Potter, Paul Schrader, Steven Soderbergh, Jaco van Dormael and Alex van Warnerdam.

Projections 4

The fourth issue contains:

Founding Father
To commemorate the centenary of cinema, Louis Lumière describes how he invented the cinema camera.

Anamorphobia
Martin Scorsese discusses screen formats.

Divisions and Dislocations: A Journal for 1994
James Toback on the LA earthquake and other events in the life of a Hollywood screenwriter.

Penn on Penn
A survey of the career of the director of *Bonnie and Clyde*.

Raising the Dead
Ken Burns – the creator of *The Civil War* – discusses his distinctive approach to documentary film-making.

The *Gone with the Wind* letters
The letters of screenwriter Sidney Howard which chart the progress of his work on one of the most famous films of all time.

Chekhov's Children
The main creator/collaborators of Louis Malle's film, *Vanya on 42nd Street*, describe the evolution of this unique film.

Sound Design: The Dancing Shadow
Walter Murch – who was responsible for the sound design of *Apocalypse Now* – describes how sound communicates its message to the audience.

Playing Cowboys and Indians
Prop master extraordinaire, Eddie Fowlie, recounts his adventures with
David Lean.

Lunch and a Book
John Seale – the cinematographer of *Rain Man* and *Witness* –
discusses how he works with directors.

An American in Paradise
The last interview with the grand master of dance, Gene Kelly.

The Tango Lesson
Sally Potter recounts her forays into the world of tango.

Creation and the Artist
One of the last interviews with the master of Italian cinema, Federico Fellini.

Missing Sandy Dennis
A poem in tribute to actress Sandy Dennis by her co-star in *The Indian
Runner*, Viggo Mortensen.

On John Ford
A tribute to John Ford in his centenary year by Lindsay Anderson.

Also, contributions by;
Percy Adlon, Kevin Brownlow, Roger Corman, Alex Cox, Andre de Toth,
Nora Ephron, Monte Hellman, Huang Mingchuan, Richard Lowenstein,
Dusan Makavejev, Arthur Penn, Vincent Sherman, István Szabó, Michael
Tolkin, Vincent Ward and Fred Zinnemann.

Projections 4½

In association with *Positif*

To celebrate their 400th issue, the editors of the French film magazine asked
film-makers to write about the films, directors and actors who have had a special significance for them. Among the eighty film-makers who responded are:

Altman and Angelopoulos, Chabrol and the Coen brothers, Eastwood and
Frears, Kazan and Kieślowski, Leigh, Linklater and Loach, Makavejev and
Marker, Ophüls, Penn and Polanski, Resnais and Rohmer, Rousselot and
Russell, Schrader and Soderbergh, Tavernier and the Taviani brothers, and
Fred Zinnemann.

There is also a tribute to Buster Keaton to mark his centenary.

Projections 5

The fifth issue contains:

Some Like It Dark
Jamie Lee Curtis chats to her father Tony Curtis.

Emotion Pictures
Quentin Tarantino discusses film with Brian De Palma.

Animation and Dynamation
The father-figure of stop-motion animation, Ray Harryhausen, discusses
his work.

A Lot Can Happen in a Second
An insight into the animated world of Nick Park, the creator of *Wallace
and Gromit*.

Bringing Things to Life by Hand
The creator of *The Nightmare Before Christmas* and *James and the
Giant Peach* discusses his approach to animation.

Cut Off their Tails with a Carving Knife
Animator Simon Pummel discusses the unique contribution of Russian
animator Ladislaw Starewicz.

Annaud on Annaud
A survey of the career of the maker of *Quest for Fire* and *The Name
of the Rose*.

A Little Tea, A Little Chat
Fred Zinnemann reflects on a life of movie-making.

Learning Your Craft
The interview with one of the quintessential stars of Hollywood,
James Stewart.

Making Safe
A series of discussions with the main creators of *Safe*: director Todd Haynes,
actress Julianne Moore, and producer Christine Vachon.

Portfolio
A celebration of American independent cinema by photographer Chris Buck.

Making Wings
A tribute to film-maker William Wellman on his centenary by his son.

Adventures in a Light Industry
A diary recounting the making of John Boorman's *Beyond Rangoon* in the
jungles of Malaysia by Walter Donohue.

In Memoriam
A tribute to Louis Malle.